Contemporary School Counseling

Theory, Research, and Practice

Christopher A. Sink, General Editor

Seattle Pacific University

Lahaska Press
HOUGHTON MIFFLIN COMPANY
Boston   New York

Publisher, Lahaska Press: Barry Fetterolf
Senior Editor, Lahaska Press: Mary Falcon
Editorial Assistant: Lisa Littlewood
Senior Project Editor: Tracy Patruno
Manufacturing Coordinator: Renee Ostrowski
Marketing Manager: Brenda L. Bravener-Greville

Cover image: The Playground (acrylic on canvas), P.J. Crook. Courtesy of Getty
Images/The Bridgeman Art Library

Lahaska Press, a unique collaboration between the Houghton Mifflin College Division
and Lawrence Erlbaum Associates, is dedicated to publishing books and offering services
for the academic and professional counseling communities. The partnership of Lahaska
Press was formed in late 1999. The name "Lahaska" is a Native American Lenape word
meaning "source of many writings." The small eastern Pennsylvania town of Lahaska,
named by the Lenape, is the home of the Lahaska Press editorial offices.

Printed in the U.S.A.

Library of Congress Control Number: 2002109671

ISBN: 0-618-21506-9

23456789-QUF-08 07 06 05 04

Brief Contents

Contents

PART ONE The Counseling Function   43

CHAPTER 2 Individual Counseling: From Good to Great   45

CHAPTER 6 **Large Group Guidance: Curriculum Development and Instruction** 189

CHAPTER 8 **Evaluating School Counseling Programs**   257

PART THREE **The Consultation Function**   295

CHAPTER 9 **School-Based Consultation**   297

Foreword

Christopher A. Sink
Seattle Pacific University

WHEN RELAYING A STORY, people tend to start with the "bad" news before launching in with "good" news, but as an optimist, let me introduce you to the profession with some positives.

The Good News: The Profession Is Changing for the Better

The school counseling profession is a very exciting field to be in right now. In fact, school counselors are experiencing a period of professional revitalization (Erford, 2003). Building on a solid foundation of theory, research, and best practices, nascent school counselors are, in my opinion, better educated and prepared for their work with students, school faculty and staff, parents, and the community at large than in any other time in the profession's almost one-hundred-year history. Moreover, contemporary counselor education programs are seemingly more thorough and intentional about the training of preservice school counselors, making use of curricular and teaching innovations from disciplines like education, counseling psychology, cognitive psychology, and developmental psychology. There is also some evidence that graduates of these counselor education programs are becoming more effective in their school-based interventions with students and their caregivers (see Chapter 8 and Whiston, 2003). By reading and studying this text, you will learn what is required to be *a successful school counselor* as well. It details many of the important changes that are taking place in school counseling programs around the nation and how you can be an integral part of the profession's transformation. And now for the downside.

The Not-So-Good News: School Counselors Are Still Saddled with Negative Public Perceptions

Even though school counseling has made considerable strides toward renewal, new counselors continue to face a less-than-complimentary public image. For too long, school counselors have heard the multitude of complaints from the students

and parents they serve. Here are just some of the sample remarks I recently gar-
nered from various teacher education students:

- "My counselor did not help me at all."
- "I didn't even know who my elementary school counselor was."
- "Yeah, we had a counselor but only the 'problem' kids went to see her."
- "He [the school counselor] told me I could never go to college. Look at me now!"
- "The counselor didn't do anything but schedule changes."
- "He didn't have a clue!"

Even if these comments are exaggerations, they are genuine feelings of preservice
teachers. If new teachers as a whole do not view school counselors as helpful to
them or their future students, their desire for collaboration (see Chapter 11) will
perhaps be less than optimal.

In the previous era (see Chapter 1), school counselors were educated to be
pseudotherapists or clinicians. By and large, they bought into the strategy of sitting in their offices and waiting for the "action" to come to them. This reactive
and crisis (traditional) orientation has served only a small percentage of students
and their families. Those children and youth in the middle—those who are *not* at
risk for school failure or those who are the high achievers—tend to receive few if
any meaningful interactions with their counselors. Regrettably, some counselors
continue to operate using outdated assumptions about school counseling and
ineffective methods of reaching students. In short, despite the improvements to
counselor education programs, school counselors remain in the shadow of the
profession's mixed history.

Even Better News: The Emergence of Comprehensive School Counseling Programs

How can school counselors emerge from this cloud of negativity and inadequate
practice? From my perspective, they must adhere more closely to the recommendations developed by the American School Counselor Association (ASCA; 1997, 1999,
2003) to enhance their interventions with students and their parents/caregivers.
Members must move beyond their conventions and fully implement a systemic-
programmatic approach—one that is proactive, prevention-oriented, and developmental in focus (see Chapters 1 and 5, and also, e.g., Gysbers & Henderson, 2001,
for detailed discussions). Since accountability is currently the catchphrase of the
educational establishment and the public at large, school counselors must also

take ownership of the varied outcomes of their programs, documenting their successes and those areas that require further development and refinement (see Chapter 8). Once school counselors are able to provide clear evidence for the efficacy of their programs and the positive impact on students, the public perception will gradually change. In brief, by adopting a comprehensive school counseling program, school counselors will be following ASCA's guidelines and serve the needs of their constituents more fully.

Target Audience and Principal Aims

This book is intended for two primary audiences. First, for graduate students in counselor education programs desiring to be K–12 school counselors, the text provides not only the baseline knowledge needed for subsequent counseling courses but also state-of-the-art information useful on the job. In addition, for those readers exploring the profession for the first time, the introductory material presented should help them make a better decision as to whether school counseling is the right plan of action. Second, school counselors already in the field can profit considerably from reading this text. It will help refocus their efforts, refresh, and update their knowledge base in accordance with the latest school counseling theory, research, and best practices. In brief, if the goal is to obtain a highly informative overview of the contemporary world of K–12 school counseling written by some of the top scholar-practitioners in the profession, then this book will prove to be quite helpful.

Organizational Framework

The text is structured around the major roles of the modern school counselor as specified by ASCA (e.g., 1997, 1999), what I call "the 3 Cs Plus." Many readers may ask why certain topics are included and others are left out and why the "how tos" of the profession are not fully detailed. The simple answer: This is an introductory text that covers the *essential* theories, research, and practice of the profession. It is my assumption that other pertinent but nonfundamental topics and application specifics are covered elsewhere in the curriculum. Resources for further reading and study, however, are included throughout the book.

ASCA's 3 Cs Plus

Nearly a century ago Frank Parsons (1909), one of the profession's earliest leaders, urged his readers to follow this advice before pursing a lifelong goal: "It is better to sail with a compass and chart than to drift into an occupation haphazard or by chance, proximity, or uninformed selection; and drift on through it without reaching any port worthy of the voyage" (p. 101). Borrowing from his wise counsel, the best way to navigate through challenging professional waters is to possess the right equipment and knowledge. Using ASCA's (1999, 2002) school counselor role statements as the map and compass, this book elucidates the key functions of the contemporary school counselor. It is organized around ASCA's "3 Cs Plus" (counseling, coordination, consultation, and the plus—large group or classroom guidance), with each well-known author (or authors) contributing a chapter relating to his or her specific area of expertise. Recently, another C, collaboration, has been discussed in the literature (e.g., ASCA, 2000; Staton & Gilligan, 2003). This important "new" role is discussed in Chapter 11.

More specifically, the first chapter is an introduction to the profession, its history, the 3 Cs Plus, and other relevant topics. Subsequently, the book is divided into four sections. Part I considers these aspects of the counseling role:

- Individual (Chapter 2)
- Group (Chapter 3)
- Peer and family counseling (Chapter 4)

Part II addresses how school counselors function as program coordinators in these areas:

- Development, implementation, and management (Chapter 5)
- Large group guidance (Chapter 6)
- Educational and career planning (Chapter 7)
- Program evaluation (Chapter 8).

Part III discusses the consultation role, both within the school (Chapter 9) and outside the school (Chapter 10). In the final section, school-based collaboration (Chapter 11) and the future of the profession (Chapter 12) are explored.

Chapter Philosophical Orientation and Structure

Each chapter overviews a particular area within the *practical* framework of K–12 comprehensive guidance and counseling programs (e.g., Gysbers & Henderson, 2001), including the ASCA National Standards (Competencies and Indicators; Dahir, 2001) and the ASCA National Model (ASCA, 2003). Comprehensive programs are designed with systems thinking (Keys & Lockhart, 1999) and developmental theory (Myrick, 2003) in mind. Further, each author has attempted to use this organizing and general rubric to guide the chapter's content: (a) introduction, rationale, and definitional issues, (b) chief theoretical orientation to the topic, (c) salient research, and (d) practical application in the context of K–12 school counseling programs. Issues of ethics, law, and diversity, as well as future trends are embedded into each chapter. Although the role technology can play in school counseling practice is not given center stage, it is addressed in several chapters.

Wading Through "Technical" Information

Occasionally I hear these remarks from promising school counselors: "Why do we study so much theory and research? Couldn't we spend more time on practical things?" I generally nod my head in tacit agreement; sometimes too much theoretical and technical information can be overwhelming and less than scintillating reading. Getting to the heart of the school counselor's job often takes readers through areas that might appear on the surface less than useful. However, try not to let this foundational material sidetrack your learning and interest. The information presented in each chapter is useful knowledge that will help you master the profession's core competencies for school counselors (see Chapter 1). In particular, by learning this information you will be able to:

- Competently use the language of school counseling and education.
- Formulate and implement a successful school counseling program.
- Skillfully support and assist students and their caregivers.
- Effectively collaborate with educational colleagues and representatives of relevant community agencies.

Some Tips to the Reader

Here are several ideas to help readers enhance their learning. First, I encourage you to discuss and debate the book's content and ideas with your fellow students and instructors. Compare and contrast the content with the realities you experience in the schools. Second, use the application material presented in each chapter to further your learning. Third, develop some specific reading goals (see below). Finally, go beyond the chapters. Use the references at the end of each chapter as a bibliography and as a guide to supplementary study. The research and best practices discussed by the authors are useful for papers assigned in other school counseling classes. It is my hope that reading and studying these chapters will further ignite your passion for school counseling.

Setting Learning Goals

Before reading any further, I suggest that you formulate a few learning goals. Use the space below each question to jot down your thoughts.

(a) I want to learn these things from this book:

what coordination + consultation looks like

(b) I can get the most from reading this book by . . . (Alternatively, these reading strategies are helpful to maximize my learning . . .)

asking questions

(c) To integrate the knowledge gained with my practical experiences, I will . . .

Use ideas in my daily work as a teacher

Acknowledgments

Permit me to thank personally each of the contributors to this text. Each individual is an important scholar in the school counseling profession, and by his or her contribution here, the profession has been further advanced. To work with this fine group has been indeed a wonderful honor for me. The publisher's representatives, Barry Fetterolf and Mary Falcon of Lahaska Press (Houghton Mifflin), should also receive my sincerest gratitude, for without their leadership, encouragement, and support, this book would have not been written. My editorial assistant, Heather Robinson Stroh, has also been very instrumental in the process of getting this book to press. I cannot go without thanking these current and former graduate students for their research assistance: Angela Bond, Kirstin Doughty, Neal Perrine, Lisa Rubel, Heather Stroh, and Amy Yillik-Downer. I want to express my appreciation to the publisher's staff, especially Merrill Peterson, and to the external reviewers (Drs. C. Marie Jackson, Elena Kimball, Ginger MacDonald, Vivian J. Carroll McCollum, Daya Sandhu, Russell Sabella) for providing their invaluable assistance in making the text better as well as a reality. Finally, Mike Bottery, University of Hull (UK) and Christian Mätzler, University of Bern (Switzerland), deserve my sincerest gratitude for hosting me as a visiting scholar while I worked on this book.

This text is dedicated to my family and to my students.

REFERENCES

American School Counselor Association. (1997). *Position statement: The professional school counselor and comprehensive school counseling programs.* Retrieved August 10, 2002, from http://www.schoolcounselor.org/pdf/counsel.pdf

American School Counselor Association. (1999). *The role of the professional school counselor.* Retrieved August 20, 2002, from http://www.schoolcounselor.org/content.cfm?L1=1000&L2=69

American School Counselor Association. (2000). *Position statement: The professional school counselor and educational planning* (adopted 1994). Retrieved November 10, 2002, from http://www.schoolcounselor.org/content.cfm?L1=1000&L2=18

American School Counselor Association. (2002). *Careers/roles.* Retrieved August 30, 2002, from http://www.schoolcounselor.org/content.cfm?L1=9

American School Counselor Association. (2003). *The ASCA National Model: A framework for school counseling programs.* Alexandria, VA: Author.

Dahir, C. A. (2001). The national standards for school counseling programs: Development and implementation. *Professional School Counseling, 4,* 320–327.

Erford, B. T. (Ed.). (2003). *Transforming the school counseling profession.* Upper Saddle River, NJ: Merrill/Prentice Hall.

Gysbers, N. C., & Henderson, P. (2001). Comprehensive guidance and counseling programs: A rich history and a bright future. *Professional School Counseling, 4,* 246–256.

Keys, S. G., & Lockhart, E. J. (1999). The school counselor's role in facilitating multisystemic change. *Professional School Counseling, 3,* 101–107

Myrick, R. D. (2003). *Developmental guidance and counseling: A practical approach* (4th ed.). Minneapolis, MN: Educational Media.

Parsons, F. (1909). *Choosing a vocation.* Boston, MA: Houghton Mifflin.

Staton, A. R., & Gilligan, T. D. (2003). Teaching school counselors and school psychologists to work collaboratively. *Counselor Education & Supervision, 42,* 162–176.

Whiston, S. C. (2003). Outcomes research on school counseling services. In B. T. Erford (Ed.), *Transforming the school counseling profession* (pp. 435–447). Upper Saddle River, NJ: Merrill/Prentice Hall.

CHAPTER 1
The Contemporary School Counselor

Christopher A. Sink
Seattle Pacific University

"Children are the world's most valuable resource and its best hope for the future."

—JOHN F. KENNEDY UNICEF appeal, July 25, 1963

Introduction

School guidance and counseling has changed quite a bit over the past several decades. In fact, the school counseling profession is in a process of significant transformation (Erford, House, & Martin, 2003). Nowadays, the school counselor's world is multifaceted, filled with variety and challenges, as well as personal rewards. Although there is a general flow to the semester and school year, the counselor's day can be unpredictable and demanding. In order to get a better feel for a school counselor's world, here are a couple "real life" scenarios.

Vignette 1: Elementary School

Ms. Conners, the school counselor, arrives to work around seven thirty in the morning to catch up on some paperwork, but within fifteen minutes, one parent calls to say a "big thanks" for helping her daughter get into middle school, while another stops in for a referral to a psychologist because her child "seems to be real depressed and hates school." The principal later arrives at her door "asking"

1

if the counselor could do lunchroom duty for the rest of the week. She checks her e-mail and finds over twenty new messages, but one is most alarming. A teacher thinks one of his students might have some type of anxiety disorder and asks the counselor to "check it out as soon as possible." On the way to this teacher's classroom another stops the counselor in the hallway, remarking that a kindergartener, who was in a small group for grieving children, is "doing much better in class." The school bell rings to start the day.

Vignette 2: Middle School

Kai, a somewhat disorientated new student, arrives at the counseling office, where the two school counselors, Ms. Ramos and Mr. Jones, work as a team. Kai was sent to the office of Ms. Ramos, who has an open "drop-in" spot in her schedule. Kai sheepishly enters and waits for Ms. Ramos to finish her phone call to a disagreeable father. Ms. Ramos waves to Kai with a smile and gestures for him to sit down in the overstuffed chair. While indicating to Kai with one hand that she'll be with him in a minute, she tries to tactfully end her phone conversation and, with the other hand, types into her computer a class schedule change for another student. Kai notices a stack of pink telephone messages on Ms. Ramos's desk and other miscellaneous papers spread out over the corner of the office. Ms. Ramos's weekly schedule is taped onto the door. With a caseload of about 475 students, almost all the time slots are filled up with counseling appointments, classroom presentations, special education meetings, and a parent education night. After finishing the phone call on a sour note while telling the principal, who stuck her head into the office, that she had no free time after school for yet another meeting, Ms. Ramos closed the door and introduced herself to Kai with a stressed smile.

From these depictions, it is obvious that school counselors are on the go, frequently with small mounds of paperwork, many follow-up telephone calls to make, a variety of administrative tasks, parent and teacher meetings to attend and conduct, classroom teaching, student testing, and so on. As you become further acquainted with the job description, the list of duties will look at times overwhelming and require significant preparation. Even so, when school counselors spend time with students, all the effort and stress seems worthwhile. To witness students change and grow, to be a significant part of their lives, gives counselors a sense of purpose and a genuine feeling of satisfaction. In short, the position is a huge privilege and a heavy responsibility. Obtaining, therefore, a reasonably clear perspective of the school counseling profession from the outset is necessary. Before moving on, however, it might be useful to do some personal reflection.

Self-Inventory

The discussion so far may have sparked some initial feelings of apprehension. For example, in the beginning I was not quite sure if school counseling was really the best career path for me. How would I find out? In time, other nagging questions came to mind:

- How does a newcomer to the school counseling profession obtain the necessary skills to be effective with kids and their parents? Can I really do all that the job requires?
- Do I need to be highly skilled in all areas to be helpful to students?
- Am I well suited to work in a school with a diverse student body?
- What age group should I work with?
- Do I have the personal qualities needed for the job?

Perhaps my concerns mirror some of your own. Take a few minutes here to jot down your preliminary thoughts and feelings about school counseling.

I need a fresh perspective — I only know how counselors function at my school.

After reading this chapter, revisit your answers. I hope you will have gained new insights and a better understanding of the profession.

Chapter Purpose and Organization

As realistically as possible, the chapter is meant to orient the reader to the school counseling profession. Because the goal is modest in scope, the wide variety of perspectives you might find in the school counseling literature have not been included. The chapter is organized in sections. The first provides a rationale for using highly trained and credentialed counselors in schools. In the second, I discuss the primary focus of school counseling. Next, the chapter summarizes several key concepts and terms used in the profession. The fourth section traces the profession's historical development. Fifth, the major roles and tasks of the contemporary school counselor are considered, along with a brief comparison of what school counselors might do at the different grade levels. To close out the chapter, I present some of the most important school counselor competency areas and a variety of personal characteristics helpful for the job.

Rationale for School Counseling

To justify the use of tax dollars for school counseling services, counselors must be able to give a convincing reply to two questions: Why are school counselors needed in today's schools? Are school counselors effective? It is obvious to most people that children and youth require extensive support and assistance as they move through the school years and beyond. The statistics concerning the general welfare (Children's Defense Fund, 2001, 2002) and mental health needs of students and their families (National Mental Health Association, 2002) reveal significant problems. Even though these numbers will fluctuate from year to year, a 2002 Children's Defense Fund report stated that for all U.S. children these sample events occur every day:

- Five children or youth under 20 years old commit suicide.
- Nine children or youth under 20 are murdered.
- Nine children or youth under 20 die from firearms.
- 180 children are arrested for violent crimes.
- 367 children are arrested for drug abuse.
- 2,861 high school students drop out.
- 4,248 children are arrested.
- 7,883 children are reported abused or neglected.
- 17,297 public school students are suspended.

Even more troubling, these concerns are often more acute for minority and disadvantaged students, and they strongly affect the school climate. Students often feel that school is not altogether a warm and nurturing place (Sink & Stroh, 2003). In short, with the number of major issues facing students today, for many, learning may take a backseat to "simply" coping with life's burdens.

Complex issues like anxiety and depression, bullying, crime, eating disorders, family problems, post-traumatic stress disorder, poverty, school violence, substance abuse, suicide, and teen pregnancy contribute to students being at risk for school failure. School counselors alone cannot make a substantial dent in these problems. Although more efficacy research is needed to clearly document the positive effect of school counselors (Whiston, 2003), the initial evidence suggests that intervention programs where educators, including school counselors, in partnership with community agencies, can help prevent (e.g., Battistich & Schaps, 1996; Illback & Nelson, 1996; U.S. Department of Education, 1999) and reduce a variety of problems faced by children and youth (see, e.g., reviews in Borders & Drury, 1992; Lewis, Sugai, & Colvin, 1998; Prout & Prout, 1998; Samples & Aber, 1998; Sink & Rubel, 2001; Whiston & Sexton, 1998; Whiston, 2003). Comprehensive school counseling programs, as discussed later, are also showing signs that they are helpful to students (e.g., Gysbers, 2001; Lapan, 2001; Lapan, Gysbers, & Petroski, 2001; Lapan, Gysbers, & Sun, 1997; Sink & Stroh, 2003). In brief, school counselors make a difference in the lives of students and their families. Since there are so many pressing issues to deal with, how do counselors prioritize their work? The following section looks at this question.

◤ The Focal Point

Like most service professions, school counseling continues to progress as innovative methods are developed and introduced into daily practice. For example, school counselors are now advised to implement "new" individual counseling methods like solution-focused interventions and multicultural techniques (e.g., Sink, Rowley, MacDonald, Jones, & Perrine, in press; Sklare, 1997; Thompson, 2002). Moreover, the advent of sophisticated technology has promising applications as well as challenges for school counseling. With constant change, school counselors often tend to feel scattered. They want to know who and what they should focus on. Fortunately, across the profession's relatively short history, the welfare of students has been at the center of the school counselor's efforts. Naturally, in different eras, certain dimensions of a student's school life were accentuated over others. Although I have more to say later about the profession's development, in the mid-1900s, for instance, school counselors overemphasized the therapeutic and emotional needs of students at risk for emotional and adjustment problems rather than attending to the whole child (Wrenn, 1957).

Recognizing that there is ongoing debate over this issue, in recent years, the core work of the school counselor can be condensed down to two major purposes: To be an ethical and a competent advocate for and facilitator of (a) student development (e.g., personal/social, educational, and career domains) and (b) a comprehensive school counseling program. The American School Counselor Association (ASCA;

1999b), the national organization representing and serving the professional needs of the nation's school counselors, reinforced these aims and added these assertions:

> School counselors, as members of the educational team, consult and collaborate with teachers, administrators and families to insure all school programs facilitate the educational process and offer the opportunity for school success for each student. School counselors are an integral part of all school efforts to insure a safe learning environment and safeguard the human rights of all members of the school community.

What are some of the primary ideas represented in this position statement? Clearly, counselors are first and foremost student-centered. In addition, notions like advisement and support, partnership, and upholding such values as equity, justice, and safety for all are embedded in the declaration. Notice that school counselors are *not* peripheral to the educational process; instead, they are vital contributors. The chapter turns next to the fundamental ideas and language of the school counseling profession.

Essential Concepts and Terminology

There are always important concepts and vocabulary that are basic to any profession. Getting a firm grasp on these should provide some specific language to frame your learning and professional growth. To begin with, school counselors should understand and use systems thinking and a developmental orientation in their practice.

Systemic-Ecological Approach

As you would expect, school counselors must take into account the larger context in which students live. Building upon the ecological theory of Bronfenbrenner (1979), university-level counselor educators and scholars like Bemak, Green, Keys, and their associates (e.g., Bemak, 2000; Green & Keys, 2001; Keys & Bemak, 1997; Keys, Bemak, & Lockhart, 1998; Keys & Lockhart, 1999) are correct when they recommend that educators cannot adequately assist students with their needs without collaborating with the significant people in students' "ecosystems." These prominent individuals might include their families, peer groups, neighborhoods, and others in the community (e.g., mental health agencies, social services, law enforcement, faith-based organizations). Figure 1.1 illustrates this social ecological perspective, with its rings showing the students' interrelated levels of functioning. Briefly then, school counselors attempt to see the bigger picture by

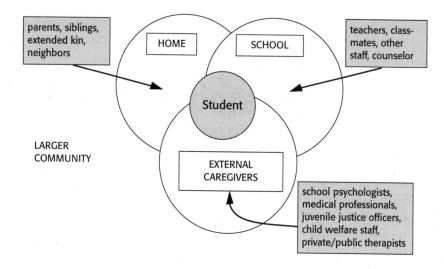

Figure 1.1 Student's Ecosystem.

using systems thinking in their work with students and their families, as well as view students as humans in progress (Amatea & Brown, 2000; Carns & Carns, 1997; Hosford & Ryan, 1970; Mullis & Edwards, 2001; Paisley, 2001; Peeks, 1997).

Middle School Example.   Curtis, age 12, was arrested the previous night, trying to shoplift his favorite CD. Although his crime was not a terribly serious offense, his court-appointed caseworker suggested to the parents that Curtis receive psychotherapy and have his school counselor follow-up. After meeting with Curtis shortly after the referral, the school counselor sensed that part of his problems might stem from unresolved concerns with the stepdad. With written permission from Curtis and Curtis's family, the school counselor hinted to the mental health counselor that the boy and his parents should obtain family therapy. The parents and Curtis reluctantly accepted this recommendation. Working with Curtis's entire system (i.e., family, mental health counselor, social worker, and teachers), the school counselor was therefore better able to manage the situation at school.

Developmental Orientation

The school counseling literature consistently underscores the need for counselors to understand the developmental issues of students. Specifically, school counseling programs and practice should be closely aligned with developmental theory and research (e.g., Borders & Drury, 1992; Dinkmeyer, 1966; Dinkmeyer & Caldwell, 1970; Erford, 2003; Green & Keys; 2001; MacDonald & Sink, 1999; Mosher & Sprinthall, 1970; Myrick, 2003; Paisley, 2001; Paisley & Benshoff, 1996; Paisley & Borders, 1995; Paisley & Hubbard, 1994; Ripley, Erford, Dahir, & Eschbach, 2003; Thompson, 2002; Zaccaria, 1966). Perhaps you have had some exposure to various developmental theories used to help explain students' thoughts, feelings, and behavior. There are, for instance, theories about how students form over time an ethnic identity (Atkinson, Morten, & Sue, 1998), as well as how they advance progressively in their cognition (Piaget, 1964/1993), moral reasoning (Kohlberg, 1984), psychosocial and interpersonal functioning (Erikson, 1950, 1968; and Selman, 1980, respectively), and career orientation (Super, Savickas, & Super, 1996). It is beyond the scope of this chapter to review each contributing theory, but there are three underlying assumptions common to most approaches that serve as the theoretical building blocks for developmental school counseling programs.

1. *Individuals move through a series of qualitatively different developmental stages at their own pace* (Lambert & McCombs, 1998; Miller, 2002; Myers, Shoffner, & Briggs, 2002; Myrick, 2003; Stroh & Sink, 2002).

Various psychologists, as alluded to above, have documented the stages of human development across many areas of functioning (see e.g., Miller, 2002, for a more in-depth presentation). Each hierarchical step typifies a phase in the student's development. The influence of new experiences, modified environments, and novel ways of understanding facilitate the ordered progression from one stage to the next. Stated another way, significant events (e.g., moving into puberty) or crises (e.g., a death of a loved one) in students' lives may cause, in Piagetian (Elkind, 1976) terminology, a sense of disequilibrium or imbalance. To resolve this cognitive "unsettledness" and its accompanying emotional upset, students often need to, in their own time, reflect on and revise their old views and emotions about a situation, substituting these for more realistic, sophisticated ones. In a nutshell, school counselors, as developmental specialists (Erford et al., 2003; Myrick, 2003), must be aware of students' general growth patterns in a variety of areas and devise guidance and counseling activities and interventions according to these different levels of functioning (Borders & Drury, 1992; Paisley, 2001).

Elementary School Example.   Thomas has lived only in an upper-middle-class European American community. Like his schoolmates, he has had very little interaction with children from different ethnicities. On a field trip to an urban city, his elementary school counselor asked all the children in Thomas's class to do a fun activity with other children from various cultures. Since Thomas has only his beliefs and feelings about these children to guide his actions, the new experience can naturally influence Thomas's future attitudes and emotions toward other playmates. Gradually, with continued exposure to children from minority cultures and further cognitive and psychosocial development, Thomas will see and appreciate the commonalities and dissimilarities among children of all backgrounds. In other words, Thomas, in time and with additional experience, will grow in his social awareness and understanding of himself and others.

2. *School counseling programs should support the healthy and normal development of students* (e.g., Borders & Drury, 1992; Clark & Stone, 2000; Dinkmeyer & Caldwell, 1970; Gysbers & Henderson, 2000; Myers et al., 2002; Myrick, 2003; Paisley, 2001; Paisley & Benshoff, 1996).

Much research has been conducted to provide educators and psychologists with at least the markers and essential characteristics of normal and abnormal human development (see, e.g., Miller, 2002, for lengthy discussion). There are, for instance, fairly specific developmental tasks (e.g., Elkind, 1976; Havighurst, 1972) and competencies (Campbell & Dahir, 1997) associated with different stages. School counselors can use these to help plan, structure, and implement guidance curriculum, individual and small group counseling, and parent meetings that promote healthy functioning.

High School Example.   The four counselors at Martin Luther King High School regularly teach and run small groups with the ninth and tenth graders about peer relationships. With the students in the later grades, the counselors go into their classrooms to work on important transition issues (e.g., job development, and career and educational planning). Later in the year, all the counselors work with students in preparation for the statewide achievement testing. They teach lessons on test-preparation and test-taking strategies as well as anxiety-management techniques. The seniors also receive additional classroom instruction as they prepare for taking college-entrance examinations.

3. *Prevention of long-term problems is central to facilitating students' psychological growth, resiliency, and school and life success* (Hamachek, 1988; Myrick, 2003; Paisley, 2001; Thompson, 2002).

Developmentally based school counseling avoids working only with students in what I call the "let's wait and see what happens" mode—that is, in the "old school" approach or remediation-focused orientation, where school counselors tend to intervene only after students' problems or issues have reached the crisis stage (Myrick, 2003). Instead, contemporary school counselors should be *proactive* in their work, assisting students through developmental stages and issues before they become debilitating concerns (Myers et al., 2002; Thompson, 2002).

Multigrade Example.   Rather than wait until the teachers refer students to him for stress-related problems (e.g., panic attacks and severe anxiety reactions), twice a year Mr. Delphino runs "Take Care" small groups for a mixture of youngsters who may or may not be at risk for significant emotional difficulties. By doing so, Mr. Delphino has used a "best practice"—intervene early and proactively.

Use of "Best Practices"

As school counselors view students more holistically and developmentally, leaders in the profession, including those representing ASCA and state school counselor associations, also highlight the need for school counselors to use *best practices* to help *all* students succeed in school (Thompson, 2002). What this educational jargon suggests is that counselors do not merely rely on past experiences to guide their work, but they implement those interventions and services that are effective in the context of the school (e.g., bibliocounseling, solution-focused counseling, play-based interventions). For counseling approaches that involve play to be considered "successful," they require a solid theoretical foundation and a research foundation that documents their usefulness with younger students. With play-like interventions, this is typically the case (Drewes, Carey, & Schaefer, 2001); the theories underlying the use of play with elementary students are largely well developed, and research studies tend to show that this strategy works, for example, with younger children who have experienced a traumatic event (see, e.g., Shen & Sink, 2002, for a review).

Guidance, Guidance Curriculum, and Counseling

Perhaps in your previous reading or from personal experiences, you have come across specific terms in education that are unclear. For example, the public often misperceives "guidance" and "counseling" as the same thing. Occasionally, you may still hear or read about the "guidance counselor," while at other times, people may refer to the "school counselor." Are these descriptors interchangeable?

Guidance.   According to Myrick (1997), the usage of the term *guidance* in American schools has changed over time. Originally, in early decades of the 1900s, it was generally viewed in relationship to vocational guidance and occupational development (Myers, 1923). For the most part, it was teachers and vocational guidance personnel who distributed vocational and occupational information to their students. Not surprisingly then, some educators and members of the public still associate guidance with the sharing of employment and career information and job placement.

At the present time, however, guidance or developmental guidance is seen as an overarching term, encompassing a set of activities and services that assist students within these content domains: personal/social, career, and educational development (Baker, 2001; Cobia & Henderson, 2003; Gysbers & Henderson, 2000; Myrick, 2003). School, mental health, and career counselors, along with teachers, nurses, and school psychologists, may team up in various ways to deliver these services and activities. Some districts and states may also use the phrase *guidance functions*. These school counseling responsibilities largely fit under the guidance umbrella. A Vermont high school, for example, uses these guidance functions: personal counseling, consultation, academic planning, college planning, career awareness, and prevention education (South Burlington High School, 2002).

Guidance Curriculum.   Most kindergarten through twelfth grade (K–12) schools now have both informal and well-developed *guidance curricula*. Taught generally in the classroom, the curricula, which often span multiple grade levels and have a scope and sequence, involve important topics of concern to students and school personnel (Cobia & Henderson, 2003; Goodnough, Pérusse, & Erford, 2003; Thompson, 2002). You might see on a counselor's shelves multiple resources that address, for example, antibullying, conflict resolution, study and test-taking strategies, methods for effective job interviewing, "kicking the habit" skills (i.e., anti–substance abuse curriculum), and how to maintain healthy relationships at school and at home.

The foci of the curricula vary somewhat from school to school. For example, at one private school in Florida, the curricular topics included these five skill areas: (a) academic issues, (b) decision making, (c) personal assessment and awareness, (d) interpersonal relations, and (e) transitional issues (Belen Jesuit Preparatory School, 2002). In contrast, Republic R-III School District's (Missouri) guidance curriculum strands (Davis, 1996) were closely aligned with those presented in the Missouri State Model Guidance Program (Gysbers & Henderson, 2000) and ASCA's National Standards for Comprehensive School Counseling Programs (Campbell & Dahir, 1997) and the ASCA National Model (ASCA, 2003), including these three domains: (a) knowledge of self and others, (b) career planning and explorations, and (c) educational and vocational development.

Counseling.   When school counselors speak of conducting a *counseling* session, they are referring to a mutually interactive and confidential process of helping students either individually or in a small group with personal, social, or other concerns (ASCA, 1999b; Myrick, 2003). As an example, one elementary school in Washington state largely provides one-to-one counseling, while another uses primarily small groups to help children work through their concerns. Importantly, school counselors help students with their "normal" developmental concerns involving, for example, identity formation, educational skills, test anxiety, family relations, and loss or grief.

Comprehensive School Counseling Programs

Over the past several decades, important members of the profession have encouraged practitioners to work in systemic and collaborative ways to assist students and their caregivers (e.g., ASCA, 1997, 1999b, 2002a; Aubrey, 1977, 1982; Campbell & Dahir, 1997; Cobia & Henderson, 2003; Dahir, 2001; Dahir, Sheldon, & Valiga, 1998; Erford, 2003; Gysbers & Henderson, 2000, 2001; Ripley et al., 2003; Schmidt, 2003; Thompson, 2002; Wittmer, 2000a, 2000b, 2000c). To accomplish this goal, ASCA's (1997, 1999a, 2002a, 2003) leadership has strongly advocated for the design and implementation of *comprehensive school counseling* (or *comprehensive guidance and counseling*) *programs*. While supporting the educational objectives of states and local school districts, school counselors operating within the context of a developmentally focused comprehensive school counseling program aid in the formation of a range of student skills (e.g., appreciation of cultural diversity, career awareness, conflict resolution, test taking). As mentioned earlier, these skills fall approximately into three major content areas. Using developmental principles (e.g., Dinkmeyer & Caldwell, 1970; Goodnough et al., 2003; Myrick, 2003), school counselors alongside teachers, nurses, administrators, and other educators work together to implement the guidance curriculum and a variety of programmatic components (e.g., individual and group counseling, educational planning, evaluation).

With a firmer grasp on some of the major concepts and vocabulary used in school counseling, a historical summary of the profession should be more intelligible. From the discussion, you will see how school counseling gradually progressed from its roots in vocational guidance to its current programmatic emphasis, linking development theory and research with a more holistic or systemic perspective.

A Brief History of School Counseling

There are numerous detailed publications addressing how school counseling evolved into a fully recognized profession and a significant part of the K–12 educational system (e.g., Aubrey, 1977; Gysbers, 1997; Gysbers, 2001; Gysbers & Henderson, 2000; Herr, 2003; Myrick, 2003; Schmidt, 2003; Wittmer, 2000b). As such, this historical review should serve as a useful introduction.

Formative Era—Vocational to Educational Guidance

Vocational Guidance.   Although there was no official school counseling profession until much later, in the early decades of the twentieth century, starting with the work of Frank Parsons (1909) in Boston and Jesse Davis (1914) in Michigan's Grand Rapids High School, leading educators expressed concern about the vocational needs of young people (e.g., Allen, 1927; Ginn, 1924; Reed, 1916). Using the terms "counseling" and "vocational guidance" liberally throughout his book, Parsons's goal was to help service providers carry out this role more effectively. Around this time as well, vocational counselors were introduced into the Boston public schools (Ginn, 1924) and through the city's Vocational Bureau, they had access to further education and training.

About a decade later, Myers (1923) argued that vocational guidance counseling, like history or mathematics, was a central part of public education. Setting the tone for a subsequent trend in school counseling, he also underscored Parsons's (1909) contention that this guidance function required specialized training and qualifications. Remarkably, Myers, predating the more formal development of a comprehensive school counseling program by approximately fifty years, suggested that for vocational guidance to be the most effective, it should be delivered not as "something added on" but as "a comprehensive program of guidance," that is, as a "unified program . . . for the entire school system" (pp. 139–140, 142). Furthermore, vocational counseling at the secondary level must first be grounded in research, and second, the guidance curriculum must meet not only students' occupational needs but their educational concerns as well.

During this period, educators also recommended several guidance "innovations." First, vocational guidance needs to begin with elementary-age children (e.g., McCracken & Lamb, 1923; Reed, 1916). Second, reflecting the view of Myers (1923), McCracken and Lamb (1923) supported the notion of integrating vocational guidance into the total school curriculum. Third, there were also hints in these early writings that vocational guidance was not enough to meet the multiple concerns of students and their families.

Educational Guidance.   By the 1930s, guidance had expanded beyond its vocational roots. At this point, "educational guidance" became the new approach, because it was seen as more prevention oriented, holistic in nature, and incorporated advances in student assessment (Brewer, 1933; Proctor, 1925; Reed, 1944; Williamson & Darley, 1937). Educational guidance took place, first, through classroom discussion, including such broad topics as vocational decision making, orientation to careers, school-related problems, home life, leisure and recreation, personal well-being, ethics, and citizenship. Moreover, the guidance role began to resemble a "position" orientation (see, e.g., Gysbers, 1997, for detailed discussion), where one educator assumed leadership of the entire guidance program. Guidance should also involve elements of individual counseling, where students have the opportunity to interview and discuss with the teacher-counselor issues of concern. Brewer saw this process, perhaps in part, as contemporary school counselors do, as an ethical practice of helping students through their normal problems (i.e., developmental issues). Finally, as a precursor to suggestions proposed in our current era (e.g., Gysbers & Henderson, 2000), Brewer advised schools to form a committee to plan and foster the aims of a comprehensive program of guidance.

It appears that during this period, the emphasis also switched to applying *scientific* techniques to educational and vocational guidance and to the more widespread use of the phrase *student personnel work* (Williamson & Darley, 1937). This shift is significant, for members of the profession were now clearly viewing students as multifaceted persons with multipotentiality. To assist students then, advanced "scientific" skills were required (e.g., the ability to administer standardized testing, understand and apply quantitative data, and perform clinical interviews). Other important developments included the need to prevent student maladjustment through periodic assessments, ongoing counseling sessions, promotion of students' social lives and extracurricular activities, parent education, and financial assistance. As a way to bring credibility to the field (i.e., "to professionalize" student personnel work), Williamson and Darley argued for increased accountability and evaluation of guidance programs.

According to Reed (1944), an early pioneer in the guidance field, the child guidance movement also had an important influence on guidance and personnel services. It was linked to society's parallel attempt to enhance the "mental hygiene" of students and the development of nursery schools and parent education programs (Faust, 1968). For example, Clifford Beers's (1908) book, *A Mind That Found Itself*, and the seminal publications in the 1920s and 1930s by William Burnham on mental issues (see Faust, for a lengthy discussion) were influential in fostering a deeper understanding and appreciation of the mental health needs of young children and set the foundation for elementary school counseling. Finally, progressive education (e.g., John Dewey's work with the University of Chicago Laboratory School) and the social reform movement of the early 1900s were also instrumental in promoting vocational guidance in schools (Aubrey, 1977).

In summary, educators in this early phase focused initially on students' vocational issues, but not long afterward, broadened their vision to include several other aspects of student functioning. The educational guidance movement, coinciding with various societal reform initiatives (Aubrey, 1977, 1982; Reed, 1944), brought together three "new" dimensions: (a) sophisticated techniques of student assessment and testing, (b) clinically oriented services, and (c) a holistic approach to guidance services. Williamson (1950) and later Froelich (1958) characterized the profession around the mid-1900s as one that provides guidance and personnel services to students and their families.

Transitional Era—Pupil-Personnel Services to Developmental Guidance and Counseling

Pupil-Personnel Services Orientation.　With the publication of several influential books on counseling and psychotherapy (e.g., Rogers, 1942; Williamson, 1950; Wrenn, 1962), the profession, by the mid-1900s, began to see that some of the roles of guidance personnel and counselors needed further modification. Specifically, pupil-personnel services had to incorporate and apply various psychotherapeutic concepts and techniques (Aubrey, 1977, 1982). Counseling became the most important service to students in the guidance program. By emphasizing human values and development, as well as clinical methods, guidance personnel's more narrow focus clearly shifted to the needs of the whole child. The ultimate outcome of individual counseling, borrowing from Rogerian psychotherapeutic language, was for "the client [student] to marshal his own resources, the resources of the institution and of the community . . . to achieve optimum adjustment of which he is capable" (Williamson, 1950, p. 209). Subsequently, Froelich (1958) argued that school counselors should not rigidly adhere to one theoretical approach to counseling; instead, they need to take an eclectic approach. Instruction and counseling were supposed to be interwoven into the guidance program with the goal aimed at helping students choose and grow (Williamson, 1950).

Moreover, Froelich (1958) offered these three main categories of pupil-personnel work designed to help students make adjustments to school and to life: (a) child accounting and regulatory services (e.g., services related to school admission, attendance, discipline), (b) referral to clinical services (e.g., psychological diagnoses and treatment) provided by outside specialists that were beyond the scope of the guidance counselor, and (c) school guidance services (e.g., counseling, consultation, research, large group guidance) administered largely by the counselor. Froelich reinforced, therefore, the "position" approach, stating that the counselor is the chief guidance worker, with teachers, administrators, and other staff members having lesser guidance roles. Froelich, however, like other educators before him, also suggested that a programmatic approach is ideally the best way to organize and coordinate guidance services.

The professionalization of guidance and personnel service in education also became a central theme during this period (see Henry, 1959). According to Tiedeman and Field (1962), three movements came together to help school guidance obtain some professional recognition. First, the American Psychological Association and the American Personnel and Guidance Association (an organization formed in 1952 and after several name changes has now evolved into the American School Counselor Association) raised professional standards by clarifying the distinctions and the educational requirements among various service providers (e.g., psychologists, counselors). Second, new legislation and funding for guidance was instrumental to the cause. The National Defense Educational Act of 1958, for example, enacted by the federal government, provided funding to improve secondary school counseling, subsidizing among other things training programs and professional institutes for guidance personnel. Additional universities also used this opportunity to create graduate programs in school counseling. At the state level, Departments of Education modified their certification requirements for counselors, making them more rigorous. Third, theoretical advancements in guidance and counseling, including leading developmental theories of, for example, Jean Piaget, Erik Erikson, and Donald Super, provided a solid foundation to structure pupil-personnel services and, later, comprehensive school counseling programs (Aubrey, 1977).

By the early 1960s, there were further calls for pupil-personnel services in elementary and secondary schools to be placed under a programmatic umbrella, where school counselors, psychologists, and social workers, as well as school attendance and health staff worked together for the benefit of the entire student body (Ferguson, 1963; Roeber, 1963). The programmatic approach, while continuing to see school guidance and counseling as a collection of services delivered to students, began to emphasize other important school counselor roles (e.g., coordination and consultation). Notably, Ferguson made a clear distinction between a guidance worker and a school counselor, arguing that the latter person is "a highly trained specialist who spends at least half of their time counseling" (p. 39). This trend has remained, as K–12 educators now use the title "school counselor" rather than "guidance counselor."

Developmental Guidance and Counseling. A stronger developmental orientation emerged around the 1950s and 1960s, extending in large part to the present (e.g., Dinkmeyer, 1966; Dinkmeyer & Caldwell, 1970; Wrenn, 1962; Zaccaria, 1966). Developmental theory and practice have their genesis in the research conducted outside of education, and thus, guidance and counseling has spent multiple decades finding better ways to infuse the advances in developmental psychology into the school context (e.g., Aubrey, 1982; Dinkmeyer & Caldwell, 1970; Mosher & Sprinthall, 1970). Through the design and implementation of comprehensive developmental guidance and counseling programs, this goal was largely accomplished. By reconceptualizing guidance and counseling, theorists like Dinkmeyer (1966) and Myrick (1997, 2003) created workable developmental models that shifted the focus away from a relatively unorganized collection of pupil-personnel services delivered by the guidance counselor and others, to one that has a clear programmatic structure. This innovation uses concepts now common in the school counseling vernacular, including, *direct* (e.g., counseling) and *indirect* (e.g., consultation) services, prevention, developmental guidance, guidance curriculum with a scope and sequence, needs-based interventions, integration of educational goals with guidance, collaboration, leadership, and positive school climate. The counselor was now seen as a coordinator of the program, a consultant to teachers and parents, a counselor for students' developmental and personal concerns, and a deliverer of classroom guidance. In summary, in the latter part of this era, school counseling began to shift from a services orientation to a systemic and developmental approach (Gysbers, 1997, 2001).

Contemporary Era—Implementation of Comprehensive School Counseling Programs

The structure and nature of developmental comprehensive school counseling programs (e.g., Gysbers, 1997, 2001; Thompson, 2002), as discussed above, continue to undergo refinements. Despite the fact that the models suggested by Dinkmeyer and Caldwell (1970) and Myrick (2003) remain very useful to structure guidance and counseling interventions (e.g., Wittmer, 2000c), the comprehensive guidance program devised in Missouri by Gysbers and Moore (1981), and later fine-tuned by Gysbers and Henderson (2000), has become the most widely used approach in the United States (MacDonald & Sink, 1999; Sink & MacDonald, 1998). By the late 1990s, the National Standards for Comprehensive School Counseling Programs (ASCA, 1997; Campbell & Dahir, 1997; Dahir, 2001; Dahir et al., 1998; Ripley et al., 2003) were also implemented in various districts as a way to supplement their comprehensive programs. So what changes are on the horizon?

This issue is considered in the last chapter; however, suffice it to say now, some of the profession's most prominent members and scholars (see Bowers & Hatch, 2002, for initial draft) have been working together for many years to create a national school counseling model using in part ASCA's national standards (ASCA, 2002b).

All this effort has come to fruition with publication of the *ASCA National Model: A Framework for School Counseling Programs* (ASCA, 2003). The keys to this framework are to (a) assist school counselors and school counseling teams design, coordinate, implement, manage and evaluate their programs for students' success; (b) clarify the school counselor's role in implementation using leadership, advocacy, and systemic change; (c) help school counselors redirect their emphasis from a service-centered approach to a program-centered approach serving all students; and (d) respond to these important questions: "What do school counselors do?" and "How are students different as a result of what we do?"

To end this section, it is important to note that some state educational leaders and many counselors in the field, for mostly legitimate reasons, have been reluctant or slow to fully implement ASCA's (1997, 1999a) directives on comprehensive guidance and counseling (Sink & Yillik-Downer, 2001). As such, the legacy of the pupil-personnel era continues to exert influence on current practice. On a positive note, however, using the programmatic approach to assist students and their caregivers, ASCA's (1997, 1999b, 2003) leadership was able to more sharply define school counselors' principal roles for the start of the twenty-first century.

Primary Roles—ASCA's 3 Cs Plus

The major areas of responsibility as defined by the profession (ASCA, 1999b; see the appendix at the end of this chapter) fall roughly into these categories: counseling, coordination, consultation, plus classroom guidance (the *3 Cs Plus*).

Counseling

To reiterate briefly this direct service, school counselors spend some of their time working confidentially with students one-to-one and in small groups on their problems and developmental concerns (ASCA, 1999b; Corey & Corey, 2002; Myrick, 2003; Newsome & Gladding, 2003; Thompson & Rudolph, 2000). Group or individual counseling involves a special type of relationship that is not a friendship per se, but nor is it a distant, professional relationship that one might have with a lawyer or a dentist. Whereas a positive student-counselor relationship is characterized by genuine caring, empathy, and support, the inappropriate counseling relationship could involve, for instance, moralizing, uninvited advice-giving, and the fostering of student dependency.

Due to various issues inherent to school settings (e.g., confidentially cannot always be assured and severe time restrictions), school counseling differs from the therapeutic processes used by mental health counselors, family therapists, or clinical psychologists. Instead, counseling in schools is geared toward helping students in the "here-and-now" more constructively handle their concerns (e.g., how to appropriately fend off a bully). Rather than looking at students' deep-seated issues (e.g., maladaptive personality and emotional disorders), counselors aim at those feelings, thoughts, and behaviors that are open to change within a relatively short amount of time. School counselors also tend to be more theoretically eclectic, using a variety of counseling techniques. For example, whereas elementary school counselors often use various play therapy techniques and behavioral methods in their work with younger children, secondary counselors might use a combination of counseling techniques derived from Adlerian theory, Glasser's reality therapy, and various methods from solution-focused brief therapy (Newsome & Gladding, 2003; Thompson & Rudolph, 2000). At all levels, school counselors aim for at least short-term behavior change.

In summary, the school counselor is a highly skilled facilitator of the counseling process, a concerned and encouraging person, and one who helps students cope more effectively with their concerns (Myers et al., 2002; Newsome & Gladding, 2003; see also, Locke, Myers, & Herr, 2001, for detailed discussions). They use evidence-based counseling techniques that are relevant to the school setting and its limitations. School-based counseling is largely on a short-term basis, and when the problem seems to require more assistance than the counselor can reasonably provide (e.g., severe depression, attempted suicide, unintended pregnancy), students are referred to external agencies or in-school support personnel (e.g., drug and alcohol specialist, intervention specialists, school social workers). A later chapter discusses how school counselors can assist families.

Consultation

This essential indirect service involves a partnership, where school counselors work closely with the key people in students' social ecologies, both inside the school and outside (Keys, Green, Lockhart, & Luongo, 2003). For example, counselors may be assisting parents with their child's substance abuse problem by providing support for the family and referrals to drug rehabilitation programs. Similarly, school counselors regularly consult with teachers, administrators, and school psychologists on a host of issues that may range from more "simple" problems (e.g., give input to a teacher on how to work with a particular student with specific learning needs) to more complex systemic issues (e.g., consult with the building administrator on how to revise the school discipline policy to be more equitable to all students). There are also times when counselors interact, on behalf of students and their families, with key representatives of mental health and other community agencies and programs (e.g., health services, government benefits office, social services). Keep in mind, however, that the goal of these consultations is "to plan and implement strategies to help students be successful in the education system" (ASCA, 1999b). This statement suggests that (a) the consultation should help students do better in school, and (b) there are limits to the consultation process.

Coordination

Similar to other roles, coordination can be a very difficult intervention, for it is generally a complex and time-consuming process. ASCA's (1999b) role statement clarified this responsibility as follows: "Coordination is a leadership process in which the counselor helps organize, manage and evaluate the school counseling program." For program coordination to work well, collaboration skills are again vital. What school counseling programs look like will vary, ranging from one that is of local origin (e.g., a school devised its program to fit the community's specific needs) to a statewide comprehensive program (e.g., Missouri's comprehensive guidance program; Gysbers & Henderson, 2000).

Within the coordinator's role, school counselors may also help oversee, facilitate, and organize, among many other things, these sample program dimensions:

- A referral network for students and their caregivers
- Prevention strategies (e.g., implementation of an anti–sexual harassment curriculum or a peer support group)
- A career development workshop
- The school-to-work transition process
- An educational assessment and program evaluation team
- School-based multidisciplinary (MDTs) or child study team meetings for at-risk students

As an example, the counselors at Gunston Middle School in Arlington, Virginia (Cook, 2001), decided to include five very practical coordination functions on their school web page. They narrowed their coordination priorities down to (a) helping locate resources for students, parents, and teachers; (b) interpreting test results;

(c) facilitating the distribution of information that is relevant to student needs; (d) assessing student needs; and (e) developing programs and choosing material/resources for parents. Of course, if you go to another middle school in a neighboring district, the major coordination activities could be very different.

In brief, the coordinator's role is a big one, requiring excellent relationship, facilitation, organizational, and leadership skills. As an indirect service to students and their families, school counselors should be able to (a) *mobilize* others in the school and the community to get involved, (b) *model* how the process should go, and (c) *manage* effectively the coordination activities.

Plus—Large Group Classroom Guidance

When visiting schools for an observational experience, you may find it a bit curious that many school counselors spend some of the day out of their office and in classrooms conducting developmentally appropriate guidance lessons (Goodnough et al., 2003). This is particularly true at the elementary level, where school counselors are more widely accepted as a regular part of the children's daily educational experience. ASCA (1999b) included this classroom teaching function in its role statement, where counselors implement a "planned, developmental program of guidance activities designed to foster students' academic, career, and personal/social development." By doing so, counselors can reach all students on a consistent basis.

For some practitioners, however, this responsibility can be quite challenging and even controversial. Good teaching and classroom management skills are needed for the effective delivery of guidance lessons. Many school counselors trained under the pupil-personnel services model received limited, if any, training in these vital classroom functions. Making the role even harder, many teachers across grade levels are quite reticent to give up precious teaching time to the counselor. Consequently, teachers may require a good deal of persuasion. Helping them understand how relevant guidance presentations can augment the educational process already going on in the classroom is one of the keys to opening closed doors. Here are three illustrations.

High School Example.   Because it is often difficult to have access to the classroom, school counselors would be wise to integrate their guidance lessons into what the teacher is already doing. Here is one good way to do this with high school students in an English literature course: In co-teaching Shakespeare's *Romeo and Juliet*, the regular teacher focuses on the "academic" elements of the play and the counselor looks at the narrative's "real life" applications (e.g., gang involvement, intolerance for cultural diversity, intimacy, conflict resolution skills).

Middle School Example.   The counselor, for instance, may co-present with the seventh-grade physical education (P.E.) teacher on the topic of "learning better with team-building." After a short introduction by the P.E. teacher, the students get into small groups and "compete" against the others on a fun, age-appropriate activity requiring student collaboration. They may also use adventure-based programs to facilitate leadership development.

Elementary School Example.   A similar approach could be used in elementary schools, where the counselor enters the art class early in the school year with the goal of having the children express their initial feelings about school through artwork. The teacher helps with the "artistic" part, and the counselor aids in dividing the children into three smaller groups. An appropriately trained adult volunteer, the counselor, and the teacher take one group each and facilitate the art activity and subsequent sharing. After group members have had a chance to talk about their paintings, the counselor could work with the entire class on the issue of "how to share your feelings." A week later, the counselor could return to the art class with a follow-up activity.

Other School Counseling Functions and Responsibilities

There are numerous "bonus" job functions and responsibilities that exceed ASCA's (1999b) 3 Cs Plus (see, e.g., Baker, 2000; Cobia & Henderson, 2003; Erford, 2003; Myrick, 2003; Schmidt, 2003; Wittmer, 2000a, for longer descriptions). Even though there is no real agreement on what are appropriate or inappropriate supplementary functions or duties (Burnham & Jackson, 2000), in recent years, the school counseling literature suggests that comprehensive programs should include at least four important dimensions (e.g., Cobia & Henderson; Erford; Myrick).

Help with Student Assessment and Program Evaluation.   Fitting nicely under the coordination and consultation roles, school counselors need to play a key part in student assessment and school counseling program evaluation (e.g., Borders, 2002; Cobia & Henderson, 2003; Guindon, 2003; Gysbers & Henderson, 2000; Lapan, 2001; Scruggs, Wasielewski, & Ash, 1999; Whiston, 2003). Unfortunately, however, school administrators frequently ask counselors to assist with achievement testing in ways that are not student-focused. Instead of engaging in important assessment-related tasks that school counselors are trained to do (e.g., interpreting test results to students, faculty, and parents), they are stuck with tedium (e.g., counting test booklets, organizing makeup tests, monitoring the test takers for hours on end). These activities use up valuable counselor time and ought to be delegated, for instance, to a trained and capable adult volunteer or a clerical staff member. Besides assisting with test interpretation, counselors should, for instance, help teachers prepare their students for academic assessments through classroom guidance activities (e.g., teaching effective test-taking strategies) and conducting more intensive small groups for underachieving or highly anxious students (e.g., these groups could be called "Beating the Testing Blues").

Like students, comprehensive guidance and counseling programs need to be evaluated regularly, looking at such areas as school climate, level of student mastery of developmental competencies, and school counselor effectiveness (Gysbers & Henderson, 2000; Lapan, 2001; Whiston, 2003). Counselors and the administrative staff must work together with perhaps an advisory team to make sure this important task is accomplished. Volunteering for the district's school counseling evaluation committee allows school counselors to voice their concerns to the administration.

Be Involved with School Reform.   By taking an active part in the educational reform movement going on around the nation, school counselors add to their creditability with the administration and teaching faculty (e.g., Adelman & Taylor, 2002; Bemak, 2000; Erford et al., 2003; Herr, 2001, 2002; House & Hayes, 2002; Paisley & Hayes, 2003; Stroh & Sink, 2002). They must be aware of evolving federal, district, and state educational mandates and policies to improve the schooling process, as well as how educational restructuring might affect their school counseling programs. For example, school counselors need to be involved with the changes prescribed in the No Child Left Behind Act of 2001 or Public Law 107-110 (U.S. Department of Education, 2002). This federal law significantly affects how school districts throughout the nation educate students and requires increased accountability for academic achievement. By attending curriculum development meetings and actively participating on educational committees, school counselors can contribute their perspectives and expertise to the debate on educational change. In brief, they must be invested in school reform, using comprehensive school counseling programs to encourage academic achievement and help close the achievement gap among various student groups (House & Hayes, 2002; Paisley & Hayes, 2003).

Contribute to School Efforts on Diversity Issues.   Because America is a highly pluralistic society, school counselors must provide leadership in promoting a healthy multicultural society (ASCA, 1999a; Borders, 2002; Green & Keys, 2001; Gysbers, 2001; Holcomb-McCoy, 2003; Lee, 2001; Paisley & McMahon, 2001; Sink, 2002). There are many good ideas on how school counselors can incorporate multicultural thinking into their interventions. For instance, multicultural education can be integrated within comprehensive guidance and counseling programs by (a) revising student competencies to include multicultural objectives, (b) using large group guidance lessons and small groups as ways to engage students in issues of diversity, (c) initiating early on the formation of multicultural thinking in students, and (d) building a multiethnic coalition of parents and community members who support multicultural thinking in schools (Sink, 2002). Multicultural competencies have also been developed for school counselors to guide their work with all students (see Holcomb-McCoy, 2003, for specifics). Finally, diversity involves students with different sexual orientations. School counselors will need to assist those students working through these issues as well.

Serve as a Professional.   To be a professional involves so many areas of behavior (see, e.g., Erford et al., 2003, and Linde, 2003, for detailed discussions), but the key ones are mentioned here. Primarily, school counselors act in a legal and ethical manner, as well as set appropriate boundaries (ASCA, 1998, section F1 "Professionalism"). To help guide their decision making, school counselors consult relevant local, state, and federal legislation and then look to ASCA's (1998) Ethical Standards for School Counselors (see the Appendix at the end of this book), as well as to the organization's position statements (see ASCA's web site at http://www.schoolcounselor.org/) on issues relevant to school counseling (e.g., AIDS, censorship, confidentiality, cross-cultural or multicultural counseling, discipline, gender equity, child abuse/neglect, peer helping, promotion of safe schools, students at risk). There are multiple resources on this topic for school counselors to peruse and implement (e.g., American Counseling Association, 1995, 1999; Fischer & Sorenson, 1995; Huey & Remley, 2003; Linde, 2003; Salo & Schumate, 1993).

Other ways school counselors model their professionalism is to join and be involved in ASCA and their state school counselor organization (ASCA, 1998, section F). By becoming professionally active and serving in leadership positions, school counselors gain access to the latest information (e.g., via regular newsletters, practical and research journals, workshops, conferences) and to a huge network of supportive colleagues. ASCA's web page (www.schoolcounselor.org) also connects counselors to various professional interest groups.

Need another good reason to be involved? ASCA's role statement (1999b; see the appendix at the end of this chapter) and ethical guidelines (ASCA, 1998, section F2) state unequivocally that school counselors must continue to hone and revitalize their skills and increase their level of knowledge using professional development activities. This means, for example, attending, as time and finances permit, district in-services, ASCA's and a state association's yearly conferences, as well as applicable community workshops. Many states require continuing education to maintain a school counseling credential or certificate. Universities conduct many useful courses just for this purpose. Finally, Table 1.1 lists a variety of relevant professional organizations alongside their web sites and publications.

Table 1.1   List of Relevant U.S. Professional Organizations and Associated Journals

Professional Organizations (Web Address)	*Sample Publications to Consult*
American Counseling Association–ACA (http://www.counseling.org/)	*Career Development Quarterly* *Counseling Today* (monthly magazine) *Counseling and Values* *Journal of Counseling & Development* *Journal of Humanistic Counseling, Education, and Development* *Journal of Multicultural Counseling and Development* *Measurement and Evaluation in Counseling and Development*
American Psychological Association–APA[a] (http://www.apa.org/)	*APA Monitor* (monthly magazine) *The Counseling Psychologist* *Psychological Assessment*
American School Counselor Association–ASCA (http://www.schoolcounselor.org/)	*ASCA School Counselor* (monthly magazine) *Elementary Guidance and Counseling*[b] (no longer published) *Personnel and Guidance Journal*[c] (no longer published) *Professional School Counseling* (1997 to present) *The School Counselor*[b] (no longer published)
National Association of School Psychologists–NASP (http://www.nasponline.org/)	*Communiqué* (monthly newsletter) *School Psychology Review* See also: *Journal of School Psychology and Psychology in Schools*
Association of Specialists in Group Work–ASGW (http://asgw.educ.kent.edu/)	*ASGW Newsletter* *Journal for Specialists in Group Work*

Note. [a] APA publishes multiple journals of interest to school counselors. For a complete inventory, see the organization's web site; [b] in 1997, these two journals were combined into *Professional School Counseling*; [c] published by the American Personnel and Guidance Association, the precursor to ASCA.

Other Duties as Assigned.   There are still other tasks to accomplish each school day. For example, most school counselors, regrettably, have responsibilities that are largely clerical in nature (e.g., collecting tickets from spectators at the basketball game, inputting students' minor schedule changes into the computer system, or typing up a newsletter). One may also be saddled with student supervision activities; for instance, many counselors have bus or lunchroom duty, while others are involved with disciplining, monitoring student attendance, overseeing study hall or the school newspaper, sponsoring a student club, and so on.

Some of the everyday tasks and functions are necessary for the maintenance and management of a school's comprehensive program. These may fall under what Gysbers and Henderson (2000) called "system support" activities. Grant writing and public relations activities are, for example, important to promote your school counseling program. The school counseling web page for Michigan's Carson High School (2002) provides additional examples of system support responsibilities, including professional development for counselors, staff and community relations/outreach, teacher consultation, advisory councils, program monitoring and assessment, and testing.

To summarize, although the percentage of time dedicated to one area (or any supplemental task) over the others varies across grade levels (Gysbers & Henderson, 2000), the job descriptions of most elementary, middle/junior high, and high school counselors include those responsibilities discussed in ASCA's (1999b) role statement. Furthermore, school counselors, just for a start, behave in a professional manner, support the development of multicultural thinking, lend a hand with student assessment, and provide their input to educational committees.

School Counseling at Different Grade Levels

At this point, you might be asking this question: How does school counseling differ from elementary to secondary schools? Some of the distinctions were previously illustrated in the sample vignettes. Drawing from various types of school counseling experiences and from recent publications (e.g., ASCA, 2002b; Cobia & Henderson, 2003; Erford et al., 2003; Myrick, 2003; Schmidt, 2003; Thompson, 2002; Wittmer, 2000a), I make a few more comparisons here.

Elementary School.   Since there is typically only one part-time or full-time counselor per school, they must coordinate the program single-handedly; as a result, counselors at this level must have strong leadership and collaboration skills. If the school is not too large, counselors generally know all the teachers and, at least by sight, most of the children and their caregivers. Elementary school counselors focus a great deal on prevention, but remediation of existing developmental and personal/social concerns is also part of the job. Using classroom visitations and developmental guidance lessons as their primary methods of contact, counselors tend to be highly visible around the building. Principals, parents, and teachers use the counselor for advice on a host of issues; hence, good consultation skills are essential. Rather than relying on verbal methods of counseling, counselors, for instance, apply structured interventions, puppets, games, illustrative story-books, and art to reach children. There are system support activities and office work to do, but they tend to be less time-consuming than at the secondary level.

Middle or Junior High School. Excluding some of the more rural schools, there are generally more students in a building than one full-time counselor can possibly handle alone. It is therefore far more difficult to get to know all students, their caregivers, and teachers very well. Accordingly, the counselors who have separate caseloads must be able to coordinate and manage their school counseling program as a team. This means collaborating and consulting with many more teachers and caregivers, and in many schools, more than one administrator. The focus here is on helping preteens and early teens with the significant developmental milestones and transitional issues that arise as they move from childhood to adolescence. Crises occur at all grade levels; however, because these students are coping with many personal, social, and physical changes, the crises seem to come at more frequent intervals. For this reason, remediation of existing school and home problems tends to consume much of the counselors' time. Excellent consultation as well as individual and group counseling skills are obviously important. Other interventions like large group guidance are still prevention-oriented, but they also have a stronger career-educational planning focus. System support and clerical tasks can be fairly heavy at times.

High School. In many large high schools today, up to four or five counselors may be required. Remarkably, counselors could have as many as 450 or more students on their caseloads. Similar to middle/junior high schools, the caseload is normally assigned based on the first letter of the students' last names (e.g., Mr. Browning works with students A to F) or by grade level (e.g., Ms. Wong has the sophomores). High school counselors are far less likely to even know half of the student body well. Given this reality, collaboration within the school counseling program is critical. Along with consultation with parents, teachers, and administrators, responsive services (e.g., individual and group counseling, making referrals) are significant responsibilities. On a more limited basis, school counselors conduct large group guidance. When they do, counselors intensify their efforts to prepare students for various life roles (e.g., higher education, intimate relationships, careers, citizenship). Finally, counselors at this level often report that the office work (e.g., telephone calls, data entry, writing letters of recommendation, transcript evaluation) and systems support tasks can be overwhelming.

Additional Resources.   Should you want to explore further the similarities and differences among elementary and secondary school counselors' job functions, these two recent texts should be helpful:

- *Elementary School Counseling: A Blueprint for Today and Tomorrow* (2nd ed.) by Kathleen O'Rourke, Claire Dandeneau, and John Worzbyt (2003). New York: Brunner-Routledge.
- *School Counseling in the Secondary School: A Comprehensive Process and Program* by Collette Dollarhide and Kelli Saginak (2003). Boston: Allyn & Bacon.

To recap, the major roles and ancillary duties of contemporary school counselors were overviewed. Because America's educational agenda continues to change, ASCA's foci and the counselors' roles will be further amended. However, for at least this decade, the job description should remain relatively consistent within each grade level and across schools.

Closing Issues

This last section considers more specifically the two reflection questions I posed early in the chapter: What are some of the key skill areas needed to be effective on the job? and What are some of the qualities of effective school counselors?

Core Competency Areas

It should now be apparent that guidance personnel in the formative era were more limited in what they needed to know and practice, but as the profession has advanced over the years so too have the school counselor requirements increased. Most of the competency areas were discussed earlier in some form; nevertheless, as a way to summarize the range of current school counselor proficiencies, I have brought them together in a single list (see Table 1.2). The interrelated competency areas were selected as a representative sample from a variety of relevant sources (e.g., Arredondo, 1999; ASCA, 1997, 1998, 1999a, 1999b; Association for

Assessment in Counseling, 1998; Cobia & Henderson, 2003; Erford, 2003; Gysbers & Henderson, 2000; Holcomb-McCoy & Myers,1999; House & Hayes, 2002; Keys & Lockhart, 1999; Lee, 2001; Myrick, 2003; National Association for College Admission Counseling, 2000; Sabella, 2000; Thompson, 2002). If you have not yet mastered the skills in some of these domains, be assured, no counselor has expertise in every area. With further experience and ongoing professional development, however, school counselors can enhance their effectiveness.

Useful Personal Characteristics

School counselors not only must be skillful, they should possess a variety of personal qualities as well. Since there are so few good empirical studies in this area, any list of "essential" characteristics will be flawed and incomplete. Having said this, there is plenty of anecdotal evidence to suggest that school counselors, principals, and teachers who comprise search committees are looking ideally for individuals

Table 1.2 Sample School Counselor Competency Areas

Areas of Competency [a, b]

- Advocacy and leadership
- Assessment and program evaluation
- Basic research skills (e.g., read research and collect, analyze, and interpret data)
- Consultation (school- and community-based)
- Coordination of school counseling program and its components
- Counseling (e.g., individual and group, multicultural, family assistance)
- Developmental theory and practice (within, e.g., personal/social, educational, and career domains)
- Educational theory and practice, including curriculum development, teaching, and classroom management skills (e.g., large group guidance)
- Interpersonal communication, including collaboration skills
- Multicultural and diversity issues, including awareness, sensitivity, and school practice
- Professionalism, including ethical and legal issues and professional development
- Systems theory and practice
- Technology, including school-based applications

Note. [a] States and school districts may have school counseling regulations and/or laws that do not completely match this list of competencies; [b] within each area, school districts, e.g., may have several skills.

who are fundamentally good people (i.e., people of character), positive, and well educated for the job. Other more specific descriptors could be included; for example, school counselors should be approachable, caring, efficient, enthusiastic, ethical, flexible, helpful, good communicators and counselors, knowledgeable, motivated, optimistic, organized, professional, responsible, teachable, tolerant, and team players. You may possess most of these qualities already, but if many do not fit you at this time, perhaps further self-reflection would be constructive.

- How might I develop these "personality" characteristics?
- What is my plan of action?
- Would personal counseling be useful for me to explore before launching into this career?

Summary and Recommendations

This chapter has served as an introduction to the school counseling profession and a glimpse into the school counselor's world. I have attempted to show how essential school counselors are to the educational process. Through a systemic and programmatic approach to school counseling, they collaborate with other educators and caregivers to facilitate student development and learning. More-

Table 1.3 Complementary Steps to Prepare for a School Counseling Career

Recommendations
1. Look into the school counselor certification requirements for your particular state (see, e.g., ASCA's web site at www.schoolcounselor.org), making sure that you know all the necessary requirements to obtain certification.
2. Spend significant time with elementary, middle/junior, and high school counselors. Do your job shadowing in all types of schools (e.g., rural, suburban, and urban public and private schools), because the schools tend to differ in each area. While you are there, do not be afraid to ask pointed questions.
3. If you have not been an educator, obtain some extended volunteer or paid school experience. At the very least take time to learn about (a) the language and culture of education, (b) the ins and outs of school operations, and (c) the teaching profession. In short, find out if school life really agrees with you.
4. Start building a professional library, including such materials as community resources, pertinent and practical articles and chapters from books, guidance curricula, lists of useful web sites, and so on.
5. Seek out some personal counseling to clarify your career choice and obtain feedback on issues that might keep you from being a successful school counselor.

over, school counselors' salient roles and functions are largely a result of the profession's key concepts and its rich history. The last section included examples of school counselor competency areas and useful personal characteristics. In the subsequent chapters, many of these issues are explored in more depth. As you read on, I suggest you also take the steps presented in Table 1.3. These should help you prepare for a meaningful career as a professional school counselor. Perhaps a quote from Frank Parsons (1909) is now appropriate: "You must learn what you are best adapted to do, and get started in that line" (p. 14).

In the next several chapters, the school counselor's use of individual, group, peer, and family counseling are explored. Following these, ASCA's second and third Cs, the coordination and consultation functions, respectively, are examined. Before wrapping up the text by looking at future school counseling trends (see Chapter 12), Chapter 11 reviews the importance of collaboration within the context of a comprehensive school counseling program.

The Role of the Professional School Counselor

American School Counselor Association (1999b)

The Role of the Professional School Counselor

The professional school counselor is a certified/licensed educator trained in school counseling. Professional school counselors address the needs of students through the implementation of a comprehensive, standards-based, developmental school counseling program. They are employed in elementary, middle/junior high, and senior high schools, and in post-secondary settings. Their work is differentiated by attention to age-specific developmental stages of student growth, and the needs, tasks and student interests related to those stages. School counselors work with all students, including those who are considered at-risk and those with special needs. They are specialists in human behavior and relationships who provide assistance to students through four primary interventions: counseling (individual and group), large group guidance, consultation, and coordination.

Counseling is a confidential relationship which the counselor conducts with students individually and in small groups to help them resolve or cope constructively with their problems and developmental concerns.

Large Group Guidance is a planned, developmental program of guidance activities designed to foster students' academic, career, and personal/social development. It is provided for all students through a collaborative effort by counselors and teachers.

Consultation is a collaborative partnership in which the counselor works with parents, teachers, administrators, school psychologists, social workers, visiting teachers, medical professionals and community health personnel in order to plan and implement strategies to help students be successful in the education system.

Coordination is a leadership process in which the counselor helps organize, manage and evaluate the school counseling program. The counselor assists parents in obtaining needed services for their children through a referral and follow-up process and serves as liaison between the school and community agencies so that they may collaborate in efforts to help students. Professional school counselors are responsible for developing comprehensive school counseling programs that promote and enhance student learning. By providing prevention and intervention services within a comprehensive program, school counselors focus their skills, time and energies on direct services to students, staff, and families. In the delivery of direct services, the American School Counselor Association (ASCA) recommends that professional school counselors spend at least 70 percent of their time in direct services to students. The ASCA considers a realistic counselor-student ratio for effective program delivery to be a maximum of 1:250.

Above all, school counselors are student advocates who work cooperatively with other individuals and organizations to promote the academic, career, and personal/social development of children and youth. School counselors, as members of the educational team, consult and collaborate with teachers, administrators and families to assist students to be successful. They work on behalf of students and their families to insure that all school programs facilitate the educational process and offer the opportunity for school success for each student. School counselors are an integral part of all school efforts to insure a safe learning environment and safeguard the human rights of all members of the school community.

Professional school counselors meet the state certification/licensure standards and abide by the laws of the states in which they are employed. To assure high quality practice, school counselors are committed to continued professional growth and personal development. They are proactively involved in professional organizations which foster and promote school counseling at the local, state, and national levels. They uphold the ethical and professional standards of these associations and promote the development of the school counseling profession.

Delegate Assembly, June 1999

Source: http://www.schoolcounselor.org/content.cfm?L1 = 1000&L2 = 69. Reprinted by permission of the American School Counselor Association.

REFERENCES

Adelman, H. S., & Taylor, L. (2002). School counselors and school reform: New directions. *Professional School Counseling, 5*, 235–248.

Allen, F. J. (Ed.). (1927). *Principles and problems in vocational guidance.* New York: McGraw-Hill.

Amatea, E. S., & Brown, B. E. (2000). The counselor and the family: An ecosystemic approach. In J. Wittmer (Ed.), *Managing your school counseling program: K-12 developmental strategies* (2nd ed., pp. 192–203). Minneapolis, MN: Educational Media.

American Counseling Association. (1995). *ACA code of ethics (eff. 1995).* Retrieved October 20, 2003, from http://www.counseling.org/site/PageServer?pagename = resources_ethics#ce

American Counseling Association. (1999). *School counseling legislation: Elementary and Secondary Education Act (ESEA) Reauthorization.* Alexandria, VA: Author.

American School Counselor Association. (1997). *Position statement: Comprehensive programs.* Retrieved October 20, 2003, from http://www.schoolcounselor.org/content.cfm?L1 = 1000&L2 = 9

American School Counselor Association. (1998, June 25). *Ethical standards for school counselors.* Retrieved October 20, 2003, from http://www.schoolcounselor.org/content.cfm?L1 = 1&L2 = 15

American School Counselor Association. (1999a). *Position statement: Multicultural counseling.* Retrieved October 20, 2003, from http://www.schoolcounselor.org/content.cfm?L1 = 1000&L2 = 2b

American School Counselor Association. (1999b). *The role of the professional school counselor.* Retrieved October 20, 2003, from http://www.schoolcounselor.org/content.cfm?L1 = 1000&L2 = 69

American School Counselor Association. (2002a). *National model & RAMP.* Retrieved October 20, 2003, from http://www.schoolcounselor.org/content.cfm?L1 = 10

American School Counselor Association. (2002b). *Careers/roles.* Retrieved October 20, 2003, from http://www.schoolcounselor.org/content.cfm?L1 = 9

American School Counselor Association. (2003). *The ASCA national model: A framework for school counseling programs.* Alexandria, VA: Author.

Arredondo, P. (1999). Multicultural counseling competencies as tools to address oppression and racism. *Journal of Counseling & Development, 77,* 102–108.

Association for Assessment in Counseling. (1998). *Competencies in assessment and evaluation for school counselors.* Retrieved August 30, 2002, from http://aac.ncat.edu/documents/atsc_cmptncy.htm

Atkinson, D. R., Morten, G., & Sue, D. W. (1998). *Counseling American minorities* (5th ed.). Dubuque, IA: Brown & Benchmark.

Aubrey, R. F. (1977). Historical development of guidance and counseling and implications for the future. *Personnel and Guidance Journal, 55,* 288–295.

Aubrey, R. F. (1982). A house divided: Guidance counseling in 20th century America. *Personnel and Guidance Journal, 61,* 198–204.

Baker, S. B. (2000). *School counseling for the twenty-first century* (3rd ed.). Upper Saddle River, NJ: Merrill.

Baker, S. B. (2001). Reflections on forty years in the school counseling profession: Is the glass half full or half empty? *Professional School Counseling, 5,* 75–83.

Battistich, V., & Schaps, E. (1996). Prevention effects of the child development project: Early findings from an ongoing multisite demonstration trial. *Journal of Adolescent Research, 11,* 12–35.

Beers, C. (1908). *A mind that found itself.* Garden City, NY: Doubleday.

Belen Jesuit Preparatory School. (2002). *Guidance department curriculum calendar.* Retrieved August 8, 2002, from http://www.belenjesuitpreparatoryschool.org/college/guidcurr.htm

Bemak, F. (2000). Transforming the role of the counselor to provide leadership in educational reform through collaboration. *Professional School Counseling, 3,* 323–331.

Borders, L. D. (2002). School counseling in the 21st century: Personal and professional reflections. *Professional School Counseling, 5,* 181–185.

Borders, L. D., & Drury, S. M. (1992). Comprehensive school counseling programs: A review for policymakers and practitioners. *Journal of Counseling & Development, 70,* 487–498.

Bowers, J. L., & Hatch, P. A. (2002). *ASCA national model for school counseling programs* [draft]. Alexandria, VA: American School Counselor Association.

Brewer, J. M. (1933). *Education as guidance.* New York: McGraw-Hill.

Bronfenbrenner, U. (1979). *The ecology of human development: Experiments by nature and design.* Cambridge, MA: Harvard University Press.

Burnham, J. J., & Jackson, C. M. (2000). School counselor roles: Discrepancies between actual practice and existing models. *Professional School Counseling, 4,* 41–49.

Campbell, C. A., & Dahir, C. A. (1997). *Sharing the vision: The national standards for school counseling programs.* Alexandria, VA: American School Counselor Association.

Carns, A. W., & Carns, M. R. (1997). A systems approach to school counseling. *The School Counselor, 44,* 218–223.

Carson High School. (2002). *Counseling center: Systems support.* Retrieved August 27, 2002, from www.resa.net/gibraltar/Organization/four_components_of_a_comprehensi.htm

Children's Defense Fund. (2001). *The state of America's children yearbook 2001: 25 key facts about American children.* Retrieved August 23, 2002, from http://www.childrensdefense.org/college/keyfacts.htm

Children's Defense Fund. (2002). *Every day in America: For all U.S. children.* Retrieved August 23, 2002, from http://www.childrensdefense.org/college/everyday.htm

Clark, M., & Stone, C. (2000). The developmental school counselor as educational leader. In J. Wittmer (Ed.), *Managing your school counseling programs: K-12 developmental strategies* (2nd ed., pp. 85–81). Minneapolis, MN: Educational Media.

Cobia, D. C., & Henderson, D. A. (2003). *Handbook of school counseling.* Upper Saddle River, NJ: Merrill/Prentice Hall.

Cook, J. (2001). *Gunston Middle School counselor's role: Coordination.* Retrieved August 26, 2002, from http://www.arlington.k12.va.us/schools/gunston/people/counsel/

Corey, M. S., & Corey, G. (2002). *Groups: Process and Practice* (6th ed.). Belmont, CA: Wadsworth.

Dahir, C. A. (2001). The national standards for school counseling programs: Development and implementation. *Professional School Counseling, 4,* 320–327.

Dahir, C. A., Sheldon, C. B., & Valiga, M. J. (1998). *Vision into action: Implementing the national standards for school counseling programs.* Alexandria, VA: American School Counselor Association.

Davis, C. (1996). *Republic R-III School District's guidance & counseling curriculum guide: Contents.* Retrieved August 8, 2002, from http://www.republic.k12.mo.us/guide/guide_co.htm

Davis, J. D. (1914). *Vocational and moral guidance.* Boston: Ginn.

Dinkmeyer, D. (1966). Developmental counseling in the elementary school. *Personnel and Guidance Journal, 45,* 262–266.

Dinkmeyer, D., & Caldwell, E. (1970). *Developmental counseling and guidance: A comprehensive approach.* New York: McGraw-Hill.

Drewes, A. A., Carey, L. J., & Schaefer, C. E. (Eds.). (2001). *School-based play therapy.* New York: Wiley.

Elkind, D. (1976). *Child development and education: A Piagetian perspective.* New York: Oxford University Press.

Erford, B. T. (Ed.). (2003). *Transforming the school counseling profession.* Upper Saddle River, NJ: Merrill/Prentice Hall.

Erford, B. T., House, R., & Martin, P. (2003). Transforming the school counseling profession. In B. T. Erford (Ed.), *Transforming the school counseling profession* (pp. 1–20). Upper Saddle River, NJ: Merrill/Prentice Hall.

Erikson, E. (1950). *Childhood and society.* New York: Norton.

Erikson, E. (1968). *Identity: Youth and crisis.* New York: Norton.

Faust, V. (1968). *History of elementary school counseling and critique.* New York: Houghton Mifflin.

Ferguson, D. G. (1963). *Pupil personnel services*. Washington, DC: Center for Applied Research in Education.

Fischer, L., & Sorenson, G. P. (1995). *School law for counselors, psychologists, and social workers* (3rd ed.). Boston: Addison-Wesley.

Froelich, C. P. (1958). *Guidance services in schools*. New York: McGraw-Hill.

Ginn, S. J. (1924). Vocational guidance in the Boston public schools. *The Vocational Guidance Magazine, 3*, 3–7.

Goodnough, G., Pérusse, R., & Erford, B. T. (2003). Developmental classroom guidance. In B. T. Erford (Ed.), *Transforming the school counseling profession* (pp. 121–151). Upper Saddle River, NJ: Merrill/Prentice Hall.

Green, A., & Keys, S. G. (2001). Expanding the developmental school counseling paradigm: Meeting the needs of the 21st century student. *Professional School Counseling, 5*, 84–95.

Guindon, M. H. (2003). Assessment. In B. T. Erford (Ed.), *Transforming the school counseling profession* (pp. 331–355). Upper Saddle River, NJ: Merrill/Prentice Hall.

Gysbers, N. C. (1997). Involving counseling psychology in the school-to-work movement: An idea whose time has come. *The Counseling Psychologist, 25*, 413–427.

Gysbers, N. C. (2001). School guidance and counseling in the 21st century: Remember the past into the future. *Professional School Counseling, 5*, 96–105.

Gysbers, N. C., & Henderson, P. (2000). *Developing and managing your school guidance program* (3rd ed.). Alexandria, VA: American Counseling Association.

Gysbers, N. C., & Henderson, P. (2001). Comprehensive guidance and counseling programs: A rich history and a bright future. *Professional School Counseling, 4*, 246–256.

Gysbers, N. C., & Moore, E. J. (1981). *Improving guidance programs*. Englewood Cliffs, NJ: Prentice-Hall.

Hamachek, D. (1988). Evaluating self-concept and ego development within Erikson's psychosocial framework: A formulation. *Journal of Counseling & Development, 66*, 354–360.

Havighurst, R. J. (1972). *Developmental tasks and education* (3rd ed.). New York: David McKay.

Henry, N. B. (Ed.). (1959). *Personnel services in education: The fifty-eighth yearbook of the National Society for the Study of Education* (part II). Chicago: University of Chicago Press.

Herr, E. L. (2001). The impact of national policies, economics, and school reform on comprehensive guidance programs. *Professional School Counseling, 4*, 236–245.

Herr, E. L. (2002). School reform and perspectives on the role of school counselors: A century of proposals for change. *Professional School Counseling, 5*, 220–234.

Herr, E. L. (2003). Historical roots and future issues. In B. T. Erford (Ed.), *Transforming the school counseling profession* (pp. 21–38). Upper Saddle River, NJ: Merrill/Prentice Hall.

Holcomb-McCoy, C. C. (2003). Multicultural competence. In B. T. Erford (Ed.), *Transforming the school counseling profession* (pp. 317–330). Upper Saddle River, NJ: Merrill/Prentice Hall.

Holcomb-McCoy, C. C., & Myers, J. E. (1999). Multicultural competence and counselor training: A national survey. *Journal of Counseling & Development, 77,* 294–302.

Hosford, R. E., & Ryan, T. A. (1970). Systems design in the development of counseling and guidance programs. *Personnel and Guidance Journal, 49,* 221–230.

House, R. M., & Hayes, R. L. (2002). School counselors: Becoming key players in school reform. *Professional School Counseling, 5,* 249–256.

Huey, W. C., & Remley. T. P. (2003). *Ethical and legal issues in school counseling.* Alexandria, VA: American School Counselor Association.

Illback, R. J., & Nelson, C. M. (Eds.). (1996). *Emerging school-based approaches for children with emotional and behavioral problems: Research and practice in service integration.* New York: Haworth Press.

Keys, S. G., & Bemak, F. (1997). School-family-community linked services: A school counseling role for changing times. *The School Counselor, 44,* 255–263.

Keys, S. G., Bemak, F., & Lockhart, E. J. (1998). Transforming school counseling to serve the mental health needs of at-risk students. *Professional School Counseling, 2,* 381–388.

Keys, S. G., Green, A., Lockhart, E. J., & Luongo, P. F. (2003). Consultation and collaboration. In B. T. Erford (Ed.), *Transforming the school counseling profession* (pp. 171–190). Upper Saddle River, NJ: Merrill/Prentice Hall.

Keys, S. G., & Lockhart, E. J. (1999). The school counselor's role in facilitating multisystemic change. *Professional School Counseling, 3,* 101–107.

Kohlberg, L. (1984). *The psychology of moral development: The nature and validity of moral stages.* San Francisco: Harper & Row.

Lambert, N. M., & McCombs, B. L. (Eds.). (1998*). How students learn: Reforming schools through learner-centered education.* Washington, DC: American Psychological Association.

Lapan, R. T. (2001). Results-based comprehensive guidance and counseling programs: A framework for planning and evaluation. *Professional School Counseling, 4,* 289–299.

Lapan, R. T., Gysbers, N. C., & Petroski, G. F. (2001). Helping seventh graders be safe and successful: A statewide study of the impact of comprehensive guidance and counseling programs. *Journal of Counseling & Development, 79,* 320–330.

Lapan, R. T., Gysbers, N. C., & Sun, Y. (1997). The impact of more fully implemented guidance programs on the school experiences of high school students: A statewide evaluation study. *Journal of Counseling & Development, 75,* 292–302.

Lee, C. C. (2001). Culturally responsive school counselors and programs: Addressing the needs of all students. *Professional School Counseling, 4,* 257–261.

Lewis, T. J., Sugai, G., & Colvin, G. (1998). Reducing problem behavior through a school-wide system of effective behavioral support: Investigation of a school-wide social skills training program and contextual interventions. *School Psychology Review, 27,* 446–460.

Linde, L. (2003). Ethical, legal, and professional issues. In B. T. Erford (Ed.), *Transforming the school counseling profession* (pp. 39–62). Upper Saddle River, NJ: Merrill/Prentice Hall.

Locke, D. C., Myers, J. E., & Herr, E. L. (Eds.). (2001). *The handbook of counseling.* Thousand Oaks, CA: Sage.

MacDonald, G., & Sink, C. A. (1999). A qualitative developmental analysis of comprehensive guidance programmes in schools in the United States. *British Journal of Guidance and Counselling, 27,* 415–430.

McCracken, T. C., & Lamb, H. E. (1923). *Occupational information in the elementary school.* Boston, MA: Houghton Mifflin.

Miller, P. H. (2002). *Theories of developmental psychology* (4th ed.). New York: Worth.

Mosher, R. L., & Sprinthall, N. A. (1970). Psychological education in secondary schools: A program to promote individual and human development. *American Psychologist, 25,* 911–924.

Mullis, F., & Edwards, D. (2001). Consulting with parents: Applying family systems concepts and techniques. *Professional School Counseling, 5,* 116–123.

Myers, G. E. (1923). A critical review of present developments in vocational guidance with reference to future prospects. *The Vocational Guidance Magazine, 2,* 139–142.

Myers, J. E., Shoffner, M. F., & Briggs, M. K. (2002). Developmental counseling and therapy: An effective approach to understanding and counseling children. *Professional School Counseling, 5,* 194–202.

Myrick, R. D. (1997). *Developmental guidance and counseling: A practical approach* (3rd ed.). Minneapolis, MN: Educational Media.

Myrick, R. D. (2003). *Developmental guidance and counseling: A practical approach* (4th ed.). Minneapolis, MN: Educational Media.

National Association for College Admission Counseling. (2000). *National association for college admission counseling statement on counselor competencies.* Retrieved August 30, 2002, from www.nacac.com/downloads/policy_couns_competencies.pdf

National Mental Health Association. (2002). *Mental health information: Fact sheets.* Retrieved August 23, 2002, from http://www.nmha.org/infoctr/factsheets/index.cfm

Newsome, D. W., & Gladding, S. (2003). Counseling individuals and groups in school. In B. T. Erford (Ed.), *Transforming the school counseling profession* (pp. 209–247). Upper Saddle River, NJ: Merrill/Prentice Hall.

Paisley, P. O. (2001). Maintaining and enhancing the developmental focus in school counseling programs. *Professional School Counseling, 4,* 271–278.

Paisley, P. O., & Benshoff, J. M. (1996). Applying developmental principles to practice: Training issues for the professional development of school counselors. *Elementary School Guidance & Counseling, 30,* 163–169.

Paisley, P. O., & Borders, L. D. (1995). School counseling: An evolving specialty. *Journal of Counseling & Development, 74,* 150–153.

Paisley, P. O., & Hayes, R. L. (2003). School counseling and the academic domain: Transformations in preparation and practice. *Professional School Counseling, 6,* 198–204.

Paisley, P. O., & Hubbard, G. T. (1994). *Developmental school counseling programs: From theory to practice.* Alexandria, VA: American Counseling Association.

Paisley, P. O., & McMahon, G. (2001). School counseling for the 21st century: Challenges and opportunities. *Professional School Counseling, 5,* 106–115.

Parsons, F. (1909). *Choosing a vocation.* Boston: Houghton Mifflin.

Peeks, B. (1997). Revolutions in counseling and education: A systems perspective in the schools. In W. M. Walsh & G. Williams (Eds), *Schools and family therapy: Using systems theory and family therapy in the resolution of school problems* (pp. 5-12). Springfield, IL: Thomas.

Piaget, J. (1964/1993). Development and learning. In M. Gauvin & M. Cole (Eds.), *Readings on the development of children* (pp. 25–33). New York: Scientific American.

Proctor, W. M. (1925). *Educational and vocational guidance.* Cambridge, MA: Riverside.

Prout, S., & Prout, H. (1998). A meta-analysis of school-based studies of counseling and psychotherapy: An update. *Journal of School Psychology, 36,* 121–136.

Reed, A. Y. (1916). *Vocational guidance report 1913–1916.* Seattle, WA: Board of School Directors.

Reed, A. Y. (1944). *Guidance and personnel services in education.* Ithaca, NY: Cornell University Press.

Ripley, V., Erford, B. T., Dahir, C., & Eschbach, L. (2003). Planning and implementing a 21st-century comprehensive developmental school counseling program. In B. T. Erford (Ed.), *Transforming the school counseling profession* (pp. 63–119). Upper Saddle River, NJ: Merrill/Prentice Hall.

Roeber, E. C. (1963). *The school counselor.* Washington, DC: Center for Applied Research in Education.

Rogers, C. (1942). *Counseling and psychotherapy.* Boston: Houghton Mifflin.

Sabella, R. A. (2000). School counseling and technology. In J. Wittmer (Ed.), *Managing your school counseling programs: K-12 developmental strategies* (pp. 337–357). Minneapolis, MN: Educational Media.

Salo, M., & Schumate, S. (1993). *Counseling minor clients* (Vol. 4). Alexandria, VA: American Counseling Association.

Samples, F., & Aber, L. (1998). Evaluations of school-based violence prevention programs. In D. S. Elliot, B. A. Hamburg, & K. R. Williams (Eds.), *Violence in American schools* (pp. 217–252). New York: Cambridge University Press.

Schmidt, J. J. (2003). *Counseling in schools: Essential services and comprehensive programs* (4th ed.). Boston: Allyn & Bacon.

Scruggs, M., Wasielewski, R., & Ash, M. (1999). Comprehensive evaluation of a K-12 counseling program. *Professional School Counseling, 2,* 244–247.

Selman, R. L. (1980). *The growth of interpersonal understanding: Developmental and clinical analysis.* New York: Academic Press.

Shen, Y-J., & Sink, C. A. (2002). Helping elementary-age children cope with disasters. *Professional School Counseling, 5,* 322–330.

Sink, C. A. (2002). Comprehensive guidance and counseling programs and the development of multicultural student-citizens. *Professional School Counseling, 6,* 130–137.

Sink, C. A., & MacDonald, G. (1998). The status of comprehensive guidance and counseling in the United States. *Professional School Counseling, 2,* 88–94.

Sink, C. A., Rowley, W. J., MacDonald, D., Jones, J. E., & Perrine, N. (in press). Models of multicultural counseling and psychotherapy: A synthesis for beginning counselors. In D. S. Sandhu (Ed.), *Alternative approaches to counseling and psychotherapy.* Huntington, NY: Nova Science.

Sink, C. A., & Rubel, L. (2001). The school as community approach to violence prevention. In D. S. Sandhu (Ed.), *Faces of violence: Psychological correlates, concepts, and intervention strategies* (pp. 417–437). Huntington, NY: Nova Science.

Sink, C. A., & Stroh, H. R. (2003). Raising achievement test scores of early elementary school students through comprehensive school counseling programs. *Professional School Counseling, 6.*

Sink, C. A., & Yillik-Downer, A. (2001). School counselors' perceptions of comprehensive guidance and counseling programs: A survey of national trends. *Professional School Counseling, 4,* 278–288.

Sklare, G. B. (1997). *Brief counseling that works: Solution-focused approach for school counselors.* Thousand Oaks, CA: Corwin Press.

South Burlington High School. (2002). *Guidance functions.* Retrieved August 6, 2002, from http://sbhs.sburl.k12.vt.us/guidance/functions.htm

Stroh, H. R., & Sink, C. A. (2002). Making the connection: Applying APA's learner-centered principles to school-based group counseling. *Professional School Counseling, 6,* 71–78.

Super, D. E., Savickas, M. L., & Super, C. M. (1996). The life-span, life-space approach to careers. In L. Brooks & D. Brown (Eds.), *Career choice and development* (3rd ed., pp. 121–178). San Francisco: Jossey-Bass.

Tiedeman, D. V., & Field, F. L. (1962). Guidance: The science of purposeful action applied through education. *Harvard Educational Review, 32,* 483–501.

Thompson, C. L., & Rudolph, L. B. (2000). *Counseling children* (5th ed.). Pacific Grove, CA: Brooks/Cole.

Thompson, R. A. (2002). *School counseling: Best practices for working in the school* (2nd ed.). New York: Brunner-Routledge.

U.S. Department of Education. (1999). Keeping schools safe: A federal report. *Education Digest, 64,* 17–26.

U.S. Department of Education. (2002). *The Left No Child Behind Act of 2001 Executive Summary.* Retrieved April 25, 2003, from http://www.ed.gov/offices/OESE/esea/exec-summ.html

Whiston, S. C. (2003). Outcomes research on school counseling services. In B. T. Erford (Ed.), *Transforming the school counseling profession* (pp. 435–447). Upper Saddle River, NJ: Merrill/Prentice Hall.

Whiston, S. C., & Sexton, T. L. (1998). A review of school counseling outcome research: Implications for practice. *Journal of Counseling & Development, 76,* 412–426.

Williamson, E. G. (1950). *Counseling adolescents.* New York: McGraw-Hill.

Williamson, E. G., & Darley, J. G. (1937). *Student personnel work.* New York: McGraw-Hill.

Wittmer, J. (Ed.). (2000a). *Managing your school counseling program: K-12 developmental strategies.* Minneapolis, MN: Educational Media.

Wittmer, J. (2000b). Developing school guidance and counseling: Its history and reconceptualization. In J. Wittmer (Ed.), *Managing your school counseling programs: K-12 developmental strategies* (pp. 2–13). Minneapolis, MN: Educational Media.

Wittmer, J. (2000c). Implementing a comprehensive developmental school counseling program. In J. Wittmer (Ed.), *Managing your school counseling programs: K-12 developmental strategies* (pp. 14–34). Minneapolis, MN: Educational Media.

Wrenn, C. G. (1957). Status and role of the school counselor. *Personnel and Guidance Journal, 36,* 175–183.

Wrenn, C. G. (1962). *The counselor in a changing world.* Washington, DC: American Personnel and Guidance Association.

Zaccaria, J. S. (1966). Developmental guidance: A concept in transition. *The School Counselor, 13,* 226–229.

PART ONE

The Counseling Function

CHAPTER 2

Individual Counseling: From Good to Great

John M. Littrell
Iowa State University

Kirk Zinck
Seldovia, AK

Introduction, Rationale, and Definitions

We begin with the assumption that you want to be a counselor who is highly effective in helping young people. Stated another way, you want to be great at helping youth develop in the direction of their potential. You want to help them discover new perspectives, develop new understanding, and modify distressing behaviors. If you do not share this assumption, you owe it to the youth that you might work with to choose another profession. Although this is an exacting standard for those preparing to become school counselors, young people in need of help deserve nothing less.

Unfortunately, too many students in the past have suffered because counselors have settled into their job. These counselors have opted to give advice, ignore pressing problems, become disciplinarians, and indulge the status quo. Overwhelmed by the expectations placed on a school counselor, or perhaps uncommitted, they seem to have forgotten that they entered the profession because they wanted to be great at helping others. In a devastating critique of the school counseling profession, Wiggins (1993) found that across K–12 settings, "more than 28% of the total group of 193 counselors were independently rated as low in effectiveness by two supervisors" (p. 382). Supervisors' statements to describe highly ineffective counselors included that they would prefer to either "fire the counselor immediately" or "release him or her at the end of his or her current contract." Because they were not included in the study, we can only guess at the students' statements. Occupying a large middle ground, approximately 50 percent of the counselors were rated as effective. Our concern is that only 21 percent were rated highly effective ("much better than average" or "no one is better in his or her field"). We want you to be in this latter group.

When more than a quarter of professionals in a field are rated as highly ineffective, the reputation of the profession suffers. Little wonder that when the economic downturns occur, school boards preserve "essential" services. They reserve budget cuts for school personnel that they deem "nonessential." In some school districts, the lack of demonstrative results by counselors means that counseling programs are likely to join "nonessential" programs (e.g., music, art, media) as the first cut. Fortunately, most school districts recognize when they have great counselors. These counselors are viewed as indispensable because they have demonstrated that they add value to the school and community. They truly help others because they persistently work at the art and craft of counseling.

Persistence

What does it take to become great at helping others? One attribute is persistence—a necessary ingredient in moving from good to great (Howe, 1999). If counselors are not persistent, lifelong learners of the art and craft of their profession, they will never become great counselors. I [JL] once heard Frank Farrelly, the coauthor of *Provocative Therapy* (1989), speak of the persistence needed to become a great counselor. He said, "The first 10,000 interviews are the hardest." Your reaction to this may be discouragement, but Farrelly was saying that the awareness, knowledge, and skills required to be really good take much practice. Dick Hackney (personal communication, July 15, 2002) believes that a graduate degree gives you the credentials to *become* a counselor. In other words, the degree only signifies the attainment of basic skills. It is now the responsibility of the degree holder to *become* a professional. Howe studied geniuses and concluded that a remarkable trait all possessed was their persistence to stay at their craft. He found that people who mastered their craft spend 10,000 hours to achieve excellence; those who were geniuses invested even more hours. In summary, much practice is required to function as a great counselor. Remind yourself of this when you expect "perfection" after your first skill-building course.

Individual Counseling

One aspect of the complex job of school counselors is providing individual counseling. The goal of individual counseling is to provide a one-to-one relationship through which students can discover satisfactory solutions to problematic situations. Stated from a problem-solving perspective, students move from saying they have a problem to saying they do not (Watzlawick, Weakland, & Fisch, 1974). Stated from a solution-focused perspective, students find solutions to their difficulties (DeJong & Berg 1998; O'Hanlon & Weiner-Davis, 1989). Individual counseling is but one way for a school counselor to help students move in the direction of maximizing their potential.

Within the context of a school, individual counseling is the best choice in some situations and the worst in others. Schools are designed for groups, whether they meet in classrooms, gyms, auditoriums, or playgrounds. Despite the focus of this chapter on individual counseling, we believe that group counseling is the preferred modality because in this way counselors can maximize their efforts and reach the greatest number of students. Meeting students' developmental needs through small groups, large groups, and classroom guidance is the most efficient way to maximize a counselor's effectiveness.

On the other hand, individual counseling is the preferred mode when students need to discuss sensitive issues. The privacy afforded by individual counseling may be most appropriate for students who are exploring issues of sexual identity, contemplating running away, learning of the death of a family member or friend, reporting physical/sexual abuse, or coping with other trauma. These are examples of developmental issues and crises that are best handled by seeing the student in a one-to-one relationship.

◤ Theoretical Orientation: Maps to Greatness

The Map Is Not the Territory

In Jim Collins's (2001) book, *Good to Great,* he described how to "take a good organization and turn it into one that produces sustained great results" (p. 15). Just as Collins provided a detailed description for companies to become great, our intent in this chapter is to provide maps for your journey from being a good counselor to becoming a great counselor. In selecting maps, we have integrated diverse and informative sources. But before proceeding on the journey, a warning: The map is not the territory (Korzybski, 1933). This means that counseling cannot be reduced to a set of procedures (i.e., maps) because counseling is a more complex phenomenon than maps could represent. Although maps may greatly assist in helping another person, they can never substitute for thoughtfulness, careful decisions, vigilant observation, flexibility, knowledge, and skill in the work of counseling.

In this chapter, we first elaborate on eight characteristics of brief counseling. When counselors holistically integrate these eight characteristics of brief counseling, they have a set of many valuable tools to swiftly help students alleviate their discomfort and reach their desired states (Littrell, 1998). Next, we present two approaches to brief counseling: (a) problem-solving brief counseling and (b) solution-focused brief counseling. We believe the combination of these two types of brief counseling offers a viable way of assisting individual students (Littrell, 1998; Littrell & Peterson, 2001b; Littrell & Zinck, 2004). Third, we explore the common factors found in successful individual change (Hubble, Duncan, & Miller, 1999). The common factors help us understand what counselors *can* influence and what they *cannot* influence in working with students. They help us direct our energy to those things we have some control over. Next, we explore six stages that people experience when making changes in their lives (Prochaska, Norcross, & DiClemente, 1994). Understanding these six stages helps counselors to individualize their approach to students and to avoid the mistake of trying to get students to act before they are prepared. We believe that having a theoretical foundation to inform one's counseling approach, awareness of common factors of change, and working knowledge of stages of change provide a school counselor with a solid foundation for doing individual counseling. Finally, we present two brief counseling cases to illustrate the above concepts.

Eight Characteristics of Brief Counseling

Eight defining characteristics of brief counseling make it especially applicable for counselors working in schools. These characteristics are explored here.

Relationship-Based.   The desperado John Dillinger robbed banks across the Midwest in the 1930s. Attributed to Dillinger is the phrase "You can get so much more out of people with a kind word and a gun—than just a gun." Since we do not condone violence as a problem-solving approach in schools, we have modified Dillinger's phrase to apply to individual counseling. We say, "You can get so much more out of students with warmth, genuineness, empathy, and brief counseling— than just brief counseling." Simply stated, Carl Rogers's (1961) facilitative conditions of warmth, genuineness, and empathy are not superficial, but are a necessary foundation for effective counseling. When these conditions are lacking, counseling degenerates into techniques done to students, rather than with students (Egan, 2002; Ivey, D'Andrea, Ivey, & Simek-Morgan (2002).

Important in individual counseling is the ability to build an alliance with students. Are you able to provide a counseling environment that is safe and comfortable? Can you create a place where students want to share their concerns? Building an alliance is not as easy as it sounds. One author [JL] remembers his first counseling lab experience.

> As a new counseling student at Indiana University in the fall of 1971, I entered a small counseling lab to practice my counseling skills with a fellow student. A huge reel-to-reel tape recorder stood ready to record our every word; my supervisor and classmates observed us from behind the one-way mirror. My anxiety ran high. The instructions about what to do had seemed simple enough: be warm, genuine, and empathic. As I began the 30-minute session, I fantasized that I understood my teacher's instructions and knew how to translate them into effective helping. Afterwards, a kind and gentle supervisor helped me realize the gulf that stood between my theoretical understanding and its practical application. (Littrell, 2001, p. 105)

During my first "counseling" session, I had tried to demonstrate warmth, genuineness, and empathy. The most memorable feedback from my counseling lab partner had nothing to do with my establishing facilitative conditions. Rather, I was told that my constant smile [albeit concealing my anxiousness] looked like a "foolish grin." Not surprisingly, my grin seriously undermined the counseling relationship that I so desperately wanted to establish. The ability to establish facilitative conditions is essential to becoming a great counselor.

Time-Limited. Based on the number of people with whom counselors interact and assist (e.g., students, teachers, administrators, parents, support staff, helping specialists), individual counseling in the school is, of necessity, constrained by time limitations and school policy. Given the collective responsibilities that school counselors have, we contend that six sessions are the maximum number of sessions that a counselor can reasonably work with one student. If more time is devoted to a single individual, the ability of the counselor to engage the many who need help is severely curtailed. Thus, when a student's problems are so severe that more than six individual sessions are required, we favor referral to counselors working in agency or private practice settings that are appropriate for more intensive counseling.

Socially Interactive. In thinking about problems, we agree with the following statement by John Weakland: "If you have a problem, life is the same damn thing over and over. If you don't have a problem, life is one damn thing after another" (cited in Thomas, 1995, p. 32). Most of the time problems are solved and we go on to the next one. Whether a problem is solved or not solved, systems theorists postulate that solutions develop in a social context. Just as students use social relationships to create meaning, form values, learn about themselves, and set goals, they use social relationships (e.g., parents, peers, teachers) to solve many of their problems (Metcalf, 2002).

Occasionally, a problem continues and key people in the student's world are not able to assist in its resolution. This is when the special one-to-one relationship of individual counseling may prove valuable. The social interaction that occurs in individual counseling provides a confidential context for sorting out meaning and learning new behaviors. While individual counseling is a special one-to-one relationship, we believe that the goal of individual counseling is to guide the student back to his or her peer group. A third grader with no friends may benefit from several individual sessions, but actual change will occur when the child applies new skills among his or her peers. Because the peer group is so important, arranging for the child to join a counseling group or other group activity oriented toward making friends is one logical outcome of brief individual counseling. In summary, brief individual counseling is a temporary relationship in which problems are defined and potential solutions developed and then applied within the context of peers, teachers, family, and community. True change occurs through the student's interaction with others. As solutions are applied, evaluated, and appropriately modified, relationships shift to accommodate and support the student's new behaviors (Murphy & Duncan, 1997)

Action-Based.   One characteristic of brief counseling is a propensity for action. Words assist in understanding and planning what is happening. Actions move students from being stuck in the present toward new solutions. Getting students to do something different breaks old patterns and allows new ones to be established (O'Hanlon & Weiner-Davis, 1989). The simple assignment of "do something different" can free students to change the viewing of the problem and/or change the doing (O'Hanlon, 1999). For example, a female adolescent complained that she and her boyfriend "always" ended telephone calls by arguing. We challenged her to "do something different, even if it is a very small change." Based on our assignment of a do-something-different task, on her own initiative she changed the nature of the call by moving the argument to the beginning of the call. Naturally, the nature of the new "argument" was quite different and the undesired situation was solved—much to her amazement. Small actions are often a major key to unlocking persistent problems. Small actions move students from constantly mulling things over in their heads into a socially interactive world. This world of other people provides a reality check and offers new opportunities for change (Berg & Steiner, 2003). Becoming a more action-based counselor who focuses on solutions helps in reaching a more diverse group of students.

Solution-Focused. Problems have a way of occupying considerable psychic energy (Csikszentmihalyi, 1990). Problems push creative thinking out of consciousness and replace it with recursive thoughts, which are attached to unpleasant feelings and emotions. Soon, problems and emotions are linked in a habitual pattern. One way of breaking students' problem focus is to clarify what they want (i.e., goals), rather than focus on what they do not want (i.e., the problem). Within a solution-focused framework new options often emerge. We have observed situations when the problem from the student's initial perspective was to stop procrastinating with homework. As the counselor facilitated a shift of emphasis to what the student wanted, the solution-focused goal became making friends with good students. Our experience has been that when we determine what students want, rather than what they do not want, the nature of counseling often changes dramatically. Students become more engaged in seeking assistance because they are headed toward something they want, rather than wallowing in the problem (Presbury, Echterling, & McKee, (2002).

Detail-Oriented. Because students are often mired in problems, rather than solution-focused, students become skilled at providing long stories about what does not work. Perhaps the most talented providers of minutiae are middle school students. Some are experts in providing the counselor with excruciating, verbatim information of who said what to whom—all very much problem-focused. In brief, counseling details are important because they offer concreteness rather than vague abstractions.

Yet brief counseling differs from other forms of counseling in the nature of the specifics collected. Our focus is on details about exceptions to the problem, goals, and ways to reach the goals (Bertolino & O'Hanlon, 2002). Information is in the service of possible solutions, not in the recitation of current problems. Students find that thoroughly describing some ways to move toward solutions becomes empowering. And not surprisingly, because solution-focused information tends to be creative and unique, counselors find more enjoyment listening to them.

Humor-Eliciting. Check the indexes in the back of counseling texts. Do you find the words *humor, fun,* or *laughter*? Probably not. If the word *humor* is found, the sentence reads, "Counselors need a sense of humor." This misplaced emphasis ignores a valuable resource most students bring to counseling—their sense of humor and playfulness. When a student's sense of playfulness is elicited, counseling becomes creative, fun, and effective (Zinck & Littrell, 2002).

Using humor and laughter are good ways to lower stress. Reduced stress facilitates better decision making and the discovery of solutions (Janis, 1983). When counseling is solution-focused, students are more apt to use humor as a way of facing change. Counselors can assist students in the exciting and often humorous process of exploring new options by eliciting the student's unique sense of humor. The counselor is not a comedian who places the focus on herself. Humor depends on rapport and fit; thus, it emerges as the counseling relationship develops. The following example illustrates humor being elicited from a student.

> COUNSELOR: Let me see if I understand. So instead of studying, you watch TV, talk on the phone with friends, play video games, and so forth. *[Counselor uses basic listening skills to summarize the student's previous responses.]* I've got a karate question for you. If you were wearing a karate belt for your expertise in procrastination, what color would your belt be? Beginner white? Intermediate green? Or even an expert black?

> STUDENT: [pauses for a moment] I'm so good at procrastinating, I think my belt would be ebony.

> COUNSELOR: Wow! That's amazing. I've worked with black belt procrastinators, but never an ebony belt one. You're really good! *[Compliments are freely given for the student's accomplishments.]* Would you be interested in using those ebony belt skills to get the studying done so as to get the teachers and your parents off your back? *[The counselor ties the skills to setting a goal.]*

In this example, the student's sense of humor was elicited based on the counselor's intriguing question that allowed for a reframing of the situation. The counselor used humor as an opportunity to compliment the student on his "expertise" at procrastinating and then turned that expertise into a resource to be used by the student to complete his studying in a timely fashion.

Developmentally Attentive.   The majority of situations that students present are their unsuccessful attempts to solve problems, which can be conceptualized as developmental tasks and challenges. The majority of these tasks and challenges deal with relationships. For example, the student who is consistently truant often cannot cooperate with teachers, make friends in school, or deal with peer pressure from those who are not in school. Brief counseling recognizes the importance of understanding personal, social, emotional, spiritual, and intellectual development. Counselors who are aware of these developmental tasks and challenges adjust their language and expectations to fit the unique needs of the individual student. They make counseling an act of co-creation during which age-appropriate goals and the strategies for achieving them are interactively developed (Berg & Steiner, 2003).

To summarize this section, counselors who integrate these eight characteristics of brief counseling (e.g., relationship-based, socially interactive, action-based, time-limited, solution-focused, detail-oriented, humor-eliciting, developmentally attentive) maximize the help they can provide students (Littrell, 1998). But more is needed to be a great counselor.

Problem-Solving Brief Counseling

Two models of brief counseling are applicable for counseling individual students. One model is *problem-solving* brief counseling; the other model is *solution-focused* brief counseling. While both models emphasize solutions, a counselor using problem-solving brief counseling begins by focusing on the current problem and historical attempts to solve it. In contrast, a counselor using solution-focused brief counseling begins by understanding when the problem is not a problem. Both models offer useful and relevant ideas to school counselors. The first model is the problem-solving brief counseling approach, popularly known as the MRI approach. The staff of the Mental Research Institute (MRI) developed the model (Fisch, Weakland, & Segal, 1982; Watzlawick et al., 1974). The MRI model has four recognizable stages:

> (1) a clear definition of the problem in concrete terms, (2) an investigation of the solutions attempted so far, (3) a clear definition of the concrete change to be achieved, and (4) the formation and implementation of a plan to produce this change. (Watzlawick et al., 1974, p. 110)

In condensed form, the theory underlying the MRI four-step model is simple. A person attempts to effectively deal with one of life's challenges. Typically, the attempt is successful and the person moves on to the next challenge. However, occasionally the person's attempted solution not only fails to achieve the desired outcome but also exacerbates the problem. When the problem is not solved by the attempted solution, the person takes what seems like a "logical" step and does more of the attempted solution—referred to as a "more-of-the-same approach." Although it seems reasonable that doing more will help, it typically makes the problem worse. To extricate the person from the more-of-the-same trap, the counselor assists the person in clarifying goals and doing activities that are not in the more-of-the-same category. This master map seems easy; it is deceptively simple in that the skills needed to guide students through the steps can be complex in their application.

An example of a more-of-the-same situation is Tom, a middle school boy, who wants to make more friends. Tom sees other boys pushing each other in a teasing way and calling each other names. Tom starts pushing kids. Because Tom doesn't have rapport with the kids he pushes, they don't like it and they withdraw from him, but not before they call him names. Now Tom is receiving attention—he just isn't making any friends. Mistakenly, Tom interprets their attention as the start of friendship and does more-of-the-same pushing. Tom's attempted solution—more pushing—results in more name-calling and attention. To make friends, Tom must cease his "more-of-the-same" pushing and begin doing something different. Tom's fear is that if he stops pushing, kids will ignore him completely. Next, a counselor helps Tom set a goal and begin implementing ways to reach it.

Solution-Focused Brief Counseling

Yet another highly useful global map is a solution-focused one (de Shazer, 1985, 1988). Rather than begin with problems, one major intervention in the solution-focused model emphasizes finding exceptions to students' problem situations. If there are exceptions to the problem, these are explored in detail. One of two tasks follows based on whether the exceptions are deliberate or spontaneous. If the exceptions are deliberate, the student is assisted to "Do more of it." If the exceptions are spontaneous, the student is helped to "Find out how." An example of helping students find exceptions to their problems is demonstrated in the following scenario.

STUDENT: I know that I should be getting my college applications filled out. It's just so boring filling out all the paperwork.

COUNSELOR: I'm curious. Given there are 168 hours each week, when do you find yourself doing just a little bit of thinking about the application or even just a very small amount of working on an application? [The counselor tries to find times when the problem is not a problem—exceptions to the problem.]

STUDENT: That's funny because just this last week I did sit down and worked on my Iowa State University application for about a half hour.

COUNSELOR: How did you do that? What was happening that you just spontaneously did that half hour? *["How" questions elicit processes that the student went through.]*

STUDENT: Well, usually my dad bugs me about filling them out and he was out of town at a conference so I just started filling it out on my own.

COUNSELOR: Wow! I'm impressed. In the absence of your dad taking responsibility, you took on the responsibility of an application for yourself. *[Credit for changes is attributed to the student.]*

STUDENT: I guess that's right.

COUNSELOR: During this next week, I'm wondering what would be the next smallest step you could take in being more responsible for the application process? *[The counselor helps the student to identify a small step toward the goal.]*

STUDENT: My dad doesn't get back for two more days. I could surprise him and get them all done.

COUNSELOR: That's a pretty big step. What would be a smaller step? *[In brief counseling the student is encouraged to make steps smaller, rather than larger, because it is less overwhelming and more likely to be completed.]*

STUDENT: No, really, I can get them done if I put my mind to it.

COUNSELOR: Let's talk in three days and you can tell me about at least one application you've completed. *[Building in an assumption that the student will have completed at least one application.]*

Counselors assist students in finding their way through the complex tasks of change. Models provide information about what is most likely to be encountered and the most common routes through the territory. However, as much as brief counselors value quality models, they know that these maps are not the territory (Korzybski, 1933). The maps make it seem as though students bring with them well-structured problems with clear paths to solution versus ill-structured problems without clear solution paths (Sternberg, 1996). As Sternberg said, "There just aren't solutions to major life problems that are as clear as the formula for finding the area of a parallelogram or the identity of the person who discovered X-rays" (p. 172). At best, models are a compendium of collective wisdom; they should serve to guide, not dictate. Thus, counselors employ a brief counseling approach as but one of many valuable tools in their repertoire to effectively help students.

Common Factors

What accounts for change in individual counseling? Why do some students change and others not? What can the counselor really control? Considerable research has identified four core ingredients that contribute to change and their contribution to the total variance (Duncan & Miller, 2000; Hubble et al, 1999). These are the counseling relationship, 30 percent; theory and techniques, 15 percent; student expectancy, 15 percent; and extratherapeutic factors, 40 percent. The counselor has more available influence with the relationship and with theory and techniques. Note that more than 50 percent of the counseling outcome is not within the direct control of the counselor. We examine each of these four common factors as they relate to how you help others.

Counseling Relationship—30 Percent.   The first characteristic of brief counseling directs our attention to the counseling relationship. Empathy is considered a hallmark of effective counseling. In examining client perceptions of empathy, Bachelor (1988) found that 44 percent of clients perceived their therapist's empathy as cognitive, 30 percent as affective, 18 percent as sharing, and 7 percent as nurturant. In other words, students will experience empathy differently. Skilled counselors have a full repertoire of relationship skills and avoid a one-dimensional approach characterized by the phrase "Give a little kid a hammer and all of a sudden everything needs pounding." No one skill is sufficient.

Theories and Techniques—15 Percent.   Second, effective counselors know what they are doing. Their interventions are grounded in theory, skill, and experience that the counselor has integrated into a unique style and approach. This grounding and integration contributes to a quality of flow within the counseling process (Csikszentmihalyi, 1990). Theory and techniques are viewed as tools to help students change (Thompson & Rudolph, 1996; Vernon, 2004). Important is the mastery of theories and techniques that are congruent with the personality of the counselor and appropriate for students within a particular school setting. Our emphasis on brief forms of counseling reflects our belief that time-limited helping is most appropriate within school settings. Other appropriate forms of counseling that lend themselves to working briefly in schools include Choice Theory/Reality Therapy (Glasser, 2001; Wubbolding, 2001) and Alderian counseling (Sweeney, 1998).

Littrell and Peterson (2001b) conducted an extensive case study of the elementary school counselor, Claudia Vangstad, who extensively used the problem-solving MRI approach (Watzlawick et al., 1974). Vangstad found that teachers and students are comfortable with counseling presented in a problem-solving language. Schools are ideally suited for nonjargon problem-solving language because it is a natural language of school.

Expectancy (Placebo Effects)—15 Percent. Third, change in counseling can be attributed to a student's belief that change is possible (Frank, 1973). School counselors who listen empathically may begin to engender hope in a student that the problematic situation does not have to stay that way.

Extratherapeutic Change—40 Percent. Finally, much of what happens in counseling does not occur in counseling; it happens in the world outside the counseling session. Counselors can facilitate the receptivity of an environment such that new student behaviors have a chance of being acknowledged and encouraged. The school counselor who plants the seeds for change outside of the counseling session is increasing the chances that extratherapeutic change will occur.

The following example demonstrates not leaving extratherapeutic change to chance. The school counselor met twice with Jim, a third-grade boy. Jim was convinced that his teacher, Mr. Foxx, did not like him. However, Mr. Foxx explained to the counselor that Jim really got on his nerves because of his whining. Keeping Jim's conversation confidential, the counselor asked Mr. Foxx to begin noting any small and positive changes that Jim made in his behavior. The counselor arranged to talk with Mr. Foxx at the end of the week to see what he had noticed. At the end of the week, Mr. Foxx described some positive changes in Jim. Meanwhile, as Jim "discovered" that his teacher really cared about him, he began to enjoy school.

By now, you may have recognized the self-fulfilling prophecy embedded in this example. The teacher was asked to look for positive change—and sure enough, he found it. When the teacher identified the change, he probably began to treat Jim differently. Conflict was transformed to collaboration based on a reciprocal change in perspective. When counselors plan and facilitate extratherapeutic changes, they extend the range of their influence beyond the confines of individual counseling sessions.

Transtheoretical Model of Change

School counselors are confronted with an amazing array of presenting problems. While knowledge of many issues is an ethical responsibility (e.g., confidentiality), we do not believe it is necessary to become a specialist in each area. The work of Prochaska and his associates has made the job easier by identifying common components of change among the major systems of psychotherapy (Prochaska & Norcross, 2002; Prochaska et al., 1994). Prochaska's transtheoretical model is grounded in the natural processes people use when attempting to change problem behaviors (e.g., smoking, problematic drinking, depression, high-fat diets, and sedentary life). The resulting good news is that a counselor can work with students in individual counseling without having to become a specialist in each problem area.

Prochaska et al. (1994) discovered three generalizations about people making changes. First, they proceed through a series of stages, each of which calls for a different approach to change. Second, those successful at changing use processes that are appropriate to a particular stage of change. Third, those unsuccessful at changing do not know the appropriate skills and can benefit from guidance. In ongoing research, Prochaska and his associates developed a theoretical model of change that integrates key constructs from many other theories of change. Described as a model of intentional change, their theoretical model focuses on decisions made by the individual: "The model describes how people modify a problem to acquire a positive behavior" (Detailed Overview, 2002).

Furthermore, Prochaska and his associates mapped the process of change in a way that we find very useful (Petrocelli, 2002; Prochaska, 1999; Prochaska et al., 1994). Prochaska's map delineates six stages or territories (see Table 2.1). To assist in conceptualizing the model, a statement of how we imagine a student might summarize his or her stage of the journey clarifies each stage.

Table 2.1   Stages in the Journey of Change[1]

1. *Precontemplation*: "I am *not* thinking about a journey of change."

2. *Contemplation*: "I have begun my journey of change. I am intending to take action in the next six months."

3. *Preparation*: "I am moving along on my journey of change. I am intending to take action within the next month."

4. *Action*: "I have really been traveling on my journey of change. I have taken action on my problem within the last six months."

5. *Maintenance*: "I've traveled far on my journey of change. I solved my problem more than six months ago."

6. *Termination*: "I don't think much about my prior journey of change. My previous behavior is no longer problematic."

[1] Modified from Prochaska, Norcross, and DiClemente, *Changing for Good,* 1994, p. 68.

Prochaska and his colleagues (1994) found that people first began by moving from the precontemplation stage to the contemplation stage. For example, students referred by teachers for disruptive classroom behavior often are in the precontemplation stage. They do not understand that they have a problem. For them, the biggest problem is that the teacher will not leave them alone. Moving into the contemplation stage implies that they are at least willing to examine the possibility that their classroom behavior is adversely affecting themselves and others. They have begun to weigh the pros and cons of continuing their present behavior.

Some students move from the contemplation stage into the preparation stage, during which they lay the foundation for changing their behavior. From the preparation stage students might move to the action stage. This is where the disruptive behavior is modified, perhaps new friends are cultivated, and new behaviors are learned. Eventually some students arrive at the maintenance stage, which involves "sustained, long-term effort" and a "revised lifestyle" (Prochaska et al., 1994, p. 204). For most people attempting change, the journey is not a linear progression from the precontemplation stage to the maintenance or termination stage, but a recycling process in which stages are frequently revisited.

For brief counselors, the usefulness of Prochaska's master model is twofold. First, the model points out that three stages precede the action stage. Many of the interventions in counseling are aimed at the action stage, where people are *doing* new things. The three steps prior to the action stage suggest that we proceed with caution. In our haste to help in a brief manner, we must not forget the necessary work people have to do prior to successful action.

Second, the students' statements in Table 2.1 remind us that the overall process of change requires time. Brief counselors believe in going only as far on the student's journey of change as is needed. Not all students need to go through all the stages of change with a counselor. Many students find one counseling session sufficient in moving from one stage of change to another (Talmon, 1990). Students are not asking us to go the whole journey—some just need help in moving from one stage to the next. Brief counselors respect students enough to stop when students have developed sufficient skills to chart their own journey. Because as counselors we find pleasure in helping people with their journeys, we sometimes overestimate how much assistance we need to provide. Brief counselors have an implicit goal: to make themselves dispensable as quickly as possible. In the words of the second author, "a counselor's job is to work themselves out of a job—over and over."

The transtheoretical change model is built around an organizing construct of a six-stage process. Into the six stages are integrated nine processes that have been identified through research as common processes that account for change across all theories of change (Prochaska, 1999; Prochaska et al., 1994). We list these common processes with the idea that readers will explore them in the original source (Prochaska et al., 1994). Moving from the precontemplation stage to the contemplation stage involves *consciousness-raising* (increasing information about self and problem) and also *social liberation* (increasing social alternatives for behaviors that are not problematic). Moving from a contemplation stage into a preparation stage may involve the processes of *emotional arousal* (experiencing and expressing feelings about one's problems and solutions) and *self-reevaluation* (assessing feelings and thoughts about self with respect to a problem). *Commitment* (choosing and committing to act, or belief in the ability to change) assists in moving from the preparation stage to the action stage. Finally, moving from action to maintenance may involve varying degrees of *reward* (rewarding self, or being rewarded by others for making change), *countering* (substituting alternatives for problem behaviors), *environmental control* (avoiding stimuli that elicit problem behaviors), and *helping relationships* (enlisting the help of someone who cares). For students to discover by themselves the change processes needed to move from one stage to another is a difficult task, often most efficiently accomplished with a guide, rather than trial-and-error learning. Counseling can be rather brief when students need guidance through only one stage, not all of them.

Salient Research

Is there research to support that we can significantly reduce the time to conduct effective counseling? The brief answer is yes. In the late 1980s, I [JL] began working with a team of graduate students at Iowa State University on a series of brief counseling research experiments. We sought answers to this question: How brief can brief be and still prove helpful to the client? Our experiments employed single-session or two-session counseling with follow-up evaluations. Our research included the following studies, which are described in considerable detail in Littrell (1998):

1. High school students with academic, career, and personal/social concerns (Littrell, Malia, Nichols, Olson, Nesselhuf, & Crandell, 1992; Littrell, Malia, & Vanderwood, 1995)
2. College students offered brief counseling with or without additional social support (Sanford & Littrell, 1997)
3. Hispanic American college students (Cruz & Littrell, 1998)
4. High school students with learning disabilities (Thompson & Littrell, 1998)

Across the four Iowa State studies reported above, one conclusion is indisputable: One- or two-session counseling demonstrated considerable benefit to many students in helping them move in the direction of the goals they set. Qualitative data indicated that the solution-oriented focus on doing something, not just talking about it, was a very affirming feature of the brief approaches. A second conclusion is that very brief counseling can rather quickly result in significant decreases in negative client affect. Qualitative data also showed that clients appreciate the focus on the positive, which fills them with hope.

An extensive ethnographic case study of an exemplary elementary school counselor has been conducted by the first author and Dr. Jean Peterson (Peterson & Littrell, 2000). In a series of articles, we have documented the successful use of brief counseling in a school, not only at the individual level but also in small groups, large groups, and classrooms. Articles focus on topics such as facilitating systemic change using the MRI problem-solving approach (Littrell & Peterson, 2001a), a model based on an exemplary counselor who used brief counseling to create a problem-solving culture (Littrell & Peterson, 2001b), establishing a comprehensive group work program in an elementary school based on using brief counseling principles (Littrell & Peterson, 2002), and creating partnerships in a school for a brief counseling program (Peterson & Littrell, 2002).

Case analysis research can clarify issues in the practice of brief counseling and demonstrate how counselors can employ brief counseling in schools. Illustrative articles address brief counseling issues and practices in school settings (Littrell & Zinck, 2004; Littrell, Zinck, Nesselhuf, & Yorke, 1997; Zinck & Littrell, 2002). In summary, we have moved beyond using anecdotal evidence to buttress the claim that brief counseling is a viable alternative to longer-term counseling. Researchers now have both qualitative- and quantitative-based findings from systematic investigations to guide counselors' actions when employing brief counseling in schools.

Practical Application

We include two examples to illustrate brief counseling in action. Kirk Zinck, a school counselor for seventeen years, helped a student in the first case, entitled *Respect Is a Two-Way Street*. The counselor in the second case was Michael Oleson, a first-year student in the school counseling program at Iowa State University. Michael's case is entitled *Healing Through Remembering*. Each counselor wrote the following case write-ups, respectively. The two counselors gave permission for their cases to be used. The identity of the clients has been disguised.

Case 1: Respect Is a Two-Way Street

This case involved sixteen-year-old Rita [pseudonym]. The intervention demonstrates how individual brief counseling helped a student cope with changes in her family structure due to a divorce and her father's subsequent remarriage. The counseling sessions occurred while Rita was living with her mother in Alaska and attempting to maintain connection with her stepmother and father who resided in the Midwest. Phone conversations and letters were critical links in her family relationship.

During our first session, Rita complained that phone conversations with her stepmother inevitably disintegrated into verbal abuse. Starting as a friendly exchange of information the conversations would become critical, with the stepmother telling her what to do, calling her names, criticizing the biological mother, and labeling any defensive reaction as disrespectful. Rita's frustrated responses aggravated the conflict. Eventually her father would get on the phone and harangue her for being disrespectful to the stepmother. The parental critiques were done under the guise of "concern," but to Rita they felt like attempts to control her thoughts and actions.

Telephone conversations inevitably ended with Rita in tears, feeling thoroughly discounted. Advice from her biological mother was simple: "Just don't talk to them." Yet, Rita felt that contact with her father and stepmother was important, and she naturally sought the approval, validation, and warmth that most young people desire from parental figures.

In exploring the problem, Rita and I determined that she wanted phone conversations to be friendly, informative, and respectful. An early aspect of the intervention helped Rita reframe her concept of "respect" from child-to-adult, to mutual. I helped her to understand two important aspects of respect: (1) she was worthy of other people's respect, and (2) self-respect is important to well-being. People treat us the way that we teach them to treat us. Adults can be taught to be respectful, even by a younger person. We determined that Rita could teach and model respect by changing her own responses in phone conversations with her stepmother.

During our initial session, Rita and I explored solutions she had attempted. She described denying her stepmother's accusations, disputing criticism, using sarcasm, and reducing contact. Rita could think of no exceptions in the conversational pattern that would help us construct an intervention task. Her attempts at solutions had failed, and her biological mother, though sympathetic, was at a loss as to how she might protect or help Rita with the telephone situation.

In a collaborative effort, Rita and I developed a simple intervention task.

When the stepmother became unfriendly or critical, Rita was to state, "This conversation is becoming hurtful and we are not resolving anything. Let's talk again when we can be respectful. I am going to hang up now. Goodbye." Rita would hang up immediately and unplug the phone for an hour to avoid receiving berating calls from her father.

Rita and I discussed how she would determine that a phone conversation was disintegrating. We decided that a critical statement from the stepmother, followed by name-calling or labeling, would be Rita's cue to follow through with the task. Rita agreed to keep her language respectful and to not swear or call names in retaliation. This was framed as teaching Rita's stepmother to treat her with respect as Rita modeled respect and asserted herself. As the session closed, we agreed that she would use the task the next time her stepmother became abusive during a phone conversation. In support of her attempts to change her stepmother's phone behavior, Rita said that her (biological) mother would naturally notice and comment on any change in how she handled phone conversations with her stepmother. This gave Rita's mother a supportive role in validating Rita's experience. Rita used the phone technique in the next weekly phone call with her stepmother and father.

Three 20-minute sessions followed the initial intervention. During our second session Rita started believing she could influence her stepmother, because the latest phone call had not ended with Rita in tears and feeling discounted. While Rita had not performed the task as she would have liked—she let some abuse occur before making the assertive response—she was confident that she would repeat the task if necessary. Together, we appraised her first attempt, reviewed the task again, and closed the session. At our next meeting, Rita reported that a well-timed response to her stepmother's disrespect allowed Rita to experience increased confidence in her ability to succeed. At a final meeting Rita reported that a phone conversation with her stepmother was cordial and enjoyable; during the conversation her father even came to the phone to say a friendly "hello." Rita's biological mother assisted very naturally by commenting on the change.

It is often difficult for adolescents to assert themselves with their parents. The simple rehearsal included in the initial session helped Rita become comfortable with the statement agreed upon. The statement was written out so that Rita could have it by the phone. In developing the change-producing task, mutual respect was emphasized so that this intervention would bring together the conflicting parties and Rita could also become comfortable with the concept of self-respect. Her performance of the task allowed her to assume some control and influence in a situation where she originally felt helpless.

A year after Rita and I worked together, she participated in a counseling group that I was facilitating. During a session, one girl expressed concern about abusive phone conversations. Rita shared her experience and taught the phone technique to the entire group. Shortly after, the group member successfully reported using the technique with a disrespectful ex-boyfriend. In teaching the technique, Rita provided a useful tool to others. In this and the girl's reporting the successful use of the task, Rita's self-respect and empowerment were reaffirmed.

How does this case illustrate brief individual counseling? It was a short-term intervention consisting of an initial 45-minute session and three 20-minute follow-up sessions. The goal was simple, immediate, and behavioral; Rita would use the script in phone conversations that became abusive. Results were observable and quickly evident. In accord with the authors' suggestions, individual counseling was used to address a situation in which a student was adjusting to a change in family structure. As summarized in the following list, all eight characteristics of brief counseling were evident:

1. *Relationship-based*: The counselor demonstrated care, empathy, and respect, and the student's preference to maintain connection with her stepmother and father was honored. The process was collaborative and specifically addressed the student's concern.
2. *Time-limited*: This intervention required only four short sessions and lasted less than a total of two hours.
3. *Socially interactive*: The counseling relationship was collaborative. Family connections were restructured and strengthened through a shift in inter-action. The process was inclusive in that Rita was encouraged to discuss our work with her mother and seek feedback—which she did.
4. *Action-based*: The plan of action involved making a statement to respect-fully terminate abusive phone calls, then hanging up immediately and unplugging the phone.
5. *Solution-focused*: Emphasis was upon an immediate, behavioral, and pos-itive shift in Rita's relationship with her stepmother and father.
6. *Detail-oriented*: The task included a specific script, actions, and attitudi-nal components. The telephone script was concrete and detailed.
7. *Humor-eliciting*: The process included some minor and nonspecific humor-ous interludes.
8. *Developmentally attentive*: The process addressed a developmental tran-sition in a family's redefinition and rejoining following divorce and remar-riage. It also reflected Rita's maturity in helping her recognize a growing ability to influence change through mature behavior, creating a task she was capable of performing, and introducing the concept of reciprocal respect.

When examined from the perspective of Prochaska's stages of change, we find that Rita began counseling in the contemplation stage. She was aware of the problem and had attempted some solutions. The counseling sessions helped Rita move to the preparation stage by providing her time to practice a detailed plan. Then Rita moved into the action stage. We believe that Rita eventually moved into the maintenance stage when she successfully taught others the assertiveness skills she had learned.

Case 2: Healing Through Remembering

Most students entering counseling programs begin with an aptitude for listening to others. Often, they are shocked when they realize that their basic listening and responding skills are not as good as they believed. Michael Oleson, a first-semester school counseling student at Iowa State University, was no exception. During a live videotaped session of basic attending skills—one watched by his peers—Michael was doing an above-average job of hearing his "counselee" until he responded with a cleverly humorous, but totally inappropriate metaphor that stopped the counselee and the counseling process cold. Michael was, in his own words, "embarrassed, discouraged, and crushed."

How does one move from being a good counselor to being a great counselor? One works at it with persistence and dedication. Michael watched his videotape several times. With his instructor he analyzed what had gone wrong and how he could have responded differently. The following case description demonstrates how Michael,[1] by dedicating many hours to practice and analysis, learned by his second semester to really hear his counselees and to use brief counseling to promote meaningful change. His session illustrates many aspects of brief counseling, which are highlighted by the authors' italicized commentary that appears in brackets. Key segments of the 25-minute session are included.

This brief counseling session was my first session with Anna, a sixth-grade student. I was a bit apprehensive when I approached Anna and her mother to suggest counseling. However, both agreed that Anna would benefit from a few sessions.

Anna was an outgoing student with a radiant smile. She lived in a rural community with her father, mother, and two younger siblings. Anna participated in numerous school events, ranging from music to sports. Her parents were actively involved in the lives of their children. During our session, Anna proved to be confident, comfortable, and personable.

[1] We thank Michael Oleson for providing this case write-up.

I thanked Anna for coming in to visit with me and quickly described brief counseling, emphasizing the importance of goal setting and the four-step process. Explaining that I was a university student, I also asked permission to record the session so that my professor could evaluate my work. *[Parent and student written permission were given to reproduce this transcript.]* We laughed as I described confidentiality and its limitations, and stated that our discussion would remain between the two of us, my professor, and the room around us.

[Second author's note: I often encourage students to discuss counseling with the child's parents. This invites support and connection. One exception is in circumstances (e.g., abuse) where a child's revelation that he or she told someone of the situation might endanger the counselee.]

MICHAEL: Hi, Anna. I appreciate that you made time to visit today. [handshake]

ANNA: No problem.

MICHAEL: I'd like to start our visit by telling you about brief counseling and what we are going to be doing today. I'm a student in the school counseling program at Iowa State University that focuses on brief counseling. And, as you may have guessed, it's called brief because that's what it is—brief!

ANNA: [laughs, smiles] Okay!

MICHAEL: [chuckle] Now, as a brief counselor, we look at things that are real and meaningful for students, and then we move forward from the past and/or present situation. Brief counseling is a solution-focused approach. Goal setting is a common way to help move forward, and we might use this strategy in our visit today. *[Omitted here is Michael's description of the four-steps of the MRI model given in the language a sixth-grader could understand.]*

ANNA: Okay, that sounds good.

MICHAEL: I also want to share with you that everything we discuss today is between you and me. Our discussion won't go any farther than the room [Anna smiles and giggles] and the tape, which will be used for grading purposes. Once my professor reviews the tape, I'll make sure that the tape is destroyed [Anna smiles broadly and laughs] and no one will see it again!

ANNA: Okay!

MICHAEL: I asked your mom if it would be okay if we met, as you left a positive impression when I met you a few weeks ago. I thought it would be neat if we did a session together since I was impressed with your maturity and outgoing personality. *[Michael provides several compliments.]* Finally, I want to clarify that I hope you will share an issue that is meaningful for you, rather than what anyone may have suggested you talk about.

ANNA: Okay.

As we began, she chose to talk about the death of her grandfather. She was extremely close to him and was grieving her loss. In addition, she had recently learned that another close relative was seriously ill. As Anna began to share some touching moments, I noticed that my vocal tone and quality was changing to match hers. My voice became soft, slow, and reassuring. Reflection of feelings and paraphrases intensified at this point in our conversation. I allowed Anna the opportunity to verbalize her emotions.

To establish rapport and solidify our relationship I did a brief self-disclosure. Anna told of writing an essay about her grandpa, and how she felt happy and warm as she visited fond memories. In response, I commented that she was courageously handling her loss. As the session progressed, writing—one of Anna's strengths—emerged and developed as a solution-focused goal. Writing about her grandpa helped Anna remember good times shared together.

MICHAEL: With all of that in mind, Anna, what is something that is real and meaningful to you that you would like to talk about? *[Focus on the counselee's world.]*

ANNA: Well, my grandpa passed away a couple of years ago from lung cancer. Just last night, my mom was telling me that a relation to me (another close relative) wasn't doing so well and I kind of thought about my grandpa and I started crying. It is really hard . . . because . . . well, I wish he could be here just one more day. And I have a lot of trouble with that.

MICHAEL: [calming, slower, and softer voice] Your grandpa passed away just a couple of years ago and last night your mom shared with you that another relation was ill.

[Note the use of counselee language. Anna uses the term "relation" for relative. Michael continues to use the counselee's language in this conversation, thus allowing her to create meaning in her own terms.]

ANNA: Mm-hmm.

MICHAEL: And that made you feel sad. *[paraphrase and reflection of feeling]*

ANNA: Yes—it brought back memories.

MICHAEL: Brought back memories. Painful memories, I'd assume.

ANNA: Exactly.

MICHAEL: You mentioned that you cried.

ANNA: Mm-hmm. Yeah—because my grandpa had cancer before, colon cancer. It was really hard because they said the one cancer was all over then it went to lung cancer.

MICHAEL: At first it started with one cancer and then went to another and then it became very complicated. *[quiet, reflective, and empathetic]*

ANNA: It was weird because they thought they could get rid of it at first, but then it kept spreading and spreading and it kept getting worse and worse and worse. Then, after all of that pain and suffering for him—he died.

MICHAEL: I'm guessing it was very hard and difficult for you to see him that way.

ANNA: Yes.

MICHAEL: It's been emotional reliving these memories that were triggered by the recent news of your relation's condition.

ANNA: Yes, very much so.

MICHAEL: It sounds like you were really close to your grandpa. *[numerous empathic statements]*

ANNA: Yeah—we were really close. We did a lot. [She looks upset.]

MICHAEL: I see this is really bringing up some sore spots for you.

ANNA: Yeah. My mom called the day it happened. We were at home and my mom was at this sort of nursing home. She was there with all of the other relatives. My dad stayed home with my younger brother and me. It was late because it was summer and we liked to stay up late. Then we got the call. My dad said he was going to drop us off at our other grandparent's house for the night because grandpa wasn't doing very well. I wasn't there, but my mom called the next morning and said that he passed away. I didn't really cry because I knew it was going to happen. She told me there were 30–40 people in the room in a circle holding hands with my grandpa. My dad was holding my grandpa's hand and he said that he could feel the life go out of him. That was kind of sad. Then just this year in school we had to do a report about a memory or memories of someone, so I wrote about my grandpa. It made me feel good to write about him. We had to read it in front of the class and it was really kind of hard. *[Note how Anna mentions a way that was helpful to her in dealing with her grandpa's death.]*

MICHAEL: Really hard.

ANNA: Yeah. A lot of the memories are also with my cousin. We wrote a lot of memories.

MICHAEL: You wrote a lot of good memories and some of the things that you did together with your cousin.

ANNA: Mm-hmm.

MICHAEL: It sounds like, Anna, as you look back, you are reflecting on the happy and good times.

ANNA: Yeah.

MICHAEL: On one hand, you feel happy when you think of all of the good times. Yet on the other hand it makes you feel sad. I remember you said you wished you could have one more day with your grandpa.

ANNA: Yes.

MICHAEL: Looking at the memories is really good in that it does make you happy and that you had a great time with him.

ANNA: Yeah—we had a lot of fun.

MICHAEL: I can tell that you did. Anna, I'd like to ask you a question.

ANNA: Okay.

MICHAEL: What grade are you in right now?

ANNA: I'm in the sixth grade.

MICHAEL: Interestingly enough, I was really close to my grandpa. [Anna smiles.] When I was your age, much like you have shared with me, the story is much the same. I remember going over to a relative's house and the next morning I woke up and my dad told me that my grandpa had passed away—I was devastated. I really feel, understand, and can relate to the pain you feel, especially when it comes up again with another death. It is a tough process. *[Michael self-disclosures.]* How long ago did your grandpa pass away? *[Michael has focused on emotions, but now moves to a cognitive focus. Subsequently, he follows with more facts.]*

ANNA: It was a year or two ago. I was in the fourth or fifth grade. I remember because I would miss school to see him. My mom is a fifth-grade teacher, and she would take off from school, stay at the hospital and spend the night with him. I didn't get to see my mom as much. I was home mostly with my dad and brother.

MICHAEL: How was that for you? *[a check to see if this is a potential issue]*

ANNA: It wasn't the same, yet it wasn't bad as we just did our normal routines. It was probably over a time of a couple of weeks. They were rough because it was about the time when he died.

MICHAEL: A rough couple of weeks.

ANNA: Yeah, they were rough.

MICHAEL: Well, from where I am sitting I see you as a very gifted person. Someone at a very young age learning how to deal with death, which is something that people much older than you—and much older than me—have a difficult time grasping. I see one of your strengths includes coping skills. What other strengths or skills do you possess? *[assessing strengths]*

ANNA: Well, I like to write.

MICHAEL: You like to write. Keeping that in mind, I want you to think about your writing. You mentioned that you are a good writer, which is excellent! I remember that you shared that you wrote a report about your grandpa, and that it made you feel good. Visiting those memories makes you feel . . .

ANNA: Happier, because of the funny and stupid things we would do. [laughter]

MICHAEL: It sounds like your grandpa was a really neat guy and played a big role in your life. When you think about him and the fun times you had you feel happy.

ANNA: Yup! And not long ago we were at a college hockey game. He was a big member of that as he ran the scoreboard for lots of years. They had a plaque dedicated to him.

MICHAEL: Wow! What an honor! That must make you feel really good, going there and representing your grandpa, being at the hockey game and seeing the plaque, realizing that his memory continues.

ANNA: Yeah, it is a really neat feeling!

Establishing and summarizing that she was missing her grandpa and that thinking about the many memories that they shared together made her feel good, I asked her what a good goal would be for her. She said that she could focus on reflecting on the positive memories and record them. She also thought visiting with her mom and grandma would be a great way to re-live some of those special moments.

MICHAEL: I can see that these positive memories make you feel happy. Looking for the positives is a great tool to use. What I am proposing to you, Anna, is that in life one way to cope is to keep things in the positive—like thinking of the good memories. This can help balance the emotions that you feel. This applies to your grandpa and also other times in the future.

ANNA: Yeah, that makes sense.

MICHAEL: If you were to think of a goal from our discussion today, what would that be?

ANNA: Well, I could write down more stories and memories, visit with my grandma, and try and recall memories and seeking out things that she can add.

MICHAEL: So you really want to spend time reflecting, remembering, and seeking out things about grandpa—thinking about the good times.

ANNA: [big smile] Yes!

MICHAEL: I see a big smile, so I see a lot of good times there.

ANNA: Yeah!

Using a whiteboard, I helped Anna formulate a positive goal. Then I asked what smaller goals she would use to reach this bigger goal. We incorporated her writing ability as a step toward goal achievement. After this was documented, I reviewed the step with her.

MICHAEL: Sounds like you are making a wonderful goal. Stating a goal in the positive is what we do in brief counseling—we want the goal to be good for you. As you build on your goal, would you like me to write it on this whiteboard?

ANNA: Yes, I'd like that!

MICHAEL: Between these two markers, which color do you like best?

ANNA: Blue. [with a giggle]

MICHAEL: Okay, I'm going to write your goal, which is: I will . . .

ANNA: Remember good times of my grandpa.

MICHAEL: That's a great goal! Now, how will you remember and what will you do to meet the goal?

ANNA: My first step will be to review the paper that I wrote for class.

MICHAEL: Okay, so you'll review the paper.

ANNA: Then I'll think about the good times.

MICHAEL: Okay—think about the good times.

ANNA: I'll visit with my mom and grandma about grandpa.

MICHAEL: Okay, you'll do some visiting. What else?

ANNA: Well, I'll write down the stories and memories.

MICHAEL: That is great! How does this make you feel?

ANNA: [big smile] Great!

MICHAEL: I see that big smile again! So let's review the steps: You'll review your paper, think of the good times, reflect and visit, and write the memories for future reflection. [short paraphrase]

ANNA: That sounds really good to me!

As we concluded our productive session, I summarized Anna's feelings and reviewed her goal. Anna agreed to a follow-up meeting. This would allow us to evaluate and validate her successes as well as make adjustments to the plan if necessary.

MICHAEL: Realizing you already have a start on this goal, how soon would you like to start writing your paper?

ANNA: In the next few days, I'll start writing.

MICHAEL: And how often will you reflect and write?

ANNA: Maybe 20–30 minutes a week for me to reflect. I'll also spend time visiting with my mom and grandma and then write those down in a journal.

[Michael gains a commitment and time frame. This encourages Anna to advance from one stage of change (preparation) to the next (action).]

MICHAEL: Okay. How does this look to you?

ANNA: Great! [big smile]

MICHAEL: I see your big smile again. You have a fantastic smile!

ANNA: Thanks!

MICHAEL: So the goal looks great. Most important, what will you gain from this goal?

ANNA: It will make it easier to think of him and talk about him. I think it will make it easier to talk about him.

MICHAEL: Help you think and talk about him, cope, and move forward.

ANNA: Yeah. Exactly.

MICHAEL: And as you move forward, you will always have the memories as you keep your journal.

ANNA: Mm-hmm.

MICHAEL: Over time, you will be able to look and read the journal and say, "I remember that!" And I'm going to guess this will make you feel really good.

ANNA: Yeah, I bet it will, too.

MICHAEL: You will have a collection of great memories and times shared.

ANNA: And that already makes me feel good.

MICHAEL: What else would you like to add to the goal?

ANNA: Nothing really. I really like how the goal is set up.

MICHAEL: Great! Everything is in your control. This is something you can do, and I see that you really want to do this. That is fantastic! You're a real trooper and I applaud you for creating your goal. If it would be okay with you, I'd like to check with you in a few weeks to see how you are doing and how the journals are progressing. How would that work for you? *[planning for a short follow-up to assess the student's progress]*

ANNA: I'd really like that!

MICHAEL: Then, if you would like, you can share a funny story and I'll bring one to share as well.

Throughout the session, Anna and I enjoyed a strong working relationship. Anna openly shared her thoughts, feelings, and emotions. Careful attending combined with warmth, genuineness, and empathy (Rogers, 1961) provided the foundation for a productive half hour. We set a positively stated goal that was real and meaningful for Anna. Interestingly, part of her goal was to remember the good times with her grandpa. I thought that my self-disclosure was appropriate and helped her feel heard.

A month later I checked with Anna to see how she was doing. She showed me her collection of memories and stories, and shared a funny moment with me. She reported that it was easier to talk about her grandpa. As we had discussed in our session, she visited with her grandma at least once a week. Anna said, "Talking about grandpa with my mom and grandma has made it easier for me to talk and think about him." Anna attained her goal, in no small part by keeping the goal in the positive and under her own control, and by having the excitement and drive to fulfill her goal.

In analyzing Michael's session with Anna, we discover that all eight characteristics of brief counseling are evident.

1. *Relationship-based*: The counselor took sufficient time to understand and acknowledge Anna's situation and, in particular, respond to her feelings. Doing counseling in a brief way requires warmth, genuineness, and empathy—three facilitative conditions that are foundational.

2. *Time-limited*: The session lasted only 25 minutes and the follow-up but 15 minutes.

3. *Socially interactive*: The counselor assisted the counselee in identifying and using Anna's mom and grandma as appropriate social supports.

4. *Action-based*: Anna left the session with a plan to think, talk to key people, and write in her journal.

5. *Solution-focused*: Although the counselor thoroughly acknowledged Anna's pain, the focus of the session was not on how to deal with the pain, but on how to remember her grandpa. The counselor helped Anna think about how her attempted solutions, resources, and strengths could be used in remembering her grandpa.

6. *Detail-oriented*: Anna's larger goal of remembering good times with her grandpa was made more concrete through Anna's ideas of reviewing the paper she had written for class, thinking about the good times, visiting with her mom and grandma, and writing down stories and memories.

7. *Humor-eliciting*: Beginning with Michael's phrase about "destroying the tape" to the promise to share funny stories with each other in the future, the session was characterized by warm humor.

8. *Developmentally attentive*: Loss can be painful at any age. Anna's memories of her grandpa were triggered by the serious illness of a relation. Helping a student find the resources to cope is an appropriate use of individual counseling.

Thinking about this case in relationship to Prochaska's stages of change, Anna had once been in the action stage in terms of dealing with her grandpa's death. The illness of her relation sent Anna back to the earlier stage of contemplation. Typical of people who recycle through the various stages, Anna had temporarily forgotten her resources. Michael helped Anna remember how she had originally dealt with her grandpa's death. Because Anna had already engaged in action in the past, the preparation that occurred during the counseling session was in many ways a review. Anna successfully moved into the action stage because of the individual counseling session.

Ethics, Law, and Diversity

Professional ethical standards provide guidelines for practice (American Counseling Association, 1995; American School Counselor Association, 1998). These ethical standards offer counselors benchmarks against which to evaluate their services. We believe that each counselor must adhere to the highest standards of individual conduct in serving youth. Counselors bring idealism, intimacy, and a willingness for in-depth exploration—three fragile elements often misunderstood in our instrumental society (Block, 2002). To listen and try to help children and youth who are also exploring the elements of idealism, intimacy, and in-depth exploration is to embark on a journey that, despite the maps provided, is unexplored territory. Again, the map is not the territory. All of the maps offered in this chapter are just that. We are not working with maps. Instead, we are working with students who are struggling, exploring, and feeling trapped, frustrated, isolated, angry, sad, and many other complex combinations of emotions.

Counselors face many ethical challenges. While it is not the purpose of this chapter to provide a course in ethics, the following is one example of the ethical challenges faced by school counselors. The three approaches to the ethical challenge of confidentiality given below are ways that counselors demonstrate that acting ethically requires caring consideration. Acting ethically also assumes that a counselor will consult, as questions arise, with professional peers or leaders in the field, and keep up with the professional literature, which offers ideas, suggestions, and (sometimes) answers to dilemmas.

During his career as a school counselor, the second author found that an ongoing ethical challenge was that of observing confidentiality. In individual counseling, meetings occur in a one-to-one, private context. While most parents approve of and appreciate the work a counselor does with their child, they also want to be involved and may even fear being cut out of their child's life when the child chooses to confide in another adult. It is this author's conviction that counseling should build bridges between a child and his or her parents. It is the counselor's job to work herself or himself out of a job through helping children strengthen their internal and external resources. In all but extreme circumstances, a primary resource is the parent-child relationship. Thus, the most effective child counseling includes parents and strengthens family ties. This inclusive approach validates parents as capable, trustworthy, and caring. There are definitely circumstances in which this openness may not be advisable. Those circumstances are exceptions.

How confidentiality with children is approached spans a range of possibilities. Some counselors interpret confidentiality as keeping what occurs in counseling between the counselor, the child, *and the parent.* If a parent inquires, he or she has a right to know what is discussed (George Pulliam, personal communication, March 2001). The authors see no ethical violation here if the child seeking counseling is informed at the outset of this policy. The dilemma is whether children will seek out the counselor if what they say is not kept strictly confidential. Age is a consideration here, as younger children are less likely to be concerned with confidentiality than older children. Some counselors observe strict one-to-one confidentiality. In this case, a counselee must give his or her consent before anything is discussed with a parent. The second author found early in his career that this strict observance of confidentiality may create problems for the child if a parent discovers that his or her child is involved in counseling or if the child refuses to discuss what has occurred in a session. Policy varies between states and/or school districts, and/or grade level regarding the requirement or lack of requirement to inform parents that a student is receiving counseling at school.

We suggest a third approach to confidentiality that satisfies ethical requirements and can build connections among family members. This is to suggest that counselees share all or parts of what is discussed with his or her parent(s) following each session. This encourages but does not force sharing. If the counselee gives consent, it may be helpful for the counselor to phone a parent and encourage making time to listen to and talk about the concerns and conclusions that are discussed in counseling sessions. Occasionally, the second author has provided both a handout and some quick education to parents on how to listen, respond, and develop an ongoing dialogue with the child. Knowledge of ethical standards and state and federal laws are but prerequisites for being a great counselor. So also are awareness, knowledge, and skills to work with children and youth who are infinitely complex. Our society recognizes age, gender, ethnicity, sexual orientation, religion, and other factors as aspects of what it means to be human. A third grader might experience bullying because she is not dressed in the latest fashion. A senior in high school might experience bullying because he identifies himself as "gay." Great counselors are able to work with these students because they are aware of discrimination and its effects, knowledgeable about the struggles these students are experiencing, and skilled at working with the complex issues at hand. Counselors need to be very informed about the topic of diversity. A thorough discussion of diversity in relationship to brief counseling can be found in a chapter entitled "Brief Counseling with Children and Adolescents: Interactive, Culturally Responsive, and Action-Based (Littrell & Zinck, 2004).

Concluding Remarks

Egan and Cowan (1979) told an insightful tale about "upstream" and "downstream" helping. Modifying their metaphor for schools, a counselor was standing by the riverbank and noticed a student floating by. The student was yelling for help, so the counselor dived into the water and rescued the student. No sooner had the student been rescued than the counselor spotted another student floating by yelling for help. Again, the counselor made a successful rescue. Thinking ahead, the counselor went upstream and spotted a bridge. On the bridge was a very large person. When a student started to cross the bridge, the very large person tossed the student into the water. To stop the reoccurrence of students being thrown into the rushing waters, the counselor enlisted the help of others to prevent future tragedies.

Students seek individual counseling for many reasons. Downstream helping (reactive) is appropriate in many situations. Conversely, upstream helping (prevention) needs to be employed much more frequently than it traditionally has been. Three examples are working to prevent teen pregnancies through education, helping create drug-free schools, and teaching abuse prevention skills. Great school counselors know that prevention efforts such as psychoeducational approaches with small groups and classroom groups are effective tools to ensure that counselors are not spending too much time with individual students to the detriment of serving many students. Great school counselors know that at times individual counseling is the most appropriate response. They recognize that it is essential to balance their time in providing services. Maintaining balance allows them to move beyond survival and to thrive within the challenging school environment. It also benefits all students that counselors must serve through making services responsive and accessible.

To become a great school counselor demands the strongest of commitments. Persistence, energy and enthusiasm, eagerness to learn, caring and empathy, and professional dedication are but a few of the attributes that highly effective counselors exhibit day after day. As examined in this chapter, individual counseling is but one tool within the repertoire of great school counselors, but it is an essential one. We wish you the best as you enter the profession of school counseling—one of the most challenging professions and one of the most rewarding. We trust that you will become a great counselor.

REFERENCES

American Counseling Association. (1995). *ACA code of ethics and standards of practice.* Retrieved October 20, 2003, from http://aca.convio.net/site/PageServer?pagename = resources_ethics

American School Counselor Association. (1998). *Ethical standards for school counselors.* Retrieved October 20, 2003, from http://www.schoolcounselor.org/content.cfm?L1 = 12&L2 = 2

Bachelor, A. (1988). How clients perceive therapist empathy: A content analysis of "received" empathy. *Psychotherapy: Theory, Research and Practice, 25,* 227–240.

Berg, I. K., & Steiner, T. (2003). *Children's solution work.* New York: Norton.

Bertolino, B., & O'Hanlon, B. (2002). *Collaborative, competency-based counseling and therapy.* Boston: Allyn & Bacon.

Block, P. (2002). *The answer to how is yes: Acting on what matters.* San Francisco: Berrett-Koehler.

Collins, J. (2001). *Good to great: Why some companies make the leap and others don't.* New York: HarperCollins.

Cruz, J., & Littrell, J. M. (1998). Brief counseling with Hispanic-American college students. *Journal of Multicultural Counseling & Development, 26,* 227–239.

Csikszentmihalyi, M. (1990). *Flow: The psychology of optimal experience.* New York: Harper and Row.

DeJong, P., & Berg, I. K. (1998). *Interviewing for solutions.* Pacific Grove, CA: Brooks/Cole.

de Shazer, S. (1985). *Keys to solution in brief therapy.* New York: Norton.

de Shazer, S. (1988). *Clues: Investigating solutions in brief therapy.* New York: Norton.

Detailed overview of the transtheoretical model. (n.d.). Retrieved October 20, 2003, from http://www.uri.edu/research/cprc/TTM/detailedoverview.htm

Duncan, B. L., & Miller, S. D. (2000). *The heroic client: Doing client-directed outcome-informed therapy.* San Francisco: Jossey-Bass.

Egan, G. (2002). *The skilled helper: A problem-management and opportunity-development approach to helping* (7th ed.). Pacific Grove, CA: Brooks/Cole.

Egan, G., & Cowan, M. A. (1979). *People in systems: A model for development in the human-service professions and education.* Pacific Grove, CA: Brooks/Cole.

Farrelly, F., & Brandsma, J. (1989). *Provocative therapy* (2nd ed.). Cupertino, CA: Meta.

Fisch, R., Weakland, J. H., & Segal, L. (1982). *The tactics of change: Doing therapy briefly.* San Francisco: Jossey-Bass.

Frank, J. D. (1973). *Persuasion and healing* (2nd ed.). Baltimore: Johns Hopkins University Press.

Glasser, W. (2001). *Counseling with choice theory: The new Reality Therapy.* New York: HarperCollins.

Howe, M. J. A. (1999). *Genius explained.* Cambridge, UK: Cambridge University Press.

Hubble, M. A., Duncan, B. L., & Miller, S. D. (1999). *The heart and soul of change: What works in therapy.* Washington, DC: American Psychological Association.

Ivey, A. E., D'Andrea, M., Ivey, M. B., & Simek-Morgan, L. (2002). *Theories of counseling and psychotherapy: A multicultural perspective* (5th ed.). Boston: Allyn & Bacon.

Janis, I. L. (1983). *Short-term counseling: Guidelines based on recent research.* New Haven, CT: Yale University Press.

Korzybski, A. (1933). *Science and sanity.* Lakeville, CT: The International Non-Aristotelian Library.

Littrell, J. M. (1998). *Brief counseling in action.* New York: Norton.

Littrell, J. M. (2001). Allen E. Ivey: Transforming counseling theory and practice. *Journal of Counseling & Development, 79*, 105–118.

Littrell, J. M., Malia, J., Nichols, R., Olson, J., Nesselhuf, D., & Crandell, P. (1992). School counseling on the cutting edge: Single-session brief counseling. *The School Counselor, 39*, 171–175.

Littrell, J. M., Malia, J. A., & Vanderwood, M. (1995). Single-session brief counseling in a high school. *Journal of Counseling & Development, 73,* 451–458.

Littrell, J. M., & Peterson, J. S. (2001a). Facilitating systemic change using the MRI problem-solving approach: One school's experience. *Professional School Counseling, 5,* 27–33.

Littrell, J. M., & Peterson, J. S. (2001b). Transforming the school culture: A model based on an exemplary counselor. *Professional School Counseling, 4,* 310–319.

Littrell, J. M., & Peterson, J. S. (2002). Establishing a comprehensive group work program in an elementary school: An in-depth case study. *Journal for Specialists in Group Work, 27,* 161–172.

Littrell, J. M., & Zinck, K. (2004). Brief counseling with children and adolescents: Interactive, culturally responsive, and action-based. In A. Vernon (Ed.), *Counseling children and adolescents* (3rd ed., pp. 137–162). Denver: Love.

Littrell, J. M., Zinck, K, Nesselhuf, D., & Yorke, C. (1997). Integrating brief counseling and adolescents' needs. *Canadian Journal of Counselling, 31,* 99–110.

Metcalf, L. (2002). *Counseling toward solutions: A practical solution-focused program for working with students, teachers, and parents.* New York: Wiley.

Murphy, J. J., & Duncan, B. L. (1997). *Brief intervention for school problems: Collaborating for practical solutions.* New York: Guilford.

O'Hanlon, W. H. (1999). *Do one thing different.* New York: Morrow.

O'Hanlon, W. H., & Weiner-Davis, M. (1989). *In search of solutions: A new direction for psychotherapy.* New York: Norton.

Peterson, J. S., & Littrell, J. M. (2000). A school counselor creates a problem-solving culture. *International Journal of Educational Reform, 9,* 311–320.

Peterson, J. S., & Littrell, J. M. (2002). Creating partnerships: A key counselor capability. *Dimensions of Counseling: Research, Theory and Practice, 30*(1), 22–26.

Petrocelli, J. V. (2002). Processes and stages of change: Counseling with the transtheoretical model of change. *Journal of Counseling & Development 80,* 22–30.

Presbury, J. H., Echterling, L. G., & McKee, J. E. (2002). *Ideas and tools for brief counseling.* Upper Saddle River, NJ: Merrill/Prentice Hall

Prochaska, J. O. (1999). How do people change, and how can we change to help many more people? In M. A. Hubble, B. L. Duncan, & S. D. Miller (Eds.), *The heart and soul of change: What works in therapy* (pp. 227–255). Washington, DC: American Psychological Association.

Prochaska, J. O., & Norcross, J. C. (2002). *Systems of psychotherapy: A transtheoretical analysis.* Belmont, CA: Wadsworth.

Prochaska, J. O., Norcross, J. C., & DiClemente, C. C. (1994). *Changing for good: The revolutionary program that explains the six stages of change and teaches you how to free yourself from bad habits.* New York: Morrow.

Rogers, C. R. (1961). *On becoming a person.* Boston: Houghton Mifflin.

Sanford, K. D., & Littrell, J. M. (1997). *Efficacy of social support task interventions in single-session counseling.* Unpublished manuscript, Iowa State University.

Sternberg, R. J. (1996). *Successful intelligence.* New York: Simon & Schuster.

Sweeney, T. J. (1998). *Adlerian counseling: A practitioner's approach* (4th ed.). Muncie, IN: Accelerated Development (Taylor & Francis).

Talmon, M. (1990). *Single-session therapy: Maximizing the effect of the first (& often only) therapeutic encounter.* Reading, MA: Addison-Wesley.

Thomas, R. M., Jr. (1995, July 16). John Weakland, an originator of family therapy, is dead at 76. *The New York Times,* p. L32.

Thompson, C. L., & Rudolph, L. B. (1996). *Counseling children:* Pacific Grove, CA: Brooks/ Cole.

Thompson, R., & Littrell, J. M. (1998). Brief counseling with learning disabled students. *Professional School Counseling, 2,* 60–67.

Vernon, A. (2004). *Counseling children and adolescents* (3rd ed.). Denver: Love.

Watzlawick, P., Weakland, J. H., & Fisch, R. (1974). *Change: Principles of problem formulation and problem resolution.* New York: Norton.

Wiggins, J. D. (1993). A 10-year follow-up of counselors rated high, average, or low in effectiveness. *The School Counselor, 40,* 380–383.

Wubbolding, R. E. (2001). *Reality therapy for the 21st century.* New York: Brunner-Routledge.

Zinck, K., & Littrell, J. M. (2002). A peaceful solution. In L. Golden (Ed.), *Case studies in child and adolescent counseling* (3rd ed., pp. 108–117). Upper Saddle River, NJ: Merrill/ Prentice-Hall.

CHAPTER 3

Small Group Counseling

Ed Jacobs
West Virginia University

Chris Schimmel
Marshall University Graduate College

Introduction, Rationale, and Definitions

An essential part of an effective school counseling program is small group counseling. Given the demands now placed on school counselors to serve all students, groups are a central part of a guidance program. The National Standards for School Counseling Programs promote the use of small group counseling as a way to reach more students and achieve the goals of an effective comprehensive school counseling program (Campbell & Dahir, 1997). Most of the groups that school counselors lead are with students, although school counselors may also find themselves leading groups with parents and faculty. This chapter focuses on leadership skills for groups of three to twelve members even though many of the skills can be applied to large group guidance activities. (A later chapter focuses on large group guidance.) In this chapter we hope to introduce to you the many wonderful possibilities that exist with the use of groups in the schools.

Value of Groups

Small groups can add much to a counselor's overall program because they allow the counselor to reach more students in more ways (Gladding, 2003; Smead,

1995). Children and young people benefit greatly from sharing their thoughts and feelings and hearing others their age do the same about such topics as bullying, shyness, anger, drugs, teenage parenting, and changing families. Counselors can offer groups to teachers on such topics as managing behavior problems, stress management, or support for new teachers. School counselors also offer parenting groups and task groups around the many issues that face the school and the community. Another value of groups is that they allow the counselor to serve more people in the same amount of time. Meeting in groups is an effective and productive way to deliver information, support, and healing to students, parents, and teachers (Jacobs, Masson, & Harvill, 2002). For adolescents, peers are often more influential than adults, so meeting in small groups is beneficial for social development. Also, group counseling triggers students to think about issues they need to work on in individual counseling sessions, such as their parents' divorce or drinking, fears, guilt, or anger.

Kinds of Groups

To help you explore the different ways groups can be used, we have divided the kinds of groups into three broad categories: psychoeducational, counseling, and task groups. Psychoeducational groups are groups where the leader is primarily responsible for providing information, but feelings may also be shared. Counseling groups are those in which personal growth and sharing regarding personal issues takes place. Task groups consist of members who meet to accomplish a specific task.

When leading a group, the leader needs to be clear about what kind of group it is and what the purpose is. Many leaders do not think about this, and if they are not careful a group can turn into some other kind of experience when the focus should stay on education or task completion. Sometimes it will be fine for a psychoeducational group to become a counseling group, but other times the leader may not want this to happen. The same goes for leading a task group. It is easy for these to become counseling groups, but often the leader needs to stick to the task and talk to members afterwards about other counseling opportunities that are available.

Below is a partial list of potential groups. This list illustrates how groups fall into three different categories. Note that the last group, "Bullying in the School," is under all three categories. We included this to show that you could conduct educational groups about bullying or have a counseling group with targets (those who are being bullied) or one with the bullies themselves. Also, if bullying is a major problem at your school, a task group could be formed to discuss what to do about it. The possibilities for the kinds of groups are almost endless. What you offer at your school depends on the specific needs of your school and community.

Psychoeducational	Counseling	Task
Parenting Skills	Changing Families	Homecoming Planning
Study Skills	Children of Alcoholics	Peer Helpers Orientation
Sex Education	New Students Group	Student Assistance Team (SAT)
Planning for College	Anger Management	Individual Educational Planning
Time Management	Pregnant Teens	Crisis Response Planning
Bullying in the School	Bullying in the School	Bullying in the School

Needs Assessment

How does one decide which groups to offer? One way to select the kinds of groups, as well as the members of those groups, is to distribute a needs assessment to students, teachers, and parents. Students would be asked to indicate a list of topics they would like to be able to discuss in small groups. Parents and teachers would indicate topics they think would be valuable for their children or students. Some counselors distribute lists of possible group topics and have students indicate if they are interested or have teachers or parents indicate if their student or child may be interested. Another method is for school counselors to provide a list of groups they are planning to conduct and have students indicate their interest in the specific group or groups they would like to join (Smead, 1995). Oftentimes, existing data are helpful in recognizing potential groups or group members. Schools maintain databases and record information regarding attendance, test scores, grade point averages, and so on, that may help identify a population of students who would benefit from group counseling.

Chief Theoretical Orientation

In your group counseling course and in group counseling trainings, you will be taught one of two perspectives: Either the group is in charge and the leader facilitates the group, or the leader is in charge and hence leads the group. From our work with numerous school districts, it is clear that the most productive model for group leading in a school setting is an active, multisensory, theory-driven, leader-directed approach. Counselors should see themselves as the leader, as the person who is primarily responsible for ensuring that the group is productive, interesting, and meaningful to the members. Too often at workshops participants share that they were taught more of a "facilitator" model, which advocates that the members are more in charge than the leader. These workshop participants feel, as a result of using the facilitator model, that their groups have not been totally successful.

Even though we emphasize an active leadership model, there are many times when the leader will be less active and will let the members take more responsibility for what is happening in the group. This is often true in task groups, some educational groups, and even in counseling groups, once the members have learned how to help one another. The amount of leading varies according to the kind of group and the members; however, for most groups in a school setting, an active leadership model works best, especially if the leader is skilled at leading. A point we emphasize is "People don't mind being led when they are led well."

Characteristics and Knowledge Base of a Competent Leader

Leading groups well is one of the most difficult, challenging, and rewarding experiences in which a counselor can engage. To be a good leader, one must have special personality traits and also possess knowledge in a number of areas. The characteristics for being a good individual counselor apply to being a good group leader:

Good listener	Kind
Cares about people	Emotionally healthy
Open-minded	Empathetic

Along with these characteristics, good leaders need additional knowledge and skills (Corey, 2000; Shechtman, 2002). They need to:

- Be clear as to the purpose of the group.
- Know counseling theory.
- Know about the topics being covered in group.
- Be creative and multisensory.
- Understand and accommodate for students from other cultures and subcultures.

Each of these characteristics is discussed below.

Is Clear as to the Group's Purpose

Anytime you lead a group, you want to know the purpose for doing it. This may sound simple, but groups are often conducted with no clear purpose in mind, causing members to shift from topic to topic rather than maintaining a clear focus and going in depth on the topic. Leaders often feel satisfied when the members are actively talking. The truth is that just getting students talking is rarely a suitable purpose for a group. If leaders get students together whose parents recently divorced or who are new to the middle school, they must understand what it is they are trying to accomplish. Clarity of purpose helps leaders plan and conduct the session(s).

Example—Lack of Purpose.   The leader of a group for high school students who are living with an alcoholic parent has just finished showing a video that depicts how life in the addicted home can be.

> COUNSELOR: Now that we have seen the video, I am interested in your reactions . . .
>
> SARA: Isn't the guy in that movie the same man that plays the President on "The West Wing"?
>
> CARLOS: Yea! I knew I recognized him from somewhere. I like him a lot!
>
> SCOTT: I don't care much for that show myself . . . my dad never wants to watch it either.
>
> COUNSELOR: So your dad doesn't let you watch much TV, Scott? What about others of you? When your parents drink do they try to restrict your activities?

Example—Purpose is Clear.   In this scenario, the same video has been shown, but this time, the leader has a better idea of the purpose of the group; therefore, she is clearer about where she wants the group to go.

> COUNSELOR: Now that we have seen the video, I want you to think about life in your own home. On a scale of 1 to 10, I want each of you to tell the group how closely this film reflects what goes on in your home. For example, if you said "10," that would mean that the film is very much like your home. If you said "1," that would mean that life is not like that in your home at all. Sara, let's start with you and go around this way.
>
> SARA: I would say an "8." It's pretty bad, but not quite that bad.

CARLOS: Mine is that bad! "10." I don't now what to do or how to act.

SCOTT: I would say between a "7" and an "8." My house is just tense all the time . . . my dad doesn't really shout and yell like that when he is drunk, everybody is just like, frozen.

PEGGY: I would say "8." Mine is a lot like Scott's, everybody is always walkin' on eggshells when my mom is drinking. We try really hard to not get yelled at.

COUNSELOR: Let's talk more about this. Let's talk about how seeing the movie maybe helped you to understand something better about your situation.

Because the leader was clear on the purpose, she directed the conversation by using the 1–10 scale and by encouraging the members to look at what they learned from the movie.

Knows Counseling Theory

We cannot emphasize enough the value and importance of being able to apply counseling theory to the group process. In dealing with personal material (such as shyness, stress, anger, guilt, relationships, friendships, or drugs), the leader must have an in-depth, working knowledge of counseling theories that can be used in a hands-on, experiential manner to assist group members. Seasoned school counselors report that they are effective because they are able to apply theories during the session. We strongly recommend Rational Emotive Behavior Therapy, Transactional Analysis, Reality Therapy, and Adlerian Therapy because they have proven effective with students, teachers, and parents. You might want to consult a good counseling theory text like Corey (2001) or Prochaska and Norcross (2003) to better understand these theories.

Example—The Leader Does Not Use Any Theoretical Orientation.

KATHY: . . . so when my mom yells at me to clean up my room, I just feel like I need to yell back at her. She makes me so mad!

ALLISON: Yea! I know just what you mean . . . my mom makes me mad too!

COUNSELOR: Who else feels that his or her mom makes them mad?

WOODY: I sure do! All parents want to do is control their kids and make them do stuff. It isn't fair! Mom and Dad both make me really mad!

COUNSELOR: Say some more about that.

WOODY: My mom is just like Kathy's, always telling me what to do and nagging me about picking up my stuff and cleaning up my messes. Dad is always on me about helping out around the house. They drive me crazy!

KATHY: That is true at my house too!

COUNSELOR: You all seem to have a lot of things in common.

Example—The Counselor Quickly Sees that the Use of Theory Can Be Helpful to the Members.

KATHY: . . . so when my mom yells at me to clean up my room, I just feel like I need to yell back at her. She makes me so mad!

ALLISON: Yea! I know just what you mean. My mom makes me so mad too!

COUNSELOR: Do any others feel that your mom *makes* you feel the way you do? That your mom creates your feelings?

WOODY: I sure do. All parents want to do is control their kids and make them do stuff. It isn't fair! Mom and Dad both make me really mad!

COUNSELOR: What if I told you all that it really isn't your mom and dad that make you mad? What if I could teach you something that would help you understand where your feelings come from so you would be able to stop fighting with them and stay out of trouble at home?

KATHY: That would be cool, but I really think my parents make me mad.

WOODY: Yea, I am not sure.

COUNSELOR: I completely understand, but I learned this thing called REBT when I was in school that really helped me learn how to control my anger and be able to stop yelling back at my parents, my friends, my teachers. It is the most important thing that I ever learned! So how about it?

MARIE: Well, if you think it could help.

ALLISON: Sure.

COUNSELOR: Great! Everybody turn your chair toward the board so you can see what I am doing. I want to show you where your anger really comes from.

At this point in the group, the counselor would go to the whiteboard or chalk-board and begin teaching a developmentally appropriate minilesson on Rational Emotive Behavior Therapy or REBT (Ellis & MacLaren, 1998; Vernon, 1995; Wilde, 1992). She would teach the idea that your thoughts cause your feelings. The counselor may teach a basic "A, B, C" approach, or she may come up with a more creative way to teach the concept. Either way, the group members would be involved in the learning and encouraged to rethink where their feelings and ulti-mately their behaviors actually come from.

The counselor in the first group seems to simply be interested in group cohe-sion and linking commonalities among members. However, the leader can and should do more to assist the members in gaining new insight into their problems with their parents. The best way to do this is to integrate counseling theory into the sessions. If students can understand their behavior, they have a much better chance of understanding how they interact with their parents, teachers, and peers. By teaching group members theory and why it works, members can begin to understand their behavior.

Knows About the Topics Being Covered in Group

Group leading in schools demands a great deal of knowledge and information on the part of the leader. Depending on the groups you lead, you may need to know about divorce, bullying, lying, dating, anger management, stress management, sex, studying, stepfamily living, teenage parenting, and so on. We suggest you start learning now as much as you can about the population of students you want to work with. Too often we hear of leaders leading when they really don't have enough knowledge of the topics to do a credible job.

Is Creative and Multisensory

Group leading with students demands creativity because you are, in a sense, competing with exciting video games and the stimulation that many kids get by interacting on the Internet. Being creative and multisensory means using props, writing, drawing, drama, movies, music, or movement to engage and stimulate the minds of the members. We have talked with many school counselors across the nation who were trained to conduct groups that consist of students sitting around talking and sharing. They report that their groups have often been boring. As Golden (1997) stated, "Our students are wired differently from students of an earlier generation. They have been developing their learning capacities through multisensory stimulation" (p. 19). Groups are more effective when the leader is creative and uses multisensory techniques. For an in-depth discussion of a multisensory approach to counseling, see *Impact Therapy* (Jacobs, 1994).

Example 1.   This example occurs during the third session of a group of seventh graders.

> COUNSELOR: . . . so what do you all think are some ways to let the name-calling not bother you as much?
>
> ROBIN: My grandma always says to just ignore it.
>
> LORI: Yea, that is what my teacher says too, but it is hard.
>
> CEVA: It is hard to ignore someone calling you an idiot!
>
> COUNSELOR: I am sure that it is difficult to "just" ignore it, but I have something I want to show you that helps me in cases just like this. Does anyone know what this is? (*holds up a 10 x 10 piece of clear Plexiglas*)
>
> DAPHNE: No.
>
> CEVA: Me neither.
>
> COUNSELOR: This is a shield. Do you know what shields do?
>
> LORI: They protect you from stuff.
>
> DAPHNE: Like in old times with knights! They used shields . . .
>
> COUNSELOR: That is right! Only I use this shield to protect myself from hurtful comments that get thrown my way. Let me show you what I mean! (*Counselor continues to teach the concept of protecting yourself by using the shield.*)

Example 2.   The following dialogue occurs during the first session of an anger management group with fifth graders.

> COUNSELOR: Each of you has said that you would like to do a better job of controlling your anger, right?
>
> STEVE: Sure.
>
> TERRI: Yes!

COUNSELOR: So I have given you each a set of fuses (*pieces of thick string cut into three different lengths: 1 inch, 5 inches, and 12 inches*). I want you to think about the size of your own fuse. Would you say you have a long fuse (*holds up longest piece of string*), meaning that it takes a long time for you to "blow up"? Would some of you say you have a medium fuse (*holds up the medium-length fuse*), meaning that it takes a little bit to get you going, but not a lot? Or would some of you say you have a very short fuse (*holds up the shortest piece of the rope*), meaning that you "blow up" very quickly?

GARY: Mine is the short one!

TERRI: Mine too. It is really short. I get it from my dad!

SCOTT: Mine is the medium one, but when I have had just sooo much, boy do I blow up!

STEVE: I think I have a pretty small fuse too.

COUNSELOR: How would you all like to learn how to lengthen your fuses? (*All nod yes.*) That is what this group is really about—teaching you how to get a longer fuse, which means you don't blow up and get into trouble as often!

Example 3. This is the second session of a personal growth group for high school girls.

COUNSELOR: (*After a brief warm-up/review of last session*) . . . it sounds like last week's session was beneficial for all of you in some way. That is great! Today I would like for everyone to take one of these cups and a pencil. (*Counselor passes out a Styrofoam cup and pencil to each girl.*) I want each of you to think for a minute about your self-worth. If this cup represents your self-worth, what happens if I pour water into it? (*Counselor pretends to pour water into cup.*)

AMBER: It would fill up the cup.

COURTNEY: Yea. It would just hold all the water you could pour in there.

COUNSELOR: Right. But what would happen if this were my cup? (*Counselor takes pencil and pokes four or five holes around the cup.*) What would happen if I poured water into this cup?

KENISHA: The water would run out all over the place. It would make a mess.

SAMANTHA: Yea, that wouldn't hold hardly any water and you sure couldn't drink out of it!

COUNSELOR: That is right! And here is what I am afraid of: I am afraid that all of you in this group have a self-worth cup that looks like this (*referring to the cup with the holes*). Do you all think that is right? (*Group nods in agreement.*) I want each of you to take your pencil and poke the number and size of the holes you feel you have in your self-worth cup. (*Girls in the group proceed in doing this.*) Good. Now I want you to label what those holes represent. One could possibly be "I am not pretty enough" or "I am not smart enough" or "I am too fat or skinny" or "I am not OK because boys don't ask me out." Label the holes in your self-worth. (*Counselor gives girls time to complete their cups.*) So what are some of the "holes" you ladies are punching out?

SAMANTHA: One of mine is about my weight. I don't think I look good. I am too fat.

AMBER: Mine are about my boyfriend breaking up with me. It seems like I can't keep a boyfriend.

COUNSELOR: Kenisha, how about you?

KENISHA: Well, I never seem to be able to do as well in school as my parents want me to. I feel dumb a lot of the time in class.

COURTNEY: Kenisha, you feel dumb?! You are kidding. You do way better than me in class! If you are dumb, then I must be really stupid.

COUNSELOR: So Courtney, you don't think Kenisha is dumb?

COURTNEY: Heck no. She is one of the smartest kids in our class.

KENISHA: You really think I am smart?

COUNSELOR: You know girls, this is exactly what this group can be about. You all are doing a great job identifying the holes in your self-worth. This group is about supporting each other and "patching" those holes. Let's get a couple of you to share some more about the "holes" in your cups and then let's start patching!

These examples show how the use of creative counseling techniques or a multi-sensory approach can add depth and impact to your groups. Creative techniques are an excellent way for the counselors in these scenarios to easily represent concepts of self-worth (the cups), creating a better temperament (the fuses), or blocking out negative comments (the shield). Not only are the concepts more easily taught with the use of creative techniques, but they also have a greater chance of sticking in the minds of the members (Jacobs, 1992).

Possesses Multicultural Understanding

Group leaders in school settings are faced with the challenge of understanding a vast array of cultural and ethnic differences among their students. The leader needs to understand the different cultures of the group members as well as understand how the members' cultures and ethnicity affect their participation in the group. The best way to learn about different cultures is to ask individuals, privately, about their cultural background and how it may affect their participation. For example, a school counselor in central Florida may have little knowledge of the Hispanic or Latino culture. However, an influx of migrant workers would necessitate that the school counselor become familiar with the cultural and ethnic issues that may exist in order to run groups based on these students' needs (Baca & Koss-Chioino, 1997).

A recognized need in many large high schools is for gay and lesbian support groups. This is yet another culture that high school counselors need to understand. Although this is a sensitive topic and must be handled as such, offering support and understanding for these students is beneficial. They struggle with issues and questions about their sexual identity. You can find excellent resources on the Internet by conducting a search for high school gay and lesbian groups (Sabella, 2003).

Practical Application

Now that you have been introduced to group work in the schools, we want to get to the nuts and bolts of group leading: stages of groups, skills, exercises, common mistakes, planning, beginning a group, and closing a group.

Stages of Groups

There is much information available regarding the stages of groups (Corey 2000; Gladding 2003; Yalom, 1995). Leaders often become distracted by the very task of trying to keep up with what stage of the process the group is in. We suggest that groups in a school setting have three very distinct stages, and a good leader will pay attention to these without becoming overwhelmed. Simply put, groups have a *beginning stage*, a *working stage*, and a *closing stage*. Special attention must be paid to time, activities, and content that is relevant to each of these three stages. We write more specifically about this later in this chapter.

Skills and Techniques

As stated earlier, effective leaders know counseling theory and have knowledge of relevant topics. However, there are many additional skills and techniques that a leader must have in order to lead a productive group. What is exciting about group leading is that the more you master these skills, the more effective your groups are. We discuss a number of skills here. For further discussion of these and other skills, see Corey and Corey (2002), Jacobs et al. (2002), or Smead (1995).

Using an Engaging, Energetic Voice.   One of the most helpful skills leaders can have in their toolbox is the use of their voice. An energetic, enthusiastic voice is helpful for setting a positive tone for most groups. When our students practice group leading, we provide feedback about how they could use their voice to better engage the group members. Some use a flat, boring voice. Others use a voice that sounds more like a teacher than a counselor. Some use the same voice no matter what grade level or topic. A different voice pattern should be used for shy kids than with students diagnosed as attention deficit hyperactivity disorder or ADHD. Also, a group that follows a major crisis requires a different voice pattern than a group on parenting. In short, an important thing to remember is to always pay attention to your voice when you are leading a group.

Using Your Eyes Effectively.   The ability to look around while members are talking is an essential skill for leaders to master. That is, it is very important for leaders to scan the group so that they can see different members' reactions. In order to keep members from being upset because the leader is not looking at them when they are talking to her, she needs to explain during the first couple of sessions the rationale behind this behavior. She needs to tell the members that she is looking around for two main reasons: (1) to see how others are reacting and (2) to encourage the talking member to look at others and not just communicate with the leader. Members looking at and talking to other members will help build cohesion in a group. Looking around as students are speaking helps the leader pick up on reactions and energy and aids in drawing out quiet members, because she sees them reacting to what is being said in the group.

Holding the Focus.   The key to group leading centers on knowing how to hold, shift, and deepen the focus. Holding the focus refers to how the leader keeps the discussion moving by "concentrating" on either a person, a topic, or an activity, so that meaningful discussion or exploration can take place. In groups, it is easy for the focus to jump from topic to topic and person to person. The skilled leader knows when and how to hold the focus. The skill of *cutting off* or interrupting is essential when holding the focus.

Example 1

This group has just completed a round that allowed the participants to rate how well they anticipate their summer will go even though they all have to visit a parent who does not have full custody of them (1 = *I think my summer will go poorly* to 10 = *I think my summer will be great*).

> COUNSELOR: So, many of you are anticipating that your summer will not go well. I heard a lot of really low numbers.
>
> PAULA: I know mine will be a "1" just because I don't get to see my friends from like June until August. It really stinks!
>
> FAWN: Mine will be a "1" because my dad is still working. I will be alone with my stepsister a lot.
>
> MARY ALICE: Mine is going to be a "9" or "10" because my dad is a farmer and I get to work with him every day on the farm. I like the farm. Have any of you ever done farm work?
>
> COUNSELOR: (*Seeing that if Mary Alice is allowed to keep talking, she will take the focus off of where the group needs to go*) Hold on a minute, Mary Alice. Paula and Fawn have just given me a good idea. I want those who think their summer is going to be good to listen to those who think theirs is going to be bad, and then let's see if we can think of some ideas that can make their summers better.

The counselor in the example above clearly sees the need to hold the focus on the *topic* of the members' perceptions as to why the summer is going to be bad. If the leader allows Mary Alice to keep talking, the focus will likely shift to farms and life on a farm, which would take the focus off of a very important topic for this group.

Example 2

This group has just completed listing all the ideas they have regarding how to make new friends, given all the members are new to this school. Takiyah has said very little since the group began three weeks ago.

TAKIYAH: I would really like to ask a couple of the girls in my class to come over to my house, but that just seems really scary to me.

COUNSELOR: Takiyah, can you tell the group why that seems so scary?

BRENDA: I know why it is scary, because you don't know if . . .

COUNSELOR: (*Hearing in Brenda's voice that she is wanting to bring attention to herself as she has a tendency to do*) Brenda, hold on one minute, let's hear more from Takiyah why *she* thinks it is scary, and then maybe we can come back to you or maybe you will have ideas on how to help Takiyah. Go ahead, Takiyah.

This counselor sees the value in holding the focus on Takiyah because this is the first time she has felt comfortable enough to speak out in the group. If the leader allows Brenda to take over, Takiyah may wait a few more weeks to share.

Shifting the Focus.   Along with knowing how to hold the focus, a leader has to know how to shift the focus to other people or other topics. If the leader does not know how to do this, one member could dominate or the group could focus on just one topic when more topics need to be discussed. Again, the skills of drawing out and cutting off help accomplish this.

Example

Roy has been talking for a long time and is starting to repeat himself.

ROY: I just think she is too hard of a teacher and she plays favorites. She . . .

COUNSELOR: (*Seeing the need to shift the focus*) Roy, let me pick up on something you said. I want to hear how others feel about your teacher and why you think you are not doing well.

Deepening the Focus.   The reason for conducting groups is to have beneficial discussion or exploration. One of the most common mistakes in school groups is the lack of depth. Topics are brought up, discussed briefly, and then another subject is brought up, then another, then another, with no real depth. We use the concept of a depth chart as a guide to how beneficial the group is. The depth chart is a 10–1 scale with "10" being the *surface of the issue* and "1" being *very deep exploration*. In order for a group to be meaningful, the discussion has to go below "7." Presented is dialogue of a group that is not going very deep. We include a diagram using "the depth chart."

Example

GLORIA: When my dad drinks, I get very scared.

SHONA: I hate it when he has been drinking and then demands that he drive when mom should do the driving. A year ago he ran off the road and we hit a tree.

LEADER: That does sound scary. Were you hurt?

SHONA: We were all jerked around and banged up a bit. Luckily, we were not going too fast. (*Tells story for three minutes*)

MAGS: My mom is the one who drinks, but only on weekends. (*Starts to cry*) She ruins almost every weekend. I want to sleep over at friends or at least go out but I can't. I don't want to leave my dad alone with her. (*Tells stories about how she takes care of mom*)

SHELLIE: It is usually not too bad at my house because my dad passes out and then we just go about our business. He is what mom says is a happy drunk. She said her father was a nasty drunk. She tells all kinds of stories about him. Her favorite one is . . . (*Tells story for five minutes*)

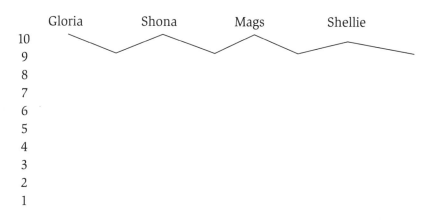

The above group would not be beneficial because the focus never went below "7." A group leader has to know how to deepen group discussion so as to have meaningful impact on the members. Below is the same example, but the leader focuses on a member and the group process moves below "7."

GLORIA: When my dad drinks, I get very scared.

SHONA: I hate it when he has been drinking and then demands that he drive when mom should do the driving. A year ago he ran off the road and we hit a tree.

COUNSELOR: That does sound scary. Were you hurt?

SHONA: We were all jerked around and banged up a bit. Luckily, we were not going too fast. It was on Jones Avenue near the big curve. We were . . .

COUNSELOR: Shona, let me hear from others about their fears or problems with their parent who drinks and then we're going to explore what we can do about it.

MAGS: My mom is the one who drinks, but only on weekends. (*Starts to cry*) She ruins almost every weekend. I want to sleep over at friends or at least go out but I don't want to leave my dad alone with her.

COUNSELOR: Mags, do you want to look at how you might do that differently?

MAGS: I can't leave my dad! (*cries more*)

COUNSELOR: Let's look at the "shoulds" you have for yourself. (*Writes SHOULDS on whiteboard*)

MAGS: I have all kinds of "shoulds." I feel like I have to take care of everyone.

COUNSELOR: Say some more about that.

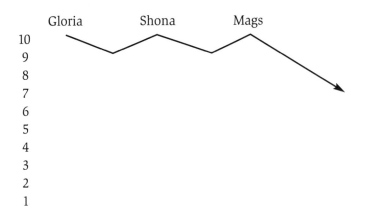

In this example, the leader holds the focus on Mags and takes her deeper into her thoughts and feelings. Deepening the focus is accomplished by asking good questions, using theory, using a multisensory technique such as a prop or movement activity or holding the focus on a member or topic as the members go to a deeper, more meaningful level. One thing that helps the leader to deepen the focus is for the leader to envision what the discussion might look like even before starting. This aids the leader in guiding the group to a deeper level of interaction.

Cutting Off.   Group members sometimes ramble, go off on tangents, or take too long to say something. Given that groups don't last long in a school setting (20–40 minutes usually), a leader has to be able to interrupt and redirect the flow of the conversation. Sometimes you will interrupt a member but continue to focus on that particular member. Other times, you will shift the focus to another person or topic. We suggest you tell members during the first session that there will be times when you will interrupt and redirect discussion to another person or topic.

Being able to cut members off is essential for high-quality group leading, yet many leaders find this skill the hardest to carry out. They feel they are being rude (Jacobs et al., 2002). In truth, leaders are not being rude but rather they are doing their jobs. A leader's job is to make sure the experience is valuable for as many members as possible. By not cutting off, leaders are being disrespectful to group members who are forced to listen to a dominant member ramble or waste valuable group time. Space does not allow us to elaborate on this skill, but we want to emphasize that it is crucial for good leading.

Drawing Out.   Another essential skill in leading school groups is being able to draw out quiet members. This skill is important because many students are hesitant to speak when they find themselves in a group. Some will never speak if they are allowed to sit quietly. Because one of the major purposes of groups in schools is to help students develop social skills, helping shy members get comfortable speaking among people they don't know well is beneficial.

There are a number of ways to draw out quiet members:

1. Use written exercises, such as sentence completions or lists, so you can then ask members to read their answers.
2. Use a round exercise, which is an activity where everyone is asked to give a word or phrase answer or a number rating.
3. Employ a kind of movement exercise where the members "speak" with their feet or hands, and then you can ask the member to elaborate. (This kind of exercise is explained in the next section.)

Using Exercises.   Knowing about exercises is essential for leading groups in schools. You want to know as much as possible about conducting an exercise, which includes the introduction and the processing of it. You also want to learn about the many different kinds of valuable exercises that are available. We discuss some of the different exercises below. You will discover excellent material with all kinds of different activities throughout your career (Vernon, 1995; Johnson & Johnson, 2000).

Choosing exercises

Many counselors mistakenly pick exercises that take too much time to conduct. For example, asking a group of elementary students to draw where they live, color it, and then cut it out would eat up much time. In elementary school groups, this would not allow enough time for discussion about life at home, which would be the leader's purpose in doing the exercise. To do the same exercise but save time for processing, the members could bring in a picture that they drew and colored at home. Many students now live in two houses, so some would feel they should do two drawings. Before using an exercise, you want to ask, "Does this exercise allow me enough time for adequate processing?"

Leaders need to also consider whether or not an exercise achieves its intended purpose. For instance, a leader who wants to focus on anger on the playground could mistakenly use an exercise that takes her from the specific topic by saying, "List three times you got angry this week." This can lead to students listing things at home, at the bus stop, or at hockey practice. This is not where the leader intended the group to go. Therefore, the exercise is not specific enough. A more direct exercise would be, "List three times you got angry on the playground in the last two weeks."

Introducing and conducting exercises

The leader needs to give thought to the introduction of an exercise. The introduction needs to be clear, concise, and usually energetic in order to get members focused. When conducting an exercise, you want to make sure members stay on task. If they are working on a drawing, writing, or working in pairs or small groups, you want to make sure they stay focused. There may be times when the exercise is serious but the members start to laugh or talk to the person next to them; in this situation, you will want to stop this behavior and refocus the members on the exercise.

Processing exercises

The most important part of doing an exercise is the processing of it; that is, the leader facilitates a discussion relating to what thoughts, feelings, or reactions were stimulated by the exercise. The majority of time following an exercise should be consumed by the processing. By thinking through the purpose of the exercise and preparing for how to discuss reactions, the leader can make the processing beneficial. Another important thing to remember throughout the processing period is to take the comments to a deeper level. Many counselors get comments from each person but do not delve further into the members' reactions or feelings. For instance, a good exercise is to ask members to name their favorite animal. The skilled leader who understands processing has the members tell the animal and then shifts into why they picked the animal. The leader asks the members to relate their comments and choice to how they see themselves today or how they would like to be in the future. This takes the group to a deeper level (below "7" on the depth chart). The leader who does not understand processing or the purpose of the exercise could easily end up with a discussion about the different animals that were chosen, which is not the purpose of the exercise. This would keep the group at a surface level. *Always remember, the key to an exercise is processing it. Exercises are never done to fill up time.*

Kinds of exercises

Rounds. A round is an exercise in which the leader goes around the room to hear briefly from everyone. It is an excellent exercise because the leader gets valuable information in a short amount of time. It also allows all members to be engaged in the group; that is, everyone has an opportunity to contribute. Often, the leader can follow up on what was said in the round. The round can be a number rating on a 1–10 scale, such as the following:

- How much do you like school? 1 = very little; 10 = a lot
- How was your week? 1 = terrible; 10 = great
- How much do you fear failure? 1 = not at all; 10 = a lot
- How would you rate today's group session? 1 = not helpful; 10 = very helpful

Rounds can also be words or phrases:

- In a word or phrase, how was your week?
- In a word or phrase, how do you feel about your parent's divorce?

- In a word or phrase, how would you describe your feelings about school?

Rounds are used during all phases of a group. During the warm-up phase, by doing a quick 1 to 10, or word or phrase go-round, you can find out about the members' weeks or days. This way the leader has an idea of what has been happening with the members without directly asking "how was your week?" and then having to listen while each member talks in depth or one member tells a long story.

The round helps in the working or middle phase as a way to get members focused on a topic. For example, the leader who wants to discuss study problems may begin by asking, "In a word or phrase, what is your biggest problem with studying? I'd like to hear briefly from each of you." After showing a twelve-minute clip from a movie, the leader could ask, "What stood out to you about that clip? Briefly, let's do a round. Who wants to start?" The round is also helpful in controlling those members who like to ramble; by asking for a word or phrase, it is much easier for the leader to break in on the member who likes to make long comments.

The round is excellent for the closing phase as well. Leaders often ask, "In a word or phrase, what stood out today?" In addition, in many groups, leaders have members share in a round what they are going to do differently during the next week.

Sentence completion exercises. Written exercises are excellent for getting members focused. Having members complete sentence stems generates interest and energy. With sentence completions, you only want to use three to five sentences in most groups. Sometimes one sentence can be all that is needed. The answers are used to generate discussion for a major part of the session. Below are various examples of some two-sentence and one-sentence exercises.

The following two sentences could be used in a group that addresses school success:

- One thing I like about school is _____
- One thing I don't like about school is _____

These sentences may be useful in a group that addresses trust issues:

- I trust those who _____
- I don't trust those who _____

The next set of sentences may be useful by themselves in the appropriate group:

- Dating is _____
- When people meet me, they _____
- I regret most that _____
- I am _____

Listing exercises. Having members list various things often gets them focused. Members enjoy hearing what is on each other's lists and get ideas from hearing others. Examples include the following:

- List characteristics of a friend.
- List ways to meet new people.
- List three things you like about yourself.
- List people you can talk to when you are down.

Rating exercises. Students like to circle ratings (e.g., 1–5 scale) and then discuss them. If you pick some provocative questions, this usually generates interesting discussion. You can find many of these in books (Canfield & Siccone, 1993), or you can make up your own. Here is an example:

	Strongly Disagree	Disagree	Neutral	Agree	Strongly Agree
I enjoy meeting new people.	1	2	3	4	5
I enjoy being by myself.	1	2	3	4	5
I like my parents.	1	2	3	4	5
I like school.	1	2	3	4	5
I think I am a good person.	1	2	3	4	5

Movement exercises. Students have lots of energy, so exercises that involve moving around are especially motivating in the schools. Of course, these activities must be age-appropriate. Movement exercises are also interesting and give the members a chance to "speak with their feet." By this, we mean that having members go to different locations in a room or move along a continuum allows them to tell something about themselves by where they move.

Example 1: The members have been talking about how they see themselves. The leader decides to use a movement exercise to further the discussion.

COUNSELOR: There are four main ways people see themselves and others. I want you to move to one of four places in reference to how you see yourself and others. In that corner over there is the position "I'm not OK, Others are OK." In the corner over there is "I'm OK, Others are not OK." In this corner is "I'm not OK, Others are not OK," and in that corner, "I'm OK, Others are OK." On a count of three, I'd like you to move to the place that represents your thoughts about yourself and others. Ready, one, two, three. (The leader has placed signs on the walls to make it easier for the members to remember which corner represents which choice.)

Example 2: The leader has a number of quiet members, so she decides to use a continuum exercise.

COUNSELOR: I want all of you to stand up. Line up here in the center of the room behind one another. . . . Now on the count of three, I want you to move along an imagined continuum or line. You can move all the way to the left or the right or anywhere in between. On this wall is "I'm a Loser" and on this other wall is "I'm a Winner." On the count of three, everyone move. Ready, one, two, three. (Note: Use of the word *loser* may seem harsh; however, this is the language that kids use. There is value in using words with which kids identify.)

In each of these examples, the leader allows different members to talk about why they positioned themselves where they did. This usually generates much interaction, and the leader can often encourage quiet members to share why they chose their spot.

Creative exercises. Earlier in this chapter we presented some examples of multisensory, creative exercises where props (e.g., shield, fuses) were used. Tapes, cups, chairs, clay, drawings, puppets, and all kinds of other things can be used as exercises to make groups more appealing. Students like these activities because they make groups more interesting and more concrete and they hold the members' attention. Today's students are bombarded with visual images in video games, computers, and television. Group leaders can make their groups more interesting by using a number of creative exercises. The key is to use activities that are meaningful and relevant and not just fun or cute. Creative exercises can be found in numerous books, including Jacobs's (1992) *Creative Counseling Techniques: An Illustrated Guide* and Canfield and Siccone's (1993) *101 Ways to Develop Student Self-Esteem and Responsibility, Volume II: The Power to Succeed in School and Beyond.*

Common reading. One very good exercise for elementary school groups is to use books that directly relate to the purpose of the group. Often, the use of books or other reading material in counseling is called *bibliotherapy*. Excellent books on divorce, fears, fighting, anger, multicultural issues, and many other relevant topics can be found in the school's library or a local bookshop. Often, leaders read a couple of pages and then spend the rest of the session discussing what was read. For middle and high school groups, many one-page readings exist that have thought-provoking points. One could use current events from a magazine or newspaper. With these, the leader has members read the paragraph or page and mark the sentence or two that stood out to them. Processing their comments and feelings usually takes much of the session.

Common Mistakes

There are a number of common mistakes that are made by group leaders in school settings. Four examples are discussed below.

Having Too Much "Fluff."   Out of fear that no one will talk, school counselors frequently fill time by having members engage in activities that are not meaningful or helpful. For example, leaders should avoid playing irrelevant games and engaging in too many arts and crafts activities. We call this having too much "fluff" in your groups. School counselors typically have access to loads of materials especially designed for group counseling. Many publishing companies also produce so-called effective programs to be implemented in groups. Although this may seem like an easy way to prepare for your groups, these materials and programs frequently contain too much "fluff" or "filler." They may be cute and keep group members busy, but they don't address the issues that members need to address in order to improve their situations.

Wasting Valuable Time.   School counselors need to be time-efficient when leading groups because the groups are quite short (20–30 minutes for elementary students and 30–40 minutes for middle and high school students). The two most frequent ways time is wasted are by (1) devoting too much time to getting started (getting seats arranged, getting members seated and ready to begin) and (2) spending too much time in the warm-up phase. The warm-up phase should not last more than five minutes for most school groups.

Using Exercises or Readings that Take Too Long.   Many counselors make the mistake of using exercises, readings, or videos that take too long. Using a twenty-minute video in a thirty-minute group does not leave ample time for discussion among group members. Ideally, counselors choose activities that take two to ten minutes to conduct, leaving the majority of the time for processing and discussion. For long movies, it is often best to show them in ten-minute segments and then process each segment as it is shown.

School counselors must be cautious not to use too many exercises in one session. Usually, one or two activities that are well thought out should generate plenty of energy and interaction among members.

Conducting One-to-One Counseling While Others Just Passively Watch.   There will be times in counseling groups when the leader will focus on one person. The mistake that is often made is the leader just focuses on the one working member and ignores the other members. It is important to include everyone in the counseling process, and this can be accomplished in several ways. Leaders can, for instance, ask questions, role-play situations, give feedback, share their perspectives, and share their own struggles with the same issue.

Planning for the Group Experience

Planning includes logistics, preparing for the series of sessions, selection of members, and most important, getting ready for the specific session you are leading. *All group sessions should be planned.*

Logistics.   The logistics of leading groups in a school setting must be given consideration. Having a group usually means getting students out of class or having students meet before school, after school, or during lunch. Lunch is often a good time for groups to meet. Getting students out of class each week at the same time is often frowned upon by teachers; therefore, counselors rotate the time at which they have a group. It is important that counselors negotiate meeting times with teachers.

Planning a Series of Sessions.   Many group experiences that center on, for example, parenting, friendship, shyness, or study skills will meet for a set number of times, and all the group sessions can be planned ahead of time. The benefit of doing this is that each session builds on the previous one and the plans can be revised and used again. This is helpful because school counselors find that their planning time is limited. Naturally, each group will be different due to the members, but the content and activities for each session can be prepared before the first session. By planning the series of sessions, the leader has the "big picture" of what he is trying to accomplish over the duration of the group experience. This also assists in deciding which students actually can benefit from being in the group.

Selection of Members.   The screening and selection of members is critical. Once the school counselor has established the types of groups she will conduct, referral boxes can be placed throughout the school and students can simply place their names in them indicating which groups they would like to be in. Many times the counselor has an idea of who may be good to have in certain groups. Teachers are a great referral source for group members. They frequently have insight into, for example, the personal and educational issues that may be bothering students. Although a less common method of referral, parents will sometimes refer their children to group counseling. Naturally, participation should be voluntary. Forcing children to attend a group can be counterproductive.

Counselors should screen for developmental appropriateness and the differing needs of students. Simply because all prospective members are in the third grade does not mean that all are at the same developmental level. As for different needs, students dealing with divorce may be at different stages, so more than one group may be needed. One way to determine the needs of the student is to interview prospective members. This method is especially effective in cases where the counselor is not already familiar with prospective members. Taking just a few minutes to determine the child's developmental level in a short interview can save having to ask a student to leave the group because of inappropriateness. The screening process can also be accomplished by consulting with teachers and parents. Teachers, especially, have great insight into whether or not a particular child could function appropriately in a small group setting. When running groups for parents and teachers, little screening is done. Counselors are just happy these members have volunteered.

Confidentiality and Parental Permission.   Confidentiality in the school setting is always a bit of an oxymoron. Can you really ensure that the members of an elementary-age group or even a group conducted at the secondary level will keep quiet about the group content outside of the group? It probably is unrealistic. However, school counselors are bound by their professional code of ethics to try to protect the confidentiality of their group members (see American School Counselor Association Code of Ethics in the appendix of this book or at www. schoolcounselor.org). You should discuss this issue with members as soon as you screen them and again as they begin to share personal information. Also, remember that confidentiality may mean different things in different cultures. For example, the following statements may help you in thinking about how to approach the issue of confidentiality:

> "What we say in group needs to stay in group. I want to make sure everyone agrees with this, and I am going to ask each of you to say you will keep things confidential. Any questions about this before I ask you to indicate that you agree?"

> "If everyone is going to feel safe sharing in this room, then we all have to agree that we won't go out of here and tell our other friends all that was said. Now if you learn something helpful in here or learn something about yourself that you want to share with your friends, that is great! But you may not go out and say 'guess what Tiana said in group today!'"

Some school counselors find it helpful to provide students with a written state-ment of confidentiality so students will know before agreeing to enter the group that they must respect the other members' right to privacy. This statement will often let potential group members know that should they choose to break confi-dentiality, then they also choose not to participate in the group. However, none of this guarantees confidentiality. That is why it is generally wise to get parental per-mission for a student to be a member of a group. You should always consult your school's policy on this issue as well as your state's policy or laws regarding parental permission/consent for children to be group members.

Planning a Session.   As we mentioned earlier, group sessions in a school setting can and should be thoroughly planned. A well-thought-out plan can ensure that the group session will be beneficial. The plan should include a good warm-up, ways to focus on important topics or issues (e.g., feeling-focused activities, thought-provoking questions, and exercises), and a relevant closing. Group plan-ning takes time. It is not easy to write good plans. However, preparation increases the possibility that the session will flow well, helping take the members to mean-ingful levels of discussion and interaction. A well-developed plan also ensures that exercises relate to the overall purpose of the group. With practice, planning becomes easier, and it is always useful. Leaders who "wing it" report that leading is frustrating, difficult, and not very beneficial or rewarding.

We suggest that leaders write out the plan, including the time it takes to com-plete each element of the session. One might also add a goal or two and those materials needed for the session. The following is a sample plan that you might use during the first session of a group for elementary-age children (possibly grades 3–5) whose parents are recently divorced (within the last 6 to 10 months). The leader has a very clear sense of the group's purpose and has built in exercises that will allow the conversation to focus on topics that these members need to address.

Sample Plan—Children of Recent Divorce

Goal(s) of the session: (Leader selects appropriate ones.)
Materials needed: (Leader selects relevant ones.)

2 min.	Warm-up: Have the students give their names, ages, and how long parents have been divorced.
1 min.	Statement of the purpose of the group: Say something like, "The purpose of this group is to discuss your feelings about your parents' divorce as well as think about ways to handle things that are going to come up with your life changing in this way, like living arrangements, holidays, school events, and so on."
2 min.	Writing exercise: Counselor says, "Write down on a piece of paper four things you have been thinking or worrying about since you heard your mom and dad were getting a divorce."
10 min.	Process exercise: Have each member share two or three things on their list. Be sure to point out common concerns. For example, you could list the most common concerns on the board. Look for ideas or themes that revolve around blame. Do any children blame themselves? (If so, address this right away. For example, "One thing that I want all of you to know before we leave this room today is that divorce is never a kid's fault." The leader might use REBT to dispute any irrational beliefs that the divorce is their fault.)
12 min.	Focus on one of these issues:

"It's my fault, because . . ."
"Life will never be OK."
"My parents don't love me."
"I will never be happy."

Use REBT to dispute their thinking.

3 min.	Closing round: Finally, the counselor could wrap things up by asking the members, "On a scale of 1 to 10, rate how you are feeling about being in this group. What stands out about today's session?"

With any plan, the leader should be flexible. We teach that leaders should stick to their plans unless what comes up in the group is of equal value to or better than what was planned. Ideally, in your group counseling course, some time will be spent on planning effective groups. If not, you may want to do additional reading (Jacobs et al., 2002).

Beginning a Group

Much thought needs to be given to the first session of any group. The leader needs to pay attention to how to open the group, how the members are feeling about being in the group, and how to focus on the content. The opening few minutes are crucial because they tend to set the tone for the group and either engage, enrage, or bore the members. Beginning leaders often make one of the following mistakes:

- Giving a long, boring introduction focusing on the rules and/or themselves
- Allowing members to take a long time to introduce themselves (which gets boring)
- Using an irrelevant, "cute" opening that actually turns people off or takes them away from the purpose of the group

The skilled leader ensures that the opening few minutes are interesting and relevant to the purpose of the group. The leader will usually want the introductions to be brief, with members just stating their names and one or two tidbits of relevant information. One common mistake is to spend lots of time on group rules right at the start. Discussing the rules without first engaging the students makes the group feel like they're beginning a class. Focusing on interesting topics or activities is usually more important than focusing on rules. We have also found that relevant, possibly fun, opening activities are better than exercises that are not relevant to the purpose of the group.

Example 1 of Nonproductive Opening.   Opening session of a group for seniors who are getting ready to go off to further their education:

> COUNSELOR: OK. Let's get started. I would like each of you to say your name, your homeroom teacher, and where you live (*pause*). Brandon, let's start with you.

Example 1 of Productive Opening.   Opening session of the same group:

COUNSELOR: OK. Let's get started. I would like each of you to say your name, what school you are thinking of attending in the fall, and state one fear or concern you have about going there. Brandon, let's start with you.

In the first example, the information gathered in the opening round (i.e., home-room teacher, where they live) would have very little relevance or importance to the group's purpose. The second example gets information that is relevant to the group's purpose as well as interesting to the other members. Each student would no doubt be interested in hearing where the other group members are heading for college and some of the concerns they have about going there. This productive opening allows for appropriate content to be brought to the table in the group.

Example 2 of Nonproductive Opening.   Opening session of a stress management group for first-year teachers in a secondary school:

COUNSELOR: Hello, I would like to welcome all of you to our group. As you know, we hope that this group will be a place where you can discuss the various obstacles you are facing as a first-year teacher. I also hope this will be a place that you all can support and assist one another in overcoming some of those obstacles that you think are creating a high level of stress. Let us begin by listing everyone's name on the board and then under your name we will list all of the courses you have been assigned to teach.

Example 2 of Productive Opening.   Here is the same scenario as above.

COUNSELOR: Hello, I would like to welcome all of you to our group. As you know, we hope that this group will be a place where you can discuss the various obstacles you are facing as a first-year teacher. I also hope this will be a place that you all can support and assist one another in overcoming some of those obstacles that you think are creating a high level of stress. Let's get started. When each of you sat down, I handed you a large rubber band. I would like to go around the room and have you say your name and then take the rubber band and stretch it out to the length that you think best represents the level of stress you are feeling as a first-year teacher.

The example of the nonproductive opening is stale and will be uninteresting to group members. In addition, the listing of courses would take too much time.

The productive opening is more interesting. It is visual. It will get the members focused quickly on their own level of stress. It will also allow members to connect with others who feel similarly overwhelmed. (Note: A group for new/beginning teachers is valuable and workable. However, many school counselors do not include this group in their overall school-counseling program.)

Considerations During the First Session. A leader never knows how a first session will go; therefore, first sessions are usually more difficult than subsequent sessions. Leaders must pay attention to how members react to being in a group, how they relate to each other, and how they relate to the purpose or content of the group. If members seem uncomfortable, bored, or confused, it is the leader's responsibility to try to fix this. Leaders often spend too much time warming up the members and not enough time on the actual content, be it friendship, parenting, stress management, or race relations. In planning and conducting a first session, you will want to make sure that a good portion of the time is focused on topics or issues relevant to the purpose and not just a session of warm-up. One common mistake is allowing the warm-up to last the entire first session. This leaves the members with unrealistic expectations about future sessions. It can leave young group members with the feeling that group is simply about having fun.

Ending a Group Session

Every group session should have a closing phase where the members review and summarize the session and tell what was significant. Most student groups last between twenty and forty minutes, so leaders have to be very careful not to run out of time and thus have either a hurried closing or no closing at all. An early mistake made by one author of this chapter was allowing the lunchtime bell to signal the end of the group. Ideally, a leader will allow two to five minutes for the closing phase of a session. One common technique used during the closing phase is to ask members to comment briefly on what they are feeling, what they learned, what stood out, or what they will do differently as a result of the session. Often, the leader will add some thoughts or support based on the members' comments. Another way to end the session is to have members write down what they learned or share in pairs and then briefly hear from each member. The key is to plan how you are going to close the session and then make sure you have enough time to do it properly.

Bringing the Entire Group Experience to a Close

For task and psychoeducational groups, the ending of the group is usually not a major event. This is not true for some counseling groups. Much thought should be given to the ending of counseling groups because some members may see the end of the group as an important loss of contact for them (Gladding, 2003). It is good to announce two or three meetings in advance that the group experience will be ending. This allows the leader to gauge how much time is needed for the closing. Usually, this is part of the last session or even the entire last session. During the ending, you want to review what has happened and how students may plan for the future. One activity that some leaders use for high school groups is a reunion activity where members act like they are having a group reunion after being away for five years. This can lead to an interesting final discussion.

Salient Research

Many articles and books can be found regarding leading various kinds of groups in the schools. However, there is a need for research on the effectiveness of different intervention techniques (Jacobs et al., 2002). In a recent article in the *Journal of Counseling & Development*, Shechtman (2002) provided a review of studies in child group interventions. Earlier, Whiston and Sexton (1998) reviewed the literature on group counseling in schools, focusing on data-based research. Although the initial research is promising, much more needs to come from practicing school counselors on what works and what does not (DeLucia-Waack, 1997).

Final Thoughts

It requires a great deal of hard work to become a competent group leader in a school setting. In her article, Shechtman (2002) wrote that "leaders of children's groups need to be acquainted with methods to enhance children's self-expressiveness and . . . need to acquire special techniques and be cautious in the handling of the group process" (p. 297). Practice is the key to learning how to lead effective groups that are interesting and helpful for students, teachers, and parents. We hope this chapter has given you a good introduction to group counseling in schools and has provided you with techniques and skills that you find useful. Our hope is that your experience in a group counseling course will add to what you have learned from this chapter.

REFERENCES

American School Counselor Association. (1998). *Ethical standards for school counselors.* Alexandria, VA: Author.

Baca, L. M., & Koss-Chioino, J. D. (1997). Development of a culturally responsive group counseling model for Mexican American adolescents. *Journal of Multicultural Counseling and Development, 25,* 130–141.

Campbell, C. A., & Dahir, C. A. (1997). *Sharing the vision: The national standards for school counseling programs.* Alexandria, VA: American School Counselor Association.

Canfield, J., & Siccone, F. (1993). *101 Ways to develop student self-esteem and responsibility, volume II: The power to succeed in school and beyond.* Needham Heights, MA: Allyn & Bacon.

Corey, G. (2000). *The theory and practice of group counseling* (5th ed.). Pacific Grove, CA: Brooks/Cole.

Corey, G. (2001). *Theory and practice of counseling and psychotherapy* (6th ed.). Pacific Grove, CA: Brooks/Cole.

Corey, G., & Corey, M. S. (2002). *Groups: Process and practice* (6th ed.). Pacific Grove, CA: Brooks/Cole.

DeLucia-Waack, J. (1997). Measuring the effectiveness of group work: A review and analysis of process and outcome measures. *Journal for Specialists in Group Work. 22,* 277–293.

Ellis, A., & MacLaren, C. (1998). *Rational emotive behavior therapy: A therapist's guide.* San Luis Obispo, CA: Impact.

Gladding, S. T. (2003). *Group work: A counseling specialty* (4th ed.). New York: Merrill.

Golden, B. (1997). A glimpse of possibilities. *Techniques: Making education & career connections, 72,* 19.

Jacobs, E. (1992). *Creative counseling techniques: An illustrated guide.* Odessa, FL: Psychological Assessment Resources.

Jacobs, E. (1994). *Impact Therapy.* Odessa, FL: Psychological Assessment Resources.

Jacobs, E., Masson, R., & Harvill, R. (2002). *Group counseling: Strategies and skills* (4th ed.). Pacific Grove, CA: Brooks/Cole.

Johnson, D. W., & Johnson, F. P. (2000). *Joining together* (7th ed.). Boston: Allyn & Bacon.

Prochaska, J. O., & Norcross, J. C. (2003). *Systems of psychotherapy: A transtheoretical analysis* (5th ed.). Belmont, CA: Wadsworth.

Sabella, R. A. (2003). *SchoolCounselor.com 2.0: A friendly and practical guide to the world wide web* (2nd ed). Minneapolis, MN: Educational Media.

Shechtman, Z. (2002). Child group psychotherapy in the school at the threshold of a new millennium. *Journal of Counseling & Development, 80,* 257–384.

Smead, R. (1995). *Skills and techniques for group work with children and adolescents.* Champaign, IL: Research Press.

Whiston, S. C., & Sexton, T. L. (1998). A review of school counseling outcome research: Implications for practice. *Journal of Counseling & Development, 76,* 412–426.

Wilde, J. (1992). *Rational counseling with school-aged populations.* New York: Accelerated Development.

Vernon, A. (1995) *Thinking, feeling, behaving: An emotional education curriculum for children grades 1-6.* Champaign, IL: Research Press.

Yalom, I. (1995). *The theory and practice of group psychotherapy* (4th ed.). New York: Basic Books.

CHAPTER 4
Peer Programs and Family Counseling

Susan C. Whiston and Jennifer C. Bouwkamp
Indiana University, Bloomington

Contemporary school counselors are not just service providers; they are an integral part of the educational mission of the school and provide a systematic curriculum that facilitates students' academic, career, and personal/social development (Campbell & Dahir, 1997). Hence, the role of school counseling involves more than solely providing individual and group counseling and can involve activities such as going into classrooms, assisting teachers in creating career development activities, and developing web sites to disseminate academic information. Furthermore, many counselors realize that students do not live in isolation and that the systems around them influence both their behavior and their emotions. In terms of influence, peers and the student's family play a particularly active role in most students' lives. Therefore, a number of counselors have instituted peer programs and counseling with students' families as methods for expanding their school counseling programs.

This chapter addresses both peer mediation and counseling programs and methods for working effectively with students' families. The first section of the chapter discusses peer programs, whereas the second portion focuses on a variety of ways in which school counselors work with families. Although working with peers and working with families may seem to be unrelated topics, both of these groups have a significant influence on the behavior of an individual student. Therefore, students' development can be enhanced if school counselors are able to design programs that increase the chance of peers and families having a positive rather than negative influence on students.

Peer Mediation and Counseling Programs

There are a variety of peer helper programs (e.g., tutoring programs); however, we will focus on the ones school counselors are most likely to be involved in (i.e., peer mediation programs and peer counseling programs). In *peer mediation*, students are trained in conflict resolution and then use these skills to resolve conflicts among their peers at school (Gerber & Terry-Day, 1999). There appears to be an increasing interest in peer mediation programs, which is reflected in Shepard's (1994) finding that since 1991 conflict resolution programs in the schools have increased by 40 percent. *Peer counseling*, on the other hand, occurs when the students are used in some capacity in the counseling process, such as providing counseling in certain situations or referring students to the school counselors for personal counseling.

Peer Mediation

In peer mediation programs, the focus is on students learning the skills to resolve conflict and then using those skills, without adult assistance, to mediate conflict situations among their peers. Therefore, peer mediation programs are conducted by students and for students and allow peers to have an active role in determining the resolution of disputes. The philosophy behind peer mediation programs is that children are exposed to violence and aggression in the media, yet have few opportunities to learn how to resolve conflicts and disputes. Peer mediation programs are designed so that students who are in the classrooms, cafeterias, and on the playgrounds will be able to identify conflicts early among other students and work to resolve these conflicts before they escalate to more violent outcomes. The logic is that violence in a school is reduced when students have the opportunity to air their grievances in the presence of a trained peer mediator who is capable of reconciling the disagreement and creating a "win-win" resolution. Another rationale is that when students are trained to mediate disputes in their schools, they will also use these skills in various other settings (e.g., home, community) throughout their lives. Hence, it is hoped that peer mediators who have advanced training in conflict resolution will experience long-term positive effects throughout their lives. Peer mediation programs are designed so that both the student mediators and the students in conflict learn conflict resolution skills (Casella, 2000).

Although there is variation in how peer mediators are trained, according to Smith and Daunic (2002) most programs focus the curricula on (a) facilitating an understanding of conflict and its determinants, (b) teaching students effective communication, problem-solving, and negotiation skills, and (c) providing a foundation for education about peace and nonviolence.

Training the student mediators often combines instruction about identifying conflicts and methods for resolving disagreements with several hours of students role-playing mediation sessions. Once the peer mediators are trained, they then work in the school environment—first, to identify potential conflicts and, second, to facilitate the resolution of the conflict among their peers. The resolution of the conflict is conducted by the peer mediator with the other students without the direct supervision of a teacher, counselor, or principal. In most schools, however, there is an adult coordinator of the peer mediation program, which is often a school counselor.

Theoretical Influences

Peer mediation programs are not grounded in one specific theoretical approach, but are influenced by several theoretical orientations. Developmental theories, particularly Kohlberg's (1984) theory of moral development, are often considered influential in peer mediation programs. It is theorized that peer mediation facilitates students in moving from Kohlberg's Level I, preconventional stage, to Level II, the conventional stage. In the preconventional stage, children's behavior is typically motivated by the need to obey rules and avoid punishment. As students develop and enter the conventional stage, their moral reasoning involves group expectations and social conventions. By actively involving peers, as compared to teachers or principals, in the resolution of conflicts, it is anticipated that moral development from the preconventional to the conventional stage will be facilitated for both the mediators and the disputants. Another theoretical foundation is behaviorism, where students learn new behaviors and are rewarded for their abilities to resolve conflicts in a positive manner. Casella (2000) also argued that peer mediation programs are influenced by social learning theories. The belief that peers will learn conflict resolution skills through the modeling of these skills by peer mediators is particularly congruent with social learning theorists' emphasis on the efficacy of modeling.

Practical Applications for Implementing a Program

In most schools, mediation programs are implemented using a "cadre" approach in which a small group of students within each school are trained to be peer mediators (Bickmore, 2002). With this approach, students are selected based on their personal characteristics and receive training in mediation outside of their regular classes. Many school counselors involve other school personnel (e.g., teachers, administrators, and nurses) in the selection process. Typically after the training, the student mediators continue to meet with an adult advisor to enhance their mediation skills and to promote nonviolent conflict resolution within their school. Bickmore found that many students indicated they would like to serve as peer mediators and that they see the role as positive. In a few schools, whole classes, grades, or the entire school will receive peer mediation training, but the more popular approach is to train a peer leadership team that is coordinated by an adult advisor.

The selection of peer mediators is often considered critical to the success of the program. Day-Vines, Day-Hairston, Carruthers, Wall, and Lupton-Smith (1996) recommended the selection of a diverse group of students in a peer mediation program. They suggested that the group include students of diverse academic abilities, gender, and cultures, which can enhance the discussions in training and assist mediators in viewing conflicts from various perspectives. The students' overall maturity and ability to empathize may be more important than other factors such as academic performance. In selecting peer mediators, school counselors should consider the students' abilities to listen, communicate, respect others, and solve problems.

Much of the training in peer mediation programs involves learning the mediation process. According to Bickmore (2002), the typical mediation process involves the following:

1. Each participant independently consenting to participate in the mediation process and agreeing to keep the proceedings confidential
2. The mediator eliciting from each participant his or her views of the situation and problem
3. The mediator assisting the participants in identifying and communicating to each other the solvable parts of their problem
4. The mediator facilitating the generation of possible solutions from all participants and negotiating a resolution that all participants can accept
5. The participants all affirming the resolution and the mediator establishing closure related to the conflict

Establishing a peer mediation program in a school requires a substantial amount of planning and school resources (Smith & Daunic, 2002). In implementing a program, individuals need to consider these questions:

- What kinds of conflicts are appropriate for the peer mediators?
- Where in the school should the mediation take place?
- How are mediators made available?
- How often can mediators miss class?

Particularly important to the success of the program is the amount of support for the program throughout the school. Programs that do not have the support of the teachers and other school personnel are bound to have little positive influence. Therefore, school counselors need to evaluate the general support for a peer mediation program and determine if there is sufficient support for the program to be successful.

Research Supporting Peer Mediation Programs

The research related to the effectiveness of peer mediation programs indicates that there can be benefits to these programs. In summarizing the research related to peer mediation programs, Carruthers and Sweeney (1996) concluded that students selected as mediators benefit from the programs in several ways. They indicated that students enjoy being mediators and their attitudes toward school improve. Johnson and Johnson (1996) found that students trained to be peer mediators generally learned the steps of conflict resolution and retained that knowledge for six or more months. There is also research indicating that younger students (i.e., elementary students) can learn and implement the steps of conflict resolution (Humphries, 1999). Furthermore, there is evidence that the conflict resolution skills students learn are applied in nonschool settings and with family members and friends (Smith, Daunic, Miller, & Robinson, 2002). Parents of mediators also have indicated that their children benefit, with the most common benefit being improvement in attitudes and grades (Carruthers & Sweeney, 1996).

In a number of studies, the peer mediation process has resulted in the disputants reaching an agreement on ways to resolve the conflict. Carruthers and Sweeney (1996) found that disputants reached agreements with the help of a mediator 80 to 95 percent of the time. Moreover, Hart and Gunty (1997) found that after implementation of a peer mediation program, teachers spent significantly less time in nonteaching activities, such as resolving conflicts. Many teachers and administrators have reported that peer mediation programs result in fewer student-to-student conflicts and fights and subsequent suspensions (Johnson & Johnson, 1996; Smith et al., 2002). Furthermore, there is evidence that peer mediation programs increase student academic engagement and achievement (Bickmore, 2002). There are, however, variations among program results, suggesting that the quality of the training may influence the outcome of the peer mediation program. The background of the adult supervisor may be especially important, and Emerson (1990) found that many of the teachers/trainers did not have (a) a thorough understanding of the mediation process, (b) an understanding of how to train peer mediators, and/or (c) good group process skills.

There are many positive benefits to peer mediation programs; however, if the goal is to reduce *serious* violence, then other programs have been found to have better efficacy. Youth violence is a national issue with 30 to 40 percent of males and 16 to 32 percent of females having committed a serious violent offense by age 17 (U.S. Surgeon General, 2001). Elliott (1998) conducted a rigorous examination of existing intervention programs for youth violence with the intent of identifying effective programs based on substantial empirical evidence. Of the 500 programs reviewed, only ten programs met the rigorous standards used. The U.S. Surgeon General and the Center for Disease Control have endorsed these ten programs as effective programs in violence prevention. Of the ten programs deemed effective, only two were counseling-related programs, and both of these were family-based counseling approaches (i.e., functional family therapy and multisystemic therapy). The other seven effective approaches were psychoeducational, residential, and community-based interventions, such as prenatal and infancy home visitations or foster care treatment.

In our opinion, there are various reasons why peer mediation programs were not identified as one of the programs deemed effective in preventing youth violence by the U.S. Surgeon General and the Centers for Disease Control. One reason is that peer mediation programs may not have an impact on some of the measures of youth violence (e.g., arrest). The most frequent agreement that is reached between the disputants in the peer mediation process is to ignore or avoid each other (Johnson & Johnson, 1996), which may have the short-term effect of avoiding a fight on the playground but does not have a long-term effect of reducing violent offenses. Another possible reason that peer mediation programs were not included in the list of effective programs is the state of research in this area. The empirical studies of peer mediation programs often have research design and methodology problems. In examining the research on the effectiveness of peer mediation programs, Gerber and Terry-Day (1999) found the positive evaluations of these programs were predominantly based on self-report and correlational data. There have been some recent studies (e.g., Hart & Gunty, 1997; Smith et al., 2002), however, that are methodologically strong, and continued research should assist school counselors in knowing the effects of peer mediation programs.

⟩ Peer Counseling Versus Peer Helping

As indicated earlier, in this chapter we are discussing two types of peer programs that might be instituted by a school counselor (i.e., peer mediation programs and peer counseling programs). Some school counselors have established peer counseling programs, where the focus is on peers providing counseling rather than mediating conflicts among students. The premise of peer counseling programs is that students may not go to their school counselors when they are experiencing slight to moderate problems, but will disclose these difficulties to their peers. Lewis and Lewis (1996) found in a sample of school counselors from the state of Washington that around 58 percent had a peer counseling program at their schools. However, peer mediation programs are still more common, and there is considerably more research related to peer mediation than to peer counseling.

Tanaka and Reid (1997) argued that peer helping programs should not be confused with peer counseling because the term *counseling* suggests the students have more expertise than they actually do. Myrick, Highland, and Sabella (1995) contended that interventions and projects can be organized around four basic peer facilitator or helper roles: (a) teacher or counselor special assistant, (b) tutor, (c) special friend, and/or (d) small group leader. As a special assistant to a counselor or teacher, students typically are trained to work in the counselor's office and are often involved in greeting visitors, answering telephones, helping collect or distribute materials or information, and working on routine office or classroom tasks. This is the oldest type of peer helper role and mostly has involved indirect types of activities and not "active" counseling of peers. Peer tutor is the second type of peer facilitator according to Myrick et al., and in these programs students provide academic assistance to other students. Sometimes the role of these tutors is also to advise or counsel peers on social issues that may be influencing their poor academic performance. The third type of peer helper is a "special friend," in which the peer facilitator is encouraged to develop a close helping relationship with another student who needs support and needs to know that others care about him or her. The fourth type of peer helper is a small group leader, where the student is trained to facilitate various types of group discussions.

In the types of helper roles described by Myrick et al. (1995), the students are not functioning as counselors but more as peer facilitators. Here precisely are the major issues that school counselors need to examine when contemplating instituting a peer counseling program (i.e., what are the roles and responsibilities of the students). Encouraging students to function in roles (e.g., peer counselor) in which they are not adequately trained can result in ethical problems and logistical nightmares.

Research Concerning Peer Counseling

The research regarding peer counseling or facilitation programs varies depending on the role of the peer facilitator and the types of programs implemented. There is very little research related to the role of special assistant to the counselor, but this role typically involves very little counseling of peers. There is considerable empirical support for peer tutoring programs (Myrick et al., 1995). Typically, school counselors do not have the responsibilities for coordinating a peer tutoring program. A school counselor, however, could be involved in training peer tutors on listening skills and methods for referring the students to the school counselor.

Concerning peer counseling programs, Lewis and Lewis (1996) found that many programs attempted to address more serious problems than academic issues. They found peer counseling programs often involved one-on-one counseling and addressed such issues as drug abuse, eating disorders, depression, and suicide. The training and background of the adult supervisor of a peer counseling program also has been found to be critical. Lewis and Lewis found a surprisingly large percentage of programs supervised by noncounselors who had little or no training in counseling. They further found that programs supervised by noncounselors had higher rates of student suicides than those programs supervised by counselors.

Morey, Miller, Fulton, Rosen, and Daly (1989) conducted research concerning levels of high school student satisfaction with the overall peer counseling experience and found that only slightly more than half of the high school students were satisfied with their interaction with their peer counselor. Morey, Miller, Rosen, and Fulton (1993) also found that in general students were only slightly satisfied with peer counseling services. Students who were self-referred to the peer counselor reported greater overall satisfaction with their interaction with the peer counselor than did students who were referred by teachers and school counselors.

On the other hand, Tobias and Myrick (1999) found that sixth-grade students who participated in six group sessions and six individual sessions with an eighth-grade peer facilitator had better grades, attended school more, and had less discipline referrals than students who did not participate in those peer-facilitated sessions. Huey and Rank (1984) found peer facilitators were equally competent as professional counselors in facilitating assertiveness groups.

Practical Applications

A school counselor considering implementing a peer helpers program should, first, clearly define the purpose and scope of the program. It is vitally important that everyone within the school understands the role of the peer facilitators and the program objectives. Some of the concerns voiced about peer counseling programs surround the issues of peer counselors attempting to address issues that are beyond the scope of the program and ones that they are inadequately trained to handle. Students must have a clear idea of what they are trained to address and what should be referred to the school counselor. In addition, school administrators need to have a clear understanding of the program and support it. Carruthers and Sweeney (1996) surveyed coordinators of peer mediation programs and found almost all of them attributed either the success or failure of the program to the support or lack of support from the school administration.

It is also crucial that the peer facilitators receive comprehensive training related to their responsibilities. In terms of peer mediation programs, Humphries (1999) stressed the importance of the peer mediators learning all of the steps in conflict resolution and having experience in "real" playground disputes as a part of the training. Morey et al. (1993) indicated that peer counseling programs have done well in training peer counselors to be empathic listeners; however, being an empathic listener may not be sufficient for many situations. They argued that peer counseling programs should focus on equipping peer counselors with effective problem-solving strategies to be used in the peer counseling process. They suggested that many of the concerns of high school students are related to relationships, and using a problem identification-resolution strategy might be particularly helpful in these types of situations.

Close supervision of any peer-facilitated program is vital to its success. Myrick (1997) suggested starting small and involving a limited number of students in the beginning. Close supervision of a peer counseling program is particularly vital and should be carried out by someone with a sound background in counseling. Lewis and Lewis's (1996) finding that people with little background in counseling are supervising peer counseling is disturbing, and school counselors need to ensure that this type of unethical practice does not occur in their own settings. Supervising a peer counseling program requires extreme dedication and requires that a helping professional always be "on-call" to consult on difficult issues that can easily arise in peer counseling situations.

Peer mediation programs often require a significant time investment. Kaufman (1991) found that many individuals who were coordinating a peer mediation program for the first time had underestimated how much time it would take to implement the program. Kmitta (1995) found that even with experienced coordinators, coordinating a peer mediation program involved around five to ten hours per week.

There are also some significant ethical and legal implications that school counselors should consider before initiating either a peer mediation or a peer counseling program. The American School Counselor Association (ASCA) in the *Ethical Standards for School Counselor* (ASCA, 1998) clearly states that the professional school counselor

> has unique responsibilities when working with peer helper programs. The school counselor is responsible for the welfare of counselees participating in peer programs under her or his direction. School counselors who function in training and supervisory capacities are referred to the preparation and supervision standards of professional counselor associations. (p. 2)

In these peer programs, there are also issues of confidentiality and standards of care. Although the students may be exceptionally mature, they are still children or adolescents who occasionally make poor choices. The school counselor holds the ultimate responsibility for the welfare of all the students and must ensure that students are provided adequate help through these programs. Those school counselors who are considering implementing a peer helpers program should also be aware of the *National Peer Helpers Programmatic Standards* (National Peer Helpers Association [NPHA], 2002), which can be retrieved from this association's web site (www.peerhelping.org). This document also includes a code of ethics for peer helpers:

> Peer Helpers shall be people of personal integrity. NPHA believes peer helpers will:
> 1. Embrace the philosophy that peer helping is an effective way to address the needs and conditions of people.
> 2. Respect the individual's right to dignity, self-development, and self-direction.
> 3. Model positive behaviors and life choices (e.g., no substance use/abuse).
> 4. Embrace the concept of service to others for the good of the community.
> 5. Maintain confidentiality of information imparted during the course of program related activities with the exceptions of child abuse, sexual abuse, family dysfunction, psychotic behavior, harm to self and others, and drug and alcohol abuse.
> 6. Refrain from tackling situations for which they have no training and preparation (e.g., peer mediation, tutoring, etc.).
> 7. Recognize, report, and know techniques to deal with stated or implied threats to their emotional or physical well being. (NPHA, 2002, p. 11)

In conclusion, for both peer mediation and peer counseling programs, the success of the programs rests on the selection of the student mentors or counselors, the quality and thoroughness of the training, and the continued monitoring and supervision of the student mediators or counselors. Quality peer programs are not implemented easily and require excellent organizational skills and perseverance. These programs need solid support from administrators, principals, and parents and must be closely monitored to ensure that situations are handled appropriately.

Family Counseling in the Schools

While the research supporting the effectiveness of peer interventions is somewhat mixed, the research supporting family counseling and intervention with parents is generally very positive (Sexton & Alexander, 2001). Often, the challenging behaviors exhibited by students stem from problematic interactional patterns and situations that exist in their homes. By failing to sufficiently attend to family dynamics, school professionals risk making clinical decisions that are unproductive, or even counterproductive, serving only to magnify an existing concern. According to Johnston and Fields (1981), the key to changing school behavioral disorders is to interrupt the cycle of maladaptive family patterns and to avoid their reenactment at school.

Family dynamics have consistently been identified in the research as important factors in the academic and behavioral adjustment of children and adolescents. As early as fifty years ago, Milner (1951) found that early reading success was correlated with family interaction patterns such as parental discipline style, training in responsibility and cooperation, and direct verbal communication. Subsequent research on the academic success of both elementary- and secondary-level students have supported and elaborated on Milner's findings. For example, Peck (1970, 1971) found that the children with reading difficulties came from families with disturbed communication patterns.

A number of studies have found a relationship among family variables and learning disabilities. Linda Perosa and colleagues (Perosa, Hansen, & Perosa, 1981; Perosa & Perosa, 1982) explored the structural interaction patterns in families with and without a child with a learning disability. Results indicated that learning disabled families tended to avoid conflicts, left conflicts unresolved, and formed two-person alliances (usually mother and child) against a third (usually father) as compared to families who did not have a child with a learning disability. Also, the learning disabled child was more likely to be the "scapegoat" and considered the cause of the family's problems than non–learning disabled children. Amerikaner and Omizo (1984) found that the fathers and mothers of learning disabled and emotionally disturbed families rated their families as significantly more chaotic, confused, and disengaged when compared to the ratings of families with normal children.

There is also evidence that parental styles influence school attendance. Little and Thompson (1983) found that the parents of the truant children were more overindulgent and overprotective, and reported more interest in having their own needs met through their children's behavior. Little and Thompson speculated that such parents become overinvolved in the children's need for immediate gratification and unwittingly participate in actions that encourage their children to avoid school.

Schools and families have many similarities; they share responsibilities for the care and education of youth (Fisher, 1986). For some students, the two most influential systems, the family and the school, are disconnected from each other and not working conjointly to facilitate the students' academic, career, and personal/social development. Given that the child is a member of both of these separate systems, it is essential that the student not be affected when there is conflict or lack of communication between the educational and home environments (Weiss, Edwards, Zelen, & Schwartz, 1991). Taylor (1982) suggested that students' academic and behavioral problems are often a result of a student's inability to successfully negotiate the friction and difficulties between home and school. Furthermore, for many students with severe academic and behavioral problems, effective treatment must involve a comprehensive approach that includes the family and the school working jointly together (Edwards & Foster, 1995). Hence, it may be with these more complicated cases that a school counselor should consider intervening in ways that involves both the family and appropriate school personnel.

We believe school counselors are in a strategic position to support and counsel families because they have an understanding of the school system, a background in child and adolescent development, and knowledge of family dynamics and counseling interventions. Because all children ages 7 to 16 are required to attend school, school counselors are one of the few mental health professionals with the potential for early recognition, treatment, and resolution of the psychological difficulties facing many youth in our society. Schools can easily connect with families with school-age children and are increasingly considered to be the primary organization for providing therapeutic information and services. Although many school counselors do not consider family counseling and interventions to be a part of their responsibilities, other professionals are arguing that school counselors are the best bridge between a student's two primary environments (i.e., home and school) (Amatea & Fabrick, 1981; Cowie & Quinn, 1997; Edwards & Foster; 1995; King, Randolph, McKay, & Bartell, 1995; Rotheram, 1989; Stone & Peeks, 1986; Wilcoxon & Comas, 1987).

In this chapter, we argue that school counselors should be providing family counseling and that functioning of the family directly impacts student learning.

Good and Brophy (1986) found that family factors accounted for more of the variance in academic achievement than curriculum or instructional variables. Thus, by improving family relations, a school counselor is indirectly influencing a child's performance in school. Nicoll (1992) contended that "school counselors are ideally situated to provide this service [family therapy] because their job description involves working as a liaison between students, families and classroom teachers" (p. 353). It should be noted, however, that school counselors have many responsibilities and most counselors are hard-pressed to find time to counsel families. Hence, what we are proposing would require a change in how the role of the counselor is viewed and a change in how counselors are trained.

Chief Theoretical Orientation: Family Systems Theories

In the last fifty years, family counseling and therapy has been influenced by a systemic view and theoretical orientation. From a systemic view, an individual's behavior cannot be understood in isolation, but must be considered within the social context and systems of the individual. Furthermore, social organizations, such as families, are more than a collection of individuals sharing a physical space; rather, they are a "system" that has properties and rules that need to be understood (Goldenberg & Goldenberg, 2000). This paradigm has been influenced by changes in the field of biology, where often the focus is on understanding how the "whole" organism functions rather than on simply trying to understand each part of the organism. Applying general systems theory, the family operates as a whole and in order to understand one part of the system (e.g., a child), a counselor would need to understand the whole system. With a systems orientation, a child's behavior in school is influenced by the family and interrelationships of the family. From this perspective, attempting to change a student's behavior without understanding the family system will probably have little effect. Unlike individual psychotherapy, clinicians with a family systems orientation focus on the family members' interdependence and the ways in which the family functions.

From a systemic approach, the school counselor recognizes that students are a part of many different systems. Family systems theories often focus on the family, but they provide an interactive perspective that considers other subsystems (school, peer, family, and community influences) and methods for bringing about positive change (Johnston & Zemitzsch, 1988). Many family members appreciate a systemic approach and feel that it reflects their problems more realistically and within a larger social context. Family systems theory can be applied not only to family-focused counseling interventions but also to other types of collaborative efforts among family members and school personnel.

Adopting a family systems perspective and learning to apply this paradigm may also address some of the criticisms of school counseling programs. School counseling programs have sometimes been criticized for not having a theoretical foundation, and systems theory can provide a sound theoretical base for school counseling interventions. In addition, counselors in schools have also been criticized for having a narrow view of student issues and ignoring subsystems that may affect students (Green & Keys, 2001). As we shall see, different family systems theories all acknowledge that individuals are members of various systems that affect their lives.

There are many family systems theories that can serve as a foundation for counseling families; however, Amatea (1989) argued that brief, problem-solving formats probably best fit in a school environment. It is important for school counselors to have some knowledge of these theories as a basis for understanding family-oriented counseling. Having an understanding of family system theories not only can assist school counselors in intervening with families but also can help a school counselor in terms of referring individuals to family therapists, who predominantly use a systemic approach in their counseling. Following is a brief introduction to three models (structural-communications, strategic, and solution-focused) that have proven to be particularly useful in school settings.

Structural-Communications Model.   Minuchin (1981) asserted that the art of family counseling is joining the family, experiencing reality as the family members do, and becoming involved in the repeated interactions that form that family's structure. It means creating a more positive way for the family to function by the counselor becoming a change agent within the structure of the family system.

According to Minuchin (1981), the four main components of the structural model are family structure, subsystems within the family structure, subsystem boundaries, and family adaptations to stress. The structure of the family is reflected in the aggregate of the operational rules the family uses to function. In a few words, the counselor's task is to enter the family's system by earning the trust of the family members. The counselor can then begin to evaluate the structure of that system by looking at the power and hierarchies, coalitions, and communication processes that have developed. Ultimately, the counselor should then be able to create situations that lead to changes in the structure that permit the family to function in a healthier manner.

Structural theorists emphasize the influence of the operation rules and hierarchical organization of the family. Minuchin (1974) argued that well-functioning families should be hierarchically organized, with the parents having more authority than the children and older children having more responsibilities and privileges than younger children. There may also be coalitions among family members that are having a negative influence. Minuchin defined coalitions as alliances between specific family members against a third member. For example, a father and son may align against the mother and disregard her wishes. In the structural-communications model, emphasis is placed on giving clear, direct, and specific communications to the child. When carried out, these assertive demands imply (a) a strong parent subsystem with correct hierarchy and (b) appropriate boundaries between the parent and child subsystem (Morrison, Olivos, Dominguez, Gomez, & Lena, 1993).

Strategic Model.   The strategic approach to family therapy assumes that when children or adolescents present problems, it is a consequence of parental disagreement on some issue. As parents disagree, the child or adolescent develops a problem in order to deflect the parents' attention away from their own crisis and onto the child or adolescent's difficulty. Madanes (1981) contended that, in this manner, the child is, in essence, helping the parents. Essentially, this approach sees the child upsetting the system by being in control of the parents with regard to the presenting concern.

A strategic model focuses on communication patterns, with the interest being in the *process* as compared to the content of the interactions. Therefore, if a female student were describing the angry fight with her mother that morning, the counselor would focus on the relationship between the mother and daughter rather than the content of the angry interchange. Watzlawick, Weakland, and Fisch (1974) suggested that the counselor's responsibilities are to break into the family's repetitive and negative cycles and understand what makes the problematic behavior persist. The counselor first carefully delineates the problem and clearly scrutinizes with the family previous attempts to change. The counselor then has an understanding of what changes are being sought and can develop a *strategy* or therapeutic plan for achieving the desired change

Another set of concepts from Watzlawick et al. (1974) that school counselors might consider is the level of change sought. *First-order changes* are the more superficial behavioral changes within the system, such as family members not "raising their voices" during family arguments. These types of changes are typically short-lived and do not influence the general functioning of the family. *Second-order changes* are more fundamental and alter the systemic interaction pattern of the family. Second-order change involves an alteration in viewpoint that would be facilitated by the counselor's use of techniques such as reframing. Strategic models encourage a focus on specific presenting problems, but the goal is on second-order change. The goal of second-order change, however, does not imply exploring the roots of a problem, but rather focuses on strategies tailored to the specific situation that will result in fundamental change within the family.

Solution-Focused Model.   The solution-focused model evolved out of strategic counseling and has been influenced by social constructionist philosophy. Similar to a strategic approach, this model downplays the clients' past history and possible underlying pathology. The focus is on identifying solutions and strategies that "work." From the beginning, the counselor joins the family in a *therapeutic conversation* related to their situation and the conflicts they hope to resolve (Goldenberg & Goldenberg, 2000). The solution-focused counselor will search with the family for what has worked thus far in the problem-solving process and attempt to discern what might work in the future (Nichols & Schwartz, 1995). A leading proponent of this approach, deShazer (1988), instructed counselors to highlight the solutions that appear to be working and then recommend those or similar solutions to the parents. deShazer described the counselor's role as providing "skeleton keys" to the family, which are interventions that work for a variety of locks. These skeleton keys do not need to fit perfectly, but they need to facilitate the evolution of solutions.

In using a solution-focused approach, a school counselor might use three kinds of questions: (a) "miracle questions," (b) exception-finding questions, and (c) scaling questions (Goldenberg & Goldenberg, 2000). A miracle question examines what the family's life would be like if by some "miracle" the problem was solved. The miracle question provides each member of the family the opportunity to speculate on the future and will often illuminate important aspects and solidify the goals of the counseling. Exception-finding questions are begun early in the process and focus on exceptions to the problem-maintaining patterns. By highlighting exceptions to the behavior, the counselor demonstrates that the problems are not pervasive and that realistic solutions are achievable. The third type of question, scaling questions, involves asking clients to quantify aspects of the situation. For example, a counselor might ask a mother to rate her frustration with her son's "talking back" and then use this scale in various counseling situations, such as gauging whether proposed solutions are having the desired effect. These three types of questions and solution-focused approaches in general are geared toward the clients' identifying possible solutions and implementing new behavior patterns. This approach is brief, and the counselor and family work actively together to jointly construct resolutions to the identified issues.

There are several other theoretical approaches to family therapy (e.g., multigenerational, humanistic, social constructionism) other than the three models briefly discussed here. These theoretical orientations were selected because of their prominence in the field of family counseling and their suitability in a school environment. School counselors interested in providing family therapy, however, need a more comprehensive understanding of family theories, which is beyond the scope of this chapter. Our intent is to increase school counselors' awareness of family therapy models so that they may seek out further information and training on their own.

Research Support for Family Therapy in the Schools

Often, school administrators and school boards are interested in the empirical support for school counseling activities, and school counselors can provide compelling evidence supporting the efficacy of family therapy. In a comprehensive review of relevant research studies, Gurman and Kniskern (1981) found that family therapy was as effective, if not more effective, as many individual treatments for problems related to family conflict. The support for the effectiveness of family therapy has continued, and numerous reviewers of research have concluded that family therapy can produce positive outcomes for clients (Alexander, Holzworth-Munroe, & Jameson, 1994; Gurman, Kniskern, & Pinsof, 1986). Meta-analytic reviews of the research have also supported the effectiveness of family therapy (Hazelrigg, Cooper, & Borduin, 1987; Shadish et al., 1993). It is somewhat surprising that school counselors do not devote more time to family-based treatments given the significant empirical support for the effectiveness of such interventions and the relative lack of empirical support for many of the activities to which school counselors dedicate much of their time (Whiston & Sexton, 1998).

Not only is family counseling generally effective, but counseling interventions with a family systems approach have also been shown to be effective in bringing about improved academic and behavioral performance. Parent counseling and consultation, for example, has been shown to positively affect student motivation, academic achievement, self-esteem, and classroom behavior (Esters & Levant, 1983; Hudgins & Stoudt, 1977; James & Etheridge, 1983). In a review of family-school effects research, Henderson and Berla (1995) concluded that there is strong evidence documenting that higher grades and test scores, better school attendance, fewer special education placements, more positive attitudes and behavior, higher graduation rates, and increased enrollment in postsecondary education are the results of schools providing support to families. In addition, Henderson and Berla concluded that family-focused school programs consistently have a positive effect beyond the immediate results with the family, also positively affecting the school and community. These benefits include improved teacher morale, higher ratings of teachers by parents, more support from families, higher student achievement, and a better reputation for the school within the community. Consequently, family counseling and therapy has been shown to have a positive affect on many school-related problems of children and adolescents.

There is also some particularly persuasive evidence that specific approaches to family therapy can be extremely effective with some of the more difficult types of behavioral problems of children and adolescents. In terms of adolescent behavior disorders, particularly students with conduct disorders, there is compelling research supporting the effectiveness of four clinical interventions programs: functional family therapy (FFT; Alexander & Parson, 1973), multidimensional family therapy (MDFT; Liddle, 1995), multisystemic therapy (MST; Henggeler, 1999), and structural family therapy (as developed by Szapocznik & Kurtines, 1989). A common thread through all of these approaches is that the counselor is active and directive as compared to more nondirective approaches to family therapy. Furthermore, there is evidence that these programs are more effective than typical forms of treatment such as individual counseling (Sexton & Alexander, 2001). As indicated earlier in this chapter, two of these programs (i.e., functional family therapy and multisystemic therapy) were deemed effective programs in preventing youth violence by the U.S. Surgeon General and the Centers for Disease Control. There is also evidence that these two approaches to family therapy are effective with clients from various socioeconomic and ethnic groups. A school counselor, however, cannot just read a little about these approaches and start using them with families. With both of these programs, a counselor needs specific training and must follow a protocol or treatment manual that specifies the "steps" to be taken in counseling the family.

Practical Applications

Although there is substantial evidence supporting the efficacy of family therapy, we are not able to thoroughly discuss all of the information necessary for providing counseling to families in schools. It should be noted that being competent in family therapy can only occur with substantial training, supervision, and continuing education. Although school counselors may have a course or two in family dynamics or family counseling, this will not provide sufficient training to initiate family therapy. It is imperative to remember that school counselors without sufficient training should refrain from providing family therapy because it is unethical to practice outside one's areas of competence. Therefore, we would like to encourage school counselors to pursue additional training in family therapy and counseling.

Family therapy, however, is not the only method for school counselors to intervene with students and their families. Approaches that center on family and school collaboration are becoming a popular way to bridge the gap between these two systems. Parent education programs and parent-teacher resource centers are just two avenues by which school counselors can engage families in educational activities that will benefit students (see Hawes, 2002).

Parent Education Programs.   Educating and consulting with parents are often considered fundamental responsibilities of a school counselor. Crase, Carlson, and Kontos (1981) found that when parents experience child-rearing problems, they often turn to school counselors for assistance. It is important to help parents develop skills that will support their children's success and achievements throughout their development. The general aim of parent education is to provide knowledge about child development, communication skills, and techniques for managing childhood behavior problems.

There are a number of commercial programs that counselors can purchase, such as *Active Parenting, Parents Effectiveness Training* (PET), and *Systematic Training for Effective Parenting* (STEP). Ritchie and Partin (1994) found that the STEP program had the most widespread use among school counselors. The STEP program is mainly based on a theory by Alfred Adler called individual psychology (Manaster & Corsini, 1982). It stresses the importance of parents using natural and logical consequences. The majority of parent education programs involve both didactic instruction of parenting practices and time for discussion. Many parents feel encouraged by sharing experiences and receiving support from other parents in similar situations. School counselors have indicated that any parent education program should include content related to self-concept enhancement, helping children succeed in school, behavioral management and discipline, decision making, substance abuse, and stepfamily issues (Ritchie & Partin, 1994).

Sometimes parent education programs are offered in schools, yet very few parents participate. School counselors need to consider ways of providing these programs that will motivate parents to attend, such as starting the program the week after parent-teacher conferences. Additional strategies for engaging family members in parenting education and other types of school programs will be discussed later in this chapter.

Parent-Teacher Resource Centers.   Parent-teacher resource centers have been launched in many schools to provide both information and training on raising and educating children and adolescents. These centers are designed so that both parents and teachers can find information regarding the influences of family dynamics on achievement and methods for facilitating child development that involve both the home and school. The intent is for parenting and teaching styles to become more congruent, which will lead to improvements in the student's social and academic adjustment. By training both parents and teachers to work with an authoritative approach to interacting with children and adolescents at home and school, better environments for child rearing can be created, leading to increased academic achievement, fewer special education placements, and improved social and emotional adjustment. A parent-teacher resource center can implement programs that facilitate home-school collaboration and parental involvement, both of which are associated with improved academic success and social adjustment. Parents may also use such centers as places where they may obtain information on available community resources and effective strategies for parental involvement in education at home.

Other Considerations in Engaging Families.   Thus far, much of the focus of this portion of the chapter has been on the effectiveness of family counseling and the importance of family and school collaboration in facilitating academic development. Nonetheless, transferring these ideas from theory to reality can pose problems, particularly when it comes to engaging family members and gaining support for family interventions in a school environment.

Engaging parents and other relevant family members in the therapeutic process can be difficult at times. Differences in perceptions regarding the cause of the child's problem and fear of criticism or blame may contribute to family resistance (McGuire & Lyons, 1985). Some parents may feel pessimistic, helpless, and angry about working with a school system because of a history of negative encounters and unsuccessful attempts to address their children's problems. Edwards and Foster (1995) suggested that parent resistance will decrease if parents are treated as experts on their children's behavior and as a critical resource in the process. Furthermore, for some families, there may be a stigma attached to family counseling that may deter parents from becoming involved in school-based family counseling. Continued and ongoing communication with the entire community about the benefits of counseling may filter down to the families and possibly increase their participation in counseling activities. In addition, Miller (2002b) contended that school counselors need to make schools more inviting to family members and offered the following suggestions:

- partner families with other families in the school community. Similar to pairing children with adult mentors, families can benefit from being paired with other veteran families;
- be flexible in school meeting hours (e.g., early morning, late evening, weekend conferencing);

- consider home visits at the convenience of families;
- access someone powerful in the hard-to-reach family's circle (e.g., employer, neighbor, religious community) to collaborate with the school;
- be vigilant that school-to-home communications use appropriate language (translation included) and appropriate reading levels, provide jargon-free information, encourage reciprocal communication instead of one-way communication, and include practical quick tips for parents to use in homework help, hygiene, development, friendship, communication skills, and family rituals;
- recognize that parents have important different, expert perspectives of their children;
- be proactive, rather than reactive. Telephone home to all children's families, emphasizing strengths;
- approach families individually, persuasively, and unconditionally; and
- focus on what works, rather than what doesn't, which sets a tone of solution building rather than pathology hunting. (p. 122)

Often, school counselors not only need to persuade family members to engage in family counseling services at their school, but they must also convince teachers and other educational personnel that schools should provide family counseling (Dicocco, Chalfin, & Olson, 1987; Goodman & Kjonaas, 1984). During an in-service meeting for teachers, the school counselor may need to explain the role of family therapy in the school and clarify the role of the school counselor as compared to others in the school. It may also be necessary to promote a paradigm shift in the school personnel to assist them in conceptualizing the child's problems contextually rather than intrapsychically (O'Callaghan, 1993). Furthermore, the school counselor may need to occasionally enlist teachers' participation in working with the family in order to assist the student in changing behaviors and achieving therapeutic goals. Teachers are more likely to become involved in family counseling activities if they feel their instructional methods are not being criticized by the counselor and the family. Hence, the school counselor must often be very diplomatic in suggesting how a teacher may interact differently with a student and his or her family.

A school counselor needs to consider the ethical and legal implications of working therapeutically with families. Of primary importance, school counselors can only provide services for which they are qualified and trained (Linde, 2003). Hence, school counselors without formal training in family therapy should not be attempting to conduct family therapy. In terms of working with parents, the Ethical Standards for School Counselors (ASCA, 1998) state that a professional school counselor should "respect the rights and responsibilities of parents for their children and endeavor to establish, as appropriate, a collaborative relationship with parents to facilitate the counselee's maximum development" (p. 2). Furthermore, these standards indicate that school counselors should adhere to laws and local guidelines when assisting families experiencing difficulties. Miller (2002a) states that in order to stay within one's area of competence, family counseling in a school should be focused on how the school and family can work together to support the student's academic success. School counselors should also adhere to the American Counseling Association's Code of Ethic and Standards of Practice (ACA, 1997), which stresses the importance of confidentiality and avoiding unwarranted disclosures of confidential information. Working with both parents and students increases the complexities associated with confidentiality, particularly when counselors may be having separate conversations with different family members. Counselors, however, must attend to issues of confidentiality, which is reflected in the ACA standards that indicate, "in family counseling, information about one family member cannot be disclosed to another member without permission. Counselors protect the privacy rights of each family member" (ACA, 1997, p. 7).

In concluding this discussion of family counseling in the schools, we want to emphasize the importance of family support in education. School counselors who are able to actively engage families in "therapeutic" or intervention activities are likely to assist the students' families in multiple ways. Even if school counselors are not providing the family therapy, they can facilitate the transition to nonschool clinicians. As Hinkle (1993) indicated, family members will be more likely to cooperate with the referral if they have developed trust in the school counselor through the initial interviews. Moreover, the validity of the initial family interviews and assessment of the problem by the school counselor is critical in making appropriate referrals to other providers. Also, when handled ethically, the school counselor may be able to provide critical information and important insights to the new therapist. Oftentimes, the outside professional will then include the school counselor as part of the problem-solving team (Whiteside, 1993).

⬛ Conclusions

In this chapter, we have discussed the role of peer and family counseling in contemporary school counseling programs. Peer programs can have some positive effects in a school, but these programs must include quality training and close monitoring. Furthermore, the school counselors must be vigilant in choosing students with appropriate attributes and ones who will understand the limits of their roles. Sometimes, peer programs are implemented in an attempt to save counselors time when, in fact, quality programs require considerable commitment of both time and resources. Although there is some research supporting the effectiveness of peer mediation and counseling programs, the state of the research in these areas is weak. Additional research is needed before one can conclude that these programs have a positive impact on students.

The second portion of this chapter addressed family counseling in schools. Kraus (1998) contended that school counselors should provide services to troubled children and their families that can alleviate the stress that may affect the students' performance in the classroom. Although there are some challenges to engaging families in counseling, school counselors should also note that there are some advantages in providing these types of services in a school environment. One of the chief advantages of school counselors' providing family counseling is that families are familiar with the school environment and may tend to feel more comfortable participating in counseling in this more familiar setting. In addition, the counseling sessions may be seen more as "conferences" than as therapy sessions, which may have less of a negative connotation. Furthermore, school personnel who have contact with young children and provide therapeutic intervention early may alleviate the need for more long-term and costly intervention later.

Although there is considerable support for the efficacy of family therapy, Shadish et al. (1993) clearly demonstrated that not all approaches to family therapy are equally effective. Therefore, school counselors cannot attempt family counseling with a generic approach but need detailed information about which models work best for which types of families and problems. Another obstacle in providing appropriate family counseling is that school counseling preparation programs often include little exposure to family therapy theoretical models, offer limited graduate coursework related to family dynamics, and typically do not provide supervised experiences in conducting family counseling. Hence, although there are many reasons for intervening with families, school counselors are often not adequately prepared to provide these services. The school counseling field needs to consider its role in providing family therapy in schools and determine whether family counseling is a part of a school counselor's responsibilities. Nicholl (2002) argued that schools may be the best place for providing family counseling; yet, most models for a comprehensive school counseling program either ignore or minimize the counselor's role in working with parents or families. As this book is designed to transform school counseling, we suggest that a primary transformation should include school counselors providing more counseling services to students' families.

Peer Programs and Family Counseling– From Knowledge to School-Based Actions

This chapter is full of great ideas; some you can explore here. First, read over Vignette 1. Second, revisit the chapter, especially those sections relating to peer interventions, and third, note your reactions to the "logistical" questions posed below.

VIGNETTE 1

Rockwell Elementary Needs a Peer Mediation Program

Rockwell is struggling with a bad case of bullying. A certain group of fifth and sixth graders on the playground and during lunchtime find it hilarious to intimidate the younger, more timid children. Mostly the bullying is verbal threats and personal teasing, but more recently, the students have been shoving their victims and asking for money. The bullies have been warned and disciplined several times by their teachers and the principal, but these interventions don't seem to have a lasting impact on behavior. You, the school counselor, just returned from a state school counselor convention and have learned how to set up and implement a peer mediation program.

The Basic Steps

1. Getting the "go ahead"
   - Besides the principal, who else should provide their input and approval?

   _____

   _____

2. Selecting the peer mediators
   - What criteria might you use? _____

   _____

- Who will suggest the possible mediators? _____

    _____

3. Training the mediators
    - How might you train the volunteers? _____

    _____

4. Carrying out the program
    - School counselors should also consider these issues:

    What kinds of conflicts are appropriate for the peer mediators?

    _____

    _____

    How should the mediation process work?

    _____

    _____

    Where in the school should the mediation take place?

    _____

    _____

    How are mediators made available? _____

    _____

    How often can mediators miss class? _____

    _____

    When do the peer mediators seek out additional help?

    _____

    _____

    Now, let's turn our attention to providing some family counseling to the school.

VIGNETTE 2

Intervention with Curtis's Family

Two months after the establishment of a peer mediation program at Rockwell Elementary, fewer bullying incidents were reported; however, one particularly aggressive boy continued to bully on the playground. After meeting individually with Curtis for several sessions, the school counselor decided to try a *solution-focused* approach with Curtis and his biological mother and stepdad.

Using a solution-focused orientation, jot down two sample questions in each category that the counselor might ask the family:

(a) Miracle questions _____

_____

(b) Exception-finding questions _____

_____

(c) Scaling questions _____

_____

What other "systems" interventions might you use with the family?

_____

_____

_____

Note: This appendix was written by Christopher Sink.

REFERENCES

Alexander, J. F., Holzworth-Munroe, A., & Jameson, P. B. (1994). The process and outcome of marital and family therapy: Research review and evaluation. In A. E. Bergin & S. L. Garfield (Eds.), *Handbook of psychotherapy and behavior change* (4th ed., pp. 595–630). New York: Wiley.

Alexander, J. F., & Parson, B. V. (1973). Short-term behavior interventions with delinquent families: Impact on family process and recidivism. *Journal of Abnormal Psychology, 81,* 219–225.

Amatea, E. S. (1989). *Brief strategic interventions for school behavior problems.* San Francisco: Jossey-Bass.

Amatea, E. S., & Fabrick, F. (1981). Family systems counseling: A positive alternative to traditional counseling. *Elementary School Guidance and Counseling, 15,* 223–236.

American Counseling Association (1997). *Code of ethics and standards of practice.* Retrieved November 20, 2002, from http://www.counseling.org/resources/ethics. htm#sp

American School Counselor Association (1998). *Ethical Standards for School Counselors.* Alexandria, VA: Author.

Amerikaner, M. J., & Omizo, M. M. (1984). Family interaction and learning disabilities. *Journal of Learning Disabilities, 17,* 540–543.

Bickmore, K. (2002). Good training is not enough: Research on peer mediation program implementation. *Social Alternatives, 21,* 33–38.

Campbell, C. A., & Dahir, C. A. (1997). *Sharing the Vision: The national standards for school counseling programs.* Alexandria, VA: American School Counselor Association.

Carruthers, W. L., & Sweeney, B. (1996). Conflict resolution: An examination of the research literature and a model for program evaluation. *The School Counselor, 44,* 5–18.

Casella, R. (2000). The benefits of peer mediation in the context of urban conflict and program status. *Urban Education, 35,* 324–355.

Cowie, K., & Quinn, K. (1997). Brief family therapy in the schools: A new perspective on the role of the rural school counseling professional. *The Family Journal, 5,* 57–69.

Crase, S. J., Carlson, C., & Kontos, S. (1981). Parent education needs and sources as perceived by parents. *Home Economics Research, 9,* 221–231.

Day-Vines, N., Day-Hairston, B., Carruthers, W., Wall, J., & Lupton-Smith, H. (1996). Conflict resolution: The value of diversity in the recruitment, selection, and training of peer mediators. *The School Counselor, 43,* 392–410.

deShazer, S. (1988). *Clues: Investigating solutions in brief therapy.* New York: Norton.

Dicocco, B. E., Chalfin, S. R., & Olson, J. M. (1987). Systemic family therapy goes to school. *Social Work in Education, 9,* 209–221.

Edwards, D. L., & Foster, M. A. (1995). Uniting the family and school systems: A process of empowering the school counselor. *The School Counselor, 42,* 277–282.

Elliott, D. S. (1998). Editor's introduction. In D. S. Elliott (Ed.), *Blueprints for violence prevention* (pp. i–xi). Boulder, CO: Center for the Study and Prevention of Violence.

Emerson, J. (1990). *Conflict resolution for students: A study of problem solving and peer conflict management.* Unpublished doctoral dissertation, University of Oregon, Eugene.

Esters, P., & Levant, R. F. (1983). The effects of two-parent counseling programs on rural low-achieving students. *The School Counselor, 31,* 159–166.

Fisher, L. (1986). Systems-based consultation with the schools. In L. C. Wynne, S. H. McDaniel, & T. T. Weber (Eds.), *System consultation: A new perspective for family therapy* (pp. 79–93). New York: Guilford.

Gerber, S., & Terry-Day, B. (1999). Does peer mediation really work? *Professional School Counseling, 2,* 169–171.

Goldenberg, I., & Goldenberg, H. (2000). *Family therapy: An overview* (5th ed.). Belmont, CA: Wadsworth.

Good, T. L., & Brophy, J. E. (1986). School effects. In M. C. Wittrock (Ed.), *The handbook of research on teaching* (3rd ed., pp. 570–604). New York: Macmillan.

Goodman, R. W., & Kjonaas, D. (1984). Elementary school family counseling: A pilot project. *Journal of Counseling & Development, 63,* 255–257.

Green, A., & Keys, S. G. (2001). Expanding the developmental school counseling paradigm: Meeting the needs of the 21st century students. *Professional School Counseling, 5,* 84–95.

Gurman, A. S., & Kniskern, P. D. (1981). Family therapy outcome research: Knowns and unknowns. A. S. Gurman & P. D. Kniskern (Eds.), *Handbook of family therapy* (pp. 750–799). New York: Bruner-Mazel.

Gurman, A. S., Kniskern, P. D, & Pinsof, W. M. (1986). Research on marital and family therapies. In S. L. Garfield & A. E. Bergin (Eds.), *Handbook of psychotherapy and behavior change* (3rd ed., pp. 565–624). New York: Wiley.

Hart, J., & Gunty, M. (1997). The impact of a peer mediation program on an elementary school environment. *Peace & Change, 22,* 76–92.

Hawes, D. (2002). Including parents and teachers. In L. D. Miller (Ed.), *Integrating school and family counseling: Practical solutions* (pp. 89–108). Alexandria, VA: American Counseling Association.

Hazelrigg, M., Cooper, H., & Borduin, C. (1987). Evaluating the effectiveness of family therapies: An integrative review and analysis. *Psychological Bulletin, 101,* 428–442.

Henderson, A. T., & Berla, N. (1995). *A new generation of evidence: The family is critical to student achievement.* Washington, DC: Center for Law and Education.

Henggeler, S. W. (1999). Multisystemic therapy: An overview of clinical procedures, outcomes, and policy implications. *Child Psychology & Psychiatric Review, 4,* 2–10.

Hinkle, J. S. (1993). Training school counselors to do family counseling. *Elementary School Guidance and Counseling, 27,* 252–271.

Hudgins, A. L., & Stoudt, J. T. (1977). HRD technology and parent training groups. *Elementary School Guidance and Counseling, 12,* 59–61.

Huey, W. C., & Rank, R. C. (1984). Effects of counselor and peer-led group assertive training on black adolescent aggression. *Journal of Counseling Psychology, 31,* 95–98.

Humphries, T. L. (1999). Improving peer mediation programs: Students' experiences and suggestions. *Professional School Counseling, 3,* 13–21.

James, R., & Etheridge, G. (1983). Does parent training change behavior of inner-city children? *Elementary School Guidance and Counseling, 18,* 75–78.

Johnson, D. W., & Johnson, R. T. (1996). Conflict resolution and peer mediation programs in elementary and secondary schools: A review of the research. *Review of Educational Research, 66,* 459–506.

Johnston, J. C., & Fields, P. A. (1981). School consultation with the "classroom family." *The School Counselor, 29,* 350–357.

Johnston, J. C., & Zemitzsch, A. (1988). Family power: An intervention beyond the classroom. *Behavioral Disorder, 14,* 69–79.

Kaufman, S. (1991). *Assessment of the implementation of conflict management programs in 17 Ohio schools: First year report school demonstration project 1990–93.* Columbus, OH: Ohio Commission on Dispute Resolution and Conflict Management.

King, B., Randolph, L., McKay, W. A., & Bartell, M. (1995). Working with families in the schools. In L. Combrinck-Graham (Ed.), *Children in families at risk* (pp. 393–413). New York: Guilford.

Kmitta, D. (1995, August/September). Struggling to survive. *The Fourth R, 26.*

Kohlberg, L. (1984). *The psychology of moral development: The nature and validity of moral stages.* San Francisco: Harper & Row.

Kraus, I. (1998). A fresh look at school counseling: A family-systems approach. *Professional School Counseling, 1,* 12–17.

Lewis, M. W., & Lewis, A. L. (1996). Peer helping programs: Helper role, supervisor training, and suicidal behavior. *Journal of Counseling & Development, 74,* 307–313.

Liddle, H. A. (1995). Conceptual and clinical dimensions of a multidimensional, multisystems engagement strategy in family-based adolescent treatment [Special issue: Adolescent psychotherapy]. *Psychotherapy: Theory, Research and Practice, 32,* 39–58.

Linde, L. (2003). Ethical, legal, and professional issues in school counseling. In B. T. Erford (Ed.), *Transforming the school counseling profession* (pp. 39–62). Upper Saddle River, NJ: Merrill/Prentice Hall.

Little, L. F., & Thompson, R. (1983). Truancy: How parents and teachers contribute. *The School Counselor, 30,* 285–291.

Madanes, C. (1981). *Strategic family therapy.* San Francisco: Jossey-Bass.

Manaster G. J., & Corsini, R. J. (1982). *Individual psychology: Theory and practice*. Itasca, IL: Peacock.

McGuire, D. E., & Lyons, J. S. (1985). A transcontextual model for intervention with problems of school underachievement. *American Journal of Family Therapy, 13*, 37–45.

Milner, E. (1951). A study of the relationship between reading readiness in grade one school children and patterns of parent-child interactions. *Child Development, 22*, 95–112.

Miller, L. D. (2002a). Overview of family systems counseling in a school setting. In L. D. Miller (Ed.), *Integrating school and family counseling: Practical solutions* (pp. 3–30). Alexandria, VA: American Counseling Association.

Miller, L. D. (2002b). Working with individual children from a family systems perspective. In L. D. Miller (Ed.), *Integrating school and family counseling: Practical solutions* (pp. 109–125). Alexandria, VA: American Counseling Association.

Minuchin, S. (1974). *Families and family therapy*. Cambridge, MA: Harvard University Press.

Minuchin, S. (1981). *Family therapy techniques*. Cambridge, MA: Harvard University Press.

Morey, R. E., Miller, C. D., Fulton, R., Rosen, L. A., & Daly, J. L. (1989). Peer counseling: Students served, problems discussed, overall satisfaction, and perceived helpfulness. *The School Counselor, 37*, 137–143.

Morey, R. E., Miller, C. D., Rosen, L. A., & Fulton, R. (1993). High school peer counseling: The relationship between student satisfaction and peer counselors' style of helping. *The School Counselor, 40*, 293–301.

Morrison, J., Olivos, K., Dominguez, G., Gomez, D., & Lena, D. (1993). The application of family systems approaches to school behavior problems on a school-level discipline board: An outcome study. *Elementary School Guidance and Counseling, 27*, 258–271.

Myrick, R. D. (1997). *Developmental guidance and counseling: A practical approach* (3rd ed.). Minneapolis, MN: Educational Media.

Myrick, R. D., Highland, W. H., & Sabella, R. A. (1995). Peer helpers and perceived effectiveness. *Elementary School Guidance and Counseling, 29*, 278–290.

National Peer Helpers Association. (2002). *Programmatic standards: National Peer Helpers Association*. Kansas City, MO: Author.

Nichols, M., & Schwartz, R. (1995). *Family therapy*. Boston: Allyn & Bacon.

Nicoll, W. G. (1992). A family counseling and consultation model for school counselors. *The School Counselor, 39*, 351–361.

Nicholl, W. G. (2002). Working with families: A rationale for school counseling programs. In L. D. Miller (Ed.), *Integrating school and family counseling: Practical solutions* (pp. 31–49). Alexandria, VA: American Counseling Association.

O'Callaghan, J. B. (1993). *School-based collaboration with families*. San Francisco: Jossey-Bass.

Peck, B. (1970). *A communication analysis of family decision making in normal and reading-problem families.* Unpublished doctoral dissertation, Bowling Green State University, Bowling Green, Ohio.

Peck, B. (1971). Reading disorders: Have we overlooked something? *Journal of School Psychology, 9,* 182–190.

Perosa, L. M., Hansen, J., & Perosa, S. L. (1981). Development of the structural family interaction scale. *Family Therapy, 8,* 77–90.

Perosa, L. M., & Perosa, S. L. (1982). Structural interaction patterns in families with a learning disabled child. *Family Therapy, 9,* 175–187.

Ritchie, M. A., & Partin, R. L. (1994). Parent education and consultation activities of school counselors. *The School Counselor, 41,* 165–170.

Rotheram, M. J. (1989). The family and the school. In L. Combrinck-Graham (Ed.), *Children in family contexts* (pp. 347–368). New York: Guilford.

Sexton, T. L., & Alexander, J. (2001). Family-based empirically supported interventions. *The Counseling Psychologist, 30,* 238–261.

Shadish, W., Montgomery, L., Wilson, P., Wilson, M., Bright, I., & Okwumabua, T. (1993). Effects of family and marital psychotherapies: A meta-analysis. *Journal of Consulting and Clinical Psychology, 61,* 992–1002.

Shepard, K. K. (1994). Stemming conflict through peer mediation. *School Administrator, 51,* 14–17.

Smith, S. W., & Daunic, A. P. (2002). Using conflict resolution and peer mediation to support positive behavior. In B. Algozzine & P. Kay (Eds.), *Preventing problem behaviors: A handbook of successful prevention strategies* (pp. 142–161). Thousand Oaks, CA: Corwin Press.

Smith, S. W., Daunic, A. P., Miller, M. D., & Robinson, T. R. (2002). Conflict resolution and peer mediation in middle schools: Extending the process and outcome knowledge base. *Journal of Social Psychology, 142,* 567–586.

Stone, G., & Peeks, B. (1986). The use of strategic family therapy in the school setting: A case study. *Journal of Counseling & Development, 65,* 200–203.

Szapocznik, J., & Kurtines, W. M. (1989). *Breakthroughs in family therapy with drug abusing and problem youth.* New York: Springer.

Tanaka, G., & Reid, K. (1997). Peer helpers: Encouraging kids to confide. *Educational Leadership, 55,* 23–31.

Taylor, D. (1982). Family consultation in a school setting. *Journal of Adolescence, 5,* 367–377.

Tobias, A. K., & Myrick, R. D. (1999). A peer facilitator-led intervention with middle school problem-behavior students. *Professional School Counseling, 3,* 27–34.

U.S. Surgeon General (2001). *Youth violence: A report of the Surgeon General.* Retrieved on September 5, 2002, from http://www.surgeongeneral.gov/library/youthviolence/

Watzlawick, P., Weakland, J. H., & Fisch, R. (1974). *Change: Principles of problem formation and problem resolution.* New York: Norton.

Weiss, H. M., Edwards, M. E., Zelen, M., & Schwartz, F. (1991). Systemic interventions produce innovative school change. *Family Therapy News, 22,* 9–12.

Whiston, S. C., & Sexton, T. L. (1998). A review of school counseling outcome research: Implications for practice. *Journal of Counseling & Development, 76,* 412–426.

Whiteside, R. G. (1993). Making a referral for family therapy: The school counselor's role. *Elementary School Guidance and Counseling, 27,* 272–279.

Wilcoxon, S. A., & Comas, R. E. (1987). Contemporary trends in family counseling: What do they mean for the school counselor? *The School Counselor, 34,* 219–225.

PART TWO

The Coordination Function

Designing, Implementing, and Managing a Comprehensive School Guidance and Counseling Program

Norman C. Gysbers
University of Missouri-Columbia

Patricia Henderson
Consultant and Formerly with Northside Independent
School District, San Antonio, Texas

Since the 1980s, school guidance and counseling has been in a "period of renewal and revitalization, where theory and practice have evolved from traditional organizational models to the widespread implementation of developmental comprehensive guidance and counseling programs" (Sink & MacDonald, 1998, p. 89).

How did guidance and counseling in the schools begin and then evolve to where it is today? What is a rationale for guidance and counseling in the schools, what is its theoretical orientation, and how is it organized and practiced currently? Finally, what research do we have concerning its effectiveness? In answering these questions, we first briefly describe the evolution of guidance and counseling in the schools from a position to a service to a comprehensive program. Then we turn our attention to the present and describe a rationale and a theoretical orientation for guidance and counseling in the schools, the comprehensive guidance and counseling program. This is followed by a section on the practical application of this concept in which the transition processes of planning, designing, implementing, evaluating, and enhancing are described—the processes that actually put the program into practice. Finally, we present salient research concerning the effectiveness of comprehensive guidance and counseling programs in the schools.

Introduction: The Evolution of Guidance and Counseling in the Schools

By the beginning of the twentieth century, the United States was deeply involved in the Industrial Revolution. It was a period of rapid industrial growth, social protest, social reform, and utopian idealism. Social protest and social reform were being carried out under the banner of the Progressive Movement, a movement that sought to change negative social conditions associated with the Industrial Revolution. Vocational guidance, as it was called then, was born during the height of this movement as "but one manifestation of the broader movement of progressive reform which occurred in this country in the late 19th and early 20th centuries" (Stephens, 1970, p. 5). As alluded to in Chapter 1, its beginnings can be traced to the work of a number of individuals and social institutions. Individuals such as Frank Parsons, Meyer Bloomfield, Jessie Davis, Anna Reed, E. W. Weaver, and David Hill were instrumental in formulating and implementing early conceptions of vocational guidance working through a number of organizations and movements such as the settlement house movement, the National Society for the Promotion of Industrial Education, and schools in Grand Rapids, Seattle, New York, and New Orleans.

During this period, vocational guidance was seen as a response to the economic, educational, and social problems of those times and concerned the entrance of young people into the work world and the conditions they might find there. Economic concerns focused on the need to better prepare workers for the workplace, while educational concerns arose from a need to increase efforts in schools to help students find purpose for their education as well as their employment. Social concerns emphasized the need for changing school methods and organization as well as exerting more control over conditions of labor in child-employing industries (United States Bureau of Education, 1914).

The Position

The implementation of guidance in the schools of the United States during the first two decades of the twentieth century was accomplished by appointing teachers to the position of vocational counselor, often with no relief from their teaching duties and with no additional pay (Ginn, 1924). They were given a list of duties to perform in addition to their regular teaching duties. No organizational structure for vocational guidance as it was called then, other than a list of duties, was provided.

A Set of Services

One solution for the lack of an organizational structure for guidance in the schools that emerged in the 1930s and continued into the 1940s and beyond was an organizational structure called pupil personnel work. What was pupil personnel work? According to Myers (1935), "pupil personnel work is a sort of handmaiden of organized education. It is concerned primarily with bringing the pupils of the community into the educational environment of the schools in such condition and under such circumstances as will enable them to obtain the maximum of the desired development" (p. 804).

In his article, Myers (1935) listed eight activities he would include in pupil personnel work in schools and the personnel who would be involved, including attendance officers, visiting teachers, school nurses, and school physicians as well as vocational counselors. In his discussion of the activities involved in pupil personnel work and the personnel involved, he stated: "Probably no activity in the entire list suffers so much from lack of coordinated program as does guidance and especially the counseling part of it" (p. 807).

In the decades of the 1950s and 1960s, guidance in the schools was being provided more and more by full-time personnel. Teacher-counselors of previous years were being replaced by full-time professional school counselors. The concept of pupil personnel work, now called pupil personnel services, continued to be the preferred organizational system.

For professional school counselors, the term *services* also was used to describe their work. Usually six services of guidance were identified. These six services were orientation, assessment, information, counseling, placement, and follow-up. One result of this organizational system for guidance and counseling was to continue to emphasize the position of counselor, not a program of guidance. As a result, guidance often was seen as an ancillary support service in the eyes of many people.

The Comprehensive Program

Beginning in the 1970s, the concept of guidance as a program began to emerge. During this period, the call came to reorient guidance from what had become an ancillary set of services delivered by a person in a position (professional school counselor), to a comprehensive, developmental program. The call for reorientation came from diverse sources, including a renewed interest in vocational-career guidance (and its theoretical base, career development), a renewed interest in developmental guidance, concern about the efficacy of the prevailing approach to guidance in the schools, and the concern about accountability and evaluation. Today, the concept of guidance as a program is the prevailing way guidance and counseling is being carried out in the schools (American School Counselor Association [ASCA], 1997, 1998, 1999; Bowers & Hatch, 2002; Gysbers & Henderson 2000).

Rationale: The Importance of Guidance and Counseling Today and Tomorrow

Why are comprehensive guidance and counseling programs required in our schools today and tomorrow? From the very beginning of guidance and counseling in schools the focus has been on meeting the needs of students as well as those of society. Today student needs are as great as they were then, and we believe they will continue to be as great into the foreseeable future. What are these needs? We have grouped them by the topics of student development, self-knowledge, decision making, changing environments, placement assistance, and relevant education.

Student Development

Students today face depersonalization in many facets of their lives as bureaucracies and impersonal relations are commonplace. They often feel powerless in the face of masses of people, mass communication, and mass everything else. They need help in dealing with these feelings, not at the expense of society but in the context of society. Their feelings of control over their environment and their own destiny, and their relations with others and institutions, are of primary importance in guidance and counseling programs. Students must be viewed as totalities, as individuals. Their development can be best facilitated by comprehensive guidance and counseling programs that begin in kindergarten and continue to be available on a systematic basis through grade 12.

Self-Knowledge

Formerly, students were brought up in a fairly stable society in which their roles were defined and relationships with others were fairly constant. Now they face an increasingly mobile society in which relationships with both people and things are becoming less and less enduring. They face an increasingly pluralistic society in which relationships with other people involve focused efforts in understanding and valuing differences as well as similarities. Society is characterized by transience, impermanence, and diversity. Traditional beliefs and ways of doing things no longer seem sufficient for coping with the environmental demands. As a result, many students have problems defining their roles and thus seek answers to Who am I? and Where do I fit in? Guidance and counseling programs can help individuals respond to such questions through the development of self-appraisal and self-improvement competencies. Through these learnings, students can become more aware of personal characteristics such as aptitudes, interests, goals, abilities, values, and physical traits and the influence these characteristics may have on the persons they are and can become. Being able to use self-knowledge in life career planning and interpersonal relationships and to assume responsibility for their own behavior are examples of needed competencies that students can acquire through participation in a comprehensive guidance and counseling program.

Decision Making

Students need help in decision making because planning for and making decisions are vital tasks in the lives of all individuals. Everyday decisions are made that influence each student's life career. Mastery of decision-making skills and the application of these skills to life career planning are central learnings in a guidance and counseling program. A preliminary task to effective decision making is the clarification of personal values. The degree of congruence between what individuals value and the outcomes of decisions individuals make contributes to personal satisfaction. Included in decision making are the skills for gathering and using relevant information. Understanding the influence of planning on the future and the responsibility each individual must take for planning are components of the life career planning process. Life career planning is ongoing. Change and time affect planning and decisions. A decision outcome that is satisfactory and appropriate for the present may become, with time or change, unsatisfactory or inappropriate. Thus, the ability to evaluate decisions in view of new information or circumstances is vital. Being able to clarify personal values, identify steps needed to make personal decisions, gather relevant information, and apply decision-making skills to life career plans are examples of desired and needed outcomes for a guidance and counseling program.

Changing Environments

Increasing societal complexity affects not only interpersonal relationships and feelings of individuality but also other life roles, settings, and events, specifically those associated with the worlds of education, work, and leisure. Changes resulting from advances in technology are perhaps more apparent because they affect the world of work. No longer are students well acquainted with the occupations of family and community members or their contributive roles to the common good of society. Parents' occupations are removed from the home and often from the immediate neighborhood.

In addition, because students over their lifetimes will be assuming a number of roles, functioning in a variety of settings, and experiencing many events, learnings in this area emphasize their understanding of the various roles, settings, and events that interrelate to form their life careers. The roles of family member, citizen, worker, and leisure participant; settings such as home, school, community, and work; and events such as birthdays, educational milestones, job entry, and job change are identified and examined in terms of their influence on lifestyles. Guidance and counseling programs can help students develop an understanding of the structure of the family and education, work, and leisure requirements and characteristics. These programs can also help students learn to accept ethnic and cultural differences among their peers. The effect of change—natural as well as unexpected, social as well as technological, in self as well as in others—is a needed major learning for students that a comprehensive guidance and counseling program can provide.

Placement Assistance

As students are and will be moving from one setting to another, they need specific knowledge and skills to make such moves as effectively as possible. They need help in placement. Although placement is defined broadly, specific attention should be given to intra- and intereducational and occupational transitions and to the personal competencies needed to make such transitions. Personal competencies needed include knowledge of the spectrum of educational courses and programs, an understanding of the relationships they may have to personal and societal needs and goals, and skills in using a wide variety of information and resources. They also include an understanding of the pathways and linkages between those courses and programs and potential personal goals. Stress is placed on the need for employability skill development, including resume writing, job searching, and job interviewing.

Relevant Education

Some of the dissatisfaction of youth with education stems from the feeling that what they are doing in school is not relevant to their lives. A comprehensive guidance and counseling program is needed to seek to create relevance in the schools and to show individuals how the knowledge, understandings, and skills they are obtaining and the courses they are taking will help them as they progress through their life careers.

Chief Theoretical Orientation: Life Career Development

The theoretical foundation for the program is a perspective of human growth and development called life career development (Gysbers, Heppner, & Johnston, 2003; Gysbers & Moore, 1975, 1981; McDaniels & Gysbers, 1992). It is defined as self-development over the life span through the integration of the roles, settings, and events in a person's life. The word *life* in the definition indicates that the focus of this conception of human growth and development is on the total person—the human career. The word *career* identifies and relates the many and often varied roles in which individuals are involved (student, worker, consumer, citizen, parent), the settings in which individuals find themselves (home, school, community), and the events that occur over their lifetimes (entry job, marriage, divorce, retirement). The word *development* is used to indicate that individuals are always in the process of becoming. When used in sequence, the words *life career development* bring these separate meanings together, but at the same time a greater meaning evolves. Life career development describes total individuals, each of whom is unique with his or her own lifestyle.

Added to the basic configuration of life career development are the influencing factors of gender, ethnic origin, spirituality, race, sexual orientation, and social class. All of these factors play important roles in shaping the life roles, life settings, and life events of all ages and circumstances over the life span. These factors are important to the conception of life career development because we live in a nation that is part of a world economy; it is increasingly diverse racially, spiritually, and ethnically, and yet has common themes that connect us all. Our nation continues to change its views on what it means to be female or male, educationally and occupationally. Social class and sexual orientation continue to play important roles in shaping an individual's socialization, and current and future status.

A major goal in using the theoretical perspective of life career development is to assist individuals to identify, describe, and understand the dynamics of their own life career development, to create within them career consciousness, that is, the ability to visualize and plan their life careers. "Included within the idea of consciousness is a person's background, education, politics, insight, values, emotions, and philosophy" (Reich, 1971, p. 15). But consciousness, according to Reich, is more than this. It is the whole person. It is the person's way of creating his or her own life. Thus, the challenge is to assist individuals to become career conscious. The challenge is to assist them to project themselves into future possible life roles, life settings, and life events; to realize the importance of gender, ethnic origin, spirituality, race, sexual orientation, and social class on their development; and then to relate their projections to their present situations for consideration and incorporation into their plans to achieve their goals or resolve their problems.

Contained in the concept of career consciousness is the notion of "possible selves" described by Markus and Nurius (1986). What are possible selves? "Possible selves represent individuals' ideas of what they might become, what they would like to become, and what they are afraid of becoming, and thus provide a conceptual link between cognition and motivation" (p. 954). Why are possible selves important? "Possible selves are important, first, because they function as incentives for future behavior (i.e., they are selves to be approached or avoided) and, second, because they provide an evaluative and interpretive context for the current view of self" (p. 954).

In the definition of life career development, the word *career* has a substantially different meaning from that in some other definitions. Here it focuses on all aspects of life, not as separate entities but as interrelated parts of the whole person. The term *career*, when viewed from this broad perspective, is not a new word for occupation. People have careers; the work world or marketplace has occupations. Unfortunately, too many people use the word *career* when they should use the word *occupation*. Further, the term *career* is not restricted to some people. All people have a career; their life is their career. Thus, the words *life career development* do not delineate and describe only one part of human growth and development.

One goal of a comprehensive school guidance and counseling program, founded on the concept of life career development, is to assist students to acquire competencies to handle the here-and-now issues that affect their growth and development. These issues may include changes in the family structure, expanded social relationships, substance abuse, sexual experimentation, changes in physical and emotional maturation, and peer pressure. Another goal is to create career consciousness in students to assist them to project themselves into possible future life roles, settings, and events; analyze them; relate their findings to their present identity and situations; and make informed, personal education and career choices based on their findings.

THE CONCEPTUAL FRAMEWORK

The comprehensive guidance and counseling program featured in this chapter and shown in Figure 5.1 consists of three elements: content, organizational framework, and resources (Gysbers & Henderson, 2000).

Content

The content element of the program identifies the competencies that students achieve through their participation in the activities of the program components of a school/district's guidance and counseling program. Competencies are usually displayed by grade level (K–12) or grade-level groupings (elementary, middle, and high school). They are often organized around domains such as career, academic, and personal/social. The American School Counselor Association (Campbell & Dahir, 1997, p. 17) uses these domains under which are listed student learnings (competencies) presented as standards:

1. Academic Development Standards
   A. Students will acquire the attitudes, knowledge, and skills that contribute to effective learning in school and across the life span.
   B. Students will complete school with the academic preparation essential to choose from a wide range of substantial postsecondary options, including college.
   C. Students will understand the relationship of academics to the world of work and to life at home and in the community.

2. Career Development Standards
   A. Students will acquire the skills to investigate the world of work in relation to knowledge of self and to make informed career decisions.

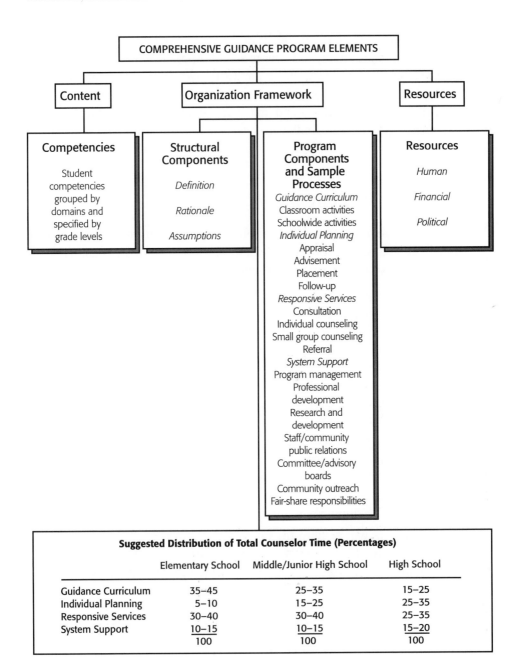

Figure 5.1

    B. Students will employ strategies to achieve future career success and satisfaction.

    C. Students will understand the relationship between personal qualities, education and training, and the world of work.

3. Personal/Social Development Standards

    A. Students will acquire the attitudes, knowledge, and interpersonal skills to help them understand and respect self and others.

    B. Students will make decisions, set goals, and take necessary action to achieve goals.

    C. Students will understand safety and survival skills.

The organizational framework of a comprehensive (developmental) guidance and counseling program consists of its structural components, program components, and use of professional school counselor time.

Organizational Framework: Structural Components

The structural components describe the ideological basis of the program. Included are the program's definition, rationale, and assumptions.

Definition

The program definition includes the mission statement of the guidance and counseling program and its centrality within the school/district's total educational program. It delineates who delivers the program, what competencies students will possess as a result of their involvement in the program, who the clients of the program are, and how the program is organized using the program components of guidance curriculum, individual planning, responsive services, and system support.

Rationale

The rationale discusses the importance of guidance and counseling as an equal partner in the educational system and provides reasons why students need to acquire the competencies that will accrue to them as a result of their involvement in a comprehensive guidance and counseling program. The rationale suggests that the guidance and counseling program is designed to help all students develop their potential through provision of developmental assistance for all students and of specialized assistance for individuals with unique needs. Although the purpose of the rationale is to express the needs for the program, it also provides direction to implementation of the program by including the conclusions drawn from the student, school, and community needs assessments and other clarifications of goals of the local and state educational system and those of the nation as a whole.

Assumption

Assumptions are the principles that shape and guide the program. They include statements regarding the contributions of professional school counselors as outlined by the American School Counselor Association (1999). They include statements regarding the contributions that guidance and counseling programs make to students' development, the premises that undergird the comprehensiveness and the balanced nature of the program, and the relationships between the guidance and counseling program and other educational programs (American School Counselor Association, 1997). Assumptions also include statements of basic expectations for professional school counselors and others who staff the program under the supervision of professional school counselors (American School Counselor Association, 1998).

◤ Organizational Framework: Program Components

The program components describe how the program is delivered to students and other guidance and counseling clients. These components are guidance curriculum, individual planning, responsive services, and system support.

Guidance Curriculum

The guidance curriculum component contains structured activities K–12 that provide all students with opportunities to master guidance and counseling competencies drawn from the content element of the program. In order for this to happen, professional school counselors are involved in teaching, team teaching, or serving as resources to those who teach a guidance curriculum. This is not a new idea; the notion of a guidance curriculum has deep, historical roots. What is new, however, is the array of guidance and counseling techniques, methods, and resources currently available that work best as a part of an organized curriculum. The guidance curriculum typically consists of competencies (organized by domains) and structured activities presented systematically K–12 through such strategies as classroom activities and schoolwide activities.

Classroom Activities.   Professional school counselors teach, team-teach, or support the teaching of guidance curriculum activities or units in classrooms. Teachers also may teach such units. The guidance curriculum is not limited to being a separate stand-alone curriculum, nor is it limited to being a part of only one or two subjects. It is included in as many subjects as possible throughout the total school curriculum. These activities may be conducted in classrooms, the guidance center, or other school facilities.

Schoolwide Activities.   Professional school counselors organize and conduct large group sessions such as career days and educational/college/vocational days. Other members of the guidance team, including teachers and administrators, may be involved in organizing and conducting such sessions. Although professional school counselors' responsibilities include organizing and implementing the guidance curriculum, the cooperation and support of the entire faculty are necessary for its successful implementation.

Individual Planning

Concern for individual student development in a complex society has been a cornerstone of the guidance movement since the days of Frank Parsons (1909). In recent years, the concern for individual student development has intensified as society has become more complex. This concern is manifested in many ways, but perhaps it is expressed most succinctly in a frequently stated guidance goal: helping all students become the persons they are capable of becoming.

To accomplish the purposes of this component of the comprehensive guidance and counseling program, activities and procedures are provided to assist students in understanding and periodically monitoring their own career, academic, and personal/ social development. Students learn about their goals, values, abilities, aptitudes, interests, and competencies so they can continue to progress educationally and occupationally. Individual planning focuses on assisting students, in close collaboration with parents, to develop, analyze, evaluate, and carry out their educational, occupational, and personal goals and plans. Individual planning is implemented through such strategies as appraisal, advisement, and placement and follow-up.

Appraisal.   Professional counselors and other trained advisors assist students to assess and interpret their abilities, interests, skills, and achievements. The use of test information and other data about students is an important part of helping them develop immediate and long-range goals and plans.

Advisement.   Professional counselors and other trained advisors assist students to use self-appraisal information along with personal/social, educational, career, and labor market information to help them plan for and realize their personal, educational, and occupational goals.

Placement and Follow-up.   Professional counselors and other educational personnel assist students to make the transition from school to work or to additional education and training.

Responsive Services

Problems relating to academic learning, personal identity issues, drugs, and peer and family relationships are increasingly a part of students' experiences. Personal counseling, diagnostic and remediation activities, and consultation and referral must continue to be included as ongoing parts of a comprehensive guidance and counseling program. In addition, a continuing need exists for a guidance and counseling program to respond in a planned way, not reactively, to the current information-seeking needs of students, parents, and teachers. The responsive services component organizes guidance and counseling techniques and methods to respond to these concerns and needs; it is supportive of the guidance curriculum and individual planning components as well. Although professional school counselors have special training and possess skills to respond to students' current needs and concerns, the cooperation and support of parents and the entire faculty are necessary for this component's successful implementation. Responsive services are implemented through such strategies as consultation, individual and small group counseling, and referral.

Consultation.   Professional school counselors consult with parents, teachers, other educators, and community agency personnel regarding strategies to help students manage and resolve personal/social, educational, and career concerns.

Individual and Small Group Counseling.   Small group and individual counseling are provided for students who have problems or difficulties dealing with relationships, personal concerns, or normal developmental tasks. The focus is on assisting students to identify problems and causes, alternatives, and possible consequences, and to take action when appropriate.

Referral.   Professional counselors refer students and their parents to other professional resources of the school and community when appropriate. These referral sources may include mental health agencies, employment and training programs, vocational rehabilitation, juvenile services, social services, and special school programs (e.g., special or compensatory education).

System Support

The administration and management of a comprehensive guidance and counseling program require an ongoing support system. That is why system support is a major program component. Unfortunately, it is often overlooked or only minimally appreciated. And yet, the system support component is as important as the other three components. Without continuing support, the other three components of the guidance and counseling program are ineffective. This component is implemented through such activities as program management, professional development, research and development, staff/community public relations, committee/advisory boards, community outreach, and fair-share responsibilities.

Program Management.   This area includes the planning and management tasks needed to support the activities of a comprehensive guidance and counseling program.

Professional Development.   Professional school counselors must regularly update their professional knowledge and skills. This may include participation in school professional development activities, attendance at professional meetings, completion of postgraduate coursework, and contributions to the professional literature.

Research and Development.   Guidance and counseling program evaluation, follow-up studies, and the continued development and updating of guidance curriculum activities are some examples of the research and development work of professional school counselors.

Staff/Community Public Relations.   The orientation of staff, parents, and the community to the comprehensive guidance and counseling program through the use of newsletters, local media, and school and community presentations are examples of public relations work.

Committee/Advisory Boards.   Serving on departmental curriculum committees and community committees or advisory boards are examples of activities in this area.

Community Outreach.   Included in this area are activities designed to help professional school counselors become knowledgeable about community resources, employment opportunities, and the local labor market. This involves professional school counselors visiting local businesses, industries, and social services agencies.

Fair-Share Responsibilities.   These are the routine "running of the school" responsibilities that all members of the school staff take equal turns doing to assure the smooth operation of the school.

◤ Organizational Framework: Use of Professional School Counselor Time

Professional school counselors are the primary providers and leaders of a school's guidance and counseling program. The use of their professional time and talents or special training is critical to the effectiveness of the program. How should they spend their time? How should their time be spread across the total program?

How professional school counselors in a school/district or school building plan and allocate their time depends on the needs of their students and their community and on the school's goals. Once chosen, time allocations are not fixed forever. The purpose for making them and adjusting them periodically is to provide direction to the program and to the administrators and professional school counselor involved.

The four program components provide the structure for making judgments about appropriate allocations of professional school counselors' time. One criterion is the concept of program balance. The assumption is that professional school counselor time should be spread across all program components, but particularly the first three. In most schools, the mission of the guidance program is to provide the kinds of activities included in all four components to and on behalf of all students. When the program is designed, decisions are made regarding the priorities for these activities based on the school/district's needs and goals. For example, if a developmentally based program is the number one priority, Guidance Curriculum and Individual Planning are allocated the largest amounts of professional school counselors' time. In another example, if helping students with problems overcome the barriers to their success in school is the number one priority, the Responsive Services component is allocated the largest amount of program time. It would be unusual for System Support, which is composed of *indirect* services to students, to be designated as the number one priority for professional school counselor time allocation.

Another criterion is that different grade levels require different allocations of professional school counselors' time across the program components. For example, at the elementary level, more professional school counselors' time is spent working in the guidance curriculum with less time spent in individual planning. In the high school, these time allocations are reversed. In the middle/junior high school, professional school counselors' time is more evenly distributed between the guidance curriculum and individual planning components. The time allocated to responsive services and system support is usually fairly constant across all three levels.

Since the program is "100 percent program," all of the professional school counselors' time must be spread across the four program components. Time allocations are changed as needs arise, but nothing new can be added unless something is removed. The assumption is that professional school counselors spend 100 percent of their time on task, implementing the guidance and counseling program.

Resources

Three major sets of resources provide the means for delivering the guidance and counseling program: human, financial, and political.

Human

Human resources for the guidance and counseling program include such individuals as professional school counselors, teachers, administrators, parents, students, community members, and business and labor personnel. All have roles to play in the guidance and counseling program. This requires a team approach: all of the individuals providing guidance to students working in concert toward mutually agreed-upon goals. While professional school counselors are the main providers of guidance and counseling activities and are the coordinators of the program, the involvement, cooperation, and support of teachers and administrators are necessary for the program to be successful. The involvement, cooperation, and support of parents, community members, and business and labor personnel also are critical.

A school-community advisory committee is recommended to bring together the talent and energy of school and community personnel. This committee acts as a liaison between the school and the community and provides recommendations concerning the needs of students and the community. A primary duty of this committee is to advise those involved in the guidance and counseling program. The committee is not a policy- or decision-making body; rather, it is a source of advice, counsel, and support and is a communication link between those involved in the guidance and counseling program and the school and community.

Financial

For a guidance and counseling program to function effectively, adequate financial support is crucial. This means that there is a budget for the program to provide for materials and equipment. This also means that appropriate facilities are provided by the school/district to house the personnel of the program.

The kinds of facilities available for a guidance and counseling program are of particular importance. Traditionally, guidance facilities have consisted of an office or suite of offices designed primarily to provide one-to-one counseling or consultation assistance. Such arrangements have frequently included reception or waiting areas that serve as browsing rooms where students have access to displays or files of educational and occupational information. Also, this space has typically been placed in the administrative wing of the school so that the counseling staff can be near the records and the administration.

The need for individual offices is obvious because of the continuing need to carry on individual counseling and consultation. A need also exists, however, to open up guidance facilities and make them more accessible to all students, teachers, parents, and community members. One way to make guidance facilities more usable and accessible is to reorganize traditional space into a guidance center.

A guidance center brings together available guidance information and resources and makes them easily accessible to students. The center is used for such activities as group sessions, student self-exploration, and personalized research and planning. At the high school level, students receive assistance in areas such as occupational planning, job entry and placement, financial aid information, and postsecondary educational opportunities. At the middle school and elementary school levels, students and their parents receive information about the school, the community, and parenting skills; they also can read books about personal growth and development.

Political

Education is not simply influenced by politics, it is politics, and thus the mobilization of political resources is key to a successful guidance and counseling program. Full endorsement of the guidance and counseling program by the board of education as a "program" or a "framework" of the school/district is one example of mobilizing political resources. Another example is a clear and concise school/

district policy statement that highlights the integral and central nature of the school/district's comprehensive guidance and counseling program to other programs in the school/district (Gysbers, Lapan, & Jones, 2000).

PRACTICAL APPLICATION: PUTTING THE PROGRAM INTO ACTION

What is required to successfully make the transition from what exists currently in guidance and counseling in a school/district to a fully functioning program? We recommend that a school/district go through a five-phase transition process consisting of planning, designing, implementing, evaluation, and enhancing. Depending on the school/district, the process can unfold over a five- to ten-year time period. Then, the program enhancement phase that follows evaluation connects back to the beginning as program redesign occurs, but at a higher level than before. Thus the complete transition process is spiral, not circular. Each time the redesign process unfolds, a more effective guidance and counseling program emerges.

Planning

The planning phase of the overall transition process involves first getting organized, then adopting the organizational system for guidance and counseling described previously, and finally doing a thorough assessment of the current status of guidance and counseling in the school/district.

Getting Organized

The goal of the entire transition process is to develop and fully implement a comprehensive guidance and counseling program for a school/district. For this to occur, careful planning is required. Our motto is plan twice and act once. This means that we understand the necessary conditions for effective change, expect resistance to change, and develop trust among school counselors and administrators.

Two standing committees are required in the getting-organized phase. The first committee is called the *Steering Committee*. The steering committee serves as the internal management group for designing a new comprehensive guidance and counseling program for the school/district. This committee is charged with the responsibility for establishing guidelines to ensure a systematic and sequential schoolwide or districtwide program. Steering committee members are key school leaders who serve as visionaries for the program and motivators for the involvement of others.

The steering committee consists of building-level administrators and professional school counselors from the school/district's elementary, middle/junior high, and senior high schools. Representatives from the school/district's central office should also be involved. The size of the steering committee is determined locally. The superintendent of schools should formally appoint the members. Ordinarily, a member of the guidance department serves as chair.

The responsibilities of the steering committee include the following:

- Becoming knowledgeable about the comprehensive guidance and counseling program
- Understanding the conditions necessary for change to take place locally
- Meeting with the administration and the board of education to gain support and secure authorization to proceed with the development and implementation of the school/district's program
- Creating the design for the comprehensive guidance and counseling program in the school/district and being responsible to see that the work is done (make the decisions, set the priorities)
- Providing progress reports to the board of education
- Appointing and supervising work groups of professional school counselors as well as others to accomplish the work to be done to fully implement a comprehensive guidance and counseling program in the school/district

Once the plans and designs are set, the Steering Committee turns the responsibility for implementation and management back to the professional school counselors to manage, coordinate, and provide to and on behalf of students.

The second committee that is required is the *School-Community Advisory Committee*. This committee is appointed by the superintendent for the purpose of providing advice and counsel concerning the development and implementation of the school/district's comprehensive guidance and counseling program. The committee provides support, offers advice, reviews present activities, and encourages new activities to meet the goals of the school/district's comprehensive guidance and counseling program. It is important to emphasize that the committee is an advisory group, not a decision-making body.

The members should have a shared enthusiasm for students and guidance. It is recommended that the members of the school-community advisory committee be appointed by the superintendent. When identifying potential members, the following points should be considered: (a) The members should represent the diversity of the school/district's patrons and business community; (b) representation should be sought from the school board, school staff, parents/guardians, and students; and (c) community members with diverse viewpoints should be included in the committee selection.

During the first year of planning, it is important for the Steering Committee to meet with the school/district board of education to present a rationale for the needed transition to a comprehensive guidance and counseling program and their plan to accomplish this task. The goal is to seek the endorsement of the board of education for the needed transition and the authorization to proceed. By endorsing the concept of a comprehensive guidance and counseling program for the school/district and by authorizing the development and implementation of the program, the board of education authorizes the administration to provide professional school counselors with the time and resources to develop and implement a comprehensive guidance and counseling program under the leadership of the steering committee.

Choosing the Organizational System and Conducting a Thorough Assessment of the Current Status of Guidance and Counseling in the School/District

In the planning phase of the transition process, one of the major tasks is to choose the organizational system for guidance and counseling in the school/district. For purposes of this chapter, we are using the system described earlier. This choice is important because the language of the system chosen becomes the common language that is used throughout the rest of the transition process.

Another major task is to thoroughly assess the current program. Groups of professional school counselors from all levels will be required to conduct the work involved. One or more work groups are needed to study and report on issues in the school/district that may have an impact on the development and implementation of the school/district's program. In addition, another work group is needed to study conditions outside of the school in the community and beyond. Finally, one work group, with members representing all levels, is responsible for organizing the professional school counselor's time and task analysis study. Each of the work groups provides periodic progress reports to the steering committee. When their work is completed, each group makes a full report of their findings to the steering committee.

The time and task analysis is a survey of the time it takes for professional school counselors to complete the tasks they are assigned in the current program. Either fifteen-minute or thirty-minute time intervals can be used. Begin collecting data on Monday, the first week. The next week collect data on Tuesday. On the third week, collect data on Wednesday. On the fourth week, collect data on Thursday, and on the fifth week, collect data on Friday. Beginning with the sixth week, repeat the process for a full school year.

Before a time and task analysis is conducted, however, it is important for all of the professional school counselors in the school/district to meet by grade level (elementary, middle, and high school) to determine where their current tasks fit into the program components. (In small schools/districts, all professional school counselors in the school/district may work together to complete this task.) This can be accomplished by having each group divide large sheets of paper into five columns. The columns should be labeled (a) guidance curriculum, (b) individual planning, (c) responsive services, (d) system support, and (e) nonguidance activities. The task is for the professional school counselors at each level to list and categorize their current tasks. The result is a chart for each level that contains all of the tasks professional school counselors are currently responsible for, categorized by the four program components and nonguidance activities. This exercise will provide all professional school counselors in a school/district with the knowledge of what current tasks go where when they fill out the time and task analysis form so that everyone will interpret the form in the same way. It is important to remember that fair-share activities are included in system support. The results of this analysis provide a basis for comparing the time and tasks involved in the current program to the time and tasks chosen for the desired school/district's comprehensive guidance and counseling program.

Designing

The design phase of the program development process is the time to design the school/district's guidance and counseling program as it should be. This phase entails establishing the priorities for delivering the program and, therefore, for allocating the program's resources. Priorities are established for the results that students will accrue due to participating in the program activities. Priorities are established not only for how the counselors spend their time, as described previously, but also for the application of their specialized talents (i.e., in guidance, counseling, consultation, coordination, assessment, program management, and/ or professional development). Priorities are established for the specific activities that comprise each of the Program Components. Priorities are also established for which categories of students will participate in the program activities; for example, *all* students in a grade level participate in guidance curriculum activities, but there may not be enough "counselors and trained advisors" available to assist *each* student in Individual Planning. Priorities would then have to be established about which students would participate in these activities. Often, students in transition from one school level to the next (i.e., elementary to middle, middle to high, high to post–high school) are given the highest priority. Typically, there is not enough counselor time available for all students to experience individual or small group counseling on a regular basis, creating the need for priorities to be set for participating students.

A major goal is to write the school/district's comprehensive guidance and counseling program manual. As with any written publication, the document must portray a cohesive whole, have a logical sequence, and be written in a consistent and concise style. As stated earlier, the written description depicts the basic structure that you have decided on and becomes the working document for you and your staff henceforth. It replaces the former guidance and counseling program handbook or plan. We recommend the write-up contain at least five sections: the structural components, the recommended design/resource allocations for the program, the position guides, the program components, and appendixes.

Structural Components

This first section should include the statements that express the philosophical basis of your program: the final versions of the rationale, the assumptions, and the program definition. In addition, the list of student competencies that are to be developed through the guidance and counseling program should be presented. Listing the specific grade-level outcomes is probably too lengthy for this section of the document, but these may be listed fully in an appendix or in a separate document.

Recommended Design/Resource Allocations

The second section of the write-up should contain statements that describe the appropriate balance among the four components, the priorities for the clients to be served, the competencies to be sought, and the professional school counselors' skills to be used. This section presents numerically what the program should look like to be considered comprehensive and well balanced.

Position Guides

The third section should describe the various jobs guidance and counseling program staff perform. This section should contain guides for not only the elementary, middle/junior, and senior high professional, but also for any counselor specialists you have in your school/district, such as vocational, special, or compensatory-education-funded counselors, and for head counselors. Job descriptions also should be included for other staff members who have been identified as having roles integral to the delivery of the guidance and counseling program, such as career center technicians, registrars, and related professionals (such as social workers, community-based licensed counselors, or school psychologists). If you are using or plan to use community volunteers, their positions also should be described here.

Program Components

The fourth section should include more detailed descriptions, each of which should begin with the definition of the component and contain the design decisions made regarding each. The strands in the guidance curriculum, the major activities that make up the individual planning component, the recurrent topics that are the focus of the responsive services, and the specific activities identified in the system support should be listed. The content priorities within and resources that support each component should be identified. The roles fulfilled by counselors, teachers, administrators, and parents in component implementation should be defined. The guidelines established for component activity implementation should be detailed and include the recommended mode of delivery for each component (i.e., small group counseling as the preferred mode for responsive services, classroom-sized groups as the preferred mode for guidance curriculum, and so on) as well as the recommended allocation of resources to the component (especially that of the professional school counselors' time). Each component description should end with statements of expectations regarding evaluation of the overall impact on students of the component's activities, each activity's effectiveness, and the quality of the competencies used by the professional staff. All of the decisions made by the program developers that relate to a component should be reflected in the write-up so as not to be lost over time.

Appendixes

It is recommended that the appendixes contain the ethical standards of the American School Counselor Association and the American Counseling Association as well as the school/district's policy on guidance and counseling. These can be easily found on these organizations' web pages.

In writing the manual it is important to highlight, when and where possible, the centrality of the guidance and counseling program within the school/district's total educational program. The more direct the link between the school/district's goals and those of the guidance and counseling program, the more clearly related the program will be to the mission of the school/district. For example, if the school/district's mission statement and strategic plan (comprehensive school improvement plan) includes such goals as helping students become good citizens, be responsible for their actions, and make informed choices, then the school/district's guidance and counseling program should be written to show how it makes a contribution to the achievement of these goals.

Implementing

This is the transition phase in which the school/district's comprehensive guidance and counseling program is put into full operation. There are three parts to this phase. The first part focuses on planning the implementation. This is followed by the second part called making the transition. The last part of this transition phase involves managing the new program.

Planning the Implementation

In this part of the implementation process, a first step is to specify changes needed to implement a comprehensive guidance and counseling program. This involves comparing and contrasting the current program with the desired program developed during the design phase. Currently, the structure in use may follow the guidance services model (orientation, assessment, information, counseling, placement, and follow-up activities), or it may be organized around the processes of counseling, consulting, and coordination, or it may be described by a list of duties.

You will be asking and answering the question, what are the discrepancies between what the school/district wants the program to accomplish and what the program is accomplishing currently? Then goals for change are established and ways to effect the changes are identified. Next a plan to accomplish the necessary improvements is developed along with expanding the overall leadership base of the program.

Making the Transition

This part of the implementation process includes developing the human, financial, and political resources needed for full program implementation. The major points to be considered in each of these areas are as follows:

Human Resources

- Implementing recommended counselor/student ratios
- Developing counselors' job descriptions
- Establishing roles and responsibilities for building guidance and counseling program leaders
- Developing job descriptions for other staff members working in the guidance and counseling program
- Clarifying organizational relationships within the guidance and counseling program

Financial Resources

- Establishing budgets for guidance departments at the school/district and building levels
- Exploring use of other-than-local funding sources
- Developing guidance and counseling program component resource guides
- Establishing guidance facilities standards and making recommendations for their application

Political Resources

- Updating policies and procedures
- Engendering support from building staff
- Working with resistant staff members
- Managing critical constituents: concerned parents

Managing the Program

In this part of the implementation process, the emphasis is on improving program activities, enhancing the role of the professional school counselor, developing the building plan for the program, and monitoring program implementation. One goal is to achieve the right program balance of activities and services. Another goal is for professional school counselors to manage their time effectively.

In improving program activities, it is important to first recognize that professional school counselors have been providing students and parents with many high-quality activities and services. It is equally important to realize that professional school counselors have been doing many tasks that are not part of the new comprehensive guidance and counseling program.

In many schools/districts professional school counselors are assigned supervisory duties, such as developing and monitoring assemblies; hall, cafeteria, bus, or restroom duty; or chaperoning school activities. Sometimes they are assigned instructional duties, such as tutoring or substitute teaching. At other times, they are given clerical duties, such as selling lunch or bus tickets, collecting and mailing progress reports, maintaining permanent records and handling transcripts, monitoring attendance, calculating grade point averages, or developing student handbooks and course guides. Sometimes they are assigned administrative duties, including developing the master schedule, covering for the absent principal, assigning disciplinary consequences, making schedule changes, or even supervising teachers.

Being responsible for such tasks takes away time that can be spent more profitably providing guidance activities and services directly to students and their parents/guardians. How much time do professional school counselors spend on such tasks? A study conducted by the Texas State Comptroller's office found that professional school counselors in Texas spend up to 40 percent of their time on activities other than counseling. The professional school counselors who participated in the study stated that spending so much time on other activities had reduced their availability to students in their schools (Rylander, 2002).

Tasks such as these are targets for displacement and/or streamlining. Displacement involves specifying the tasks that are done and either eliminates them or shifts responsibility for doing them to someone else. Streamlining, on the other hand, may necessitate doing tasks more efficiently. This involves analyzing tasks to pinpoint inefficiencies. It may also involve using technology to streamline such tasks as scheduling by using the Internet.

Enhancing the role of professional school counselors is critical in managing the guidance and counseling program. This means ensuring that professional school counselors' work is appropriate to their training and expertise by establishing appropriate job descriptions for them in each building. It also means helping professional school counselors recognize the potential number of students who will benefit from their activities and services. Finally, it means helping professional school counselors manage their time through effective planning and calendaring.

At this point, it is very important to develop building plans that provide very specific descriptions of what is planned to happen in a school's comprehensive guidance and counseling program: how many guidance lessons are taught at each grade level, by whom, and what the topics are; what individual planning activities are done for each grade level, how they are organized, what the outcomes are, and how they relate to the past and future planning activities; what the small group counseling service offers, to how many children at which grade levels, and on what topics. Parent education and staff consultation plans are included. Further, the time frames for conducting the planned activities are established and laid out for the upcoming school year.

By now, all involved are well into the implementation of a comprehensive guidance and counseling program. As difficult as planning and designing the program is, it is even more difficult to maintain the momentum for change and the improvements so that the program does not revert back to its original traditional form. Systems for monitoring progress toward the established goals and for monitoring overall improved program implementation are developed and used. Staff continues to be encouraged to try the new activities and be reinforced in their efforts. Finally, program adjustments are made as a result of monitoring the changes.

Evaluating

Now that the planning and designing phases of the program improvement process have been completed and the implementation phase is well under way, we are ready to discuss the next phase of the process: evaluation. Three kinds of systematic evaluation are required to achieve accountability for your guidance and counseling program. Personnel evaluation, the first kind of evaluation, describes the procedures used by your school/district to evaluate professional school counselors and other personnel who may be assisting the professional school counselors in implementing the school/district's guidance and counseling program. Program evaluation, the second kind, examines your school/district's written guidance and counseling program to see if it is the same as the actual implemented program. Results evaluation, the third kind, focuses on the impact that guidance activities in your school/district's program are having on students, the school, and the community.

Personnel Evaluation

A key part of comprehensive guidance and counseling program implementation and management is a professional school counselor performance improvement system. The basic purpose of such a system is to assist professional school counselors reach and maintain their professional potential. Such a system includes helping individuals define their jobs, providing professional supervision, conducting fair performance evaluation, and setting goals for professional development (Henderson & Gysbers, 1998).

The purposes of evaluating professional school counselors' performance are to improve the delivery to and impact of the program on the students it serves and to provide for communication among professional school counselors, guidance and counseling program staff leaders, and school administrators. For professional school counselors, evaluation specifies contract status recommendations and provides summative evaluation as to their effectiveness. For the school/district, evaluation defines expectations for professional school counselors' performance and provides a systematic means of measuring their performance relative to these expectations.

Program Evaluation

Program evaluation asks two questions: Does the school/district have a written comprehensive guidance and counseling program? Is the written program of the school/district being implemented fully in the school buildings of the school/district? Answers to these questions are provided through the program evaluation process, the goal of which is to examine the written program carefully and verify through documentation that it is the implemented program.

Whether or not a written guidance and counseling program exists in the school/district and whether or not any discrepancies exist between the written guidance and counseling program and the actual implemented program become clear as the program evaluation process unfolds.

The first step in setting up such a process is establishing standards for guidance and counseling programs. Program standards are defined as acknowledged measures of comparison or the quality criteria used to make judgments about the adequacy of the size, nature, and structure of a comprehensive guidance and counseling program. Program standards are derived from the model used to establish the written guidance and counseling program.

How many program standards are required to establish whether a comprehensive guidance and counseling program is in place and functioning? The answer is enough standards to ensure that judgments can be made on whether a complete comprehensive guidance and counseling program is actually in place and functioning to a high enough degree to benefit all students, parents, teachers, and the community fully. Once a sufficient number of program standards are written to represent a comprehensive guidance and counseling program fully, the next step is to write indicators for each standard. Indicators are defined as statements that specify important aspects of the standards; thus, enough indicators need to be written for each standard to provide evaluators with the confidence that each standard is in place and functioning.

Results Evaluation

Once it has been established that a guidance and counseling program is in place and functioning as it should in a school/district through program evaluation, and professional school counselors and other staff members are being evaluated on their job descriptions using a schoolwide or districtwide performance-based system, the next step is results evaluation. Johnson (1991) suggested there are long-range, intermediate, and immediate results that need to be considered. According to Johnson, long-range results focus on how programs affect students after they have left school. Intermediate results emphasize what impact the program has had on students some period of time after they have participated in guidance and counseling program activities, and immediate results are results that describe the impact of specific guidance activities soon after the activities have been completed.

What format should we use to organize and carry out results evaluation? We recommend that if a school/district used the model for guidance and counseling programs described previously, then the four program components—guidance curriculum, individual planning, responsive services, system support—can provide the needed format to organize and carry out results evaluation. For each program component, the activities to be evaluated are listed followed by the anticipated results and the documentation required to provide evidence of results attainment. The documentation column can be subdivided into immediate, intermediate, and long-range results, if desired, to focus attention on the time period in which data will be collected. This recommended format is adapted from one developed by the professional school counselors of the Omaha Public Schools, Omaha, Nebraska (Maliszewski, 1997).

Enhancing

The enhancing phase of the transition process uses the data gathered from program, personnel, and results evaluations to redesign and enhance the comprehensive guidance and counseling program that has been in place in a school/district for a number of years. The program enhancement process connects back to the beginning as program redesign unfolds but at a higher level. The enhancement process is spiral, not circular. Each time the redesign process unfolds a new and more effective school/district comprehensive guidance and counseling program emerges. Evaluation data regarding the effectiveness of the school/district's comprehensive guidance and counseling program, its personnel, and its results provide a basis for sound decision making and should be analyzed to determine what changes are necessary to improve the comprehensive guidance and counseling program. The following examples illustrate program changes that might be indicated as a result of the evaluation process.

- *Professional school counselor time allocation.* The time that the professional school counselor devotes to the various program components may need to be adjusted because evaluation data show that the allocations need to be increased or decreased in order to more effectively carry out the activities and services of the various program components.
- *Student competencies.* Additional student competencies may need to be added and/or new activities may need to be developed to respond to changing student needs.
- *Professional development.* Additional time may need to be devoted to school counselor professional development in order to keep current with best practices.
- *Public relations activities.* More emphasis may need to be given to public relations activities because evaluation data show a lack of understanding in the community about the school/district's comprehensive guidance and counseling program.
- *Nonguidance activities.* The evaluation data might show that the school/district's comprehensive guidance and counseling program is not yet fully implemented because of nonguidance activities assigned to the professional school counselor. In order to more fully implement the school/district's comprehensive guidance and counseling program, consideration needs to be given to nonguidance activity reassignment.
- *Professional school counselor/student ratio.* Additional staff may need to be added to accommodate an increase in student population and/or increased needs of students. Additional staff may be needed to improve professional school counselor/student ratios in order to fully implement the school/district's comprehensive guidance and counseling program.
- *Clerical support.* Evaluation results may indicate that the comprehensive guidance and counseling program requires the addition of clerical support in order to free up the professional school counselor's time to more fully implement the school/district's comprehensive guidance and counseling program.

The redesigning process involved in the enhancing phase is based not only on conclusions drawn from evaluation data but also on observations gained by using the school/district's comprehensive guidance and counseling program over time. Changes in the makeup of the school/district and economic base of the community may also affect the redesign process. Most important, the redesign process does not involve changing the organizational framework of the program. Instead, the redesign process involves making internal changes, such as in program content, activities, and time allocations.

In addition, it is important to remember in all phases that annual reports to the board of education are required to fully inform them of any changes that are being planned in the school/district's comprehensive guidance and counseling program.

Salient Research

What have we learned from evaluation efforts so far? While Chapter 8 examines the research in depth, we summarize some of it here. For example, in a study of seventy-five Missouri high schools that had begun the implementation of the Missouri Comprehensive Guidance and Counseling Program Model between 1984 and 1988, Gysbers and Hughey (1989) found that the model provided more organization and structure, and that it formalized the program by establishing priorities, goals, and activities. This study also found that nonguidance activities decreased and that more time was being spent in the classroom conducting guidance curriculum activities. Barriers to implementation included the time involved in implementing the program, the professional school counselor–student ratio, and funding.

A 1990 survey of students, parents, and teachers who had participated in some way in the activities of the comprehensive guidance and counseling programs in their schools found that they generally felt positive about and valued the work of the professional school counselor in their schools (Hughey, Gysbers, & Starr, 1990). Eighteen high schools from across Missouri were included in this study. Data were obtained from students, parents, and teachers in fourteen of the eighteen high schools.

In a study conducted in high schools in Missouri, Lapan, Gysbers, and Sun (1997) found that students in high schools with more fully implemented guidance and counseling programs were more likely to report that they had earned higher grades, their education was better preparing them for their future, their school made more career and college information available to them, and their school had a more positive climate. In Utah, Nelson and Gardner (1998) found that students in schools with more fully implemented guidance and counseling programs rated their overall education as better, took more advanced mathematics and science courses, and had higher scores on every area of the ACT.

In their review of outcome research in school counseling, Sexton, Whiston, Bleuer, and Walz (1997, p. 125) made the following points:

- Reviews of outcome research in school counseling are generally positive about the effects of school counseling.
- Research results do indicate that individual planning interventions can have a positive impact on the development of students' career plans. There is some support for responsive services activities such as social skills training, family support programs, and peer counseling. Consultation activities are also found to be an effective school counseling activity.

In a study conducted in middle schools in Missouri, Lapan, Gysbers, and Petroski (2001) found that when middle school classroom teachers indicated that there was a more fully implemented guidance and counseling program in their schools, seventh graders reported that they had earned higher grades, school was more relevant for them, they had positive relationships with teachers, they were more satisfied with their education, and they felt safer in schools. In addition, data from 424 high schools in the High Schools That Work Network from 1996 to 1998 indicated that there was a strong association of changes in the amount that students talked with a teacher or professional school counselor and changes in school achievement levels in science, mathematics, and reading. Controlling for demographic characteristics, those schools that increased the amount that students talked to teachers and counselors about their high school program increased their achievement rates; those that decreased this time had declines in their average achievement levels (Kaufman, Bardby, & Teitelbaum, 2000).

A Final Note

Our vision for guidance and counseling in the twenty-first century is fully implemented comprehensive guidance and counseling programs in every school/district across the country, serving all students and their parents, staffed by active, involved professional school counselors. When guidance and counseling is conceptualized, organized, and implemented as a program, it places professional school counselors conceptually and structurally in the center of education and makes it possible for them to be active and involved. As a result, guidance and counseling becomes an integral and transformative program, not a marginal and supplemental activity. It provides professional school counselors with the structure, time, and resources to fully use their expertise.

APPENDIX

Comprehensive Guidance and Counseling Programs—Further Exploration

Here is an opportunity to apply some of the major ideas discussed in Chapter 5.

Exercise 1

A key theme in this chapter was the development of student competencies or standards. These could also be called student outcomes—i.e., what you want students to accomplish through the implementation of a comprehensive program. Gysbers and Henderson suggested that programs should use academic, career, and personal/social development standards. Others in the profession have recommended that these standards are not inclusive enough. Emotional, citizenship, character/moral, multicultural, and spiritual development, for instance, receive limited or no attention in the ASCA National Model and in other comprehensive programs. A couple of all-important questions are: What should students be able to do (be competent at) when they finish high school? What is the school counselor's role in facilitating the attainment of these competencies?

Brainstorm the FIVE MOST critical outcomes for students to accomplish.

All Grade 12 students will be able to . . .

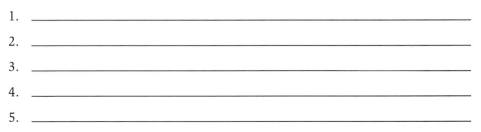

1. _____

2. _____

3. _____

4. _____

5. _____

Now go through the ASCA National Model and the National Standards for School Counseling Programs and compare your competencies with those presented in these publications (go to the web site, www.schoolcounselor.org, for copies of the documents).

How do your values and emphases match up with the profession's student outcomes?

Exercise 2

An important aspect of the *implementation process* discussed in Chapter 5 is developing the human, financial, and political resources required to make the program work well. Think through these areas and list some options.

Human Resources

- Implementing recommended counselor/student ratios *(What are the "target" ratios for elementary, middle/junior high, and high schools?)*

- Elementary ___:___ middle/junior high ___:___ high school ___:___

- Developing counselors' job descriptions *(What are the key functions that school counselors would do regardless of their grade level? You might want to review Chapter 1 for some ideas.)*

  _____

  _____

- Establishing roles and responsibilities for building guidance and counseling program leaders *(What are the major duties of the program leaders?)*

  _____

  _____

Financial Resources

- Establishing budgets for guidance departments at the school and district and building levels *(What things might each counselor need to buy?)*

  _____

  _____

- Exploring use of other-than-local funding sources *(Where might school counselors obtain additional funds to make their programs go?)*

  _____

  _____

Political Resources

▪ Engendering support from building staff *(Record your ideas below.)*

_____

_____

▪ Working with resistant staff members *(Record your ideas below.)*

_____

_____

▪ Managing critical constituents: Concerned parents *(Record your ideas below.)*

_____

_____

Exercise 3

"Don't Reinvent the Wheel." The authors presented the notion that school counselors already do job tasks that fit into one of the four program components. For those counselors you've shadowed, what tasks fit under which component?

Program Components

Guidance _____

_____

Individual Planning _____

_____

Responsive Services _____

_____

Support Services _____

_____

Note: This appendix was written by Christopher Sink.

REFERENCES

American School Counselor Association. (1997). *The professional school counselor and comprehensive school counseling programs.* Position statement: Comprehensive programs. Alexandria, VA: Author.

American School Counselor Association. (1998). *Ethical standards for school counselors.* Alexandria, VA: Author.

American School Counselor Association. (June, 1999). *The role of the professional school counselor.* Alexandria, VA: Author.

Bowers, J. L., & Hatch, P. A. (2002). *ASCA national model for school counseling programs (draft).* Alexandria, VA: American School Counselor Association.

Campbell, C. A., & Dahir, C. A. (1997). *Sharing the vision: The national standards for school counseling programs.* Alexandria, VA: American School Counselor Association.

Ginn, S. J. (1924). Vocational guidance in Boston Public Schools. *The Vocational Guidance Magazine, 2,* 3–7.

Gysbers, N. C., & Henderson, P. (2000). *Developing and managing your school guidance and counseling program* (3rd ed.). Alexandria, VA: American Counseling Association.

Gysbers, N. C., & Hughey, K. F. (1989). Missouri comprehensive guidance: How's the model working? What's next? *The Counseling Interviewer, 21*(4), 21–27.

Gysbers, N. C., & Moore, E. J. (1975). Beyond career development: Life career development. *Personnel and Guidance Journal, 53,* 647–652.

Gysbers, N. C., & Moore, E. J. (1981). *Improving guidance and counseling programs.* Englewood Cliffs, NJ: Prentice-Hall.

Gysbers, N. C., Heppner, M. J., & Johnston, J. A. (2003). *Career counseling: Process, issues, and techniques* (2nd ed.). Needham Heights, MA: Allyn & Bacon.

Gysbers, N. C., Lapan, R. T., & Jones, B. (2000). School board policies for guidance and counseling: A call to action. *Professional School Counseling, 3,* 349–355.

Henderson, P., & Gysbers, N. C. (1998). *Leading and managing your school guidance and counseling program staff: A manual for school administrators and directors of guidance.* Alexandria, VA: American Counseling Association.

Hughey, K. E., Gysbers, N. C., & Starr, M. (1990). Evaluating comprehensive school guidance and counseling programs: Assessing the perceptions of students, parents, and teachers. *The School Counselor, 41,* 31–35.

Johnson, C. D. (1991). Assessing results. In S. K. Johnston & E. A. Whitfield (Eds.), *Evaluating guidance and counseling programs: A practitioner's guide* (pp. 43–55). Iowa City, IA: American College Testing Program.

Kaufman, P., Bardby, D., & Teitelbaum, P. (2000). *High schools that work and whole school reform: Raising academic achievement of vocational completers through reform of school practice.* Berkley, CA: National Center for Research in Vocational Education, MPR Associates.

Lapan, R. T., Gysbers, N. C., & Petroski, G. F. (2001). Helping seventh graders be safe and successful: A statewide study of the impact of comprehensive guidance and counseling programs. *Journal of Counseling & Development, 79*, 320–330.

Lapan, R. T., Gysbers, N. C., & Sun, Y. (1997). The impact of more fully implemented guidance and counseling programs on the school experiences of high school students: A statewide evaluation study. *Journal of Counseling & Development, 75*, 292–302.

Maliszewski, S. J. (1997). Developing a comprehensive guidance system in Omaha public schools. In N. C. Gysbers & P. Henderson (Eds.), *Comprehensive guidance and counseling programs that work—II* (pp. 195–219). Greensboro, NC: ERIC Counseling and Student Services Clearinghouse.

Markus, H., & Nurius, P. (1986). Possible selves. *American Psychologist, 41*, 954–969.

McDaniels, C., & Gysbers, N. C. (1992). *Counseling for career development: Theories, resources, and practice.* San Francisco: Jossey-Bass.

Myers, G. E. (1935). Coordinated guidance: Some suggestions for a program of pupil personnel work. *Occupations, 13*, 804–807.

Nelson, D. E., & Gardner, J. L. (1998). *An evaluation of the comprehensive guidance and counseling program in Utah public schools.* Salt Lake City: Utah State Office of Education.

Parsons, F. (1909). *Choosing a vocation.* Boston: Houghton Mifflin.

Reich, C. A. (1971). *The greening of America.* New York: Bantam.

Rylander, C. E. (2002). *Guiding our children toward success: How Texas school counselors spend their time (A report authorized by S.B. 538, 77th Legislature).* Austin, TX: Office of the Comptroller.

Sexton, T. L., Whiston, S. C., Bleuer, J. C., & Walz, G. R. (1997). *Integrating outcome research into counseling practice and training.* Alexandria, VA: American Counseling Association.

Sink, C. A., & MacDonald, G. (1998). The status of comprehensive guidance and counseling in the United States. *Professional School Counseling, 2*, 88–94.

Stephens, W. R. (1970). *Social reform and the origins of vocational guidance.* Washington, DC: National Vocational Guidance Association.

United States Bureau of Education (1914). *Vocational guidance.* Papers presented at the organization meeting of the Vocational Guidance Association, Grand Rapids, Michigan, October 21–24, 1913. Prefatory Statement (Bulletin, 1914, No. 14, Whole Number 587). Washington, DC: U.S. Government Printing Office.

CHAPTER 6

Large Group Guidance: Curriculum Development and Instruction

Susan Jones Sears
The Ohio State University

In the school counselor role and function statement by the American School Counselor Association (1999), large group guidance is one of the four primary counselor interventions (individual and group counseling, consultation, and coordination are the other three). Group interventions have become more and more popular as a means of assisting children and youth with a wide range of problems (Gibson & Mitchell, 1999). An earlier chapter espoused the value of small group counseling. This chapter focuses on large group guidance as an important vehicle for delivering a comprehensive school counseling program.

Definitions and Rationale

School personnel have utilized large groups to disseminate information to students for years. However, simply bringing students together to disseminate information in a large setting is not group guidance. There are many definitions of large group guidance. The American School Counselor Association (ASCA) Role Statement defines it as "a planned, developmental program of guidance activities designed to foster students' academic, career, and personal/social development" (ASCA, 1999). Wittmer and Thompson (2000) suggested a similar definition:

"Large group guidance is the systematic delivery of age-appropriate, preventative (developmental) guidance concepts and units to large groups of students, usually in a school classroom setting" (p. 11). The definitions suggest that large group guidance is sometimes viewed as a delivery system (e.g., Wittmer & Thompson, 2000), while other times it is described as a curriculum (e.g., ASCA, 1999). For the purposes of this chapter, large group guidance is defined as an intervention to deliver a curriculum or a series of planned activities to help students anticipate problems before they occur or to help them cope effectively with problems after they occur. This definition expands the scope of topics seen as appropriate for large group guidance interventions. A rationale for a broader definition is presented in the next section of the chapter.

A Rationale for Large Group Guidance

An obvious rationale for utilizing large group guidance as a counseling intervention is that it enables school counselors to reach a greater number of students to cover a wide range of issues. Another important reason is that counselors can introduce themselves and the counseling program to a greater number of students. Once students know what their counselors can offer, they may be more inclined to seek their assistance. Another reason is that large group guidance, by enabling counselors to see students interact with their peers in classroom settings, helps them identify students who need additional assistance in the form of small group or individual counseling.

Students benefit from large group guidance in several ways. Children and youth

- hear or are exposed to others' comments or feelings about issues with which they may be grappling,
- can participate in the group even though they may not choose to speak in the group,
- have opportunities to try out their ideas and receive feedback from their peers,
- acquire important information or knowledge that they can use to make effective decisions, and
- gain skills needed to deal with problems at school or in their daily lives.

Group guidance enables counselors to demonstrate to teachers that they can contribute to students' knowledge, skills, and well-being. It also gives counselors the opportunity to establish alliances with teachers desiring to help their students by integrating life skills with subject matter content or with teachers who identify specific issues they want addressed in the classroom.

Chief Theoretical Orientation

Historically, large group guidance has been used as a means of delivering information and providing experiences to help students prepare for problem situations before they arise. For example, large group guidance in elementary schools can be used to help younger students learn skills such as how to make friends, resolve conflicts, and take tests. In middle and high school, large group guidance interventions are used to help students make transitions from middle to high school, select courses in high school, and learn about college or financial aid information.

In both the ASCA Role Statement (1999) and Wittmer and Thompson's (2000) definitions, large group guidance is described as developmental. Myrick (1997) defined the developmental approach as an effort to identify specific skills and experiences that students need to be successful at school. Developmental counseling and developmental counseling programs focus on primary prevention and seek to promote positive development by delivering a prevention curriculum. The curriculum is called the guidance curriculum by some (Gysbers & Henderson, 1999). Large group guidance is the delivery system for the guidance curriculum.

If large group guidance is supposed to be developmental in nature, how do counselors determine what skills and experiences should be included in a developmental guidance curriculum? They do so by drawing upon human development theories, concepts, and principles such as those proposed by Piaget, Erikson, Kohlberg, Gilligan, Selman, Super, and Havighurst (Paisley & Benshoff, 1996). For example, advocates of developmental guidance propose using human developmental tasks as guides to identifying students' needs. A review of specific tasks will describe how they can be used to meet student needs.

Developmental Perspectives

Robert Havighurst (1972) noted that to progress through different stages of development, children and youth have to be successful in achieving or coping with certain tasks. He referred to them as developmental tasks and defined them in the following way:

> A developmental task is a task which arises at or about a certain period in the life of the individual, successful achievement of which leads to his or her happiness

and to success with later tasks, while failure leads to unhappiness in the individual, disapproval by the society, and difficulty with later tasks. (p. 8)

Havighurst (1953) described the following developmental tasks as ones that school-age children and youth must achieve:

Infancy and Early Childhood (ages 0–5)

1. Learning to walk,
2. Learning to eat solid food,
3. Learning to talk,
4. Learning to control elimination of body wastes,
5. Learning sex differences and modesty,
6. Forming concepts and learning language to describe social and physical reality,
7. Getting ready to read,
8. Learning to relate emotionally to family members, and
9. Learning to distinguish right and wrong and beginning to develop a conscience.

Middle Childhood (ages 6–11)

1. Learning physical skills necessary for ordinary games,
2. Building wholesome attitudes toward oneself and a sense of self-concept,
3. Learning to get along with age mates,
4. Learning to be tolerant and patient,
5. Learning appropriate social roles,
6. Developing concepts necessary for everyday living,
7. Developing conscience and morality, and
8. Achieving personal independence.

Adolescence (ages 12–19)

1. Achieving new and more mature relationships with peers,
2. Achieving sex-role identity,
3. Accepting one's physique and using the body effectively,
4. Achieving emotional independence of parents and other adults,
5. Preparing for marriage and family life,
6. Preparing for an economic career,

7. Acquiring a set of values and an ethical system as a guide to behavior, and
8. Desiring and achieving socially responsible behavior. (pp. 81–83)

Using developmental theories and concepts as a foundation for designing school counseling programs makes good sense and is not a new idea. Those employing this approach tend to see human development as a process of orderly, systematic, and continuous change in a valued direction (Blocher, 1987). Havighurst's (1953) developmental tasks represent this view of human development. Developmental school counselors can spend much of their time helping students gain skills to understand themselves, develop effective relationships with others, learn conflict resolution skills, set educational and career goals, value diversity, and make effective decisions. Their large group guidance interventions reflect students' developmental needs.

Expanding Perspectives

Some professionals question the use of human development theories and concepts as a foundation on which to build school counseling programs and counseling interventions. They suggest that nothing assures that change in the developing organism will be orderly, systematic, or even progress in a valued direction (Blocher, 1987; Sears, 2002). Having spent considerable time in urban schools, we can attest to the large number of children and youth whose lives are not unfolding in an orderly manner. In fact, they are experiencing significant gaps between the demands of their environment and their capacity to cope. These young people need assistance in acquiring the skills needed to cope with or even survive environmental demands such as serious poverty, health-related problems, dysfunctional family situations, and crime-ridden neighborhoods. To expect that a developmental guidance curriculum is going to meet all their needs is not realistic.

It is clear that children in many of our urban schools need more than developmental or preventative counseling (Gross & Capuzzi, 1996). They come to school not having accomplished the developmental tasks of early childhood. Their neighborhood and family environments have not been as supportive as those of children in more advantaged homes and communities such as the suburbs in which most educators live. How can large group guidance interventions serve the at-risk students who are populating our schools in larger and larger numbers? The answer to this question lies in expanding group guidance and school counseling in general to include more action-oriented or activist counseling (Sears, 2001). Activist school counseling recognizes that many students need more than developmental or preventative interventions. It recognizes that school counseling interventions must include student advocacy and systemic change if today's urban students are to succeed in school. Professional school counselors serve a social function to help students bridge the major discontinuities in their lives and overcome the barriers standing in the way of their positive growth and development (Blocher, 1987).

Moreover, school counselors, particularly in urban schools, are in a position to assist students who are at risk of not succeeding and help them acquire the skills to survive and grow. One important way to do this is by using large group guidance to help students learn skills they should have learned earlier either at home or at school. Many students need to learn how to replace dysfunctional responses to their environments with ones that increase their chances for success. For example, school counselors can include units focusing on self-control, anger management skills, and conflict-resolution skills in large group guidance classes in elementary, middle, and high school so those students who have not mastered those skills have additional opportunities to do so. Group guidance units for at-risk youth may need to be more intensive, thus taking longer than typical classroom guidance activities. In other words, school counselors need to be prepared to modify traditional, developmental group guidance to include guidance units focusing on issues that they may have only seen as appropriate in small groups or individual counseling.

A more activist approach to large group guidance builds on resiliency research that maintains there is a biological imperative for growth and development if protective environmental supports such as caring relationships, high expectations, and opportunities for meaningful participation are in place (Henderson, 2000). Large group guidance is one way to provide opportunities for students to participate meaningfully in discussions about important life skills and for counselors to model caring relationships and to demonstrate that they expect students to achieve and succeed.

Salient Research

Research about the effectiveness of large group guidance is sparse. In their review of school counseling outcome research, Whiston and Sexton (1998) cited twelve studies that could be characterized as interventions that were designed to serve all students and were classroom or group guidance activities. Several of those articles are reviewed in this section of the chapter and were chosen to illustrate the broad range of topics upon which large group guidance activities can be based.

Self-Esteem

Five studies used large group guidance to try to enhance the self-esteem or self-concept of elementary-age students, but three of the five studies found little or no differences between experimental and control groups. However, one study in which classroom guidance was used to promote wellness resulted in increased knowledge about wellness and increased self-esteem (Omizo, Omizo, & D'Andrea, 1992). Sixty-two fifth graders from two classrooms and ranging in age from 9.6 to 11.1 years participated. One classroom constituted the experimental group, and the other classroom was the control. This study is somewhat unique because the researchers trained a teacher to conduct the ten weekly guidance sessions lasting forty-five to sixty minutes each. The study attempted to promote lifestyle changes by teaching the children ways to remove obstacles to wellness and to increase their basic understanding of wellness, including nutrition, physical exercise, and stress management. Children who participated had higher levels of self-esteem (measured by the General Self-Esteem Scale) and increased knowledge about wellness (measured by Wellness Knowledge Test).

Study Skills

Carns and Carns (1991) reported that a study skills guidance program resulted in significant increases in students' standardized test scores. The program was designed to increase the self-efficacy, awareness of metacognitive skills, and knowledge of learning styles of 118 fourth graders. Participants in the program were pretested in the spring of third grade and posttested in the spring of their fourth-grade year. On average, those who participated improved three years and one month in grade equivalents on the California Test of Basic Skills. However, it is important to note that the students were all from upper-middle to upper class homes and no control group was used.

Multicultural Group Guidance

D'Andrea and Daniels (1995) described a study on multicultural group guidance in which the guidance program was effective in increasing social development of elementary students. The goal of this intervention was to help 117 third-grade elementary students in Honolulu to develop a variety of social and interpersonal skills to resolve conflicts that resulted from negative cultural or ethnic prejudices. The students were from low to low-middle socioeconomic backgrounds and were Hawaiian, Filipino, Korean, African American, European American (white), and from other Pacific Island groups. The Multicultural Guidance Project consisted of ten guidance sessions, once a week for ten weeks, and the lessons were delivered during students' homerooms. Teacher and student forms of the Social Skills Rating Inventory (SSRI) were used to assess students' social skills. Researchers reported there was a significant increase in the teachers' ratings of the students' social skills and a significant decrease in problem behaviors.

Career Guidance

Lapan, Gysbers, Hughey, and Arni (1993) reported on the evaluation of a program enhancing both the writing skills and the career development of high school juniors. All honors and nonhonors juniors (166) attending a suburban midwestern public high school participated in thirteen guidance sessions during eight weeks. School counselors and teachers teamed on a language arts and career guidance unit in which students had the opportunity to take aptitude and interest inventories and use occupational and educational reference materials and computerized career information to explore occupations related to their interests and aptitudes. The English teachers emphasized selecting and using references, organizing information for personal use, summarizing information, and using various sources of information. More than 90 percent of the students said that the guidance and language arts unit was beneficial. Significant changes in pre-post vocational identity scores were found for both boys and girls.

Counselors need to conduct more research on large group guidance as an effective intervention. The studies reviewed above demonstrate the breadth of topics that can be researched. Later in this chapter, the evaluation of large group guidance interventions is discussed. Carefully planned evaluations of group interventions can be a first step toward more research on the effect of this important counseling intervention.

Practical Applications

When *guidance,* the term applied to what we now call school counseling, first appeared in schools, it had a curriculum that evolved from the social reform movements of the latter nineteenth and early twentieth centuries (Baker, 1992). For example, Jess B. Davis, a high school principal in Grand Rapids, Michigan, set one period a week in the English composition classes for vocational and moral guidance (Baker, 1992; Gibson & Mitchell, 1999). School counselors engage in instructional or pedagogical activities when delivering many group programs (Baker, 1992). Given that reality, school counselors must learn how to instruct effectively.

Large Group Guidance Facilitation Skills

Today, many school counseling trainees are coming from outside the field of education. Thirty-nine states do not require school counselors to be certified or licensed as teachers prior to becoming school counselors. It is important, therefore, that school counselors acquire some of the facilitation skills that teachers use, such as planning, instructing, applying, and evaluating.

Planning

Effective planning requires that school counselors determine target populations, assess student needs, write measurable objectives, and design the group guidance lesson or unit.

Determining Target Population. The student-to-counselor ratio in many schools is so high (600 or 700 students to one counselor) that counselors may need to be creative in how they determine their target groups. For example, Mr. Jay Young is one elementary school counselor in a school with 750 students in kindergarten through grade 5. Mr. Young decided to schedule his guidance interventions monthly. In October he worked with the kindergarten students, in November with the first-grade classes, in December, the second-grade classes, and so on, until he progressed through the fifth grade.

Students in some grades or classrooms may need the counselor's help more than others. Mr. Young may have to decide if he should work more with one grade than with the others. For example, Ms. Jones's third-grade class may be fighting more on the playground or causing more disruptions in the lunchroom. Mr. Young, probably in consultation with the principal and teachers, needs to determine the best use of his time. Spending more time with the third-grade class may create a better learning environment in the entire school. While it may seem that Mr. Young is not serving students equally, he is contributing to a more stable environment for all students.

Assessing Student Needs. Collecting data to ensure you are planning guidance units that meet students' needs is critical. Counselors can collect two kinds of data: archival data, or data that already exists, and survey data, or data that you create. Examples of archival data are attendance records, discipline records, test scores, and dropout rates. Survey data can be collected using short questionnaires that counselors create and administer to students, staff, or both. Low test scores may suggest that the students need to improve their learning and study skills and/or their test-taking skills. Also, discipline records often indicate which students are experiencing adjustment problems or having trouble controlling their anger.

If the target population consists of elementary-age students (or students in middle or high school), it is possible to focus on helping students to achieve one of Havighurst's (1953) developmental tasks. Havighurst suggested that students from ages six to twelve should learn how to be tolerant and patient. Therefore, a large group guidance unit in which students learn about the strengths of different cultures would be appropriate. This type of guidance unit could be integrated into a social studies class at the elementary, middle, or high school, providing an opportunity for the counselor to team with a teacher or teachers.

Writing Measurable Objectives to Meet Needs. A measurable objective is a clear, concise statement of a goal including how to determine if the goal has or has not been reached. Writing measurable objectives helps you think systematically about what you want to accomplish, and it also lays the groundwork for evaluating your large group guidance interventions. Examples of measurable career objectives for high school students appear below:

At the end of the first year of high school, students will:

- Describe two areas of interest using the Harrington-O'Shea (Harrington, 2000) classification system.
- Identify three careers that reflect their interests and abilities.
- Describe the course of study available in their high school to help them prepare for the careers they have chosen to explore.

Designing the Group Guidance Unit. Researching the content of the guidance unit and developing the lesson plan are important parts of the planning process. To prepare a thorough unit, you will have to locate and read books and journals as well as exploring web sites.

The topics of group guidance can be varied: social and emotional competency skills, problem solving, anger management, conflict resolution, alcohol and other drug awareness, grade-level transitions, grief and loss, financial aid, selecting colleges, sexual harassment, test-taking skills, and so on. Remember, you currently are learning skills in your counselor education program that can be translated into large group guidance lessons/units later in your career. Some examples are communication skills, decision-making processes, how to change irrational thinking, career planning and exploration, clarifying values, and managing stress. While you are preparing to become a school counselor, you should begin to build a resource library that you can draw upon once you graduate.

Once you have researched the content of the guidance unit, you are ready to develop the lesson plan. Lesson plans consist of several components: measurable objectives, the content and activities designed to implement the objectives, materials and resources needed, homework if appropriate, and evaluation strategies. Review the sample lesson plan provided.

SAMPLE LESSON PLAN FOR A GROUP GUIDANCE UNIT

(Middle or High School Students)

TITLE: Identifying My Interests

OBJECTIVES: After completing this group guidance unit, students will:

1. Identify two career interest areas.
2. Identify two careers related to their interest areas.
3. Describe the skills needed to succeed in each career.
4. Describe the working conditions and salary associated with each of the careers.

CONTENT AND ACTIVITIES

Session One: Ask students to define interests and discuss how interests are acquired. Give examples of how interests relate to occupational/career choices. Introduce them to the Harrington-O'Shea Career Decision-Making System (Harrington, 2000) and have them complete the interest inventory. Explain how they can score the interest inventory and see their results immediately (use transparencies to make certain students understand how to score and interpret the instrument). Collect the instruments and place them in manila folders.

Session Two: Return the interest inventories to the students. Use two of the students' results to demonstrate how to interpret the inventory (seek the permission of the two students to use their results prior to the session). Use a laptop computer and the Internet connection in the classroom (use the school library if classrooms do not have Internet connections) and log onto the *Occupational Outlook Handbook* (OOH; http://stats.bls.gov/ocohome.htm). Using one of the student's interests, demonstrate to the other students how they can find information about occupations that relate to their interests. If possible, use an LCD projector to project the information on a large screen so the students can follow easily. If an LCD is not available, create a handout that allows students to follow your demonstration or use transparencies to assist them in viewing your demonstration. Illustrate how the OOH can help them find related occupations, skills needed to succeed in occupations, working conditions, and salary. Inform them that session 3 will meet in the computer lab (after consultation with the teacher) and, with the help of the technology teacher, each student will have the opportunity to explore occupations related to his or her interests.

Session Three: Students report to computer lab. Counselor and teacher working together show students how to locate the *Occupational Outlook Handbook* and explore occupations related to their interests. Both the teacher and counselor are available to assist students in their searches. Students are encouraged to go to related Internet sites to continue their occupational explorations. Distribute a Career Profile sheet that asks students to record two interests, two occupations that are related to those interests, skills needed to succeed in those occupations, as well as the working conditions and salaries.

MATERIALS/RESOURCES

Harrington-O'Shea Career Decision-Making System Revised (Harrington, 2000) for thirty students, access to the computer lab and Internet connection, fifteen copies of the *Occupational Outlook Handbook* (if computers are not available), overhead transparencies, and Career Profile worksheets (forms that a counselor designs for this unit).

EVALUATION

During the last fifteen minutes of the 60-minute session, lead a discussion focusing on what the students learned about their interests, skills, and possible occupational choices. Collect the Career Profile to evaluate the effectiveness of the three sessions and to maintain a career profile on each student. Use these records again when helping the students develop or review their educational plans for high school.

Instructing

Instructing includes the behaviors that professionals need to communicate clearly and accurately, use questioning and discussion techniques, engage students in learning, provide feedback to students, and demonstrate flexibility.

Communicate Clearly and Accurately.   You have learned how to communicate clearly and accurately with individuals and small groups. In large group guidance, you need to be able to use those same skills with many more clients all congregated in the same space. Just as you practice your individual and small group counseling skills, so do you need to practice your large group guidance skills. Standing in front of a classroom of twenty-five or thirty students can be challenging. You must have thought carefully about what you intend to say. The volume and tone of your voice is important. To be heard in a large room, you will have to learn how to project your voice. This is a skill that requires repetition to perfect. Your tone is critical. Have you learned to sound both businesslike and warm? Try audiotaping or videotaping classroom guidance sessions during your internship. Ask you instructor or peers to critique your communication skills.

Use Questioning and Discussion Techniques. Asking open-ended questions such as, "What do you think?" or "What is your reaction to that idea?" or "What interests you?" are the types of questions that invite students to give their opinion. As students share their opinions and beliefs, continued group discussion can be fostered if you continue to ask questions or invite comments, including for example: "Who agrees with that opinion and why?" and "Who holds a different opinion and why?"

Engage Students in Learning. The main reason for using questioning and discussion techniques is to engage students in learning. It is also important to involve students in activities to foster their learning. Dividing students into smaller groups ranging from dyads to groups of five or six to complete an activity designed to implement your objectives is another useful way to engage them. Note the activity in the Sample Lesson Plan above. Students actually take an interest inventory and then access the Internet to explore occupations. Regardless of the age group (elementary, middle, or high school students), involving students in appropriate activities is more effective than just asking them to listen to information.

Provide Feedback to Students. In large group guidance discussions, you must be able to give feedback quickly and succinctly. "Interesting comment," "I like that idea," "You sound like you have given the issue a lot of thought," and "Say a little more about that" are all examples of feedback. You may feel like you are repeating yourself over and over again. But students hear what you say to them, and if you say nothing in response to their comments, they can misread your silence as rejection.

Demonstrate Flexibility and a Sense of Humor. Anyone who has worked with large groups, particularly classroom groups, has discovered that flexibility and a sense of humor are valuable tools. Students often are unpredictable both in actions and in speech. Sometimes they say and do things to draw attention, but in other instances they are just expressing their ideas openly, not recognizing the implications of what they are saying. Elementary-age children, in particular, may tell you and their classmates private, personal information that you will want to acknowledge but then quickly move on. Discussions on various topics can go in directions you had not anticipated. If the discussion seems relevant, you will want to be flexible enough to deviate from your lesson plan and take advantage of what teachers refer to as a teachable moment.

If you utilize large group guidance interventions extensively, you will make mistakes. You may say something that makes no sense or leaves an impression other than the one you intended. You may misspell a word on your handout or transparency. Students are quick to pick up on and point out any and all mistakes. Learning how to laugh and poke fun at your own mistakes allows students to see you as a human being who can make mistakes but handles them well.

Anytime you are facilitating classroom guidance, you are modeling for the students. Ideally, you should model an open communicator who values their ideas and opinions and is there to help them confront life's challenges.

Applying

One of the primary goals of group guidance is to help students transfer the information and skills they are acquiring to situations in their own lives. Whether or not students generalize the skills and information to other situations is the true test of whether the large group guidance intervention is worth the time and energy spent. Therefore, counselors should design activities in which students can apply what they are being taught and then receive feedback on their work. An example may illustrate this point. Jane Jones, a high school counselor, is conducting group guidance sessions to help students learn how to conduct college searches. First, she presents students with ideas on what to look for when deciding which colleges they want to visit, such as academic majors offered, the scope of extracurricular activities available, geographical location, and cost. Second, students develop a checklist to help them gather information when they visit the college either in person or via the Internet. Third, Ms. Jones organizes a field trip to a local college, and the students use their checklist to gather information. Upon returning to the school, Ms. Jones leads a discussion in which the students share the information they gathered plus the perceptions gained through their on-site experiences. The students conclude the experience by profiling the students who may possibly benefit by attending that particular college. The field trip to the college has enabled them to apply the checklist of relevant information in a real-world assignment. Regardless of whether the students attend that college, they have acquired the information and skills needed to conduct college searches.

Evaluating

Evaluating group guidance interventions lets you know if you are meeting the needs of your target populations, provides you with information about the success or effectiveness of your guidance program, and improves your guidance program.

Accountability is very important in today's schools, and you need to be able to provide evaluative information to the principal, teachers, and parents. Two kinds of data are useful: quantitative data (How many students did you serve as a result of group guidance interventions?) and qualitative data (What did the students think about your guidance sessions?). Some ways you can collect data include the following:

- Administer a pre- and postlesson questionnaire to determine what the students learned as a result of the intervention. For example, review our Sample Lesson Plan again. A pre-post test for that group guidance intervention could be as easy as asking students to list two interests, list two careers that relate to their interests, and describe the skills, working conditions, and salary associated with those careers. The pretest and posttest responses should be quite different and will allow you to determine how well students mastered the desired objectives.
- Develop and administer a questionnaire that targets the objectives at the end of the guidance sessions. Don't ask students to put their names on the questionnaires.
- Conduct exit interviews with representative samples of students, asking them questions that help you determine if they have mastered the objectives the intervention was designed to achieve.

Multicultural and Diversity Issues

The ASCA National Standards for School Counseling Programs, while not addressing multicultural issues directly, include a standard that promotes students' respect for themselves and others: Standard A: Students will acquire the attitudes, knowledge, and interpersonal skills to help them understand and respect self and others (Dahir, Sheldon, & Valiga, 1998, p. 12).

Large group guidance is one way that counselors can increase students' understanding of the values and behaviors of different cultures or subcultures. In many schools, multicultural and diversity issues are discussed in the social studies classes. Offering to work with social studies teachers to develop classroom guidance activities to apply the multicultural concepts being taught in their classes can result in positive collaboration between counselors and teachers as well as increase the respect that students have for individual differences.

Counselors must also be conscious that their behavior toward different cultures, ethnicities, and religions in their schools can set a model for others to emulate. If counselors demonstrate inclusive behaviors by interacting with all students in a positive and supportive manner, then they are modeling acceptance and respect. Students learn from the behavior of adults. In addition, counselors also model acceptance and respect for all students when they commit to removing barriers to student learning such as watered-down curricula or low teacher expectations for student success. By advocating for a rigorous education for and fairness to students regardless of ethnicity, religion, disability, cultural background, or sexual orientation, they are modeling the acceptance and respect that students should be able to expect from the staff in their schools.

Legal and Ethical Issues

When students feel comfortable with counselors, they share information about themselves and their family. In individual counseling sessions, only counselors hear personal information or family problems. Thus, counselors have time to process whatever the student says and can remind students that confidentiality protects them in most situations. However, confidentiality does not exist in large group guidance, but be aware that some students still share personal information. Counselors need to be prepared for comments or responses they are not expecting. Elementary students, in particular, may blurt out, "My dad beats me with a belt when he is angry" or "My dad hit my mother." Responding to comments like these can be challenging, and students will observe closely how counselors respond both verbally and nonverbally. Counselor responses such as "That's important so let's you and I talk about that privately" are usually effective enough to prevent the student's comment from diverting the attention of the entire class. Completing the group guidance session and then following up with the student is a reasonable way to proceed.

In the example used above, child or spousal abuse might be a problem in that student's home. Most states require counselors or any school staff who suspects child abuse to report their suspicions to the proper authorities. Counselors need to know the laws relating to child abuse in their states so they can act both legally and ethically when needed.

While confidentiality does not apply in large group guidance, counselors can still help students and teachers understand that students' privacy is important. Counselors should establish ground rules in large group guidance just as they do in small group counseling. Ground rules can bring discipline and order to large group guidance without limiting students' expression. Examples of appropriate rules include the following:

- One person talks at a time.
- Don't interrupt when someone else is talking.
- Listen to what others are saying.
- Show respect for different ideas and opinions.
- When others make personal comments, respect their privacy.

Ground rules also are one way that counselors can take reasonable precautions to protect students from other students and can help keep in check the students who like to tease or intentionally demean other students.

Counselors frequently use large group guidance to provide interpretations of career interest inventories, aptitude tests, or achievement tests. Counselors are obligated to provide the clear and understandable interpretation of whatever tests they are explaining and should also be very careful not to divulge the results or scores of any students. Developing a fictitious example of a student's scores to explain test results can facilitate a good explanation without discussing an individual student's test results.

Closing Comments

Large group guidance is one of the four primary interventions that school counselors can use to help students succeed in school and in life. It can be used as a delivery system for both preventive and remedial counseling and enables counselors to reach large numbers of students. Large group guidance requires careful planning, effective instruction, opportunities for students to apply what is being learned, and systematic evaluation to determine its effectiveness.

This chapter included a sample lesson plan for you to review. The plan focused on the career development needs of high school students. The appendix in this chapter provides another example of a large group guidance unit. This one is appropriate for third- through fifth-grade students. The unit can be used as is or modified to meet the needs of your students. Working with classroom or large groups can be challenging. Practice will improve your skills.

Any School District
School Counseling Program:
Classroom Guidance Curriculum

Grades 3–5: Lessons for Three Class Periods

Title: Good Study Habits Can Lead to Academic Success

ASCA National Standard.   Academic Standard A: Students will demonstrate the attitudes, knowledge, and skills that contribute to effective learning in school and across the life span.

Objectives:

After completing this guidance unit, students will:

1. Describe how to get organized to study.
2. Identify effective and ineffective study habits.
3. Describe how to improve their study area at home.
4. Describe what they need to do before, during, and after a test to ensure their best performance.

Content and Activities:

Lesson One: Begin the lesson by asking if anyone knows the definition of a study habit. Allow time for responses. It should be explained that *study habits* are what people do each time they do homework or engage in other study activities. Explain that habits may be effective or ineffective. Using the whiteboard or chalkboard or a transparency, make two columns. Label one column "Effective Study Habits" and the other column "Ineffective Study Habits." Give the following example, and ask students to categorize it as effective or ineffective. *Note: This example illustrates to students that they must plan time to study. It is not effective to try to watch television and do homework at the same time.*

Example: Suzy is on the floor in front of the television with her homework in front of her. She is really interested in the program on television and only looks at her books during the commercials. Is this a good study situation? Is Suzy doing her best work? What should she do? Should we list this on the chart as an effective way to study? Why?

Use the list of habits below and ask the students to categorize the items on the list as effective or ineffective study habits. (Putting these on an overhead transparency or chart paper will make it easier for students to read and think about each habit.)

Study Habits

1. Doing your homework when the radio is playing very loudly
2. Studying at home in a nice quiet study area with a desk and a chair
3. Starting your homework after dinner
4. Developing a study schedule and sharing it with your mother or other family member
5. Asking your brother or sister to help you with math if you get stuck
6. Completing your homework and putting it in your backpack or notebook before you watch any evening television

Then, distribute the handout entitled "Ready . . . Set . . . Get Organized: Tips" (see handout for lesson one, page 209). The handout includes five effective study habits. Discuss each of the tips with the students and ask them if they are currently practicing these habits:

1. Write down all assignments and when they are due.
2. Write down when tests are scheduled.
3. Check off completed assignments.
4. Write down special instructions.
5. Ask questions if you are confused.

Lesson Two: Effective Study Habits: Finding a Place to Study   Direct students to complete the "Finding a Place to Study" worksheet (see handout for lesson two, page 210). Read/work through the questions on the worksheet and encourage a brief discussion of each question. Once you complete the worksheet, ask students to describe how they can improve their study area at home. List their responses on the chalkboard or on a transparency. Ask students to write their name and one way they intend to improve their study area on an index card.

At the end of lesson two, collect the index cards and review them. In one week, return them to the class and ask students to share how they have improved their study area. Take the cards they completed the week before to remind you (and them) of what they wrote.

Lesson Three: Preparing and Taking Tests   The counselor should explain to students that tests are one way that students can show teachers and parents what they have learned. Also, tests influence the grades students receive on their report cards, so they should do the best work they can. Divide students into three groups. Designate group 1 as the "Before the Test" group, group 2 as the "Taking the Test" group, and group 3 as the "After the Test" group. *Note: If you have over twenty students in the classroom, you may want to form two groups designated as 1, 2, and so on. The groups should have no more than five or six students.*

Give all students index cards. Ask the students in group(s) 1 to write tips or things they should do to prepare before the test. Ask group 2 to write what they should do while taking the test. Ask group 3 to write what they should do after the test. This part of the activity should take ten to fifteen minutes. While the students are working, tape three large sheets of construction or chart paper on the wall. Ask each group, taking turns, to tape the index cards with their tips to the chart that coincides with the number of their group. After the students have completed placing their tips on the charts, read several of the tips on each chart to the class. Ask students to discuss briefly if they think the tip would help them or not. Distribute the handout for Lesson Three (page 210), "Test Taking." Ask the students to review it and add any additional tips that would help them. Encourage the students to keep the worksheet in their notebook so they can refer to it as needed.

Materials/Resources Needed:

Whiteboard or chalkboard, markers or chalk, worksheets, transparencies for overheads

Evaluation:

Students have learned tips for getting organized, the difference between effective and ineffective study habits, how to find a quiet place to study, and how to prepare and take tests. In other words, they have identified study skills that are necessary for academic success. You can evaluate this activity in several ways. You can ask each student to write, from memory, four or five study skills that can help them achieve and then collect what they have written so you can evaluate the effectiveness of the unit. Or you could give each student a postcard and ask them to write three study skills they plan to practice. Ask them to address the card to themselves, collect the cards and, in two weeks, mail them to the students as a reminder of the skills they have committed to practice. This latter evaluation lets you review what they have written and reinforce their learning later.

Handout for Lesson One
Ready . . . Set . . . Get Organized "Tips"

- Write down all assignments and when they are due.
- Write down when tests are scheduled.
- Check off completed assignments.
- Write down special instructions.
- Ask if you are confused.

Handout for Lesson Two
Finding a Place to Study

Planning time to study is not enough for success. You also need a place where you can concentrate on your work. The best place is one where you feel motivated to study. For some students, that means absolute quiet. Others prefer music playing softly in the background. A place of study should have certain things. The lighting should be bright so you can read easily. It should have space for you to spread out your work, and it should have a dictionary and materials such as paper and pencils for you to use.

Is the area where you study at home the best place for you? Do you need to change things to make it better? Answer the following questions to help you decide.

1. Where do you study? _____

2. Is the place where you study away from loud talking and noises that break your concentration? If not, what can you do about it?

_____

3. Does the place have good lighting? If it doesn't, what can you do about it?

_____

4. Is there a table or desk where you can spread out your work and study materials? If not, how can you make more space?

_____

Here are some things you should have on hand when you are studying. Put a check next to the things you have.

_____Paper	_____Eraser	_____Stapler or paper clips
_____Scratch paper	_____Ruler	_____Clock or watch
_____Pencils	_____Scissors	_____Waste basket
_____Pens	_____Tape	_____Dictionary

What else do you need to help you study effectively?

Handout for Lesson Three
Test Taking
"1-2-3"

1 = Before the Test
- Study and do your homework.
- Go to bed early the night before.
- Eat breakfast.
- Bring the right tools (pencils, scratch paper, etc.).
- Relax.
- Think positive.
- Breathe deeply.

2 = Taking the Test
- Make sure you understand the directions.
- Ask for help if you are confused.
- Work at your own speed—it's not a race.
- Use time wisely—pay attention and stay on task.
- Write neatly.
- Answer easy questions first.
- Guessing is okay if you choose the "best guess" from the possible answers.
- Look for "key words" such as *only, never, always,* and *all.*
- Never give up! Keep working.
- Check over your test when you are finished.

3 = After the Test
- Remain quiet if others are still testing.
- Remember that tests have value—they tell us what we know and what we still need to learn.
- Learn from the results.

REFERENCES

American School Counselor Association. (1999). *Role statement: The school counselor.* Alexandria, VA: Author.

Baker, S. B. (1992). *School counselors for the twenty-first century.* New York: Macmillan.

Blocher, D. H. (1987). *The professional counselor.* New York: Macmillan.

Carns, A. W., & Carns, M. R. (1991). Teaching study skills, cognitive strategies, and metacognitive skills through self-diagnosed learning styles. *The School Counselor, 38,* 341–346.

Dahir, C. A., Sheldon, C. B., & Valiga, M. J. (1998). *Vision into action: Implementing the national standards for school counseling programs.* Alexandria, VA: American School Counselor Association.

D'Andrea, M., & Daniels, J. (1995). Helping students learn to get along: Assessing the effectiveness of a multicultural development guidance project. *Elementary School Guidance and Counseling, 30,* 143–154.

Gibson, R. L., & Mitchell, M. H. (1999). *Introduction to counseling and guidance* (5th ed.). Upper Saddle River, NJ: Prentice Hall.

Gross, D. R., & Capuzzi, D. (1996). Defining youth at risk. In D. Capuzzi & D. R. Gross (Eds.), *Youth at risk: A prevention resource for counselors, teachers, and parents* (2nd ed., pp. 3–17). Alexandria, VA: American Counseling Association.

Gysbers, N. C., & Henderson, P. (1999). *Developing and managing your school guidance program* (3rd ed.). Washington, DC: American Counseling Association.

Harrington, T. F. (2000). *The Harrington-O'Shea Career Decision-Making System Revised.* Retrieved November 7, 2002, from http://www.arbeitsamt.de/laa_bb/international/InhaltKongressB/B61Harrington.pdf

Havighurst, R. J. (1953). *Human development and education.* New York: Longmans, Green.

Havighurst, R. J. (1972). *Developmental tasks and education* (3rd ed.). New York: David McKay.

Henderson, N. (2000). Resiliency in schools: Making it happen. In N. Henderson, B. Benard, & N. Sharp-Light (Eds.), *Schoolwide approaches for fostering resiliency* (pp. 3–8). San Diego, CA: Resiliency in Action.

Lapan, R. T., Gysbers, N., Hughey, K., & Arni, T. J. (1993). Evaluating a guidance and language arts unit for high school juniors. *Journal of Counseling & Development, 71,* 444–451.

Myrick, R. D. (1997). *Developmental guidance and counseling: A practical approach* (3rd ed.). Minneapolis, MN: Educational Media.

Omizo, M. M., Omizo, S. A., & D'Andrea, M. J. (1992). Promoting wellness among elementary school children. *Journal of Counseling & Development, 71,* 194–198.

Paisley, P. O., & Benshoff, J. M. (1996). Applying developmental principles to practice: Training issues for the professional development of school counselors. *Elementary School Guidance and Counseling, 30,* 163–169.

Sears, S. J. (2001). *Activist counseling.* [Brochure]. Columbus, OH: Author.

Sears, S. J. (2002). School counseling now and in the future: A reaction. *The Professional School Counselor, 5,* 164–172.

Whiston, S. C., & Sexton, T. (1998). A review of school counseling outcome research: Implications for practice. *Journal of Counseling & Development, 76,* 412–426.

Wittmer, J., & Thompson, D. (2000). *Large group guidance activities: A K-12 sourcebook.* Minneapolis, MN: Educational Media.

CHAPTER 7

Preparing Students for the Future: Career and Educational Planning

Kenneth F. Hughey
Kansas State University

Preparing students for their future is a critical task and responsibility for schools. It involves school counselors and key stakeholders (e.g., teachers, administrators, parents) playing an integral role in facilitating the career development of students. Career and educational planning and preparation are important components of facilitating students' career development. As stated by Herr and Cramer (1996), "Career development proceeds—smoothly, jaggedly, positively, negatively—whether or not career guidance or career education exists. As such, career development is not an intervention but the object of an intervention" (p. 32). It follows, then, that to enhance and facilitate the career development of students and their career and educational planning, school counselors should work collaboratively with key stakeholders to implement relevant programs, activities, and interventions in a systematic, intentional manner.

Career development has been defined as the "total constellation of psychological, sociological, educational, physical, economic, and chance factors that combine to shape the career of any given individual over the life span" (Sears, 1982, p. 139). Given the breadth of this definition, addressing issues that prepare students for the future is integral to their educational program, spans their educational career, and continues into the future. Further, given the complexities and challenges students will face, it is imperative that they be effectively prepared for the future.

Parsons (1909) addressed the importance of preparing students for the future. He stated:

> We guide our boys and girls to some extent through school, then drop them into this complex world to sink or swim as the case may be. Yet there is no part of life where the need for guidance is more emphatic than in the transition from school to work—the choice of a vocation, adequate preparation for it, and the attainment of efficiency and success. The building of a career is quite as difficult a problem as the building of a house, yet few ever sit down with pencil and paper, with expert information and counsel, to plan a working career and deal with the life problem scientifically, as they would deal with the problem of building a house, taking the advice of an architect to help them. (p. 4)

The complexity of today's world requires that career and educational planning and preparation for students be a priority for the educational systems, including school guidance and counseling programs. Wrenn (1962) stated: "The adolescent faces increasingly a world of new conditions and new opportunities, a world where occupations change as well as values" (p. 7). As will be discussed, these changes continue and emphasize the need for making career development programs a priority for all students (Feller & Davies, 1999; Hughey & Hughey, 1999).

In particular, school counselors implementing comprehensive school guidance and counseling programs (Gysbers & Henderson, 2000) have a critical role to play in addressing the career and educational planning needs of students. Through their collaborative efforts with key stakeholders, students can be more effectively prepared for career and educational opportunities. These collaborative efforts have been advocated by Hoyt (1981) and Hoyt and Wickwire (1999), and are essential to effectively prepare students for their future.

Positive outcomes have been found for schools with more fully implemented comprehensive guidance and counseling programs. Lapan, Gysbers, and Sun (1997), for example, showed that schools with more fully implemented programs had students who reported they were better prepared for the future. In addition, students reported that more information regarding educational and career opportunities was available to them. As a result, a focus on enhancing the career development of students in the context of comprehensive school guidance and counseling programs seems important and productive. Further, based on a meta-analysis of career education interventions, Baker and Taylor (1998) stated the following:

> Given the continuing need to help children and adolescents prepare for the transitions from school to work, the career education goals, first presented about three decades ago, still seem to be salient. Consequently, interventions designed to achieve those goals seem salient as well. (p. 382)

Helping students explore, plan, and make educational and career decisions, and develop career and educational goals are critical responsibilities of school counselors, educators, and key stakeholders. The challenge is to effectively prepare students to be contributing members of society. As noted in *Breaking Ranks* (National Association of Secondary School Principals, 1996), "A young person who grows into adulthood unequipped to reach his or her full potential will possess neither the knowledge nor the will to contribute to making this a better society" (p. 4).

The purpose of this chapter is to present information that addresses issues relevant to student career development, facilitating career and educational planning, and preparing students for the future. First, the changing workplace and the skills needed to be successful will be addressed. Understanding the changes occurring is essential for professionals and should be addressed through the learning experiences provided for students and in the information provided to parents. This will be followed by a discussion of three career development theories presented to help conceptualize interventions to facilitate student career development. Then, issues and considerations for career and educational planning activities at the elementary, middle, and high school levels will be considered. Following this, examples of activities are presented. The intent is to provide an overview of relevant issues and to present resources for further study and exploration. It is hoped that a case will be made for the importance of career and educational planning for all students and that readers will be energized to make this a high priority in their work with students and key stakeholders.

The Changing Workplace and Implications for Student Planning

As professionals work to facilitate the career and educational planning of students, it is important to consider the changing workplace. Over the past twenty years, there have been a number of changes in the workplace that likely impact students' career and educational planning. As an example, consider the following ideas for today's students and compare these to the way it was for their grandparents: job security, workplace competitiveness, and rate of change. Feller (2002) noted these contextual factors as being significantly different. In general, there is a lowered sense of security, workplace competitiveness has increased, and the rate of change has increased. In addition, consider the impact of a global economy and technology. Clearly, these issues have the potential to impact the manner in which students are prepared for the future and the skills needed to be successful.

To summarize, the changing workplace requires students to be adequately prepared to enhance their competitiveness and help them become valuable contributors to society.

Changing Workplace

The workplace has evolved and changed, resulting in factors that must be considered as school counselors and stakeholders work with students to enhance and facilitate their career development and effectively prepare them for the future. Over time, the workplace has changed from being characterized as agricultural to industrial to information-oriented, knowledge-based (Toffler & Toffler, 1995). The emerging workplace is characterized by organizations that have become flatter as a result of fewer layers of management (Feller, 1996a). In the traditional workplace, mass production is emphasized "by workers who are not asked to think about what they are doing" (Secretary's Commission on Achieving Necessary Skills [SCANS], 1991, p. 3). In contrast, work in the emerging workplace is "problem-oriented, flexible, and organized by teams; labor is not a cost but an investment" (SCANS, 1991, p. 3). The evolving workplace emphasizes quality, variety, customization, convenience, service exceeding expectations, and time-based competition (Feller, 2002). Also, the emerging workplace values innovation, acceptance of broader responsibilities, and greater agility (Feller, 2002). The following summarizes changes noted by Feller (1996b):

Traditional Workplace	Emerging Workplace
Centralized control	Decentralized control
Individual worker tasks	Work teams, multiskilled workers
"That's not my job" view	Increased "dejobbing" view
Mass production	Flexible production
"Entitlement ethic"	"Psychology of earning ethic"
Company dependent career	"Own your own job, skills, and career"
Workers as a cost	Workers as an investment
Advancement by seniority	Advancement by skill documentation
Narrow skills for some	Broader skills for all
Little concern for foreign markets	Great concern for foreign markets and alliances

DeBell (2001) noted additional changes that included the following: demographic changes, racial and ethnic change, changes in educational level achieved, gender distribution of the workforce, changes in wages and hours worked, labor unions and reform, globalization, and technological changes. Reardon, Lenz, Sampson, and Peterson (2000) noted a change in the social contract. Being loyal to the organization resulted in workers being kept as employees; however, this contract has changed. Being aware of these changes and understanding their impact provides information to help understand the environment for which students are preparing. Further, this information is relevant to parents and teachers who work with students to facilitate their career and educational planning.

Skills for the Future

According to the SCANS (1991) report,

> A strong back, the willingness to work, and a high school diploma were once all that was needed to make a start in America. They are no longer. A well-developed mind, a passion to learn, and the ability to put knowledge to work are the new keys to the future of our young people, the success of our businesses, and economic well-being of the nation. (p. 1)

With the changes noted, it is important to consider the skills and knowledge needed to successfully prepare students for the future. Developing these skills would enhance the career and educational preparation and the career development of students. In addition to the skills that add value to the individual, it is important to know the rules of the workplace, some of which have changed or been adapted over time.

The following competencies were identified in the SCANS (1991) report as important:

1. Resources: Identifies, organizes, plans, and allocates resources;
2. Interpersonal: Works with others;
3. Information: Acquires and uses information;
4. Systems: Understands complex inter-relationships; and
5. Technology: Works with a variety of technologies. (p. xvii)

In addition, the SCANS report identified three foundation skills:

1. Basic skills: Reading, writing, mathematics, listening, and speaking;
2. Thinking skills: Creative thinking, decision making, problem solving, seeing things in the mind's eye, knowing how to learn, and reasoning; and
3. Personal qualities: Individual responsibility, self-esteem, sociability, self-management, and integrity.

Hartley, Mantle-Bromley, and Cobb (1996) identified themes related to basic skills needed to be successful. The basic skills include (a) learning to learn; (b) reading, writing, and mathematics; (c) communication; (d) problem solving; (e) personal/career development; (f) interpersonal skills; (g) organizational effectiveness; (h) technology; (i) science; and (j) family. In general, it seems important that school counselors and educators involved in the career and educational planning of students inform students of the skills needed to be successful and seek ways to make these a part of students' educational programs. To be prepared, students, as prospective workers, will need both technical skills and interpersonal skills (Rojewski, 2002). In addition, they will need skills that involve flexibility, creative thinking, conflict resolution, and reflection skills. It follows, then, that knowledge is a valuable and essential resource in the emerging workplace (Drucker, 1994; Toffler & Toffler, 1995).

In addition, as noted, some of the rules have changed. The following are examples: "Work hard, and you will always have a job" and "If you work hard, you will be rewarded." Moses (1998) presented the following: "If your company is profitable, your job is secure" (p. 8) and "If you receive outstanding performance ratings, you should be confident of a rosy future" (p. 8).

In summary, the level of skills needed to be successful in the changing workplace has increased. Helping students and their parents become aware of these changes is important as students prepare for the future. Further, these skills can be addressed as part of students' educational programs and further developed as they determine appropriate next steps.

Implications for Professionals

There are a number of implications for school counselors, teachers, and key stakeholders as they work collaboratively to facilitate the career development of students and effectively prepare them for their future. These ideas may be used by school counselors to impact decisions that influence the career and educational planning of students. Implications include the following:

1. According to Hull (2000), "The issue is not 'skills versus knowledge' for some students. Rather, it is the appropriate combination of skills and knowledge for all students" (p. 3).
2. Lifelong or continuous learning is a requirement for the future.
3. Effective career guidance and planning are essential for the evolving workplace.
4. Success is related to improvement (Feller, 2002).

5. Help and encourage students to seek ways to add value personally and in relation to society.
6. Expand learning opportunities for students.
7. Provide challenging, relevant learning experiences for students.
8. Encourage students to try. As Feller (2002) noted, "Talent comes from focused effort and directed commitment" (p. 10).
9. Encourage students to view jobs as problems to be solved (Feller, 2002).

Readers are encouraged to consider additional implications (e.g., economic, social, workplace) that follow from the changes and the potential impact these may have on student career and educational planning and preparation. These can be used as the basis for developing and implementing activities and interventions as part of comprehensive school guidance and counseling programs or in classes.

Career Development Theories

In addition to being aware of the impact of workplace changes and their implications, career development theories provide a means to understand issues relevant to student development. Further, these theories provide a means to conceptualize activities and interventions designed to facilitate the career development of students. Again, the goal is to effectively prepare students for the future and to facilitate their career and educational planning. To this end, three theories will be briefly discussed. The intent is to present relevant information for school counselors and to encourage readers to further explore these and other theories. The theories presented are Holland's theory, Super's developmental theory, and Krumboltz's learning theory of career counseling.

Holland's Theory of Vocational Personalities and Work Environments

Holland's (1997) theory is a practical approach to relating one's personality to work environments (e.g., occupations, majors). Holland (1997) presented four assumptions to guide his theory:

1. Most people can be categorized as one of six personality types (Realistic [R], Investigative [I], Artistic [A], Social [S], Enterprising [E], or Conventional [C]).
2. Environmental types include the same six types.
3. "People search for environments that will let them exercise their skills and

abilities, express their attitudes and values, and take on agreeable problems and roles" (p. 4).

4. "Behavior is determined by an interaction between personality and environment" (p. 4).

Each of the personality types is described with the premise that one will be most satisfied in an environment (occupation) that matches the personality type. A key concept from Holland's (1997) theory is congruence, the degree of compatibility between one's personality type and environmental type. The following are some descriptors of the personality types and environments (Holland, 1997; Reardon & Lenz, 1998):

1. Realistic (R)—conforming, genuine, hardheaded, persistent, practical, reserved. R types typically prefer outdoor activities and have mechanical and athletic skills. R types prefer R occupations including auto mechanic, farmer, machinist, or electrician.
2. Investigative (I)—analytical, complex, independent, intellectual, precise, reserved. I types typically prefer working independently to solve problems and demonstrate math and science skills. I types prefer I occupations including chemist, dentist, actuary, or nurse anesthetist.
3. Artistic (A)—complicated, expressive, idealistic, imaginative, introspective, nonconforming. A types typically prefer artistic and creative situations, are imaginative, and have artistic skills. A types prefer A occupations including musician, painter, art teacher, art director, or photojournalist.
4. Social (S)—cooperative, empathic, friendly, helpful, idealistic, patient, persuasive, sociable. S types typically like to interact with people, teach, and help people solve their problems. S types prefer S occupations including teacher, nurse, counselor, or psychologist.
5. Enterprising (E)—adventurous, assertive, energetic, extroverted, forceful, self-confident. E types typically are involved in leadership activities, are adept at persuading others, and like influencing others. E types prefer E occupations including salesperson, manager, supervisor, or head coach.
6. Conventional (C)—careful, conforming, conscientious, efficient, methodical, orderly, practical, unimaginative. C types typically have clerical, math, and organization skills. C types prefer C occupations such as bookkeeper, accountant, banker, or secretary.

Holland (1997) realized that a person would not exhibit all of the characteristics of a specific type. Most are represented by a combination of types, and generally three of the types are used to characterize an individual. For example, a person's Holland code might be SEA, presented in order of interests from highest to lowest. Also, occupations are characterized by three-letter codes. The idea is for individuals to explore occupations, majors, or activities congruent with their Holland type. One's Holland type may be assessed formally or informally. For example, the Self-Directed Search (Holland, 1994) may be used with high school students or the Career Explorer (Holland & Powell, 1994) with middle school students. In addition, the Career Interests Game is available at the web site for the Career Center of the University of Missouri (http://career.missouri. edu/article.php?sid = 146). It is imperative that these not be used to determine the "right" occupation for students. Rather, these are designed to be helpful to students in their educational and career planning. Further, these resources may be used to help students become aware of options. In addition, Holland's ideas may be helpful in providing information to students that represent the range of Holland types.

Holland's (1997) model is typically presented as a hexagonal model and has been described as the RIASEC model. In addition to congruence, Holland identified other constructs related to the theory including consistency, differentiation, calculus, and identity. Holland codes are described as consistent if individuals identify with types close to each other on the hexagon. For example, a high level of consistency is shown by a code of SEC, whereas SRI shows a low level of consistency. Levels of consistency have been used to predict the ease of career decision making.

Differentiation was described by Holland (1997) as the extent to which one's personality is clearly defined. A highly differentiated person would be one who closely resembles one type. For example, a person may be a very, very strong R, with the other types not having an impact. Calculus refers to the degree of relatedness between types. The closer types are to one another, the more similar they are. For example, S and E are more similar than S and R. Finally, identity is described as the extent to which a person possesses "a clear and stable picture of one's goals, interests, and talents" (Holland, 1997, p. 5).

Based on Holland's (1997) theory, it is important to provide experiences in each of the six areas (RIASEC). Holland recommended that students be provided with "accurate and accessible information about themselves and the world of work over a long time span rather than at a few critical periods" (p. 214). Holland's theory can be used to help students understand the relationship between personal characteristics and occupations or majors. In addition, the theory provides a means to organize occupational and educational information.

In summary, Holland's (1997) theory provides practical ideas that have been widely used in the profession. In addition, the approach is readily understandable by students in their career and educational planning.

Super's Developmental Theory

Super (1990) described his theory as "a loosely unified set of theories dealing with specific aspects of career development, taken from developmental, differential, social, personality, and phenomenological psychology and held together by self-concept and learning theory" (p. 199). Related to his theory, Super presented propositions, which are summarized by Gysbers, Heppner, and Johnston (2003):

> The first three propositions emphasize that people have different abilities, interests, and values, and because they have, they may be qualified for various occupations. No person fits one occupation; there are a variety of occupations available for an individual and occupations accommodate a wide variety of individuals. The next six propositions focus on the self-concept and its implementation in career choices, on life stages with their mini and maxicycles, and on the concepts of career patterns and career maturity. The next five propositions deal with the synthesis and compromise between individual and social factors and work and life satisfactions. Finally, the last proposition looks at work and occupation as the focus for personality organization as well as the interplay of such life roles as worker, student, leisurite, homemaker, and citizen. (p. 23)

The life-career rainbow (Super, Savickas, & Super, 1996) is one schema that supports Super's developmental theory. Presented on the outside of the rainbow are the stages of development: growth (ages 4 to 13); exploration (ages 14 to 24); establishment (ages 25 to 44); maintenance (ages 45 to 65); and disengagement (65 plus). Even though ages are associated with the stages, not everyone goes through the stages at the ages noted. Super et al. (1996) described the tasks associated with the stages as follows:

1. Growth: "becoming concerned about the future, increasing personal control over one's life, convincing oneself to achieve in school and work, and acquiring competent work habits and attitudes" (p. 131)
2. Exploration: "crystallizing, specifying, and implementing an occupational choice" (p. 132)
3. Establishment: "stabilizing, consolidating, and advancing in an occupation" (p. 133)
4. Maintenance: "holding on, keeping up, and innovating" (p. 134)

5. Disengagement: "deceleration, retirement planning, and retirement living" (p. 134)

Career maturity, a relevant construct from Super's theory, "denotes readiness
to engage in the developmental tasks appropriate to the age and level" (Gysbers
et al., 2003, p. 24) of the individual. Also, within the life-career rainbow, various
life roles, including child, student, leisurite, citizen, worker, and homemaker, are
depicted. The various life roles interact and take varying amounts of time and
energy over the course of one's career. Multiple roles can positively or negatively
impact one's life. Questions based on roles include the following: "What roles do
you anticipate having in your life/career? How strong or intensely will you be
involved in those roles? At what age or ages will those roles be active? How is
your participation in these roles determined? "Which forces are internal and
which are external?" (Reardon et al., 2000, p. 14).

Self-concept is another construct associated with this theory. Super (1963)
defined self-concept as a "picture of the self in some role, situation, or position,
performing some set of functions, or in some web of relationships" (p. 18). The
Career Archway Model (Super, 1990) depicts personality factors (e.g., interests,
values, needs) and social factors (e.g., economy, school, family, society) that
influence the development of self-concepts and lead to the keystone, self. The factors making up the archway interact with and influence each other. According to
Niles and Harris-Bowlsbey (2002), "Because self-concepts continue to develop
over time, the need to make choices and the process of adjusting to the choices
implemented represent lifelong tasks" (p. 38).

Based on Super's theory, career planning is more than choosing an occupation or a program of study. It involves consideration of the various roles in which
one is or will be involved and the importance or salience of the roles. Career
development is a lifelong process and, as a result, appropriate career interventions need to be provided for all students. Gysbers et al. (2003) noted that differential interventions may be needed based on students' level of career maturity.
This seems particularly relevant for high school students and, to an extent, middle school students. There are, however, career needs relevant to all students in a
particular group, and such similarities result in presenting career and educational
planning activities to all students. Career guidance activities based on developmental concepts must take into account a variety of factors and may vary depending on the diverse needs and career maturity of students.

Learning Theory of Career Decision Making/Career Counseling

Krumboltz (1996) stated the following regarding career counseling:

> Conceiving of career counseling as a learning experience positions it as one of the central educational goals of the nation. It is no longer merely a matchmaking service, a frill for those who ought to have been able to figure out a good match for themselves. The economic welfare of the nation depends on its citizens learning career-relevant skills and characteristics and learning to adapt to a constantly changing work environment. (p. 75)

It follows that learning theory provides a way of conceptualizing career development programs and career and educational activities in schools. The social learning theory of career decision making (SLTCDM) addressed "how learning experiences combine to shape each person's career path" (p. 60). The learning theory of career counseling, which adds to the SLTCDM, "outlines goals, assessment strategies, and interventions" (Krumboltz, 1996, p. 60) to facilitate career development.

According to SLTCDM, the following four factors influence career decision making (Mitchell & Krumboltz, 1996):

1. Genetic endowment and special abilities include factors such as gender, ethnicity, artistic ability, or physical appearance.
2. Environmental conditions and events include "social, cultural, political, and economic forces, as well as such forces as natural disasters and the location of natural resources" (Mitchell & Krumboltz, 1996, p. 238). Many of these are not under the individual's control.
3. Learning experiences include instrumental and associative learning experiences.
4. Task approach skills include skills developed as a result of the interaction of the previous three factors. These include problem-solving skills, emotional responses, and work habits.

These four factors influence people's beliefs about themselves and the world of work, and the actions they take. Ways in which the four factors influence career decision making follow:

1. Self-observation generalizations are "overt or covert statements evaluating one's own actual or vicarious performance or assessing one's own interests or values" (Mitchell & Krumboltz, 1996, p. 244). These may be related to abilities, values, or interests.

2. Worldview observations are generalizations about the world in which persons live and are used to predict the future. The accuracy of these observations is dependent upon the learning experiences on which they are based.

3. Task approach skills are "cognitive and performance abilities and emotional predispositions for coping with the environment, interpreting it in relation to self-observation generalizations, and making covert and overt predictions about future events" (Mitchell & Krumboltz, 1996, p. 246). Task approach skills that are essential to career and educational planning include decision making, problem solving, gathering information, and clarifying values (Niles & Harris-Bowlsbey, 2002).

4. Actions are the result of learning experiences related to making career and educational decisions. Examples of actions include selecting courses, deciding on a postsecondary institution, or deciding on a program or major.

Based on this approach, career decision making is a learned skill. As a result, it is critical that this be taught as part of students' educational programs. School counselors and other stakeholders have a key role in teaching career decision-making skills. Krumboltz (1996) described interventions that followed from this approach as being developmental and preventive interventions and targeted and remedial interventions.

A more recent addition to this approach is planned happenstance theory (Mitchell, Levin, & Krumboltz, 1999). It is "a conceptual framework extending career counseling to include the creating and transforming of unplanned events into opportunities for learning. The goal of a planned happenstance intervention is to assist clients to generate, recognize, and incorporate chance events into their career development" (p. 117). While this approach seems different from other approaches, it is reasonable to consider ways to help students learn to be proactive in their career and educational decision making and seek opportunities. The skills noted by Mitchell et al. (1999) to assist persons to recognize and create opportunities include the following:

1. Curiosity: exploring new learning opportunities
2. Persistence: exerting effort despite setbacks
3. Flexibility: changing attitudes and circumstances
4. Optimism: viewing new opportunities as possible and attainable
5. Risk Taking: taking action in the face of uncertain outcomes (p. 118)

These skills are appropriate to develop and foster in students to enhance their career development and facilitate their career and educational planning. Students need to be aware of and seek opportunities that will facilitate and enhance their career development.

In summary, the goal of this approach "is to facilitate the learning of skills, interests, beliefs, values, work habits, and personal qualities that enable each client to create a satisfying life within the constantly changing work environment" (Krumboltz, 1996, p. 61). A key factor in this approach is learning with the activities and interventions designed to enhance student learning. This focus is consistent with and complements schools' emphasis on learning.

Final Thoughts from Career Theories

The intent of this brief overview of three career theories was to provide information that may serve as the basis for the conceptualization of activities and interventions implemented as part of the effort to enhance students' career and educational planning. Clearly, there are other theories; however, it is hoped that this presentation created an interest to pursue further reading and study in this area. In part, the purpose of theory is to conceptualize interventions designed to enhance students' career development. As a result of effectively applying theory to activities and interventions, it is intended for students to develop the skills needed for effective career and educational planning. In the process, the intent is that students will be effectively prepared for their future.

Career and Educational Opportunities for Students

As school counselors, educators, and key stakeholders work with students to facilitate their career and educational planning and preparation, a question that follows is "What are the career and educational opportunities available to students?" Based on the workplace issues, one might be somewhat pessimistic; however, there are many opportunities for students' consideration. Regardless of how one views the opportunities, it should be clear that a particular option will not be in the range of choices for a student if he or she does not know about the option. As a result, one of the goals of activities and interventions, implemented as part of a program, is to help students become aware of a variety of career and educational options. Further, students need to be well prepared in order for options to be available to them.

The challenge in working with students is to help them learn about the options and become well prepared for any option they might choose. There are a variety of educational alternatives that should be presented to students (e.g., college/university, community college, technical college, proprietary institution). One option is not better than another. Rather, the task involves helping students and their parents become aware of and explore options in order to make informed choices. While obtaining a bachelor's degree is an appropriate option for students, as Gray and Herr (1995) stated, there are "other ways to win," other appropriate, reasonable options for consideration. Helping students and parents broaden their knowledge and exploration of postsecondary education options (Hoyt, 2001) and the occupations associated with these is a critical responsibility of school counselors.

Career and Educational Planning: Preparing Students

Making Career Development a Priority

Based on the workplace issues and the career theories, it follows that career development should be a priority for all students (Feller & Davies, 1999; Hughey & Hughey, 1999). Further, as Feller (2000) recommended, career development should be addressed as a program for all students, and career and educational planning should be an integral part of school guidance and counseling programs. According to Hull (2000), "Preparing students to select career pathways and guiding them in plans to enroll in coursework that will lead them to achieve their career goals is essential to helping them meet the challenges of the twenty-first century" (p. 14). Hull (2000) also described the purposes as developing essential skills and facilitating learning opportunities. It is imperative that students be provided guidance in their career decision making and in learning the skills needed for the future.

As noted by Gysbers and Henderson (2000), a program involves specific characteristics. These include the following: student competencies, activities to meet the competencies, professional personnel, resources, and evaluation. Further, programs are developmental and comprehensive, and involve a team effort. Providing learning experiences to help prepare students for the future is an important part of school guidance and counseling programs. Understanding the implications of the changing workplace and applying the career theories provide a framework that serves as the basis for programs to meet students' career and educational needs. Consequently, students will learn to make career and educational decisions and be contributing citizens.

Stakeholders' Roles in Preparing Students for Their Future

The Role of School Counselors

School counselors have a critical role to play in the career and educational planning of students. According to the Role of the Professional School Counselor (American School Counselor Association [ASCA], 1999), school counselors are involved in program implementation through counseling, large group guidance, consultation, and coordination. In addition, it is noted that school counselors work to promote the career development of all students. The Ethical Standards for School Counselors (ASCA, 1998) address counselors being concerned with the educational and career needs of students and "encourages the maximum development of each counselee" (A.1.b.). Counselors also have a responsibility to assist in the development of "educational procedures and programs to meet the counselee's developmental needs" (ASCA, 1998, D.2.) and treat each student "with respect as a unique individual" (ASCA, 1998, A.1.a).

Based on the model presented by Gysbers and Henderson (2000), school counselors would most likely address career and educational planning through the guidance curriculum and individual planning. There may, however, be times when career and educational planning issues are addressed as part of responsive services or systems support. Further, school counselors serve as advocates for students to promote the development, including the career development, of students (ASCA, 1999). School counselors are key professionals in advocating for activities and interventions that address the career and educational planning needs of all students. As advocates, school counselors have a critical role in striving to provide solid learning opportunities for students and working to facilitate student learning (Campbell & Dahir, 1997). Not only do counselors fulfill an advocacy role with teachers and administrators, they also serve as advocates with other stakeholders (e.g., parents, community). In addition, counselors advocate for the appropriate placement of students (e.g., students with special needs) and advocate for the appropriate placement of students in courses that most effectively meet their needs. Further, school counselors collaborate with key stakeholders (e.g., parents, teachers, administrators) to facilitate the career development of students. It follows that school counselors have a critical role to play in helping students prepare for their future and involving other stakeholders in this process to facilitate and enhance the development of all students.

Roles of Administrators and Teachers

Administrators and teachers work collaboratively with school counselors to meet the career development needs of students. School administrators support the collaborative efforts of teachers and counselors to facilitate the career and educational planning of students. Further, administrators provide resources for the various activities and programs implemented to prepare students for the future.

Teachers work collaboratively with school counselors to effectively prepare students for the future. Teachers may integrate activities and lessons into the classroom curriculum that address career and educational planning or focus on skills needed for the future. Career education (Hoyt, Evans, Mackin, & Mangum, 1972) addressed the collaborative role of teachers and counselors in preparing students for the future. As noted in Hoyt et al. (1972), career education was defined by Hoyt as

> the total effort of public education and the community aimed at helping all individuals to become familiar with the values of a work-oriented society, to integrate these values into their personal value systems, and to implement these values into their lives in such a way that work becomes possible, meaningful, and satisfying to each individual. (p. 1)

Within this context, Hoyt (1981) identified important and relevant competencies or skills to be addressed as part of the curriculum. These included the following: enhancing student learning, effective work habits, career decision making, and relevance of subject content to students.

In addition, teachers can help students make connections between the content being learned and real-world applications. Contextual teaching and learning is defined as "teaching and learning that helps teachers relate subject matter content to real world situations and motivates students to make connections between knowledge and its applications to their lives as family members, citizens, and workers and engage in the hard work that learning requires" (U.S. Department of Education, n.d.). The development of skills and knowledge that helps students see the relevance of the work completed in school to their future is essential. Berns and Erickson (2001) identified several approaches for implementing contextual learning and teaching, including problem-based learning, cooperative learning, project-based learning, service learning, and work-based learning. Further, Berns and Erickson (2001) recommended that lessons be developmentally appropriate, include learning groups, support self-regulated learning, consider student diversity, address multiple intelligences, include appropriate questioning, and include authentic assessment. Activities implemented by teachers that help students make the connection to the real world and prepare students for the future are important. Working collaboratively with teachers and administrators, school counselors enhance the chances of facilitating student development and career and educational planning. Further, these collaborative efforts provide opportunities for students to develop skills needed for the changing workplace and their future.

The Role of Parents

Parents have a significant role to play in the career development of their children. Young (1994) stated that parental influence is most helpful when it is "intentional, planned, and goal-directed action" (p. 197). Earlier, Young and Friesen (1992) noted that parents are active in influencing their children in a range of issues related to career development (e.g., acquiring skills, independence, personal responsibility). As a result, it is important for school counselors to work with parents in these areas.

Parents can serve as models for their children relative to their approach to work and their occupations. Brown (2003) noted that parents have a significant influence on children and, as such, parental knowledge and views of the world of work and education can have a significant influence on their children. According to Brown (2003), parents can provide a range of activities to facilitate their children's career development and facilitate their career and educational planning. Parents can serve as an information source for their children, they can help their children learn about the educational and occupational opportunities available, and they can provide and support opportunities for career decision making. Parents can help their children seek out learning experiences that will help them become aware of their interests, skills, and values and relate these to career and educational opportunities.

Counselors can provide opportunities to enhance parents' knowledge and understanding of the world of work and to help parents work with their children on their career and educational planning. Helping parents become aware of the workplace changes and the implications of these for their children is an appropriate task for school counselors. Further, counselors can provide consultation to parents and experiences that will help them effectively utilize their influence with their children. According to Otto (2000), "The opportunity is there. The challenge is for counselors to develop ways to multiply their effectiveness by working with parents to help young people make career decisions" (p. 118).

Student Competencies

Addressing student competencies is an important characteristic of comprehensive school guidance and counseling programs (Gysbers & Henderson, 2000). School counselors working collaboratively with teachers, administrators, and stakeholders determine the competencies to be addressed to facilitate the career development of students. The personnel in each district determine the competencies and the level(s) at which the competencies are to be addressed. One goal is that all students will be effectively prepared to make career and educational decisions and, then, upon graduation make an effective transition. Conceptually, the process has been presented with a focus in the elementary school on awareness, the middle school on exploration, and high school on decision making and preparation. While this may be a helpful framework, it seems important to note that these areas of emphasis overlap and consideration of the developmental needs of students is critical to the development and implementation of programs and activities designed to effectively prepare students for the future.

The National Standards for School Counseling Programs (Campbell & Dahir, 1997) provide standards that may be used to conceptualize and respond to student needs with respect to career and educational planning. The following are academic development and career development standards that relate to preparing students for the future:

Academic Development

Standard A: Students will acquire the attitudes, knowledge, and skills that contribute to effective learning in school and across the life span.

Standard B: Students will complete school with the academic preparation essential to choose from a wide range of substantial postsecondary options, including college.

Standard C: Students will understand the relationship of academics to the world of work, and to life at home and in the community. (p. 17)

Career Development

Standard A: Students will acquire the skills to investigate the world of work in relation to knowledge of self and to make informed career choices.

Standard B: Students will employ strategies to achieve future career success and satisfaction.

Standard C: Students will understand the relationship between personal qualities, education and training, and the world of work. (p. 17)

Student competencies are identified under each of these standards and serve as the impetus for student development and achievement. Campbell and Dahir (1997) provided a list of competencies that can be used as a guide by school counselors. As school counselors work collaboratively with stakeholders to determine and address student competencies, it is important that these be relevant, timely, developmentally appropriate, and address the diverse needs of students.

In addition to the National Standards, the National Career Development Guidelines (Kobylarz, 1996) provide a framework for preparing students for the future. The areas around which competencies are presented are self-knowledge, educational and occupational exploration, and career planning. Specific competencies have been identified by grade level and may be used in the development of programs designed to enhance students' career development.

Another way of conceptualizing career competencies was developed by Gysbers and Moore (1981). The life career development model uses three domains: self-knowledge and interpersonal skills; life roles, settings, and events; and life career planning. Each domain includes goals and student competencies to be addressed as part of the program to facilitate student development.

Regardless of the framework used to conceptualize and address students' career development needs, the goal is to effectively prepare students for the changing and evolving workplace. Further, students are being prepared to be successful in life and to make contributions to society. In doing so, the program should be developmental, addressing the needs of students at particular levels, and sequential. In addition to the above frameworks, there are a variety of programs and activities to facilitate the development of students (e.g., Gysbers, Starr, & Magnuson, 1998; Omaha Public Schools, 1998).

Addressing the Career and Educational Planning Needs of All Students

It is imperative that school counselors and key stakeholders address the needs of all students "regardless of gender, race, ethnicity, cultural background, sexual orientation, disability, family structure and functionality, socioeconomic status, learning-ability level, language, level of school involvement, or other special characteristics" (Gysbers, 2001, p. 103). Lee (2001) noted the importance of school counselors being culturally responsive and implementing culturally responsive programs and activities. As a result, counselors are facilitators of student development, serve as student advocates, and work with diverse families and communities. Being knowledgeable of the diverse needs of students is imperative as school counselors work collaboratively with key stakeholders to prepare students for the future. Even with the information available regarding various student characteristics, it is important that the student be helped as an individual.

Issues and recommendations have been provided by various authors that emphasize the importance of considering student characteristics in planning and implementing programs and activities to facilitate student career and educational planning and decision making. Examples of topics to be considered by school counselors include multicultural issues (e.g., Herring, 1998; Mau, 1995; Mau & Bikos, 2000; Murrow-Taylor, Foltz, Ellis, & Culbertson, 1999), gifted and talented students (e.g., Colangelo, 1997; Perrone, 1997; Rysiew, Shore, & Leeb, 1999), employment-bound youth (Herr, 1995), students with disabilities (e.g., Bowen, & Glenn, 1998; Fox, Wandry, Pruitt, & Anderson, 1998; Kosciulek, 2003; Schwiebert, Sealander, & Bradshaw, 1998), gender issues (e.g., Sellers, Satcher, & Comas, 1999; Trusty, Robinson, Plata, & Ng, 2000), and at-risk students (e.g., Aviles, Guerrero, Howarth, & Thomas, 1999; Ladany, Melincoff, Constantine, & Love, 1997; O'Brien, Dukstein, Jackson, Tomlinson, & Kamatuka, 1999; O'Brien et al., 2000).

For some students, there are legal issues that need to be considered. For example, the Individuals with Disabilities Act (IDEA, PL 101-475) requires that an Individual Education Program (IEP) include transition services for students with disabilities no later than age 16. In some cases, it is appropriate to begin this at age 14. According to Clark and Kolstoe (1995), the transition goals "should address the needed match between graduation requirements and postschool outcomes such as postsecondary education, vocational training, integrated employment, and community living, and should include socialization skills for each of these outcome environments" (p. 172). School counselors may be involved in the process of developing an IEP and addressing transition needs of students with disabilities.

According to Herr and Cramer (1996), it is especially important for specific groups to address "reduction of stereotypes, discrimination, environmental barriers, and other forms of bias that may impede the career development of such groups" (p. 257). A key issue in working with all students is helping them effectively prepare for their future and reach their potential. Two premises presented by Lee (2001) seem relevant in considering the needs of diverse students and in the development of programs and activities to facilitate students' career development. These are "All young people can learn and want to learn," and "cultural differences are real and cannot be ignored" (p. 259). In a different context, Feller

(2002) noted that for all students, learning should be the constant and time the variable. This principle is a relevant consideration in working to prepare all students for the evolving, changing environment.

Preparing Students for Their Future: Activities and Interventions

According to Schmidt (2003), "The essential goal for all services of a comprehensive school counseling program is to help schools create appropriate learning activities, design individual educational plans, and incorporate adequate career exploration for all students throughout their school years" (p. 223). Career preparation is a process that is initiated in elementary school and continues through the school years and beyond. The activities and interventions provided should be planned to prepare students for their careers and be part of a sequential, developmental program. Further, the activities and interventions should follow from the student competencies and be targeted toward student growth and development. Similar activities or interventions may be implemented at various levels; however, the outcomes may vary depending on the needs of students, developmental level, or level of career maturity. The level of complexity and focus of the activities and interventions may vary by level.

Various authors (e.g., Brown, 2003; Herr & Cramer, 1996; Niles & Harris-Bowlsbey, 2002; Zunker, 2002) provide descriptions of career programs, including student competencies and activities, at the elementary, middle, and high school levels. The following sections present examples of activities that might be implemented at the various educational levels. Even though these are discussed at a particular level, they may be adapted at other levels. The activities and interventions discussed are intended to be part of comprehensive school guidance and counseling programs that are integral to the educational program. Clearly, one activity, a number of loosely related activities, or unrelated activities, do not make a program. To effectively prepare students for the future and to facilitate their educational and career planning requires a coordinated effort of school counselors with key stakeholders in the school. Some activities may be facilitated by school counselors, some by teachers, and some may be co-facilitated. Some activities may be infused in the curriculum, while others may be implemented using small groups of students or classes. In addition, other interventions may be individual. Some may involve community members or students going into the community. To be most effective, a coordinated effort is needed to systematically, intentionally, and professionally implement activities. Activities may focus on various topics including enhancing awareness (self and career), promoting exploration, facilitating decision making, and developing skills needed for the future.

As school counselors implement activities to facilitate students' career development and prepare students for the future, technology should be considered an appropriate and effective resource. For example, online resources are available to facilitate students' career and educational planning (e.g., Harris-Bowlsbey, Riley Dikel, & Sampson, 1998; Sabella, 2003; Van Horn & Myrick, 2001).

School counselors must be cognizant of their level of involvement in the activities and determine the most effective and efficient use of their time. To help with this, Dykeman (2002) identified levels of involvement in activities. These included conducting, consulting, and coordinating. A key consideration is determining the relevant learning activities or interventions, and then addressing the appropriate level of involvement needed to facilitate student mastery of the competencies.

Enhancing the relevance and applicability of the content to students will create opportunities for students to use the knowledge and skills learned. It is increasingly important that school counselors and teachers help students understand the connection between the learning that takes place in the classroom and the work world. Johnson (2000), in a study involving sixth and ninth graders, found that students had limited understanding of the relationship of school to the real world. In addition, they had little awareness of the skills and knowledge needed to be successful. As a result, an overriding goal is to provide learning experiences that encourage students to become well prepared for their future, whatever option they might choose. Also, it is necessary that they be aware of the skills needed in the future and have the opportunity to develop these skills. In the process, "The sacred right of every student to make his or her own life choices must always be the top concern of the school counselor" (Hoyt, 2001, p. 11); however, providing students the skills needed to make the career and educational choices to help them achieve their goals is a responsibility of school counselors and stakeholders.

Elementary School

Niles and Harris-Bowlsbey (2002) noted the need for elementary students to learn about themselves and the educational and occupational options. Becoming aware of the options and learning about the variety of opportunities is critical for elementary students and involves school counselors working collaboratively with teachers. It is important as students learn about the options and opportunities that they not make choices prematurely (Herr & Cramer, 1996). The activities of the elementary school guidance and counseling program provide the foundation on which skills are further developed and knowledge is enhanced in middle school, high school, and beyond. It is imperative that program activities have a solid educational purpose and be integrated into the school guidance and counseling program and curricular activities. Examples of activities will be provided; however, these are not intended to be a complete program. Rather, these are presented to provide ideas for consideration and integration into a program.

Enhancing student awareness is one on the goals of an elementary program designed to provide a foundation for appropriate career and educational planning. Beale (2000) and Beale and Nugent (1996) recommended using creative strategies to enhance student awareness. Beale (2000) described a career awareness activity that involved a visit to the hospital. A number of activities were conducted in preparation for the visit, during the visit, and following the visit. Feedback from students and adults was positive. This activity could be replicated for other workplaces. Beale and Nugent (1996) described Project Pizza Connection, a visit to a restaurant. They noted that the key to a positive learning experience is a "teacher or counselor who leads the group, guides classroom discussions, and highlights and relates salient features of the tour to children's classroom experiences" (p. 298).

Beale and Williams (2000) described activities for effectively planning a career day designed to have a significant impact on students. The goals of the activity, which involved parents and adults in the community, were to help students become aware of traditional and nontraditional occupations, to understand the importance of responsibility and effective work habits, and to understand the interrelationships of workers. Various introductory activities were encouraged to prepare students for the activity. Murrow-Taylor et al. (1999) described the implementation of a multicultural career fair that involved a variety of occupations and cultures and included the opportunity for students to hear from representatives of both genders. Providing exposure to a variety of models and addressing gender and ethnic stereotyping is important as career activities are implemented. This is particularly important as children tend to choose stereotypical occupations by gender (Sellers et al., 1999).

One elementary school counselor uses a careers-on-wheels day to help students become familiar with occupations. Various workers come to the school and meet with small groups of students to discuss their work. All workers bring their equipment or vehicles to the school. Students learn about occupations and the importance of school subjects to the occupations. Occupations represent various levels of education (e.g., college, technical school, community college, on-the-job training). Teachers are actively involved in the process. Another activity is a mini–job fair in which local business professionals discuss with fifth graders the characteristics they expect of part-time high school employees, and the skills needed to be successful. In both examples, preparatory work is completed to ready students for effective participation in the activities.

Bachay and Rigby (1997) described a career intervention implemented with Haitian third-grade students who had limited English proficiency. The purpose of this intervention was to help students become familiar with the world of work and to understand the relationship to what was learned in school. The intervention, which involved a field trip, was experiential and targeted to the developmental needs of the students involved.

Stereotyping is an important topic to be addressed throughout students' educational career (Wahl & Blackhurst, 2000). This must begin during the elementary years and continue through high school. It can be addressed in classroom guidance or group activities or may need to be addressed with individual students. As an example, having both genders represented in activities and programs to provide for diversity in participants is important. Consider appropriate responses or actions to address the following comments made by students:

An elementary boy states, "Only boys can be engineers."

An elementary girl who is a leader in class states, "I cannot be the president of the United States."

Encouraging students to become aware of and explore a variety of occupations and to become as well prepared as possible is an important message for elementary students. In addition, it is important that this be continued through the next levels of schooling. At times, units based on career and educational competencies may be implemented. Gillies, McMahon, and Carroll (1998) described a career education unit that included ten lessons facilitated by teachers. The focus of the intervention was helping students develop a better understanding of themselves and the variety of life roles. In their evaluation of the intervention, the authors reported a positive impact on students' knowledge of occupations, and students were able to make connections between learning in school and various occupations.

The focus at the elementary level is helping students become aware of the career and educational opportunities. Providing learning experiences that enhance student awareness and help them explore opportunities is important. Involving teachers and other stakeholders in the process will benefit students' career and educational planning.

Middle School

Middle school is a time of transition. One of the goals of the middle school is for students "to learn about themselves and the world of work and then translate this learning into an educational plan for the remainder of their secondary education" (Niles & Harris-Bowlsbey, 2002, p. 285). Students should be provided learning opportunities that enable them to explore various educational and occupational options. Further, middle school students will be initiating the career planning process and relating this to the world of work. Herr and Cramer (1996) offered the following considerations:

1. Provide students the opportunity to explore their personal characteristics and the educational options available.
2. Since there is a range of career maturity in middle school students, various types of interventions should be used to address individual differences.
3. Accurate, relevant information is needed as students initiate career and educational planning.
4. Concrete experiences enhance student exploration.
5. Encourage students' exploration of their personal characteristics (e.g., feelings, interests) and relate these to career and educational planning.

O'Brien et al. (1999) implemented an extensive career program for at-risk seventh graders. The program involved career exploration and self-awareness classes and classes that addressed math and science careers. This program resulted in increases in participants' "career planning and exploration efficacy, educational and vocational development efficacy, number of careers they were considering, and congruence between interests and career choice" (p. 224). The authors provided a number of recommendations including lengthening the intervention, providing individual career assistance, beginning interventions in the elementary school, and considering cultural influences. Similarly, Fouad (1995) described a one-year intervention, reported to be moderately successful, designed to enhance culturally diverse middle school students' awareness of math and science careers.

Students can begin the process of learning about their interests and exploring occupations related to these. For example, the Self-Directed Search Career Explorer (Holland & Powell, 1994) or the Career Key (Jones, 2002) are interest inventories designed to be used with middle school students. Both instruments are based on Holland's (1997) theory and provide a means to help students understand their interests and explore career and educational options. Counselors and teachers can make effective use of instruments such as these and help students integrate the results into the career and educational planning efforts.

Middle school students may be offered a career class to facilitate their career and educational planning. As an example, one rural school offers an elective, semester course to eighth-grade students. The students are provided learning experiences to develop skills in understanding and using career information; to acquire knowledge of various occupations; to become aware of the changing roles of men and women; to become aware of the career decision-making process; to develop positive attitudes toward work; and to understand the importance of and relationship of personal qualities, education, and the opportunities in the work world. Various learning activities are used to help students achieve these goals. Activities include completing the Self-Directed Search Career Explorer (Holland & Powell, 1994) and learning to use various career information resources (e.g., *Occupational Outlook Handbook*). Students complete research on an occupation and use this information to prepare an oral presentation and a product (e.g., PowerPoint presentation, poster). The presentation and product are designed to enhance students' learning about various occupations and to address additional skills (e.g., research and communication skills). In addition, students shadow workers and prepare a report of their activities. A speaker panel addresses topics designed to help students with their career exploration and planning.

It is imperative to integrate into activities information to challenge gender-role stereotyping and to encourage students to consider a variety of options. The goal of activities and interventions should be to expand options as opposed to limiting choices.

The Real Game (Barry, 2001) is designed to be used as part of career programs in middle schools (see Jarvis & Keeley, 2003, for descriptions of Real Game programs across grade levels). This game is designed to help students learn about work roles and other responsibilities. Students assume a particular occupational role and role-play situations experienced in one's career. The learning principles that serve as the foundation for The Real Game activities are "Change is constant," "Learning is ongoing," "Focus on the journey," "Follow your heart," and "Access your allies." One elementary school teacher used The Real Game effectively with fifth-grade students and was very pleased with the outcomes and students' response.

As information is gathered and integrated to help students learn about themselves and explore occupational and educational options, students can use this to facilitate planning. In the process of preparing students, it is important that students have access to and know how to use relevant, timely, and accurate career and educational information (Herr & Cramer, 1996).

The career and educational planning process should be initiated during middle school and continued throughout high school. Student portfolios can be used to help students and their parents with this planning process. The use of portfolios could be initiated in elementary school, and continued in middle school and high school. Further, this process can be used to help students learn the skills to make career and educational decisions. In some cases, this effort was described as the development of four-year plans. Bottoms, Presson, and Johnson (1992) noted that "Increasingly, counselors and other educators are realizing that a coordinated plan, implemented no later than eighth grade, is the way to prepare students for work and further education" (p. 172). Gray and Herr (1995) described the process as the development of individual career plans. They defined an individual career plan as "a process that leads to a product (the plan) that assists students and parents in relating each student's career interests and postsecondary higher education aspirations to individual aptitudes and achievements" (pp. 116–117). The goal should not be to have a firm decision in eighth grade; however, goals should be for students to develop plans that help provide direction and focus, and to learn the career decision-making process. Students should be encouraged to plan challenging programs of study to effectively prepare for the future. Clearly, parental involvement in this planning effort benefits the students. It helps parents understand the process and learn ways to help their children with career and educational planning.

Middle school is a critical time for students to explore career and educational opportunities. The students' learning experiences at this level should prepare them for the programs, activities, and interventions implemented at the high school level.

High School

Continuing the career and educational planning efforts initiated in elementary and middle school is important at the high school level. While some of the activities may be similar to those at earlier levels, the depth and focus will likely vary. High school students are a very diverse group and are at various developmental levels (e.g., levels of career maturity), with some having needs that are consistent with earlier levels. Although some students may be decided about their next steps, not all students will complete high school with a specific career or educational decision. It is hoped that students will know the process of making career and educational decisions and be able to apply this skill in the future. A goal is to effectively prepare them for the transition from high school to their selected option (e.g., postsecondary education, job, technical education, military service).

Gray and Herr (1995) stated, "The principal emphasis in career guidance at the high school level should be on secondary and postsecondary academic and career planning" (p. 113). They further noted that the "career guidance program activities in the senior high school must take each student from where he or she is in coping with developmental tasks integral to career development and lead that person to create a specific set of preferences and plans for achieving these goals" (p. 113). In other words, planned, systematic, and intentional work on the development of relevant individual career plans must be implemented.

Dykeman et al. (2001) developed a taxonomy of high school career interventions that may be used to help school counselors conceptualize interventions. Their categorization of interventions included work-based interventions (e.g., job shadowing, mentoring programs), advising interventions (e.g., academic planning, career counseling, career assessment), introductory interventions (e.g., career day, classroom guidance activities), and curriculum-based interventions (e.g., infusion of career information into the curriculum, career academy). This conceptualization of activities is designed to help school counselors and stakeholders who implement career activities.

As noted, the development of plans is a critical task, ideally initiated in middle school, to be implemented in high school. Encouraging students to take challenging programs of study (Bottoms et al., 1992) is critical to their preparation. In addition, working with teachers to help students see the relevance of these courses to the future is valuable. Continued involvement of parents in this process with high school students is essential. This career and educational planning may occur in classrooms, small groups, or individually. Regardless of context, working with and understanding the individual and his or her specific needs are critical.

Career portfolios may be used to help students with their career and educational planning. There are a variety of types and, in some cases, the process may begin during elementary school with the portfolio following the student through middle school and on to high school. Planned activities, some involving parents, can be implemented to help make the portfolio a useful tool for effective planning.

In addition to individual career and educational planning, some students will likely require individual career counseling to facilitate their planning and development. There may be challenges or barriers, internal or external, that need to be addressed; multiple options from which they feel pressured to choose; conflicts about parental expectations and what the student is considering; or other issues (e.g., interests, values, beliefs) that impact their career decision making and may be most effectively addressed by individual career counseling. Students may experience challenges in making choices about which postsecondary educational institution to attend. Gati and Saka (2001) conceptualized high school students' career difficulties around issues related to lack of readiness, lack of information (the process, self, options), and inconsistent information. School counselors are in a critical position to effectively work with individual students and/or their parents and, if required, to make an appropriate referral.

Classroom learning activities can be co-facilitated by school counselors and teachers. One example is a career and language arts unit offered to high school juniors (Hughey, Lapan, & Gysbers, 1993; Lapan, Gysbers, Hughey, & Arni, 1993). This thirteen-session intervention provided the opportunity for students to explore and obtain information about occupations and educational options. English teachers focused on language arts skills including selecting and using references, and organizing and summarizing information. Guidance competencies addressed career exploration based on interest assessment results, career and educational planning, nontraditional occupations, and enhanced understanding of students' interests, aptitudes, and abilities. According to Hughey et al. (1993), students, teachers, and counselors reported a positive impact of the unit. Further, Lapan et al. (1993) noted that students achieved guidance competencies and their perception of themselves increased over the course of the unit.

Kraus and Hughey (1999) assessed the impact of a career intervention based on Crites's (1978) career choice competencies and adapted from the work of Savickas and Crites (1981). The intervention was designed to teach the career choice competencies (accurate self-appraisal, gathering occupational information, goal selection, making future plans, and problem solving) and provide students the opportunity to apply these competencies. While no differences were found between the treatment and control groups, males in the control group had higher levels of career decision-making self-efficacy than females in the control group, and females in the treatment group had higher levels of career decision-making self-efficacy than females in the control group.

As part of learning career decision-making skills and making career and educational plans, students need accurate, current, and meaningful information about occupational and educational options. Students need to become familiar with a variety of resources and strategies to obtain information. The effective use of these resources should be taught to help students prepare for the future. Imel, Kerka, and Wonacott (2001) prepared a resource that addresses the use of online occupational information and resources to facilitate career planning. For example, the *Occupational Outlook Handbook* (U.S. Department of Labor, 2002) is a current source of occupational information, and information on educational options is available from various publishers as well as online. School counselors may use Internet resources to facilitate students' educational and college searches. Helping students and their parents become familiar with relevant Internet resources can facilitate their career and educational planning efforts. In addition, it would be helpful for high schools as part of the school guidance and counseling program to have computerized career guidance systems (e.g., DISCOVER, CHOICES). Further, videos such as *Tour of Your Tomorrow* (Feller & Vasos, 2001), which follows from the Harrington-O'Shea Career Decision-Making System (Harrington & O'Shea, 2000), provide information that can be used by students as they plan their careers.

To help students with their planning, one high school offered a program titled "Is There Life After High School?" This activity, coordinated by a school counselor, involves a panel of graduates enrolled in various kinds of postsecondary institutions (e.g., college, technical college) and represents diversity of students. A moderator facilitates the presentation, which addresses topics including recommendations for success, balancing work and academics, comparing high school with postsecondary education, challenges encountered, time management, and managing money. Students and teachers have responded positively to this activity.

Helping students learn about and understand the evolving workplace and the skills needed to be successful are relevant topics. Further, helping students understand the relationship between what they are learning in school and the world outside of school can be helpful. Blank and Harwell (1997) presented a number of ideas for helping students connect with the real world (e.g., project-based learning, mentoring, service learning).

To prepare for their next steps, students need assistance with job search activities. Students, regardless of their postsecondary plans, will likely need to be taught skills related to resume writing, writing cover letters, job search strategies, and job interviewing. This might be accomplished through classroom guidance activities or as part of classes.

The development of career academies or career pathways may be used to help students organize their programs and to make their education more relevant. For example, one high school used Holland's (1997) theory to develop pathways that encouraged students to take challenging courses based on students' career goals, interests, and needs. Students were taught relevant aspects of Holland's theory and completed the Self-Directed Search as part of a guidance activity.

Preparing students for the future is a critical responsibility for high school counselors, teachers, and other stakeholders. It involves taking into account the diverse needs of students as they make the transition from high school to the next level of their career. School counselors have an essential role in providing learning experiences, interventions, and activities that facilitate students' career development and enhance their career and educational planning.

◤ Concluding Thoughts

There are significant opportunities for students as they develop in their careers and prepare for their future. In addition, it is important to help students develop the skills needed to prepare for the challenges of the changing workplace. Helping students develop and work toward career and educational goals that effectively prepare them for the future is a critical responsibility for school counselors. Snyder, Feldman, Shorey, and Rand (2002) emphasized the importance of instilling hope in students. They stated that hope "is that which enables people to set valued goals, to see the means to achieve those goals, and to find the drive to make those goals happen" (p. 298). School counselors working collaboratively with key stakeholders should use their professional expertise to coordinate and conduct activities to help students develop goals, implement plans to achieve the goals, and facilitate development. Making career and educational planning and preparation a priority and an integral part of each student's educational program is imperative. Further, facilitating students' knowledge, skills, and attitudes relative to preparation for the future is a responsibility that should not be left to chance. Rather, systematic, intentional, and relevant learning experiences are needed to prepare students for the future. According to Krumboltz and Worthington (1999), "Students should be empowered to take action, not merely to decide on a future occupation" (p. 318). Providing learning experiences that result in students taking an active role in their career would seem to enhance their opportunities for success.

Career development is a lifelong process, and learning is lifelong and a job requirement. Preparing students for the future, facilitating their career development, preparing them for transitions, and providing learning experiences that enhance their development are critical tasks that involve school counselors collaborating with stakeholders, including parents, teachers, administrators, and the community. The goal is that students will be successful and add value to their lives, their community, society, and the organizations with which they are associated. Understanding contextual factors (e.g., the economy, the workplace) and applying career theories in the development of programs, activities, and interventions are critical to helping students plan their careers. Preparing students for the future offers challenges and opportunities that must be addressed.

Based on several sources (Feller, 2003; Herr & Cramer, 1996; Niles & Harris-Bowlsbey, 2002), the following are questions for school counselors to consider as they work with stakeholders to effectively prepare students for the future:

1. Do students know how to make career decisions?
2. Are students aware of their characteristics (e.g., interests, skills) and occupational and educational opportunities?
3. Do students know that the career choices involve more than choosing an occupation?
4. Do students understand the evolving workplace and the skills needed to be successful?
5. Do students have the basic skills needed to be successful, and are they well prepared academically and occupationally?
6. Do students know how to respond to transition and change?
7. Do students know how to seek and recognize opportunities?
8. Do students realize that learning is a lifelong process and that maintaining currency with respect to skills is essential?
9. Do students understand the importance of being culturally aware and responsive?
10. Do students know to be assertive and entrepreneurial, and how to search for jobs?

Affirmative responses to these questions will likely result in positive outcomes for students as they seek to find their place in the future and make contributions to their community and society.

APPENDIX
Try Your Hand at Educational and Career Planning

Case Study: "Kinesha Wants to Jumpstart Her Education"

Kinesha is an African American eleventh grader who is looking toward an Ivy League school for college, and she sees medical school in her future. She is an excellent student, the class president, and volunteers regularly at her church's youth group. In her initial meeting with her school counselor, Dr. Jones, Kinesha admits that the whole "college application thing" is overwhelming. At this point, Kinesha has not visited any of the schools she's interested in, but she has researched them online. Kinesha is worried that her grades (3.86 GPA) aren't good enough to get into a place like Yale. Her PSAT scores are at the National Merit Scholarship level. Financially, her caregivers don't have the means to help her through an expensive university.

Based on this scenario, use the chapter's information to help Kinesha achieve her dreams. Walk through the planning process by jotting down your reactions to these questions:

1. Which stage of Donald Super's developmental theory is Kinesha most likely to "fit" within and why? _____

   _____

   _____

2. By understanding the characteristics of this stage, how might you, the high school counselor, better work with Kinesha in her educational and career planning? _____

   _____

   _____

3. What ethical and legal issues may apply to this case study?

   _____

   _____

4. How might Kinesha's ethnicity and gender influence your assistance?

_____

_____

_____

5. How might you involve the school staff and faculty in the planning process? How might you involve her family? _____

_____

_____

_____

6. Review the activities suggested in this chapter under "high school." Which ones seem to be the most relevant to Kinesha's situation?

_____

_____

_____

7. **Making a plan**. Use the space provided below and sketch out a plan that will clarify the steps that would be most supportive of Kinesha as she thinks through her educational and career options. Again, assume you're her high school counselor.

Note: This appendix was written by Christopher Sink.

Kinesha's Educational/Career Plan

Educational goals: _____

_____

_____

Career goals: _____

_____

_____

What does she need to do and when? (Note steps she's already taken.)

Plan A Steps:

1. _____
2. _____
3. _____
4. _____
5. _____

Others? _____

Plan B Steps:

1. _____
2. _____
3. _____

Others? _____

As counselor what do I need to do to help and when?

_____

_____

What things can the family do to assist the student?

_____

_____

Other issues to consider: _____

REFERENCES

American School Counselor Association. (1998). *Ethical standards for school counselors.* Retrieved on October 24, 2002, from http://www.schoolcounselor.org/content.cfm? L1 = 1&L2 = 15

American School Counselor Association. (1999). *The role of the professional school counselor.* Alexandria, VA: Author.

Aviles, R. M. D, Guerrero, M. P., Howarth, H. B., & Thomas, G. (1999). Perceptions of Chicano/Latino students who have dropped out of school. *Journal of Counseling & Development, 77,* 465–473.

Bachay, J. B., & Rigby, E. T. (1997). Welcome to our school community: A career development intervention for the newcomer. *Professional School Counseling, 1,* 13–14.

Baker, S. B., & Taylor, J. G. (1998). Effects of career education interventions: A meta-analysis. *The Career Development Quarterly, 46,* 376–385.

Barry, B. (2001). *The Real Game facilitator's guide* (2001 rev.). St. John's, Newfoundland, Canada: The Real Game.

Beale, A. V. (2000). Elementary school career awareness: A visit to a hospital. *Journal of Career Development, 27,* 65–72.

Beale, A. V., & Nugent, D. G. (1996). The pizza connection: Enhancing career awareness. *Elementary School Guidance & Counseling, 30,* 294–303.

Beale, A. V., & Williams, J. C. (2000). The anatomy of an elementary school career day. *Journal of Career Development, 26,* 205–213.

Berns, R. G., & Erickson, P. M. (2001). *Contextual teaching and learning: Preparing students for the new economy.* Columbus, OH: CTE National Dissemination Center.

Blank, W. E., & Harwell, S. (Eds.). (1997). *Promising practices for connecting schools with the real world.* Tampa: University of South Florida.

Bottoms, G., Presson, A., & Johnson, M. (1992). *Making high schools work.* Atlanta, GA: Southern Regional Education Board.

Bowen, M. L., & Glenn, E. E. (1998). Counseling interventions for students who have mild disabilities. *Professional School Counseling, 2,* 16–25.

Brown, D. (2003). *Career information, career counseling, and career development* (8th ed.). Boston: Allyn & Bacon.

Campbell, C. A., & Dahir, C. A. (1997). *Sharing the vision: The national standards for school counseling programs.* Alexandria, VA: American School Counselor Association.

Clarke, G. M., & Kolstoe, O. P. (1995). *Career development & transition education for adolescents with disabilities.* Boston: Allyn & Bacon.

Colangelo, N. (1997). Counseling gifted students: Issues and practices. In N. Colangelo &

G. A. Davis (Eds.), *Handbook of gifted education* (2nd ed., pp. 353–365). Boston: Allyn & Bacon.

Crites, J. O. (1978). *Career Maturity Inventory: Theory and research handbook* (2nd ed.). Monterey, CA: California Test Bureau/McGraw-Hill.

DeBell, C. (2001). Ninety years in the world of work in America. *The Career Development Quarterly, 50,* 77–88.

Drucker, P. E. (1994, November). The age of social transformation. *The Atlantic Monthly, 274,* 53–80.

Dykeman, C. (2002, August 21). *Practical ideas for busy school counselors* (Webcast). Columbus, OH: CTE National Dissemination Center. Retrieved September 23, 2002, from http://www.nccte.org/events/profdevseries/20020821/index.asp

Dykeman, C., Herr, E. L., Ingram, M., Pehrsson, D., Wood, C., & Charles, S. (2001). *A taxonomy of career development interventions that occur in US secondary schools.* Minneapolis, MN: National Research Center for Career and Technical Education.

Feller, R. W. (1996a). The future of work. *Vocational Education Journal, 71*(4), 24–27.

Feller, R. W. (1996b). Redefining "career" during the work revolution. In R. W. Feller & G. Walz (Eds.), *Career transitions in turbulent times: Exploring work, learning, and careers* (pp. 143–154). Greensboro, NC: ERIC/CASS.

Feller, R. W. (2000, September). *Changing workplace: Keeping the boats afloat.* Presentation to the Manhattan-Ogden USD 383 Schools, Manhattan, KS.

Feller, R. W. (2002). Aligning school counseling, the changing workplace, and career development assumptions. *Professional School Counseling, 6,* 262–271.

Feller, R. W., & Davies, T. G. (1999). Career development for all. In A. J. Pautler, Jr. (Ed.), *Workforce education: Issues for the new century* (pp. 115–128). Ann Arbor, MI: Prakken.

Feller, R. W., & Vasos, J. (2001). *CDM career video series: Tour of your tomorrow* (2nd ed.). Ft. Collins, CO: Valer Productions.

Fox, R. W., Wandry, D., Pruitt, P., & Anderson, G. (1998). School to adult life transitions for students with disabilities: Forging a new alliance. *Professional School Counseling, 1*(4), 48–52.

Fouad, N. A. (1995). Career linking: An intervention to promote math and science career awareness. *Journal of Counseling & Development, 73,* 527–534.

Gati, I., & Saka, N. (2001). High school students' career-related decision-making difficulties. *Journal of Counseling & Development, 79,* 331–340.

Gillies, R. M., McMahon, M. L., & Carroll, J. (1998). Evaluating a career education intervention in the upper elementary school. *Journal of Career Development, 24,* 267–287.

Gray, K. C., & Herr, E. L. (1995). *Other ways to win: Creating alternatives for high school graduates.* Thousand Oaks, CA: Corwin Press.

Gysbers, N. C. (2001). School guidance and counseling in the 21st century: Remember the past into the future. *Professional School Counseling, 5,* 96–105.

Gysbers, N. C., & Henderson, P. (2000). *Developing and managing your school guidance program* (3rd ed.). Alexandria, VA: American Counseling Association.

Gysbers, N. C., Heppner, M. J., & Johnston, J. A. (2003). *Career counseling: Process, issues, and techniques* (2nd ed.). Boston: Allyn & Bacon.

Gysbers, N. C., & Moore, E. J. (1981). *Improving guidance programs.* Englewood Cliffs, NJ: Prentice-Hall.

Gysbers, N. C., Starr, M., & Magnuson, C. S. (1998). *Missouri comprehensive guidance program model* (Rev. ed.). Columbia, MO: Instructional Materials Laboratory.

Harrington, T. F., & O'Shea, A. J. (2000). *The Harrington-O'Shea Career Decision-making System Revised.* Circle Pines, MN: AGS.

Harris-Bowlsbey, J., Riley Dikel, M., & Sampson, J. P., Jr. (1998). *The Internet: A tool for career planning.* Columbus, OH: National Career Development Association.

Hartley, N., Mantle-Bromley, C., & Cobb, R. B. (1996). Building a context for reform. In N. K. Hartley & T. L. Wentling (Eds.), *Beyond tradition: Preparing the teachers of tomorrow's workforce* (pp. 23–52). Columbia, MO: University Council for Vocational Education.

Herr, E. L. (1995). *Counseling employment bound youth.* Greensboro, NC: ERIC.

Herr, E. L., & Cramer, S. H. (1996). *Career guidance and counseling through the lifespan* (5th ed.). New York: HarperCollins.

Herring, R. D. (1998). *Career counseling in schools: Multicultural and developmental perspectives.* Alexandria, VA: American Counseling Association.

Holland, J. L. (1994). *Self-directed Search, Form R* (4th ed.). Odessa, FL: PAR.

Holland, J. L. (1997). *Making vocational choices: A theory of vocational personalities and work environments* (3rd ed.). Odessa, FL: PAR.

Holland, J. L., & Powell, A. B. (1994). *Self-directed Search Career Explorer.* Odessa, FL: PAR.

Hoyt, K. B. (1981). *Career education: Where it is and where it is going.* Salt Lake City, UT: Olympus.

Hoyt, K. B. (2001). Helping high school students broaden their knowledge of postsecondary education options. *Professional School Counseling, 5,* 6–12.

Hoyt, K. B., Evans, R. N., Mackin, E. F., & Mangum, G. L. (1972). *Career education: What it is and how to do it.* Salt Lake City, UT: Olympus.

Hoyt, K. B., & Wickwire, P. N. (1999). Career education: Basic concepts and current status. In A. J. Pautler, Jr. (Ed.), *Workforce education: Issues for the new century* (pp. 49–63). Ann Arbor, MI: Prakken.

Hughey, K. F., & Hughey, J. K. (1999). Preparing students for the future: Making career development a priority for students. *Journal of Career Development, 25,* 203–216.

Hughey, K. F., Lapan, R. T., & Gysbers, N. C. (1993). Evaluating a high school guidance-language arts career unit: A qualitative approach. *The School Counselor, 41,* 96–101.

Hull, D. M. (2000). *Education and career preparation for the new millennium: A vision for systemic change.* Waco, TX: CORD.

Imel, S., Kerka, S., & Wonacott, M. E. (2001). *Using online occupational information for career development.* Columbus, OH: Center on Education and Training for Employment. Retrieved August 12, 2002, from http://ericacve.org/docs/pfile04.htm

Jarvis, P. S., & Keeley, E. S. (2003). From vocational decision making to career building: Blueprint, Real Games, and school counseling. *Professional School Counseling, 6,* 244–250.

Johnson, L. S. (2000). The relevance of school to career: A study of student awareness. *Journal of Career Development, 26,* 263–276.

Jones, L. K. (2002). *The Career Key.* Retrieved August 8, 2002, from http://www.careerkey. org/english/

Kobylarz, L. (Ed.). (1996). *National career development guidelines k-adult handbook.* Stillwater, OK: NOICC Training Support Center.

Kosciulek, J. F. (2003). An empowerment approach to career counseling with people with disabilities. In N. C. Gysbers, M. J. Heppner, & J. A. Johnston, *Career counseling: Process, issues, and techniques* (2nd ed., pp. 139–153). Boston: Allyn & Bacon.

Kraus, L. J., & Hughey, K. F. (1999). The impact of an intervention on career decision-making self-efficacy and career indecision. *Professional School Counseling, 2,* 384–390.

Krumboltz, J. D. (1996). A learning theory of career counseling. In M. L. Savickas & W. B. Walsh (Eds.), *Handbook of career counseling theory and practice* (pp. 55–80). Palo Alto, CA: Davies-Black.

Krumboltz, J. D., & Worthington, R. L. (1999). The school-to-work transition from a learning theory perspective. *The Career Development Quarterly, 47,* 312–325.

Ladany, N., Melincoff, D. S., Constantine, M. G., & Love, R. (1997). At-risk urban high school students' commitment to career choices. *Journal of Counseling & Development, 76,* 45–52.

Lapan, R. T., Gysbers, N. C., Hughey, K. F., & Arni, T. J. (1993). Evaluating a guidance language arts unit for high school juniors. *Journal of Counseling & Development, 71,* 444–451.

Lapan, R. T., Gysbers, N. C., & Sun, Y. (1997). The impact of more fully implemented guidance programs on the school experiences of high school students: A statewide evaluation study. *Journal of Counseling & Development, 75,* 292–302.

Lee, C. C. (2001). Culturally responsive school counselors and programs: Addressing the needs of all students. *Professional School Counseling, 4,* 257–261.

Mau, W. (1995). Educational planning and academic achievement of middle school students: A racial and cultural comparison. *Journal of Counseling & Development, 73,* 518–526.

Mau, W., & Bikos, L. H. (2000). Educational and vocational aspirations of minority and female students: A longitudinal study. *Journal of Counseling & Development, 78,* 186–194.

Mitchell, L. K., & Krumboltz, J. D. (1996). Krumboltz's learning theory of career choice and counseling. In D. Brown, L. Brooks, & Associates, *Career choice and development* (3rd ed., pp. 233–280). San Francisco: Jossey-Bass.

Mitchell, K. E., Levin, A. S., & Krumboltz, J. D. (1999). Planned happenstance: Constructing unexpected career opportunities. *Journal of Counseling & Development, 77,* 115–124.

Moses, B. (1998). *Career intelligence: The 12 new rules for work and life success.* San Francisco: Berrett-Koehler.

Murrow-Taylor, C., Foltz, B. M., Ellis, M. R., & Culbertson, K. (1999). A multicultural career fair for elementary students. *Professional School Counseling, 2,* 241–243.

National Association of Secondary School Principals. (1996). *Breaking ranks: Changing an American institution.* Reston, VA: Author.

Niles, S. G., & Harris-Bowlsbey, J. (2002). *Career development interventions in the 21st century.* Upper Saddle River, NJ: Merrill/Prentice Hall.

O'Brien, K. M., Dukstein, R. D., Jackson, S. L., Tomlinson, M. J., & Kamatuka, N. A. (1999). Broadening career horizons for students in at-risk environments. *The Career Development Quarterly, 47,* 215–229.

O'Brien, K. M., Bikos, L. H., Epstein, K. L., Flores, L. Y., Dukstein, R. D., & Kamatuka, N. A. (2000). Enhancing the career decision-making self-efficacy of upward bound students. *Journal of Career Development, 28,* 277–293.

Omaha Public Schools. (1998). *Comprehensive competency-based guidance management system.* Omaha, NE: Author.

Otto, L. B. (2000). Youth perspectives on parental career influence. *Journal of Career Development, 27,* 111–118.

Parsons, F. (1909). *Choosing a vocation.* Boston: Houghton Mifflin.

Perrone, P. A. (1997). Gifted individuals' career development. In N. Colangelo & G. A. Davis (Eds.), *Handbook of gifted education* (2nd ed., pp. 398–407). Boston: Allyn & Bacon.

Reardon, R. C., & Lenz, J. G. (1998). *The self-directed search and related Holland career materials: A practitioner's guide.* Odessa, FL: PAR.

Reardon, R. C., Lenz, J. G., Sampson, J. P., & Peterson, G. W. (2000). *Career development and planning: A comprehensive approach.* Belmont, CA: Wadsworth/Thomson.

Rojewski, J. W. (2002). *Preparing the workforce of tomorrow: A conceptual framework for career and technical education.* Columbus, OH: National Dissemination Center for Career and Technical Education, The Ohio State University.

Rysiew, K. J., Shore, B. M., & Leeb, R. T. (1999). Multipotentiality, giftedness, and career choice: A review. *Journal of Counseling & Development, 77,* 423–430.

Sabella, R. A. (2003). *SchoolCounselor.com 2.0: A friendly and practical guide to the World Wide Web.* Minneapolis, MN: Educational Media.

Savickas, M. L., & Crites, J. O. (1981). *Career decision making: Teaching the process.* Unpublished manuscript, Northeastern Ohio Universities College of Medicine, Rootstown, OH.

Schmidt, J. J. (2003). *Counseling in schools: Essential services and comprehensive programs* (4th ed.). Boston: Allyn & Bacon.

Schwiebert, V. L., Sealander, K. A., & Bradshaw, M. (1998). Preparing students with attention deficit disorders for entry into the workplace and postsecondary education. *Professional School Counseling, 2,* 26–32.

Sears, S. (1982). A definition of career guidance terms: A National Vocational Guidance Association perspective. *The Vocational Guidance Quarterly, 31,* 137–143.

Secretary's Commission on Achieving Necessary Skills. (1991). *What work requires of schools: A SCANS report for America 2000.* Washington, DC: U.S. Department of Labor.

Sellers, N., Satcher, J., & Comas, R. (1999). Children's occupational aspirations: Comparisons by gender, gender role identity, and socioeconomic status. *Professional School Counseling, 2,* 314–317.

Snyder, C. R., Feldman, D. B., Shorey, H. S., & Rand, K. L. (2002). Hopeful choices: A school counselor's guide to hope theory. *Professional School Counseling, 5,* 298–307.

Super, D. E. (1963). Self-concepts in vocational development. In D. E. Super, R. Starishevski, N. Matlin, & J. P. Jordaan (Eds.), *Career development: Self-concept theory* (pp. 17–32). New York: College Entrance Examination Board.

Super, D. E. (1990). A life-span, life-space approach to career development. In D. Brown, L. Brooks, & Associates, *Career choice and development* (2nd ed., pp. 197–261). San Francisco: Jossey-Bass.

Super, D. E., Savickas, M. L., & Super, C. M. (1996). The life-span, life-space approach to careers. In D. Brown, L. Brooks, & Associates, *Career choice and development* (3rd ed., pp. 121–178). San Francisco: Jossey-Bass.

Toffler, A., & Toffler, H. (1995). *Creating a new civilization.* Atlanta, GA: Turner.

Trusty, J., Robinson, C. R., Plata, M., & Ng, K. (2000). Effects of gender, socioeconomic status, and early academic performance on postsecondary educational choice. *Journal of Counseling & Development, 78,* 463–472.

U.S. Department of Education. (n.d.). *Contextual teaching and learning: Helping students make the connection.* Retrieved August 5, 2002, from http://www.contextual.org

U.S. Department of Labor. (2002). *Occupational outlook handbook* (2002–03 ed.). Retrieved August 12, 2002, from http://www.bls.gov/oco/home.htm

Van Horn, S. M., & Myrick, R. D. (2001). Computer technology and the 21st century school counselor. *Professional School Counseling, 5,* 124–130.

Wahl, K. H., & Blackhurst, A. (2000). Factors affecting the occupational and educational aspirations of children and adolescents. *Professional School Counseling, 3,* 367–374.

Wrenn, C. G. (1962). *The counselor in a changing world.* Washington, DC: American Personnel and Guidance Association.

Young, R. A. (1994). Helping adolescents with career development: The active role of parents. *The Career Development Quarterly, 42,* 195–203.

Young, R. A., & Friesen, J. D. (1992). The intentions of parents in influencing the career development of their children. *The Career Development Quarterly, 40,* 198–207.

Zunker, V. G. (2002). *Career counseling: Applied concepts of life planning* (6th ed.). Pacific Grove, CA: Brooks/Cole.

CHAPTER 8

Evaluating School Counseling Programs

Richard T. Lapan
University of Missouri-Columbia

Introduction, Rationale, and Definitions

The primary objective of this chapter is to help both preservice and practicing professional school counselors more fully understand how evaluation research can be a formidable ally for improving counseling services provided to students K–12 and in advocating for effective comprehensive programs with key decision makers (Cramer, Herr, Morris, & Frantz, 1970; Fall & Van Zandt, 1997; Herr, 1982). While significant gaps in our knowledge base are clearly evident and the methodological rigor of several studies has been criticized, the overall results of more than forty years of evaluation research suggest that within the school setting counselors can effectively impact critical aspects of student development in two distinctive ways. First, professional school counselors enhance student development directly by providing sophisticated counseling services to students (e.g., individual and group counseling, as well as classroom guidance curriculum and social skills training). Second, professional school counselors work to shape and maintain key school, family, and community contexts that nurture optimal student growth and development (Lapan, 2001). This chapter will familiarize the reader with an evolving knowledge base that supports counselor effectiveness to deliver these two kinds of services. Evaluation research can be used both to improve counseling services provided to all students K–12 and to advocate for the support of effective comprehensive programs with local school district, state, and federal policymakers.

Personal Assumptions and Beliefs

Two beliefs significantly influence my interpretation of the research reported in this chapter and how it has been organized. First, I have a great deal of respect and admiration for those professional school counselors who have made serious attempts to implement a comprehensive program concept in their schools (Campbell & Dahir, 1997; Gysbers & Henderson, 2000). Each year for the past thirteen years, I have had the opportunity to teach a school counseling practicum course. This past semester four of my students did their practica in four different elementary schools in one school district. I was struck with how each of the elementary school counselors, who provided on-site support for my students, had adapted the comprehensive program concept to best serve the differing needs of students, fit the unique circumstances of their individual schools, and match their own personal and professional strengths. The same comprehensive program model (Gysbers & Henderson, 2000) served as a general framework that had evolved into four uniquely individualized approaches, finely tuned to the particular circumstances of each school. The service delivery methods implemented by these counselors dramatically varied across schools (e.g., individual play therapy, structured group counseling, social skills training and friendship groups, and evening support groups for parents of special needs children). Over a period of several years, the program implemented in each school had been refined and tailored to the point where the principal, parents, and students expressed a great deal of satisfaction and valuing of their counselor's work.

Second, I have a certain amount of trepidation and caution in writing a chapter on evaluation of school counseling programs. Unfortunately, for a number of reasons evaluation research has been a somewhat problematic area for school counselors. Many school counselors have received little if any training in how to conduct general program evaluation activities (Trevisan, 2000). Even fewer counselors have been exposed to strategies for conducting practical evaluation research on the impact of their program within a school setting (Trevisan & Hubert, 2001). Because of such factors, it is not surprising that a number of school counselors develop negative attitudes toward program evaluation (Fall & Van Zandt, 1997). In addition, far too many school counselors have had less than positive encounters with their required graduate-level statistics courses and experience unnecessarily high levels of mathematics anxiety. Unfortunately, this anxiety is often associated with program evaluation and research.

Evaluation research can be a very positive force for the development of our profession. In this chapter, I have attempted to clearly demonstrate this connection. To accomplish this objective, findings from numerous individual studies have been summarized and lengthy discussions of any one particular study have been avoided. The reader is encouraged to study the original sources cited in this chapter. The research findings reviewed in this chapter are reported in a way that counselors can use the data to inform their practice, improve their programs, and advocate for their profession.

Why Evaluate School Counseling Programs?

A professional school counselor's day is filled with a wide range of tasks that demand immediate attention. Given the challenges and sometimes hectic nature of this job, it is legitimate to ask why a practicing school counselor should be concerned with research and actually attempt to carry out her or his own program evaluation activities. One counselor's experience provides a partial answer to this question. Hughes and James (2001) described how an elementary school counselor's work role was in serious jeopardy of being radically altered because of impending budget cuts. Working with a counselor educator colleague, the school counselor gathered data that would inform local decision makers about the range of vital activities and roles that were currently being implemented as part of the school counseling program. The resulting report and presentation to the decision-making committee led to a discussion of how the needs of students could be better served in the school, and a greater awareness and recognition for the counseling program's role in assisting students. Hughes and James concluded that to protect and support their program, professional school counselors should regularly collect accountability information and then report the findings to school-based decision makers.

Evaluation research can be a catalyst for improving counseling services that are provided to help all students more effectively cope with the range of significant challenges they now confront in K–12 schools. For example, when approving a state-mandated comprehensive counseling program for the state of Texas, the Texas Education Agency (1996) argued that "the problems students face are becoming increasingly more serious and complex. These problems include poverty, violence, gang involvement, dysfunctional families, child abuse, substance abuse, increasing numbers of students who are at risk of dropping out, and students who lack needed personal and social skills" (p. 53).

The Ethical Standards of the American School Counselor Association require practicing professional school counselors to evaluate the effectiveness of their comprehensive programs (please review at www.schoolcounselor.org and Chapter 1 in this text). To develop counseling programs that better meet the needs of students and the unique challenges posed by markedly different school settings (i.e., urban, rural, and suburban schools), evaluation research can become "a dynamic that motivates a pace of innovation and improvement" (Slavin, 2002, n.p.). It enhances the counseling profession's ability not to rely solely on opinion or conjecture but to use evidence as an important part of the basis and justification for one's practice (Sexton & Whiston, 1996). Evaluation practices can highlight the direct relationship between the work of the school counselor and the enhanced academic achievement of K–12 students. This information can be used collaboratively with school administrators in reform efforts to improve schools and student learning. As counselors more clearly demonstrate their effectiveness and justify the need for additional resources to enhance critical components of their counseling programs, public recognition and support for our efforts will be strengthened.

Chapter Organization

The remainder of this chapter has been organized into four sections. The first section discusses comprehensive school counseling programs as results-based systems that evolve to better meet the needs of students. These needs vary depending on the school, family, and community contexts within which young people live. As the needs of students change across these contexts, the program activities and interventions employed by school counselors must be adapted to more effectively assist students. The next three sections of this chapter use ASCA's National Standards for School Counseling Programs (Campbell & Dahir, 1997) and the ASCA National Model: A Framework for School Counseling Programs (American School Counselor Association, 2003) to summarize a wide range of research that suggests that professional school counselors can play an important role in promoting K–12 students' academic achievement and career, social, and emotional development.

Results-Based Systems

During the last part of the twentieth century, a process was set in motion to re-energize and redesign the profession of school counseling (Paisley & Borders, 1995). Leaders in the field recognized that because school counselors had organized their work in schools around ancillary position orientations they were having difficulty helping students effectively cope with increasingly problematic and diverse issues (Sprinthall, 1981). For example, results from national longitudinal studies had suggested that students from minority families, economically disadvantaged homes, and rural areas were much less likely to receive counseling services

(Lee & Ekstrom, 1987). The Commission on Precollege Guidance and Counseling (1986) found also that students most in need of effective school counseling services were the least likely groups to receive such interventions. Many teachers believed that school counselors were mostly ineffective in addressing the significant problems posed by at-risk students (Peterson & Maddux, 1988).

By implementing a comprehensive program concept, it was hoped that school counselors would make a significant contribution to the learning climate in each school (Myrick, 1987). The work of the school counselor would be integrated with the central concerns and goals of each school and become a motivating force to enhance student academic achievement, career development, social and emotional growth, as well as intergroup understanding and acceptance (e.g., ASCA/NACAC, 1986; Gysbers & Henderson, 2000; Herr, 1995; Johnson & Johnson, 1982; Myrick, 1997). The ASCA National Standards for School Counseling Programs (Campbell & Dahir, 1997) reflect the goals and accomplishments achieved by this more than forty-year effort to transform the field of school counseling around a comprehensive program model.

An important component of this change process has been and continues to be a commitment to a results-based orientation (Lapan, 2001). Johnson and Johnson (1982) argued that school counseling should be reconceptualized as a results-based program. From this perspective, essential outcomes critical for all students to attain are first identified. Then, counselor duties and work tasks evolve and adapt in ways that maximize student attainment of these critical outcomes. Mitchell and Gysbers (1978) suggested that to continually strive to enhance student development, a comprehensive program should become a self-correcting system based on four interrelated processes (i.e., planning, designing, implementing, and evaluating). This defines an ongoing process for program improvement, where counselor roles and duties are not static but continually adapt to better meet the needs of all students. For example, Paisley (2001) described how strategies for team building and community-based systemic interventions could now help school counselors reshape and redesign their comprehensive program. Results-based systems challenge counselors not to lapse into outdated, rigid, and marginally effective work roles. Instead, attainment of outcomes is consistently evaluated, and on the basis of this information counselor roles and work tasks are adapted to better help students.

Many of the early pioneers who paved the way for the comprehensive program movement had a commitment to establishing and improving the effectiveness of school counseling services through conducting evaluation research studies. For example, Caravello (1958), noting the absence of studies examining the effectiveness of counseling in the schools, conducted a longitudinal experimental/

control group study of 300 high school seniors. Analyzing written reports gathered from students one year after they graduated, Caravello concluded that seniors who received counseling from a full-time counselor or guidance specialist were more likely to continue their educational and vocational training after graduation, and to develop vocational goals and make career decisions earlier in high school than students who did not receive such counseling services. Sanborn (1964) compared outcomes for 1,193 seniors who attended four different high schools, each having distinctively different school counseling services. Two years after graduating from high school, significant advantages were found for those students attending high schools where they received regularly scheduled group guidance activities by a full-time counselor. These students expressed greater satisfaction with the counseling they received in high school and indicated a greater tendency to use this counseling to address both personal and family problems.

The most significant study from this era was arguably John Rothney's (1958) classic five-year longitudinal study of high school seniors. Rothney assessed the impact of receiving counseling services during high school over the five-year period immediately following graduation. Collecting data for students attending four different high schools, Rothney compared a random sample of students who received counseling services while in high school to a control group of high school students who did not receive counseling services. He found that students receiving counseling services while in high school (a) had slightly higher academic achievement while in high school and during the five-year period after graduating from high school; (b) were more satisfied with their high school and postsecondary educational experiences; (c) had a better understanding of their strengths and weaknesses as high school seniors; (d) were more consistent in expressing a vocational choice, entering a career related to that choice, and remaining longer in that chosen area after high school; (e) made more progress in their post–high school employment; (f) were more likely to both enter and then graduate from postsecondary educational training programs; (g) expressed greater satisfaction with their lives five years after graduating from high school; (h) joined in more self-improvement activities in the five years following high school graduation; and (i) reported very positive attitudes about the counseling they received while in high school.

When considering the lessons that could be learned from this study, Rothney (1958) concluded:

> When so many small and a few large differences in the directions hypothesized by guidance workers can be obtained under representative high school counseling conditions, it seems likely that greater differences would appear if counseling were

done under more ideal circumstances. Such circumstances would seem to require more acceptance of counseling as a regular part of secondary school experience, more enthusiastic support from parents and school personnel, and better techniques of evaluation. (pp. 482–483)

In many respects, the conclusions Rothney drew from his very sophisticated and time-consuming study have forecasted some of the most important challenges and opportunities currently faced by the school counseling profession. Over the past twenty-five years, published reviews of the research on school counselor effectiveness have consistently found many small and a few large effects related to interventions conducted by school counselors. These reviews have also consistently criticized methodological problems with some studies and exposed glaring gaps in the knowledge needed to guide counselor practice (e.g., Borders & Drury, 1992; Gerler, 1985, 1992; Lee, 1993; Schmidt, Lanier, & Cope, 1999; St. Clair, 1989; Whiston & Sexton, 1998). Practitioners and researchers have continued to struggle to have school counseling be a more accepted part of the K–12 experience and more fully integrated into the central core of a school's mission (e.g., Watkins, 2001). Obtaining more enthusiastic support from key school personnel (e.g., principals, teachers, and school board members) and parents has not yet been adequately realized (e.g., Gysbers, Lapan, & Jones, 2000; Shoffner & Williamson, 2000).

Fortunately, the school counseling profession is now in a better position to improve upon the conclusions that can be drawn from Rothney's (1958) study. Efforts of professional school counselors across the United States are beginning to coalesce around the implementation of a common comprehensive program framework (Campbell & Dahir, 1997; Gysbers & Henderson, 2000) that holds greater promise for increasing the role counselors can play in promoting more holistic, positive development for all students (Sink & MacDonald, 1998). In addition, better methods, tools, and strategies for conducting program evaluation research are now both available and being put to productive use. Qualitative approaches for conducting rigorous methods of inquiry have been developed in the larger discipline of educational and psychological research. Such methods are now beginning to be very successfully used to study the development of school counselors and school counseling programs. For practical examples of how to conduct qualitative program evaluation research, please review the methods used in the following studies (Brott & Myers, 1999; Cinamon & Helman, 2002; Hughey, Lapan, & Gysbers, 1993; Jackson & White, 2000; MacDonald & Sink, 1999). Also, Schmidt (1995) outlined a systematic strategy for using external reviewers to satisfy the accountability demands currently placed on counselors to evaluate their school counseling programs.

Professional school counselors' ability to use quantitative analyses to conduct practical evaluation studies has been enhanced in two ways. First, commercially available software products can now place very powerful yet extremely user-friendly data analysis tools on each counselor's desktop computer (e.g., Statistical Package for the Social Sciences [SPSS], 2001). Graduate training programs need to assist counselors in becoming competent in using such programs to compute basic statistics (e.g., percentages, means, standard deviations, t-tests, and correlations) and then to present such data through informative/interesting graphical displays. In the vast majority of cases, practicing professional school counselors will only need these basic statistical tools to quantitatively evaluate their program and bring this information effectively to the attention of key decision makers.

Second, extending correlational analyses, multiple regression, and factor analysis, the field of multivariate statistics has developed new analytic procedures that can be used to analyze program evaluation data. For example, hierarchical linear modeling techniques enable evaluators to test for benefits to students across multiple levels and contexts (e.g., classrooms, schools, school districts, and communities) (Arnold, 1992). Recently, such procedures have shown promise in the evaluation of possible outcomes for students who participate in more fully implemented comprehensive counseling programs (Lapan, Gysbers, & Petroski, 2001; Lapan, Gysbers, & Sun, 1997). Practicing professional school counselors and counselor educators can come together and combine their skills to apply these slightly more complex and time-consuming quantitative procedures. These multiple methods of research enable the field of school counseling to gain a clearer understanding of the benefits students derive from specific counselor efforts and how comprehensive programs can be improved to be of greater assistance to all students.

A Framework for Program Planning and Evaluation

Considerable progress has been made implementing comprehensive counseling program models across the United States. Several states have adopted program frameworks that clearly reflect the vision for change advocated by reformers for more than three decades. With the support of strong leadership from state supervisors of guidance, several states have mandated comprehensive counseling program guidelines to structure the work of counselors in schools and their graduate-level training (e.g., Missouri, Texas, and Utah). For example, in 1988 the Utah Comprehensive Guidance Program (UCGP) was implemented as a major statewide school restructuring effort. Since then, more than 2,000 administrators, teachers, and school counselors have received intensive training in how to put this model in place in each school in the state of Utah. Implementation of the UCGP has led to dramatic changes in counselor roles, work tasks, and benefits for students (Nelson & Gardner, 1998). Utah school counselors are now providing students substantially more career planning, advisement, and classroom guidance curriculum. Counselors are now more likely to gain the support and involvement of parents in counseling program activities. Because of the success of the UCGP and demonstrated benefit to students, key policymakers and stakeholders (e.g., the governor of Utah, the State Board of Education, and the Utah Parent-Teacher Organization) have worked with the Utah State Legislature to provide sustainable state funding for this initiative since 1993 (Utah State Office of Education, 2000).

As will be more fully described later in this chapter, positive advantages for students have been associated with changes in counselor roles and work tasks that follow from implementation of a comprehensive program model. Positive effects for counseling interventions have been found across a diverse range of students—for example, low-achieving students, gifted students, learning disabled students, disruptive students, and students from divorced families (for a review see Borders & Drury, 1992). Students have reported that they are now more likely to meet with their school counselors and that these sessions are both important and meaningful to them (Hughey, Lapan, & Gysbers, 1993). Professional school counselors report that as the implementation of a comprehensive program model moves forward they find that they are more likely to (a) spend more time with students, teachers, and parents; (b) spend a greater amount of time in classrooms; (c) generate greater public understanding and support for their program; and (d) spend far less time on nonguidance tasks such as clerical and fill-in roles (Gysbers, Lapan, & Blair, 1999).

Although these initial reports have been encouraging, serious concerns have been raised. Researchers have noted problems related to (a) the quality of program implementation efforts, (b) the adequacy of the research base to support these efforts, and (c) the prioritizing of certain counselor work tasks and roles over others. Sink and MacDonald (1998) found that nearly half of all U.S. states had by 1997 begun to abandon outdated models and were attempting to implement a comprehensive program framework. However, these implementation efforts were seriously hampered by (a) a lack of attention to ethnic and multicultural issues, (b) poor integration of developmental theory into the guidance curriculum, and (c) an imbalance between remediation and prevention activities (MacDonald & Sink, 1999; Paisley & Peace, 1995). Keys, Bemak, and Lockhart (1998) criticized the delivery models of developmental counseling programs for not adequately addressing the mental health needs of at-risk youth. Critical policy directives, such as state school board associations' policies for school counseling, have not kept pace with changes in the field (Gysbers et al., 2000).

While finding evidence that school counselors were performing the roles and duties suggested by a comprehensive program model, Burnham and Jackson (2000) noted serious discrepancies and significant variations across counselors and schools. House and Hayes (2002) argued that school counselors need to assume a more proactive leadership role in efforts to reform schools to better meet the learning needs of all students. Hampering the more complete assumption of such critical leadership roles, however, is the reality that far too many school counselors continue to spend an excessive amount of their work time performing noncounseling tasks. For example, a recent statewide study in Texas found that school counselors spend only approximately 60 percent of their time on counseling tasks (Rylander, 2002). A substantial amount of counselor time was spent performing administrative duties. Counselors in Texas reported that the performance of these administrative duties greatly reduced their availability and effectiveness in working with students.

Whiston and Sexton (1998) contended that there was a "dearth of outcome studies" published between 1988 and 1995 that could provide a research basis to support comprehensive program reforms (p. 422). As school counselors attempt to implement programs in varied and diverse settings, disagreements over counselor roles and work tasks have arisen. For example, when drawing conclusions from their excellent review of the literature, Borders and Drury (1992) suggested that the role of a coordinator might be deemphasized. However, counselor educators attempting to meet the challenging and unique needs of students attending urban schools have strongly argued that in this particular setting the coordinator role may be one of the most important work roles performed by school counselors and should be emphasized in a counselor's day-to-day work tasks and duties (Green & Keys, 2001). From a results-based perspective, these are empirical questions that can be answered through program evaluation research.

Figure 8.1 presents a heuristic framework professional school counselors can use to guide their results-based program planning and evaluation activities. In this process, the essential work tasks and roles of the school counselor evolve to better enhance the academic achievement, career development, and social and emotional development of all students in each school. Counselors distribute their time to promote student development in two ways. First, counselors work directly with students and parents using empirically supported individual, group, and classroom guidance procedures. Second, counselors work with key stakeholders (e.g., teachers, parents, community leaders, and students) and policymakers (e.g., principals,

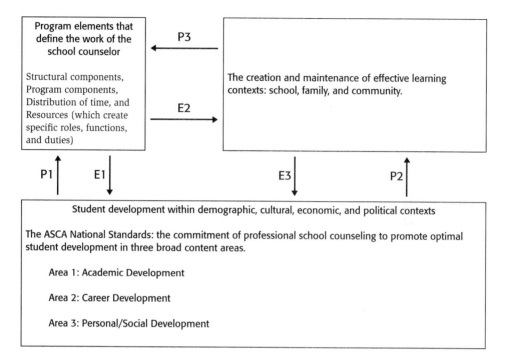

Six Planning and Evaluation Processes

Program planning from results to be attained
P1 – Describe the direct relationship between the attainment of desired student outcomes and the performance of specific counselor work roles and duties.
P2 – Describe the relationship between the attainment of desired student outcomes and key aspects of school, family, and community learning contexts in a particular school.
P3 – Describe the direct relationship between the creation and maintenance of effective learning contexts and the performance of specific counselor roles and duties.

Evaluation of attained results
E1 – Gather information linking the attainment of valued student outcomes to specific roles and work duties performed by the school counselor.
E2 – Gather information linking the creation and maintenance of effective learning contexts to specific roles and work duties performed by the school counselor.
E3 – Gather information linking the attainment of valued student outcomes to the creation and maintenance of effective learning contexts.

Figure 8.1   A results-based program planning and evaluation framework.

school board members, and elected public officials) to maintain school, family, and community contexts necessary for nurturing optimal student development.

The school counselor as a reflective, investigative professional needs to engage in consistent information-gathering activities that lead to improved answers to important program evaluation questions such as the following:

1. How can counselor roles, duties, functions, and interventions be transformed to be of greater benefit and impact for all students?
2. How can counselor time on task be redistributed to maximize benefits for all students?
3. How can a program be tailored to better meet the needs of each local school?
4. How can the program become central to the overriding mission of each school?
5. How can better partnerships between school personnel, parents, and business and community leaders be established?
6. How can counselors better advocate for their programs with local, state, and national policymakers?

The continuing development of school counseling depends on our profession's ability to improve answers to such program evaluation questions. Public acceptance and support for professional school counseling will be enhanced by a discipline that can be trusted to benefit students through practices grounded in respected, rigorous methods of inquiry.

Figure 8.1 suggests that a straightforward four-step approach be used to effectively carry out program planning and evaluation activities. First, using a coherent developmental framework (e.g., the ASCA National Standards for School Counseling Programs, the ASCA National Model, or the formative/summative outcomes outlined by Lapan, 2001), school counselors should identify (with the input of key stakeholders and policymakers) critical student outcomes that will become the objectives to be attained by the comprehensive program. Many practical and user-friendly methods are available and can be readily employed to gather this information (e.g., needs surveys or focus groups). Second, an action plan would then be developed that highlights both the direct counseling services most likely to impact desired student outcomes, as well as strategies for shaping specific aspects of school, family, and community contexts that nurture this growth. Third, a counselor would then collect, analyze, and synthesize information related to this action plan. Finally, counselors should engage in discussions of their results with key policymakers and stakeholders. These discussions would focus on the use of the evaluation information to document desired gains for students (step 1), improve the action plan to be used in the future to better meet student needs (step 2), and advocate for effective counseling practices with key policymakers and stakeholders (step 3).

It is important to reiterate that basic descriptive statistics (e.g., percentages, means, and standard deviations), bivariate correlations, t-tests, and an ability to graph these results provide practicing school counselors more than enough quantitative tools to conduct program evaluation activities. Because this is a strength of school counselors, the emphasis should be on gathering information through interpersonal exchanges. For a practicing school counselor, conducting program evaluation and accountability activities is not the same thing as doing an impractical and overwhelming project in multivariate statistics. The core of a results-based program evaluation process is grounded in an ability to observe important interpersonal events and abstract the meaning of these encounters. This is one of the strengths professional school counselors bring to their local schools.

A results-based approach to program planning and evaluation clearly recognizes that there may be no context-free best way to implement a comprehensive program in widely diverse school and community settings. More than three decades ago, Herr and Cramer (1972) extended to school counseling Paul's (1969) challenge to psychotherapy researchers that they identify specific treatments that are effective for different people, who have different problems, live in different circumstances and conditions, and understand why certain positive changes come about as a result of the counseling/psychotherapy intervention. Herr and Cramer (1972) challenged school counselors to develop programs that aligned the specific resources needed by learners for their different types of needs, under different kinds of school conditions, for promoting different types of student development, and attempting to achieve different purposes. The importance of making such distinctions can be seen in program evaluation research on critical school-based interventions. For example, extensive evaluations of early childhood education programs have led to the empirically supported conclusion that depending on the types of learners and the needs of these learners, either a student-centered or a more didactic approach produces the best results (Paris & Cunningham, 1996).

A comprehensive counseling program creates greater opportunities to enhance student development when the conditional fit among learners, the counselor, the school, the students' families, and the community are maximized. This approach emphasizes the necessity of professional school counselors to provide culturally competent counseling services to an increasingly diverse student population and work to have students realize the benefits of attending schools that have culturally responsive learning environments (Constantine & Yeh, 2001; Lee, 2001). From this situational perspective, it may be that in some contexts the coordinator role should be deemphasized while in others (e.g., more urban settings) it might need to be highlighted. This becomes an empirical question that can be answered by either qualitative or quantitative evaluation research methods. Depending on the particular school, family and community contexts, the needs of students, and the strengths and weaknesses of the counselor, a coordinator's role may be critical in some situations but not in others. A results-based evaluation process would attempt to gather information to shed light on this question and then feed these insights back into the program-planning activities that connect counselor time to specific work roles in a particular school.

The evolving specialty of school counseling needs reflective, investigative practitioners. Professional school counselors must make very difficult decisions in allocating their time and resources in ways that best benefit an increasingly diverse student population. A counselor's ability and willingness to make informed decisions regarding how they will focus their efforts and spend their time are necessary conditions for engaging in a results-based process of program improvement. To successfully integrate a comprehensive program model in their schools, counselors must be able to thoughtfully plan, design, implement, evaluate, and then use the insights gained from this process to improve their efforts (Gysbers & Henderson, 2000). Within each school, a results-based process of program development leads to the creation of richly elaborated knowledge structures that can be used to guide counselor practice and enhance outcomes for all students.

An example is briefly described to illustrate how a results-based approach can be used to transform the essential work of the school counselor to better meet the needs of students in a local school district. Approximately six years ago, secondary school counselors in a suburban/urban Missouri school district were approached by their principal to reduce the number of physical fights that were occurring between students. The counselors developed and then put in place a peer mediation and conflict resolution program (Profitt, 1996). First, counselors trained a diverse group of students in peer mediation and communication skills. Supervision and space were provided to peer counselors to interact with fellow students in ways that would proactively resolve disputes before they escalated into physical confrontations. The program was a major success. The counselors validated their work by graphing the dramatic decline, over a two-year period, in the number of student referrals to the principal's office for fighting.

Over time, this intervention became a regular and expected part of the school environment and the comprehensive counseling program. Eventually, it took less and less counselor time to manage it effectively. Counselors then re-allocated some of this saved time to develop more intensive anger management training options for those students whose needs were clearly not being effectively met by the peer counseling intervention. Over a six-year period, work roles and duties engaged in by these counselors changed dramatically as they explored, conceptualized, implemented, and evaluated various options. In the peer mediation phase, counselors developed materials, trained peer counselors, and provided necessary supervision. As clusters of students were identified that did not successfully respond to peer mediation, the school counselors allocated work time to help these students by providing them with more intensive interventions, such as cognitive-behavioral counseling, functional behavioral analyses, and family counseling.

To better meet the anger management needs of all the students, these counselors developed a richly elaborated knowledge structure tailored to what would work in their particular school. The counselors gathered information from key stakeholders to identify critical outcomes that needed to happen for students in their school. Learning from experience, they then created a two-level approach that better fit the situation in their school. This multilevel approach identified different strategies for assisting counselors to know how to help students better manage their anger. Over time, these professional school counselors gained insight in how to maximize the fit between learner, counseling approach, counselor, and school (Herr & Cramer, 1972). For example, they became more knowledgeable about which students, under what conditions would need more time-intensive interventions (e.g., family counseling or applied behavioral analysis) if the student were to develop more effective anger management skills. By engaging in an ongoing process of reflective, investigative inquiry and debate, these counselors came to understand how best to help students in their particular school. This understanding was then used to adjust counselor roles, duties, time allocations, and resources to better maximize results for all students. Their principal came to understand the counselors as essential colleagues in her attempt to create and maintain a more effective learning environment in the high school for all students.

As both this example and the remainder of this chapter demonstrate, professional school counselors have consistently shown an ability to positively promote the academic, career, social, and emotional development for diverse student populations. Counselors can use the results of the many high-quality studies conducted to date to advocate for the support of their efforts with key policymakers and stakeholders. One potentially effective strategy that is currently being used in the state of Missouri is to develop and disseminate policy briefs. A policy brief summarizes the results of local, state, and national research findings into user-friendly documents that target critical stakeholders (e.g., parents, school board members, local and state legislators, and other key decision makers). A policy brief clearly highlights student needs and how professional school counselors are responding to assist students. When a counselor has only a few minutes of a key policymaker's time, a policy brief provides an effective way to interject critical results-based information into those decision-making processes that greatly impact students and actual support for comprehensive school counseling programs. Examples of policy briefs can be reviewed online at http://schoolweb. missouri.edu/msca/.

Academic Achievement

Leaders in the attempt to transform the field of school counseling have consistently emphasized that one of the primary purposes of a comprehensive program is to assist the instructional process in schools and enhance student academic achievement (e.g., Myrick, 1987). Major reviews of school counseling research conducted since the 1970s have concluded that professional school counselors can use a variety of intervention strategies to improve the academic achievement of students who have differing needs and come from diverse backgrounds. For example, Gerler (1985) critiqued several studies demonstrating that elementary school counselors can significantly influence the development of more positive classroom learning environments and improve in-class behaviors associated with higher levels of academic achievement. Among the effective strategies used by counselors to achieve these results was the development of consultation relationships with classroom teachers. In addition, teachers who developed a productive consultative relationship with their school counselor also expressed greater satisfaction in their job as a teacher. These findings were corroborated a few years later by Conoley and Conoley (1981). They found that teachers who developed productive consultative relationships with their school counselors (a) created a better learning environment for students in their classrooms, (b) were more positive when interacting with their students and complimentary of their students, and (c) had a more positive perception of themselves as teachers.

Borders and Drury (1992) reviewed a number of studies supporting the position that a wide range of counselor interventions could be used to improve student academic achievement, persistence, school attendance, and classroom behavior. For example, group counseling interventions have been effectively employed to improve student attitudes toward school and others. Bowman and Myrick (1987) used a peer facilitation procedure to improve the classroom behavior and school attitudes of second and third graders. Consultation with teachers and parents by school counselors was again found to be associated with better grades, higher achievement test scores, improved classroom behavior, and student motivation to learn (e.g., Bundy & Poppen, 1986; Medway, 1982). These results were found across a wide range of student populations and school settings (e.g., minority, gifted, disruptive, low-achieving, and learning disabled students, and students experiencing significant disruptions in their families). Lapan, Kardash, and Turner (2002) summarized and integrated available research to suggest strategies school counselors could use to empower all students to become self-regulated learners (i.e., students who take charge of their own learning; see Zimmerman & Schunk, 2001, for details).

Whiston and Sexton (1998) highlighted how classroom guidance curriculum activities had been shown to be capable of positively impacting student academic achievement. Studies found that classroom guidance curriculum interventions could be tailored to improve students' reading scores (Hadley, 1988), mathematics achievement (Lee, 1993), study skills, standardized achievement test scores (Carns & Carns, 1991), and composition skills (Lapan, Gysbers, Hughey, & Arni, 1993). Integrating career development activities and programs into the classroom curriculum has been repeatedly found to enhance student learning and measured academic achievement levels (Baker & Taylor, 1998; Evans & Burck, 1992). In contrast to fears and reservations expressed by some school administrators that time spent on classroom guidance curriculum activities would hurt student academic achievement, the opposite has actually been found. Connecting student learning to meaningful real-life issues and valued possible futures appears to enhance student motivation and learning. Interestingly, the connection of student learning to meaningful experiences and desired future career directions is also one of the central recommendations of a major policy statement authored by secondary school principals for radically reforming high schools in the United States (National Association of Secondary School Principals [NASSP], 1996).

Results from initial evaluations of statewide implementations of comprehensive counseling program models have suggested that student academic achievement can be positively impacted by the adoption of such a framework in each school. For example, students attending Utah schools where the UCGP was being more fully implemented were found to score higher on the ACT standardized achievement test (on almost every area of the test) and take more advanced mathematics, science, and technical courses than students in schools where the UCGP was less fully implemented (Gardner, Nelson, & Fox, 1999). Students attending a school that was more fully implementing the UCGP expressed greater satisfaction in the education they were receiving and felt that their school counselors were more effective in assisting them. In addition, statewide samples of both middle and high school students reported earning higher grades in schools that were more fully implementing the state-mandated Missouri Comprehensive Guidance and Counseling Program (Lapan et al., 1997; Lapan et al., 2001).

Career Development

One of the most consistent findings in the literature has been that school-based interventions can have a major impact on students' career development. In those schools that were more fully implementing a comprehensive program model, statewide samples of both seventh graders (n = 22,601) and high school students (n = 22,964) reported that considerably more career and college information was now being made available to them (Lapan et al., 2001; Lapan et al., 1997). Peterson, Long, and Billups (1999) demonstrated how a computer-assisted classroom career intervention could be effectively used by school counselors to improve eighth graders' decisions about the courses they should take in grades 9 through 12. Career interventions have been found to increase foresight, direction, and positive time perspective in adolescence (e.g., Savickas, 1990). Researchers have described practical and effective ways in which counselors can work with parents to help them become more productively involved in promoting their children's career development (e.g., Palmer & Cochran, 1988). Career interventions offered by school counselors have been associated with positive outcomes for a wide range of students, including minority students (Dunn & Veltman, 1989; Haas & Sullivan, 1991), students with learning disabilities (Hutchinson, Freeman, Downey, & Kilbreath, 1992), and gifted students (Hong, Whiston, & Milgram, 1993; Kerr & Ghrist-Priebe, 1988).

Several studies have described procedures counselors can use to promote career development through classroom guidance activities and integrate career development into the academic curriculum. For example, a joint program offered by the language arts department and the school counselors resulted in measured gains in both the career development and academic achievement of high school juniors (Hughey et al., 1993; Lapan et al., 1993). In this joint program, school counselors presented extensive in-class career exploration exercises while the language arts teachers worked with students on composition skills (e.g., organization, grammar, and paragraph construction). After statistically controlling for prior academic achievement differences between students, gains in career competencies identified by this state's comprehensive counseling program significantly predicted higher grades earned by students on a research paper focusing on career and life plans. It is important to note that the grades were assigned by the language arts teachers based solely on the composition skills students demonstrated in their research papers.

Solberg et al. (1998) developed a classroom approach for enhancing the vocational identity development of adolescents. This approach connected family involvement, self-efficacy expectations, and a focus on stress and time management to facilitate expectations and behaviors related to success in college. Findings from two independent meta-analyses investigating the impact of school-based career development activities on student development and academic achievement have each supported the positive influence of such career interventions (Baker & Taylor, 1998; Evans & Burck, 1992). School counselors and teachers can create seamless programs that enhance the career development and academic achievement of all students. To maximize benefits to both areas of student development, school counselors can create a synergy between students' motivation to learn and the crystallization of desired possible futures.

Increasingly, school counselors and counselor educators have emphasized the need to create community-based partnerships to more effectively accomplish the varied and multiple goals of their comprehensive counseling program (e.g., Keys & Bemak, 1997; Paisley, 2001; Taylor & Adelman, 2000). Community-based partnerships provide counselors efficacious intervention strategies to enhance the career development of all students. Lapan and Kosciulek (2001) developed an evaluation framework school counselors could use to evaluate the impact of such community-based career partnerships. The potential of community partnerships to improve dramatically the career development of an increasingly diverse K–12 student population can be seen in the evaluation results of those community-career partnerships funded by the School-to-Work Opportunities Act of 1994.

In their initial report to Congress evaluating the benefits to students who participated in school-to-work community partnerships, Hershey, Silverberg, Haimson, Hudis, and Jackson (1999) reported significant benefits to students related to partnership implementation efforts in eight states. Instead of training students in industry-specific skill certificates as some had feared, partnerships were much more likely to engage students in the exploration of broad career pathways. Because of these partnerships, students were now getting greater support and guidance in how to plan their high school coursework around a career goal and use elective courses to follow their career interests. Non–college bound students were taking many more classes focusing on a career goal than they had in the past. Four-year college bound students were as likely to participate in partnership programs as non–college bound students. Women, especially African American women, were more involved in activities connecting school and the workplace. Students, particularly African American students, were now taking many more high school classes that matched their career interests (Hershey et al., 1999). Establishing and maintaining community-based partnerships has the potential to enable school counselors to more effectively meet the academic achievement, career development, and social-emotional needs of all their students.

Two qualitative studies conducted outside the field of school counseling have provided additional support for the position that students' career development is improved when school counselors engage in job duties that are central to the more complete implementation of a comprehensive program model. In a recent national study conducted by the Sloane Foundation on student educational and occupational aspirations and plans, Schneider and Stevenson (1999) argued that the most effective schools had counselors who actively engaged students in career planning and positive human development activities across the high school years. Essentially, they described many of the central components and likely outcomes of a comprehensive school counseling program that could be implemented in all schools by professional school counselors (Campbell & Dahir, 1997; Gysbers & Henderson, 2000).

Blustein, Phillips, Jobin-Davis, Finkelberg, and Roarke (1997) conducted a theory-building investigation of more adaptive school-to-work transitions for work bound youth. Among several interesting findings, the authors pointed out that job satisfaction in young adulthood (for students who went straight into the workforce after high school) was strongly connected to student experiences with school counselors in high school. Young adults who were fortunate enough to have school counselors who were proactive in reaching out to them and providing emotional and instrumental support expressed greater satisfaction with their current job and career situation. In contrast, young adults who reported that their school counselors did not engage them in any meaningful way (usually because of their large caseloads) were not as satisfied with their job and career situation. It is important to note that as the number of complications increase in a student's life, the gains from career interventions that have been found to be effective in other situations may diminish. For example, in a particularly well designed study on middle school, inner-city youths, Fouad (1995) did not find significant gains for students related to the implemented career intervention. This is a very important area for future research to address.

Social and Emotional Development

Professional school counselors are in an important frontline position assisting students K–12 to become socially competent and productive young adults. Young people face significant challenges and barriers to their ability to create more desired and satisfying life structures (Super, Super, & Savickas, 1996) in young adulthood. The recognition has begun to emerge from various constituencies in our society that schools must effectively respond in more holistic ways to help students cope with the major dilemmas of our day. For example, the George

Lucas Educational Foundation stated, "Academic achievement isn't just about good grades and getting into the right college. It's also about the social and emotional development that is vital for students to master" (p. 25). The commitment to positively impact the social and emotional development of all students has historically been a central focus of professional school counseling. For example, Gerler's (1985) review of the research concluded that interventions carried out by elementary school counselors resulted in positive gains in students' ability to get along with peers, parents, and teachers. Schlossberg, Morris, and Lieberman (2001) demonstrated how developmental guidance units led by school counselors can improve ninth graders' attitudes and behaviors toward school. These are the very same behaviors that leading educational psychologists today continue to identify as bedrock skills essential for successful academic achievement in schools (e.g., Ladd, 1999; Wentzel, 1999).

Whiston and Sexton (1998) pointed out that approximately half of all the school counselor outcome studies published between 1988 and 1995 could be classified into what Gysbers and Henderson (2000) labeled "responsive services," thus suggesting more of a focus on remediation than on development and prevention. From a slightly different perspective, one could argue that this emphasis on responsive services studies also reflects the overriding daily work reality of counselors desperately trying to assist students who face major challenges to their social and emotional development. Even a casual review of any leading counselor journal would reveal that professional school counselors are using a number of counseling methods to work directly with students on the most important challenges faced today by a young person growing up in our society (e.g., family relationships, multicultural identity development, anger management, drug abuse, sexual development, and school violence). An overview of some of these studies and intervention methods used by school counselors is presented below.

Somewhat paralleling the demographic changes in the United States, the reaffirmation of the need for intergroup cooperation to make a pluralistic democracy function effectively, and a commitment to social justice, school counselors have begun to emphasize multiculturalism and diversity in their work. For example, Lee (1996, 2001) outlined criteria professional school counselors could implement to provide culturally competent counseling and create culturally responsive schools for an ever-diversifying student population. D'Andrea and Daniels (1995) demonstrated how multiculturally based group guidance procedures could be used to facilitate the social development of minority elementary students. Mason (1996) evaluated a program that could be implemented to successfully train school counselors to work with Mexican American students to prevent alcohol and drug problems. Carter and El Hindi (1999) described some of the basic issues and more effective practices school counselors could use when counseling Muslim students. Lee and Cramond (1999) found that a formal mentoring program could improve the aspirations of economically disadvantaged students. Nishimura (1995) pointed out how school counselors could more effectively meet the needs of biracial children. Finally, Graham and Pulvino (2000) showed how a multicultural conflict resolution program could be effectively used to de-escalate potentially violent situations and help third graders appreciate cultural and individual differences.

Unfortunately, and as highlighted by the Columbine shooting tragedy, school violence and student safety have become major issues for students, parents, school personnel, and policymakers. Sandhu (2000) described strategies counselors could use in working with alienated students to curb school violence. Besley (1999) showed how a well-defined coaching process could be adopted by counselors in combination with other counseling procedures to help angry students internalize more adaptive cognitions and act in less aggressive ways. Omizo, Hershberger, and Omizo (1988) demonstrated how school counselors could work with students to reduce their hostile and aggressive behavior. Lapan et al. (2001) used teacher observations (4,868 middle school teachers) of school counselor performance of counseling tasks central to the implementation of a comprehensive program (e.g., assisting students with personal concerns) to study the impact for middle school students (22,601 seventh graders). Seventh graders attending schools where counselors were more fully implementing a comprehensive program reported (a) feeling safer at school, (b) having better relationships with teachers, (c) feeling that their education was more relevant and important to their future, (d) being more satisfied with the quality of education they were receiving in their school, (e) having a better interpersonal climate between students, and (f) earning higher grades. These results replicated similar findings for high school students found in an earlier statewide study (Lapan et al., 1997).

Major reviews of school counseling research have consistently found that school counselors can significantly and effectively enhance the social skill development of students (e.g., Borders & Drury, 1992; Gerler, 1985; Schmidt et al., 1999; Whiston & Sexton, 1998). Counselors have employed various intervention strategies to improve the social skill development of students with behavior problems (Verduyn, Lord, & Forrest, 1990), learning disabled students (Omizo & Omizo, 1988a; Utay & Lampe, 1995), and gifted students (Ciechalski & Schmidt, 1995). Brake and Gerler (1994) worked with elementary students with behavior problems to significantly reduce their inappropriate behaviors. Interpersonal relationships between middle school students have also been improved by interventions that can be offered by school counselors (e.g., Galassi & Gulledge, 1997;

Hutchins & Cole, 1977; St. Clair, 1989). The ability to relate effectively to others is critical for both success in school and well-being in adulthood. School counselors can make a major contribution to students' ability to make friends, develop empathy for others, and internalize the interpersonal behaviors needed for success in the workplace.

School counselors have worked with adolescents on a range of issues related to their sexual development. For example, several studies have outlined the special needs of adolescent mothers and fathers and suggested effective counseling interventions (e.g., Griffin, 1998; Kiselica, Gorczynski, & Capps, 1998). School counselors have advocated for the rights of gay and lesbian students and recognized the need to protect students in schools (e.g., McFarland & Dupuis, 2001). Stone (2000) discussed the ethical and legal responsibilities incumbent upon school counselors to advocate for the rights of students who have been sexually harassed. Finally, across the United States many school counselors have implemented sexual abuse and prevention programs that meet the criteria for program effectiveness found by leading abuse prevention researchers (e.g., Reppucci & Haugaard, 1989).

School counselors have positively influenced students' social and emotional development by providing a variety of counseling services to families. For example, counselors have helped young people cope with major disruptions to one's family (e.g., divorce) (Omizo & Omizo, 1988b; Richardson & Rosen, 1999; Rose & Rose, 1992). Morrison, Olivos, Dominguez, Gomez, and Lena (1993) used a family systems approach to help minority children (e.g., Hispanic American, Asian American, and African American elementary students) resolve school behavior problems. The authors reported that 77 percent of the students successfully met their objectives and only 22 percent of these successful students relapsed (i.e., needing referral for additional treatment). In addition, counselors have demonstrated an ability to successfully teach parents effective behavior contracting practices and involve mothers and fathers in needed parent education training (Beale, 1999; Gerler, 1985; Smith, 1994).

School counselors have also been active assisting students with a variety of health problems and issues related to well-being. For example, Cox (1994) demonstrated an effective method for helping an eight-year-old student with cystic fibrosis learn needed self-care practices at school. Katz, Rubinstein, Hubert, and Blew (1988) described how school counselors can help students recovering from cancer to reintegrate and improve their adjustment to school. Richburg and Cobia (1994) reported a successful intervention in working with a student who was an elective mute. Cobia, Carney, and Waggoner (1998) outlined counseling procedures school counselors could implement to help children and adolescents infected with the HIV virus. School counselors have also focused on suicide prevention activities (Hazell & Lewin, 1993). Haines (1994) conducted a cognitive behavioral stress management intervention for high school students that seemed to be especially effective for students experiencing high levels of emotional arousal. Finally, Romano, Miller, and Nordness (1996) documented the need for elementary students to participate in stress prevention and well-being programs that could be effectively offered by school counselors.

Professional school counselors have employed a wide range of individual, group, family, and classroom counseling techniques to facilitate the social and emotional development of K–12 students. For example, a brief individual counseling approach was shown to be effective in assisting high school students make progress toward reaching their goals and resolving their concerns (Littrell, Malia, & Vanderwood, 1995). A comparison between brief versus a more traditional counseling approach found that after treatment, second through seventh graders who received a brief counseling intervention felt that they were making more progress to reach their goals and solve their problems than students who received more traditional counseling (Bruce & Hopper, 1997). It is important to note, however, that the differences between these two methods of counseling decreased over time with students in both interventions reporting positive affective, cognitive, and behavioral changes. Solution-focused group counseling approaches were found to hold promise for use in developmental school counseling programs (LaFountain, Garner, & Eliason, 1996). Play therapy was shown to be an effective method for helping elementary students whose coping skills hurt their learning in school to develop more effective self-efficacy beliefs and learning behaviors (Fall, Balvanz, Johnson, & Nelson, 1999). Group counseling has consistently been found to be an effective method of counseling for helping students to develop a more positive affect and attitude toward school (e.g., Prout & Prout, 1998; Zinck & Littrell, 2000). As stated earlier, school counselors have also used family systems approaches to help students (Widerman & Widerman, 1995).

Peer counseling and conflict mediation procedures have been shown as effective ways school counselors can assist students (Johnson, Johnson, Dudley, Ward, & Magnusson 1995; also see Chapter 4 in this book). For example, Whiston and Sexton (1998) reviewed six studies that found peer counseling interventions to be of significant help for (a) inner-city students (Diver-Stamnes, 1991), (b) high school students (Robinson, Morrow, Kigin, & Lindeman, 1991), (c) fourth through sixth graders (Gentry & Benenson 1992), (d) elementary students who then were able to generalize these positive behaviors both at home and in school (Johnson et al., 1995), and (e) in discussing future plans and school-related problems with high school students (Morey, Miller, Fulton, Rosen, & Daly, 1989). Based on observations of students participating in a mediation process as well as student reflections on their experiences, Humphries (1999) suggested steps for improving peer mediation programs. Finally, Tobias and Myrick (1999) found that eighth-grade peer facilitators could be effective in helping sixth-grade students with behavior problems improve their attendance, grades, and attitudes toward school.

Conclusion

Professional school counselors are at the vanguard and on the front lines assisting students to cope more effectively with a range of formidable obstacles and challenges to their academic, career, social, and emotional development. For example, counselors have employed sophisticated group counseling approaches to improve school outcomes for adolescent females at risk for dropping out of school (Zinck & Littrell, 2000). While not formally tied to early research on the role of school counselors in preventing students from dropping out of school (e.g., Gerler, Drew, & Mohr, 1990), more recent work like Zinck and Littrell's demonstrated professional school counseling's unbroken commitment to address critical national issues in education. Comprehensive school counseling programs are by their very nature designed to move a counselor's work into the heart and center of the most important issues faced by schools (Sprinthall, 1981; Watkins, 2001). They are an indispensable part of any serious attempt to reform K–12 education in ways that will benefit all students (American School Counselor Association, 2003). There is an evolving knowledge base that professional school counselors can use to both improve benefits to students and advocate for effective programs and practices with key policymakers. Professional school counselors should fully understand this evolving knowledge base. This information needs to be translated into our counseling work with K–12 students and policymaking discussions with key stakeholders.

APPENDIX

The Evaluation Process in Action

This section gives you an opportunity to explore the chapter's content in a practical way.

VIGNETTE

Evaluating a School Counseling Program and the Students' Successes

You are a middle school counselor and part of the districtwide school counseling committee. The district's school counseling program received a large three-year federal grant to fund additional school counselors in those buildings that have a significant number of students at risk for school failure. There's one major "catch." For the grant to be refunded each year, the school counselors must be *accountable* for positive student and program outcomes. In other words, counselors need to document the "successes" of their comprehensive school counseling program in meeting the educational needs of these students with special needs.

If you took a "results-based" approach as advocated for in this chapter, what might your evaluation processes and procedures look like? Perhaps you might want to do the following:

- First, as you consider the evaluation issues that arise in this practical scenario, review the information presented in Chapter 8 (e.g., Figure 8.1).
- Second, it might be useful to define for yourself (and for the district?) what "educational success" would mean for the program and for the students. How could you measure success, both qualitatively and quantitatively?
- Third, to help guide your planning, think over these questions and jot down your ideas in the space provided below:

  1. What do we want to measure? (What are the outcomes?)

  2. What kinds of data do you want to collect? (e.g., grades, test scores, "feelings," perceptions, self-reports of "educational success," others?)

3. How might we measure these data?

4. When will the evaluation(s) take place? How often?

5. Who is in charge?

- What folks are going to lead and take overall ownership of the evaluation process?

- What folks are going to collect, analyze, and report the data?

6. What resources might be available in the district (a director of research?) and elsewhere to help with the planning and implementation of the evaluation process? (Check published materials on evaluation?)[1]

- Finally, you might also want to check out the ASCA *National Model for School Counseling Programs* available at ASCA's web site (www.schoolcounselor.org) and see if your plan reflects the evaluation ideas presented in the National Model. What other ideas might you use from ASCA's National Model?

_____

_____

_____

_____

_____

_____

_____

_____

_____

_____

_____

[1] A good practical example of an evaluation of a school district's secondary counseling program can be found in a recent issue of ASCA's journal, *Professional School Counseling.* See Curcio, C. C., Mathai, C., & Roberts, J. (2003). Evaluation of school district's secondary counseling program. *Professional School Counseling, 6*(4), 296–303.

	How might the overall school counseling program be evaluated?	How might the students' accomplishments within the program be evaluated?
What do we want to measure? (Outcomes)		
How will we measure the "whats"? (Methods)		
When? (Time frame)		
By whom? (Responsible parties)		
Resources? Internal: External:		
Other issues of concern?		

Note: This appendix was written by Christopher Sink using a real-life scenario.

REFERENCES

American School Counselor Association. (2003). *The ASCA National Model: A Framework for School Counseling Programs*. Alexandria, VA: Author.

American School Counselor Association/National Association of College Admission Counselors. (1986). *Professional development guidelines for secondary school counselors: A self-audit.* Alexandria, VA: Author.

Arnold, C. L. (1992). An introduction to hierarchical linear models. *Measurement and Evaluation in Counseling and Development, 25,* 58–90.

Baker, S. B., & Taylor, J. G. (1998). Effects of career education interventions: A meta-analysis. *The Career Development Quarterly, 46,* 376–385.

Beale, A. V. (1999). Involving fathers in parent education: The counselor's challenge. *Professional School Counseling, 3,* 5–12.

Besley, K. R. (1999). Anger management: Immediate intervention by counselor coach. *Professional School Counseling, 3,* 81–90.

Blustein, D. L., Phillips, S. D., Jobin-Davis, K., Finkelberg, S. L., & Roarke, A. E. (1997). A theory-building investigation of the school-to-work transition. *The Counseling Psychologist, 25,* 364–402.

Borders, L. D., & Drury, S. M. (1992). Comprehensive school counseling programs: A review for policy makers and practitioners. *Journal of Counseling & Development, 70,* 487–498.

Bowman, R. P., & Myrick, R. D. (1987). Effects of an elementary school peer facilitator program on children with behavior problems. *The School Counselor, 34,* 369–378.

Brake, K. J., & Gerler, E. R. (1994). Discovery: A program for fourth and fifth graders identified as discipline problems. *Elementary School Guidance & Counseling, 28,* 170–181.

Brott, P. E., & Myers, J. E. (1999). Development of a professional school counselor identity: A grounded theory. *Professional School Counseling, 2,* 339–348.

Bruce, M. A., & Hopper, G. C. (1997). Brief counseling versus traditional counseling: A comparison of effectiveness. *The School Counselor, 44,* 171–184.

Bundy, M. L., & Poppen, W. A. (1986). School counselors' effectiveness as consultants: A research review. *Elementary School Guidance & Counseling, 20,* 215–222.

Burnham, J. J., & Jackson, C. M. (2000). School counselor roles: Discrepancies between actual practice and existing models. *Professional School Counseling, 4,* 41–49.

Campbell, C. A., & Dahir, C. A. (1997). *Sharing the vision: The national standards for school counseling programs.* Alexandria, VA: American School Counselor Association.

Caravello, S. J. (1958). Effectiveness of high school guidance services. *The Personnel and Guidance Journal, 5,* 323–325.

Carns, A. W., & Carns, M. R. (1991). Teaching study skills, cognitive strategies, and metacognitive skills through self-diagnosed learning styles. *The School Counselor, 38,* 341–346.

Carter, R. B., & El Hindi, A. E. (1999). Counseling Muslim children in school settings. *Professional School Counseling, 2,* 183–188.

Ciechalski, J. C., & Schmidt, M. W. (1995). The effects of social skills training on students with exceptionalities. *Elementary School Guidance & Counseling, 29*, 217–222.

Cinamon, R. G., & Helman, S. M. (2002, April). *Stages of career development in Israeli school counselors*. Paper presented at the annual meeting of the American Educational Research Association, New Orleans, LA.

Cobia, D. C., Carney, J. S., & Waggoner, I. M. (1998). Children and adolescents with HIV disease: Implications for school counselors. *Professional School Counseling, 1*, 41–45.

Commission on Precollege Guidance and Counseling. (1986). *Keeping the options open: Recommendations*. New York: College Entrance Examination Board.

Conoley, J. C., & Conoley, C. W. (1981). Toward prescriptive consultation. In J. C. Conoley & C. W. Conoley (Eds.), *Consultation in schools* (pp. 265–293). New York: Academic Press.

Constantine, M. G., & Yeh, C. J. (2001). Multicultural training, self-construals, and multicultural competence of school counselors. *Professional School Counseling, 4*, 202–207.

Cox, J. E. J. (1994). Self-care in the classroom for children with chronic illness: A case study of a student with cystic fibrosis. *Elementary School Guidance & Counseling, 29*, 121–128.

Cramer, S. H., Herr, E. L., Morris, C. N., & Frantz, T. T. (1970). *Research and the school counselor*. Boston: Houghton Mifflin.

D'Andrea, M., & Daniels, J. (1995). Helping students learn to get along: Assessing the effectiveness of a multicultural development guidance project. *Elementary School Guidance & Counseling, 30*, 143–154.

Diver-Stamnes, A. C. (1991). Assessing the effectiveness of an inner-city high school peer counseling program. *Urban Education, 26*, 269–284.

Dunn, C. W., & Veltman, G. C. (1989). Addressing the restrictive career maturity patterns of minority youth: A program evaluation. *Journal of Multicultural Counseling and Development, 17*, 156–164.

Evans, J. H., & Burck, H. D. (1992). The effects of career education interventions on academic achievement: A meta-analysis. *Journal of Counseling & Development, 71*, 63–68.

Fall, M., Balvanz, J., Johnson, L., & Nelson, L. (1999). A play therapy intervention and its relationship to self-efficacy and learning behaviors. *Professional School Counseling, 2*, 194–204.

Fall, M., & Van Zandt, E. E. Z. (1997). Partners in research: school counselors and counselor educators working together. *Professional School Counseling, 1*, 2–3.

Fouad, N. A. (1995). Career linking: An intervention to promote math and science career awareness. *Journal of Counseling & Development, 73*, 527–533.

Galassi, J. P., & Gulledge, S. A. (1997). The middle school counselor and teacher-advisor programs. *Professional School Counseling, 1*, 55–60.

Gardner, J. L., Nelson, D. E., & Fox, D. G. (1999). *Level of program implementation and pupil-counselor ratios within the comprehensive guidance program in Utah public schools.* Salt Lake City, UT: Institute for Behavioral Research in Creativity.

Gentry, D. B., & Benenson, W. A. (1992). School-age peer mediators transfer knowledge and skills to home settings. *Mediation Quarterly, 10,* 101–109.

George Lucas Educational Foundation Staff. (2001). Educating the heart and mind. *The School Counselor, 39,* 25–27.

Gerler, E. R. (1985). Elementary school counseling research and the classroom learning environment. *Elementary School Guidance & Counseling, 20,* 39–48.

Gerler, E. R. (1992). What we know about school counseling: A reaction to Borders and Drury. *Journal of Counseling & Development, 70,* 499–501.

Gerler, E. R., Drew, S. R., & Mohr, P. (1990). Succeeding in middle school: A multimodal approach. *Elementary School Guidance & Counseling, 24,* 263–271.

Graham, B C., & Pulvino, C. (2000). Multicultural conflict resolution: Development, implementation and assessment of a program for third graders. *Professional School Counseling, 3,* 172–179.

Green, A., & Keys, A. (2001). Expanding the developmental school counseling paradigm: Meeting the needs of the 21st century student. *Professional School Counseling, 5,* 84–95.

Griffin, N. C. (1998). Cultivating self-efficacy in adolescent mothers: A collaborative approach. *Professional School Counseling, 1,* 53–58.

Gysbers, N. C., & Henderson, P. (2000). *Developing and managing your school guidance program* (3rd ed.). Alexandria, VA: American Counseling Association.

Gysbers, N. C., Lapan, R. T., & Blair, M. (1999). Closing in on statewide implementation of a comprehensive guidance program model. *Professional School Counseling, 5,* 357–366.

Gysbers, N. C., Lapan, R. T., & Jones, A. (2000). School board policies for guidance: A call to action. *Professional School Counseling, 3,* 349–355.

Haas, N. S., & Sullivan, H. (1991). Use of ethnically matched role models in career materials for Hispanic students. *Contemporary Educational Psychology, 16,* 272–278.

Hadley, H. R. (1988). Improving reading scores through a self-esteem intervention program. *Elementary School Guidance & Counseling, 22,* 248–252.

Haines, A. A. (1994). The effectiveness of a school-based, cognitive behavioral stress management program with adolescents reporting high and low levels of emotional arousal. *The School Counselor, 42,* 114–125.

Hazell, P., & Lewin, T. (1993). An evaluation of postvention following adolescent suicide. *Suicide and Life-Threatening Behavior, 23,* 101–109.

Herr, E. L. (1982). Perspectives on the philosophical, empirical, and cost-benefit effects of guidance and counseling: Implications for political action. *Personnel & Guidance Journal, 60,* 594–597.

Herr, E. L. (1995). *Counseling employment bound youth.* Columbus, OH: ERIC/CASS.

Herr, E. L., & Cramer, S. H. (1972). *Vocational guidance and career development in schools: Toward a systems approach.* Boston: Houghton Mifflin.

Hershey, A. M., Silverberg, M. K., Haimson, J., Hudis, P., & Jackson, R. (1999). *Expanding options for students: Report to Congress on the National Evaluation of School-to-Work Implementation.* Princeton, NJ: Mathematica Policy Research.

Hong, E., Whiston, S. C., & Milgram, R. M. (1993). Leisure activities in career guidance for gifted and talented adolescents: A validation of the Tel-Aviv Activities Inventory. *Gifted Child Quarterly, 37,* 65–68.

House, R. M., & Hayes, R. L. (2002). School counselors: Becoming key players in school reform. *Professional School Counseling, 5,* 249–256.

Hughes, D. K., & James, S. H. (2001). Using accountability data to protect a school counseling program: One counselor's experience. *Professional School Counseling, 4,* 306–309.

Hughey, K. F., Lapan, R. T., & Gysbers, N. C. (1993). Evaluating a high school guidance-language arts career unit: A qualitative approach. *The School Counselor, 41,* 96–101.

Humphries, T. L. (1999). Improving peer mediation programs: Student experiences and suggestions. *Professional School Counseling, 3,* 13–20.

Hutchins, D. E., & Cole, C. G. (1977). A model for improving middle school students' interpersonal relationships. *The School Counselor, 25,* 134–136.

Hutchinson, N. L., Freeman, J. G., Downey, K. H., & Kilbreath, L. (1992). Development and evaluation of an instructional module to promote career maturity for youth with learning difficulties. *Canadian Journal of Counselling, 26,* 290–299.

Jackson, S. A., & White, J. W. (2000). Referrals to the school counselor: A qualitative study. *Professional School Counseling, 3,* 277–286.

Johnson, C. D., & Johnson, S. K. (1982). Competency based training of career development specialists or "let's get off the calf path." *Vocational Guidance Quarterly, 32,* 327–335.

Johnson, D. W., Johnson, R., Dudley, B., Ward, M., & Magnusson, D. (1995). The impact of peer mediation training on the management of school and home conflicts. *American Educational Research Journal, 32,* 829–844.

Katz, E. R., Rubinstein, C. L., Hubert, N. C., & Blew, A. (1988). School and social reintegration of children with cancer. *Journal of Psychosocial Oncology, 6,* 123–140.

Kerr, B. A., & Ghrist-Priebe, S. L. (1988). Intervention for multipotentiality: Effects of a career counseling laboratory for gifted high school students. *Journal of Counseling & Development, 66,* 366–369.

Keys, S. G., & Bemak, F. (1997). School-family-community linked services: A school counseling role for changing times. *The School Counselor, 44,* 254–263.

Keys, S. G., Bemak, F., & Lockhart, E. J. (1998). Transforming school counseling to serve the mental health needs of at-risk youth. *Journal of Counseling & Development, 76,* 381–388.

Kiselica, M. S., Gorczynski, J., & Capps, S. (1998). Teen mothers and fathers: School counselor perceptions of service needs. *Professional School Counseling, 2,* 146–152.

Ladd, G. W. (1999). Peer relationships and social competence during early and middle childhood. *Annual Review of Psychology, 50,* 333–359.

LaFountain, R. M., Garner, N. E., & Eliason, G. T. (1996). Solution-focused counseling groups: A key for school counselors. *The School Counselor, 43,* 256–267.

Lapan, R. T. (2001). Results-based comprehensive guidance and counseling programs: A framework for planning and evaluation. *Professional School Counseling, 4,* 289–299.

Lapan, R. T., Gysbers, N. C., Hughey, K., & Arni, T. J. (1993). Evaluating a guidance and language arts unit for high school juniors. *Journal of Counseling & Development, 71,* 444–452.

Lapan, R. T., Gysbers, N. C., & Petroski, G. (2001). Helping seventh graders be safe and successful: A statewide study of the impact of comprehensive guidance programs. *Journal of Counseling & Development, 79,* 320–330.

Lapan, R. T., Gysbers, N. C., & Sun, Y. (1997). The impact of more fully implemented guidance programs on the school experiences of high school students: A statewide evaluation study. *Journal of Counseling & Development, 75,* 292–302.

Lapan, R. T., Kardash, C., & Turner, S. (2002). Empowering students to become self-regulated learners. *Professional School Counseling, 5,* 257–265.

Lapan, R. T., & Kosciulek, J. F. (2001). Toward a community career system program evaluation framework. *Journal of Counseling & Development, 79,* 3–15.

Lee, C. C. (1996). *Multicultural issues in counseling: New approaches to diversity.* Alexandria, VA: American Counseling Association.

Lee, C. C. (2001). Culturally responsive school counselors and programs: Addressing the needs of all students. *Professional School Counseling, 4,* 257–261.

Lee, J., & Cramond, B. (1999). The positive effects of mentoring economically disadvantaged students. *Professional School Counseling, 2,* 172–178.

Lee, R. S. (1993). Effects of classroom guidance on student achievement. *Elementary School Guidance & Counseling, 27,* 163–171.

Lee, V. E., & Ekstrom, R. B. (1987). Student access to guidance counseling in high school. *American Educational Research Journal, 24,* 287–310.

Littrell, J. M., Malia, J. A., & Vanderwood, M. (1995). Single-session brief counseling in a high school. *Journal of Counseling & Development, 73,* 451–458.

MacDonald, G., & Sink, C. A. (1999). A qualitative developmental analysis of comprehensive guidance programmes in schools in the United States. *British Journal of Guidance & Counselling, 27*, 415–430.

Mason, M. J. (1996). Evaluation of an alcohol and other drug use prevention training program for school counselors in a predominantly Mexican American school district. *The School Counselor, 43*, 308–316.

McFarland, W. P., & Dupuis, M. (2001). The legal duty to protect gay and lesbian students from violence in school. *Professional School Counseling, 4*, 171–179.

Medway, F. J. (1982). School consultation research: Past trends and future directions. *Professional Psychology, 13*, 422–430.

Mitchell, A., & Gysbers, N. C. (1978). Comprehensive school guidance and counseling programs: Planning, design, implementation, and evaluation. In *The status of guidance and counseling in the schools. A series of issues papers.* Washington, DC: American Personnel and Guidance Association.

Morey, R. E., Miller, C. D., Fulton, R., Rosen, L. A., & Daly, J. L. (1989). Peer counseling: Students served, problems discussed, overall satisfaction, and perceived helpfulness. *The School Counselor, 37*, 137–143.

Morrison, J. A., Olivos, K., Dominguez, G., Gomez, D., & Lena, D. (1993). The application of family systems approaches to school behavior problems on a school-level discipline board: An outcome study. *Elementary School Guidance & Counseling, 27*, 258–272.

Myrick, R. D. (1987). *Developmental guidance and counseling: A practical approach.* Minneapolis, MN: Educational Media.

Myrick, R. D. (1997). *Developmental guidance and counseling: A practical approach* (3rd ed.). Minneapolis, MN: Educational Media.

National Association of Secondary School Principals. (1996). *Breaking ranks: Changing an American institution.* Reston, VA: Author.

Nelson, D. E., & Gardner, J. L. (1998). *An evaluation of the comprehensive guidance program in Utah schools.* Salt Lake City, UT: Institute for Behavioral Research in Creativity.

Nishimura, N. J. (1995). Addressing the needs of biracial children: An issue for counselors in a multicultural school environment. *The School Counselor, 43*, 52–57.

Omizo, M. M., Hershberger, J. M., & Omizo, S. A. (1988). Teaching children to cope with anger. *Elementary School Guidance & Counseling, 22*, 241–245.

Omizo, M. M., & Omizo, S. A. (1988a). Group counseling's effects on self-concept and social behavior among children with learning disabilities. *Journal of Humanistic Education and Development, 26*, 109–117.

Omizo, M. M., & Omizo, S. A. (1988b). The effects of participation in group counseling sessions on self-esteem and locus of control among adolescents from divorced families. *The School Counselor, 36*, 54–60.

Paisley, P. O. (2001). Maintaining and enhancing the developmental focus in school counseling programs. *Professional School Counseling, 4,* 271–277.

Paisley, P. O., & Borders, L. D. (1995). School counseling: An evolving specialty. *Journal of Counseling & Development, 74,* 150–153.

Paisley, P. O., & Peace, S. D. (1995). Developmental principles: A framework for school counseling programs. *Elementary School Guidance & Counseling, 30,* 85–93.

Palmer, S., & Cochran, L. (1988). Parents as agents of career development. *Journal of Counseling Psychology, 35,* 71–76.

Paris, S. G., & Cunningham, A. E. (1996). Children becoming students. In D. C. Berliner & R. C. Calfee (Eds.), *Handbook of educational psychology* (pp. 117–147). New York: Macmillan.

Paul, G. L. (1969). Behavior modification research: Design and tactics. In C. M. Franks (Ed.), *Behavior therapy: Appraisal and status* (pp. 29–62). New York: McGraw-Hill.

Peterson, D., & Maddux, D. C. (1988). Rural regular and special education teachers' perceptions of teaching hyperactive students. *Rural Special Education Quarterly, 9,* 10–15.

Peterson, G. W., Long, K. L., & Billups, A. (1999). The effect of three career interventions on educational choices of eighth grade students. *Professional School Counseling, 3,* 34–42.

Profitt, K. (1996, October). *Peer counseling and conflict resolution.* Paper presented at the annual meeting of the Missouri Counselor Educators, Columbia, MO.

Prout, S. M., & Prout, H. T. (1998). A meta-analysis of school-based studies of counseling and psychotherapy: An update. *Journal of School Psychology, 36,* 121–136.

Reppucci, N. D., & Haugaard, J. J. (1989). Prevention of child sexual abuse: Myth or reality. *American Psychologist, 44,* 1266–1275.

Richardson, C. D., & Rosen, L. A. (1999). School-based interventions for children of divorce. *Professional School Counseling, 3,* 21–26.

Richburg, M. L., & Cobia, D. C. (1994). Using behavioral techniques to treat elective mutism: A case study. *Elementary School Guidance & Counseling, 28,* 214–220.

Robinson, S. E., Morrow, S., Kigin, T., & Lindeman, M. (1991). Peer counselors in a high school setting: Evaluation of training and impact on students. *The School Counselor, 39,* 35–40.

Romano, J. L., Miller, J. P., & Nordness, A. (1996). Stress and well-being in the elementary school: A classroom curriculum. *The School Counselor, 43,* 268–276.

Rose, C. C., & Rose, S. D. (1992). Family change groups for the early age child. *Special Services in the Schools, 6,* 113–127.

Rothney, J. W. M. (1958). *Guidance practices and results.* New York: Harper.

Rylander, C. K. (2002). *Guiding our children toward success: How Texas school counselors spend their time.* Austin, TX: Texas Education Agency.

Sanborn, M. P. (1964). A comparison of four high school guidance programs in terms of four criteria. *The Personnel and Guidance Journal, 3,* 293–298.

Sandhu, D. S. (2000). Alienated students: Counseling strategies to curb school violence. *Professional School Counseling, 4,* 81–85.

Savickas, M. L. (1990). The career decision-making course: Description and field test. *The Career Development Quarterly, 38,* 275–284.

Schlossberg, S. M., Morris, J. D., & Lieberman, M. G. (2001). The effects of a counselor-led guidance intervention on students' behaviors and attitudes. *Professional School Counseling, 4,* 156–164.

Schmidt, J. J. (1995). Assessing school counseling programs through external reviews. *The School Counselor, 43,* 114–123.

Schmidt, J., Lanier, S., & Cope, L. (1999). Elementary school guidance and counseling: The last 20 years. *Professional School Counseling, 4,* 250–257.

Schneider, B., & Stevenson, D. (1999). *The ambitious generation: America's teenagers motivated but directionless.* New Haven, CT: Yale University Press.

Sexton, T. L., & Whiston, S. C. (1996). Integrating counseling research and practice. *Journal of Counseling & Development, 74,* 588–589.

Shoffner, M. F., & Williamson, R. D. (2000). Engaging preservice school counselors and principals in dialogue and collaboration. *Counselor Education and Supervision, 40,* 128–140.

Sink, C. A., & MacDonald, G. (1998). The status of comprehensive guidance and counseling in the United States. *Professional School Counseling, 2,* 88–94.

Slavin, R. (2002, April). *Evidence-based education policies: How they will transform educational practice and research.* Paper presented at the annual meeting of the American Educational Research Association, New Orleans, LA.

Smith, S. E. (1994). Parent-initiated contracts: An intervention for school related behaviors. *Elementary School Guidance & Counseling, 28,* 182–187.

Solberg, V. S., Gusavac, N., Hamann, T., Felch, J., Johnson, J., Lamborn, S., et al. (1998). The Adaptive Success Identity Plan (ASIP): A career intervention for college students. *The Career Development Quarterly, 47,* 48–95.

Sprinthall, N. A. (1981). A new model for research in the science of guidance and counseling. *The Personnel and Guidance Journal, 59,* 487–493.

Statistical Package for the Social Sciences. (2001). *SPSS for Windows (Version 10.0).* Chicago, IL: Author.

St. Clair, K. L. (1989). Middle school counseling research: A resource for school counselors. *Elementary School Guidance & Counseling, 23*, 219–226.

Stone, C. B. (2000). Advocacy for sexual harassment victims: Legal support and ethical aspects. *Professional School Counseling, 4*, 23–30.

Super, D. E., Super, C. M., & Savickas, M. L. (1996). The life-span, life-space approach to careers. In D. Brown, L. Brooks, & Associates (Eds.), *Career choice and development.* (3rd ed., pp. 121–178). San Francisco: Jossey-Bass.

Taylor, L., & Adelman, H. S. (2000). Connecting schools, families, and communities. *Professional School Counseling, 3*, 298–307.

Texas Education Agency (1996). *Texas School Counseling and Guidance Programs: Final Study Report*. Austin, TX: Research and Evaluation Division, State of Texas.

Tobias, A. K., & Myrick, R. D. (1999). A peer facilitator-led intervention with middle school problem-behavior students. *Professional School Counseling, 3*, 27–33.

Trevisan, M. S. (2000). The status of program evaluation expectations in state school counselor certification requirements. *American Journal of Evaluation, 21*, 81–94.

Trevisan, M. S., & Hubert, M. (2001). Implementing comprehensive guidance program evaluation support: Lessons learned. *Professional School Counseling, 4*, 225–228.

Utah State Office of Education. (2000). *1989-1999: A decade of progress and change in the delivery of comprehensive guidance programs grades 7-12*. Salt Lake City, Utah: Author.

Utay, J. M., & Lampe, R. E. (1995). Use of a group counseling game to enhance social skills of children with learning disabilities. *Journal for Specialists in Group Work, 20*, 114–120.

Verduyn, C. M., Lord, W., & Forrest, G. C. (1990). Social skills training in schools: An evaluation study. *Journal of Adolescence, 13*, 3–16.

Watkins, C. (2001). Comprehensive guidance programs in an international context. *Professional School Counseling, 4*, 262–270.

Wentzel, K. R. (1999). Social-motivational processes and interpersonal relationships: Implications for understanding motivation at school. *Journal of Educational Psychology, 91*, 76–97.

Whiston, S. C., & Sexton, T. L. (1998). A review of school counseling outcome research: Implications for practice. *Journal of Counseling & Development, 76*, 412–426.

Widerman, J. L., & Widerman, E. (1995). Family systems-oriented school counseling. *The School Counselor, 43*, 66–73.

Zimmerman, B. J., & Schunk, D. H. (2001). *Self-regulated learning and academic achievement*. Mahwah, NJ: Erlbaum.

Zinck, K., & Littrell, J. M. (2000). Action research shows group counseling effective with at-risk adolescent girls. *Professional School Counseling, 4*, 50–59.

PART THREE

The Consultation Function

CHAPTER 9
School-Based Consultation

Keith M. Davis
Appalachian State University

Introduction, Rationale, and Definitions

The next two chapters focus on the consultative function of school counselors: (a) school-based consultation and (b) community-based consultation. While school-based consultation places an emphasis on school counselors providing direct and indirect services to those within a school environment, community-based consultation places a primary emphasis on consultation with various professionals and constituents outside the school. Although two different foci for consulting, both school-based and community-based consultation share a common goal: maximizing the best possible educational experience for children and adolescents.

Consultation has long been recognized as an integral function for counselors in a variety of settings (Baker, 2000; Brown, Pryzwansky, & Schulte, 2000; Dinkmeyer & Carlson, 2001; Dougherty, 1999; Kahn, 2000; Kampwirth, 2002; McCarthy & Sorenson, 1993; Mendoza, 1993; Myrick, 2003; Newman, 1993; Randolph & Graun, 1988; West & Idol, 1993). For school counselors, consultation has further been recognized as one of the American School Counselor Association's 3 Cs (i.e., counseling, consultation, and coordination), with collaboration later being added as the fourth C (Baker, 2000; Myrick, 2003).

In this chapter, you should gain an understanding of the following school-based consultation areas: (a) introduction to consultation, including its rationale and definition; (b) theoretical orientations and models; (c) research; (d) practical implications for use in K–12 school counseling programs; (e) issues of diversity; (f) ethical issues; and (g) future trends.

What's more, throughout this chapter is the assumption that effective school-based consultation is a collaborative effort between the consultant and consultee. Collaborative consultation has clearly been recognized as the preferred method for conducting consultation within the schools (Baker, 2000; Davis, 2003; Dinkmeyer & Carlson, 2001; Dougherty, 1999; Kampwirth, 2002), although continued research is needed regarding the interactive nature of this approach.

School counselors are in a position to provide collaborative and consultative services for the benefit of the student body. In fact, they are required to work with various school professionals in order to provide a better educational experience for children and adolescents (ASCA, 1998). For example, counselors work collaboratively inside the school environment with parents (Mullis & Edwards, 2001) and with a variety of professionals, including school psychologists (Rowley, 2000), special educators (Idol & Baran, 1992), teachers (Clemente & Collison, 2000; Davis & Garrett, 1998), administrators (Cole, 1991; Kaplan, 1995; Ponec & Brock, 2000), and the nurse (Moore & Davis, 2002).

Rationale for School-Based Consultation

The need for school counselors to develop skills in school-based consultation has been well documented in various publications (Brown, Pryzwansky, & Schulte, 2000; Brown, Spano, & Schulte, 1988; Davis, 2003; Dinkmeyer & Carlson, 2001; Dougherty, 1999; Kampwirth, 2002), and professional organizations and accrediting bodies have also noted this important school-based function. For example, the Council for the Accreditation of Counseling and Related Educational Programs (CACREP; 2001) has recently included within its standards for accreditation of graduate school counseling programs curricular experiences in theories, models, processes, and applications of consultation. Equally, the American School Counselor Association (ASCA, 1998) has included competencies in its professional development guidelines for school counselors at all levels.

School-based consultation presents school counselors with an effective avenue to help create change within the school environment. Although the ASCA's (1997) position statement regarding counselor-to-student ratio currently stands at 1:250, the reality is that many school counselors face much larger ratio discrepancies. Given these large discrepancies, Dinkmeyer and Carlson (2001) and Kampwirth (2002) both reported that in order for school counselors to deliver more services to students, consultation can be employed as a more time-efficient and cost-effective strategy for providing services to students. Dinkmeyer and Carlson (2001) summarized this observation as follows:

The school counselor who works with one client impacts one person and his or her life. The consultant who works with one teacher indirectly affects the lives of 30 or more children. The consultant who works with one parent education group may affect the lives of 20 to 30 children. (p. 11)

Imbedded within this rationale are two assumptions. School counselors (a) are in the best position to work with those individuals who have the most consistent contact and impact within the educational experiences of children and adolescents, and (b) when acting as consultants are more likely to coordinate services that can facilitate change in the environment of children and adolescents. Specifically, Dinkmeyer and Carlson (2001) suggested that it is teachers, administrators, and parents who are the first to identify concerns in children and adolescents, and given their regular contact with students, it becomes even more important for school counselors to coordinate such services in a collaborative manner. School-based consultation is one way to facilitate that change.

Definitions of Consultation and Collaboration

Definitions of consultation are prolific throughout the professional literature. Mentioned earlier was the importance of collaborative relationships between school counselors and other school professionals. It is also difficult to talk about school-based consultation without considering the importance of collaboration within the consultative process. To understand more clearly the terms *consult, consultation,* and *collaboration,* I borrowed from Kampwirth's (2002) work. Using *Webster's Collegiate Dictionary* (1997), his publication summarized them as follows:

1. Consult: seeking guidance or information, giving professional or expert advice;
2. Consultation: the act of consulting; a meeting for deliberation or discussion; and
3. Collaborate: to work, one with another; cooperate. (p. 3).

Drawing largely upon the excellent work of Kampwirth (2002) once again, further definitions, distinctions, and characteristics of consultation and collaboration are offered. After reviewing all the literature on consultation, collaboration, and collaborative consultation (a reading of pp. 3–5 in Kampwirth is recommended), he offered the best explanation to date of collaborative consultation:

Collaborative consultation is a process in which a trained, school-based consultant, working in an egalitarian, non-hierarchical relationship with a consultee, assists that person in her efforts to make decisions and carry out plans that will be in the best educational interest of the students. (p. 3)

Two important words used by Kampwirth (2002) in this definition are *egalitarian* and *non-hierarchical*. Kampwirth noted these as consultees are more likely to engage in the consultation process when they believe they share with the consultant at least an equal amount of input into the planning process. He recognized that collaboration and consultation are not necessarily interchangeable because consultation may not always be a collaborative process. He cited the work of Brown et al. (2000), who suggested the inappropriateness of using the two terms when referring to the same process since two or more people collaborating are providing a direct service to one another, and consultation has traditionally been defined as an indirect service for a third-party interaction. However, according to Kampwirth, it makes sense to use the two terms together because collaboration refers to "mutual problem solving by equal partners and the consultation part referring to the third-party interaction" (p. 6). To emphasize the importance of collaboration, this writer also noted that collaboration refers to a unique kind of consultation, characterized by "a reciprocal arrangement between individuals with diverse expertise to define problems and develop solutions mutually" (as cited in Pugach & Johnson, 1988, p. 3). Finally, Kampwirth concluded that when collaboration is defined in this way,

> [It] may seem very different from forms of consultation practiced in the business, medical, or military arenas because it is not clear from this definition that any one person is the expert. Resolution of this dilemma revolves around the belief that consultation can take place between or among two or more people, with the role of expert shifting periodically among partners in this enterprise. (p. 6)

Inherent in this statement, and supported in the current professional literature on collaborative consultation, is that school-based consultants need not necessarily be experts in the content of consultation, but rather experts in the process of conducting school-focused consultation (Baker, 2000; Davis, 2003; Dinkmeyer & Carlson, 2001; Kampwirth, 2002) with each person involved contributing varying degrees of expertise in the problem-solving process.

Theoretical Orientations and Models for School-Based Consultation

West and Idol (1987) conducted a comprehensive examination and review of school-based consultation in terms of how it has been studied and applied in a variety of educational settings (e.g., special education, learning disabilities, school psychology, school counseling). In this review, the authors sought to analyze various theories, models, and related research in school-based consultation, an emphasis placed on the planned progression from formulation of consultation theory to model building to implementation of applied research in school-based consultation. They discovered the existence of ten models contributing to the overall knowledge base of consultation, of which six contained a clearly identifiable theory or theories. They finally concluded that research on theory and model building in school-based consultation could benefit from additional conceptualization and testing. Although West and Idol's (1987) review is somewhat dated at this point, when examining the more current school-based consultation literature, not much has changed since their initial conclusions. Current research in school-based consultation is discussed later.

Given that school-based consultation is still in its "infancy," it is proposed here a combination of several "established" theories, as well as emerging approaches to school-based consultation for school counselors in training to consider. Specifically, the established theory of behavioral consultation is discussed, as well as its variation of conjoint behavioral consultation (CBC). In addition, two emerging approaches to school-based consultation, (a) solution-focused consultation and (b) family systems consultation, are discussed. Imbedded within these approaches is the importance placed on collaboration.

Behavioral Consultation

Behavioral consultation is one approach to consultation that is appropriate for the school setting and firmly rooted in theory. Conoley and Conoley (1992) noted that this approach is predicated on the theories of learning established by Skinner, Bandura, and Meichenbaum. The basic tenet from a behavioral standpoint is that a person's actions are a function of environmental stimuli, primarily the environmental contingencies that support them (i.e., antecedents and consequences to behavior). Although radical behaviorism was not concerned with the internal events of people due to the fact that internal events could not be observed, Meichenbaum (1977) noted that it was the internal cognitions of individuals that could be observed and worked with. In addition, Bandura (1977) proposed a theory of social learning, which posits that people learn by observing models. Humans observe role models and rehearse specific behaviors they observe, but only under conditions where the observed behaviors result in positive reinforcement for those behaviors.

The consultant's job in this approach is to help facilitate the consultee in analyzing how a student's problem behavior is maintained by reinforcements through an understanding of antecedents and consequences of the behavior. Antecedents are internal or external events that precede and are thought to be functionally related to the behavior that follows the antecedent's occurrence. Internal antecedents might include hunger, anger, or sadness over a preceding event, or a student's self-talk (Kampwirth, 2002). External antecedents might include a teacher asking a student to do something, the behavior of another student sitting next to the target student, or a change in the classroom routine. Consequences are the effects or results of a behavior, which can be positive, neutral, or negative. This approach often involves the school-based consultant observing how classroom dynamics play a role in maintaining problem behaviors.

Conjoint Behavioral Consultation

Conjoint behavioral consultation is similar to the behavioral approach to consultation. Here too, the school-based consultant engages in the analysis of the antecedents and consequences that maintain problem behavior in the student. The only distinction made here is that the consultant should equally include the family of the student, along with the teacher, as a consultee in this process. The idea is to bring congruency and consistency between the school and home in the establishment of interventions (Sheridan & Colton, 1994; Sheridan, Eagle, Cowan, & Mickelson, 2001; Sheridan & Kratochwill, 1992).

A Generic Approach to the Consultation Process

Although various theories and approaches to school-based consultation are abundant throughout the consultation literature, many of the steps described in these approaches share similar stages and/or steps in the process. Gutkin and Curtis (1990) surveyed varying approaches, steps, and stages to consultation established in the literature and identified several commonalities. They are summarized here.

Define and Clarify the Problem.   The study by Bergan and Tombari (1976) is among the most frequently cited references in the consultation literature, identifying the importance of the problem identification stage. If the correct problem is not recognized, then both the consultant and the consultee spend unnecessary time defining the problem. The consultant's role at this point is to help facilitate the consultee in operationally defining as much as possible the exact behaviors that constitute the problem. This may include the frequency, duration, intensity, and onset of the problem. The assumption is that if this initial stage is successful, the chances of a positive outcome in the consultative process are increased.

Analyze the Forces Impinging on the Problem.   At this stage, the consultant gathers information on the ecology of the student's life and classroom behaviors, noting possible sources and the interrelated expectations within both the student's life and the classroom. This may include possible influences of the "student's parents, the classroom situation, the curriculum, sociocultural phenomena, and any other sources of influence that could be related to the behavior(s) of concern" (Kampwirth, 2002, p. 181).

Brainstorm Alternative Strategies.   After the ecology of the problem is understood, the consultant and consultee begin to discuss the implementation of possible strategies. Although dated, the suggestions by Pfeiffer and Jones (1974) are nevertheless important:

1. Avoid evaluating the potential strategies as they are being discussed;
2. As many interventions as possible should be generated; and
3. When generating possible interventions, creativity and novelty are important considerations.

What should come from this process is a collection of collaborative ideas between the consultant and consultee.

Evaluate and Choose Among Alternative Strategies.   In this step, the consultant's job is to help the consultee choose a strategy (or strategies) to implement that has the maximum impact for minimal effort. Known as the "mini-max principle," the strategy for implementation of an intervention by the consultee should have as minimal an intrusion as possible on the ecology of the classroom or the child's family dynamics. It is a wise consultant who will realize that the consultee at this point may try to defer power to the consultant in the formulation of a strategy and implementation. The consultant's job is to help facilitate the consultee in co-creating the strategy. Furthermore, it is critically important that the final strategy be acceptable to the consultee.

Specify Consultant and Consultee Responsibilities. Here, the consultant collaborates with the consultee on defining exactly what each other's responsibilities will be in the remainder of this process—in other words, mutually agreeing on who, what, when, where, and how each will carry out their individual responsibilities.

Implement the Chosen Strategy. This is the moment of truth! Here is where everything up to this point in the process is tested. The consultant's job now is to help provide support to the consultee. Specifically, the consultant will want to monitor whether (a) the problem changes in focus, (b) something might have been missing from the original strategy, (c) there is something that prevents the consultee from carrying out the strategy, or (d) the third party (most likely the student) reacts in some unexpected way. It may be necessary to repeat some of the previous steps, recognizing that these steps are not inevitably linear. Equally important, it is here that resistance in the consultee might first be manifested.

Evaluate the Effectiveness of the Action and Recycle if Necessary. The consultant's job now is to continue monitoring, and if necessary (more often likely), collect information from the consultee and situation about the progress and possible changes in the strategy. It is also critically important for the consultant to reinforce the efforts of the consultee. As in the previous step, it may once again be necessary to recycle through some or all of these stages. Effective consultation is more of a trial-and-error process than a static and sequential process.

Emerging Approaches to School-Based Consultation

Like many of the other theories and perspectives on school-based consultation, the newer emerging approaches have not been fully and empirically tested for their efficacy. Nevertheless, there are two approaches that warrant some consideration here: (a) solution-focused consultation and (b) consultation through an understanding of family systems.

Solution-Focused Consultation. Many of the prevailing theories and models of school-based consultation are grounded in a problem-solving approach. While these approaches focus on deficits (i.e., exploration of weaknesses), solution-focused interventions concentrate on solutions and strengths. The recent emergence of solution-focused interventions in schools has been well documented in the literature. For example, Kahn (2000) cited successful solution-focused interventions in schools, including individual counseling (Metcalf, 1995; Mostert, Johnson, & Mostert, 1997; Murphy, 1994, 1997; Sklare, 1997; Van, 1999; also see

Chapter 2 in this book), small group counseling (LaFountain & Gerner, 1996), supervision (Juhnke, 1996; Santa Rita, 1996), and school leadership (Paull & McGrevin, 1996).

Using Kahn's (2000) excellent article and case study on solution-focused consultation in the schools, I briefly describe the steps to this strength-based approach to consultation below.

Presession and Initial Structuring. The initial goal of this first step is for the consultant to facilitate the consultee in identifying strengths and resources in the current situation of concern. Using what de Shazer (1985) called the "language of change," the consultant carefully constructs questions for the consultee that are future oriented. These types of questions can be found in Juhnke (1996), and Kahn (2000) includes examples like "How would you like the student to be?" "How would you like to be with your student?" "With your class?" and "How will you know when the consultation is successful?" (p. 250). The purposes of such presuppositional words as *when* and *will* are to instill hope in the consultee by setting the stage for future change.

Establishing Consultation Goals. Unlike traditional consultation, which is problem-solving focused, this approach spends minimal time on exploration of the problem before establishing consultation goals. Exploration of the problem is only done in terms of exceptions or examples in which the problem did not occur. The reasoning here is that too much exploration of the problem takes away valuable time from generating solutions. Example questions for goal generation include the following: "What's the minimal amount of change that you are willing to accept?" or "What are you willing to do to make your life easier in the classroom?" (Kahn, 2000, p. 251). It is critically important that solutions be defined behaviorally and concretely.

Examining Attempted Solutions and Exceptions. Once goal setting has been established, the consultant explores with the consultee any previous attempts at solutions and exceptions. If consultees are at a loss to recall any previous solutions or exceptions, then a question such as "When was a time that it happened just a little?" (Kahn, 2000, p. 251) may help establish a base for a small change. Sometimes, consultees truly cannot find an exception. In this case, Kahn (2000) suggested that the consultant do the following:

(a) give the teacher a homework assignment of looking for exceptions throughout the coming week; (b) ask the consultee to recall or imagine a master teacher (e.g.,

How would this person handle the problem?); and, (c) ask the consultee for permission to observe in the classroom and provide feedback about exceptions. (p. 251)

Helping Consultees Decide on a Solution. For this step, Kahn (2000) cited the work of Berg (1994), who in turn offered three rules in this decision-making process: (a) "If it ain't broke, don't fix it"; (b) "Once you know what works, do more of it"; and (c) "If it does not work, don't do it again" (p. 16). While moving the emphasis of change from the student's behavior to the consultee's behavior, Kahn recommended the following questions: "When was the last time you found him/her doing what you want?" "What was different?" "How did you get him/her to do that?" and "What do you need to do to make that happen again?" (Kahn, 2000, p. 251). Again, the consultant has the consultee describe these solutions behaviorally and concretely. Helping the consultee choose the best solution, Kahn once again recommended good questions: "Which solution is best given your resources? the student's resources? the time of year? the cooperation of the family? the severity of the problem?" (p. 251).

Summarizing and Complimenting. Although complimenting should take place throughout the consultation, it is even more important in this step as a way to end the session in a positive manner. Furthermore, complimenting and giving praise for successful exceptions in the past helps foster in the consultee attributes of internal success. All positive comments should describe specific behavioral accomplishments.

To conclude, Kahn's (2000) article also provided a useful case study in solution-focused consultation by a school counselor. The case study includes an example of how a dialogue representing this approach would look between the school-based consultant and consultee. Thus, a reading of this article is highly recommended.

Family Systems Concepts and Techniques in School-Based Consultation. The concepts and techniques in this approach to school-based consultation share with conjoint behavioral consultation inclusion of the family in the consulting process. Similarly, this approach can share with solution-focused consultation a strength-based approach for working with children through parents at the school. Centered on systems theory and understanding systems and family systems dynamics (Haley, 1986; Madanes, 1981; Minuchin, 1974; von Bertalanffy, 1968), particularly within the school (Davis, 2001; Hinkle, 1993; Hinkle & Wells, 1995; see also Chapter 4 in this book), school-based consultation can provide insight into how a student's problem behavior at school can be a symptom of ineffective family interaction patterns.

Recognizing the need for school-based interventions with children and their families by school counselors has largely been influenced by an understanding that schoolchildren belong to a much larger social system that includes an interfacing of both family and school (Fine & Carlson, 1992; Hinkle, 1993; Hinkle & Wells, 1995). For students belonging in two such social systems, it becomes necessary for school counselors to recognize that problem behavior in schoolchildren may not be idiosyncratic, but rather a manifestation of dysfunctional family patterns and interactions (Davis, 2003; Fine, 1992; Fine & Carlson, 1992; Hinkle, 1993; Hinkle & Wells, 1995). Thus, to intervene with the student without consideration of potential familial influence on the problem behavior may result in ineffective treatment strategies.

An understanding of structural family dynamics is one of many methods for conducting school-based family interventions. Developed by Minuchin (1974), structural family dynamics can be described as an approach based on a framework that is directed toward changing the organization of a family through analyzing the process of family interactions. Minuchin identified three essential components of structural family theory: (a) family structure, (b) subsystems within the family, and (c) boundaries. Family structure is thought of as the organized patterns in which families interact. Family interactions are largely governed by transactions within the family, often involving a group of covert rules, which govern those transactions. Within the family structure, often there is a hierarchical structure, with adults and children having differing degrees of authority and power. Subsystems differentiate family members who come together to perform various family functions. All members of the family belong in at least one subsystem. For example, subsystems may be determined by generation (i.e., parents, children, grandparents) or gender (e.g., mother/daughter subsystem or father/son subsystem). Finally, boundaries are often the invisible barriers that regulate interpersonal interactions among individuals and subsystems within the family, as well as the entire family with the external world.

One of the primary goals in understanding structural family dynamics is for the school-based consultant to help facilitate the family in solving its own problems through altering the family structure. This is accomplished by the school-based consultant "joining" the family system in an effort to help the family members change their existing structure. Specifically, the consultant helps the family with the creation of an effective hierarchical structure, a structure that usually expects the parent(s) to function as a cohesive executive subsystem in charge of the family system. Through altering boundaries and realigning subsystems, the consultant helps the family change existing behaviors and experiences of each family member. Commonly, structural problems in families are seen as general shortcomings in their ability to adjust to changing circumstances (e.g., divorce, remarriage, addition/subtraction of family members, and adjustment to child developmental needs). Throughout the remainder of the consulting relationship, the consultant helps facilitate the family to modify their interactions and challenge their assumptions concerning how they relate to one another.

Strategic approaches to school-based family consulting are based on techniques (i.e., strategies and/or directives) employed by the consultant to help the family change their thinking, behaviors, and interactions with one another (Haley, 1980; Madanes, 1981, 1984, 1990). Strategic approaches are designed with the assumption that malfunctioning hierarchies and/or structures within the family result in dysfunctional family behaviors and interactions among family members. Thus, the primary goals of strategic interventions in consulting are designed to reorganize the family structure, in particular, the family's hierarchy and generational boundaries. Strategic interventions are most commonly directives given by the consultant to the family to help change family behaviors and interactions.

Specifically, the consultant introduces new behaviors (i.e., directives) into the existing set of family transactions and interactions, having the family practice these new behaviors in between consulting sessions. The purpose of the family practicing new behaviors is to change existing behavior patterns that have served to maintain dysfunctional interaction patterns within the family. There are too many specific directives to delineate here, and directives need to be customized to meet the needs and particularities of each family's problem. However, literature on specific strategic directives, customized to fit specific family problems, can be found in a variety of resources (Coyne, 1987; Coyne, Kahn, & Gotlib, 1987; Fisch, Weakland, & Segal, 1982; Haley, 1986, 1987; Hinkle & Wells, 1995; Madanes, 1981, 1984; Papp, 1983; Stanton, 1981; Stanton, Todd, & Associates, 1982; see also Chapter 4 in this book).

Although this approach at first glance may seem more like conducting therapy, it is important for the consultant to keep in mind that consulting with the family is an effort in helping to change the behavior of the student. Using Dinkmeyer and Carlson (2001) as a way to illustrate the differences between consultation and counseling, the following is offered:

> It is consultation when:
> 1. The main focus of the relationship is a third person (often a student).
> 2. The relationship is characterized by collaboration on ways to help this third person.
>
> It is counseling when:
> 1. The main focus of the relationship is the person seeking the help.

2. The relationship is characterized by collaboration on ways to help the person seeking the help. While a third person may be discussed, the goal of the relationship is focused on the help seeker. (pp. 66–67)

Research in School-Based Consultation

Although many articles and books have been published regarding the importance of school counselors conducting school-based consultation, empirically derived research specifically germane to the interactive processes and outcomes of school counselors conducting school-based consultation is woefully limited. Most of the empirically derived research studies in school-based consultation are found within the school psychology and special education literature, and many are quite dated. Therefore, analogies to school counseling might be tenuous at best given their differing roles in schools.

Alderman and Gimpel (1996) found that

teacher consultees believe that the most effective consultation includes (1) personal support with contact and listening, (2) suggestions that have proven to work, and (3) suggestions that are practical and part of a plan. The collaborative model stresses these approaches. (p. 307)

Kampwirth (2002) provided further insight into the school-based consultation research when referencing the work by Hughes (1994), which suggested that current research on the effectiveness of consultation is not well documented. Rather than focusing on improved student behavior and achievement, existing school-based consultation research was based on irrelevant outcomes such as teacher attitudes toward consultation and process refinements. Lacking in particular are follow-up studies determining the effectiveness of consultation interventions, consultation approaches, and processes of consultation. Kampwirth noted Hughes's concerns that the question "What consultation approaches result in what effects with which clients and consultees?" (p. 82) was perhaps a more important point of inquiry. To answer Hughes's question, I propose that what is needed in the school-based consultation literature from school counselors is more single-case experimental design studies that examine specific consultation approaches and processes used, with whom, and with which clients.

Practical Applications in K–12 School-Based Consultation

When considering the practical applications for conducting K–12 school-based consultation, there is perhaps no larger issue than time. Since the majority of school-based consultation will take place between the school counselor and the teacher, school counselors need to be cognizant of the time demands placed upon teachers in an age of increased accountability for educational achievement. Gone are the days when school counselors and teachers could sit and have lengthy and detailed conversations about students. Given these time constraints, it is my experience as a school counselor, as well as the experiences of the school counselors I supervise, that teachers much more prefer the briefer approaches to consultation (i.e., solution-focused and behavioral approaches).

Given the demands placed on classroom teachers, it is important once again to remind school counselors of the intervention acceptability for the consultee of the final strategy agreed upon. Many teachers share with school counselors ratio discrepancies between them and students. Therefore, interventions must be agreed upon that have the best chance of succeeding. This was referred to earlier as the mini-max principle. Using Kahn's (2000) solution-focused approach to consultation, described previously, as one example, a case study and application are offered here.

Case Study

You get a referral from the fourth-grade teacher. In the referral, the teacher states that a student, David (a European American male), has become increasingly aggressive toward other students in his class (i.e., bullying, shoving, knocking things off other students' desks). You, as the consultant (an elementary school counselor), have worked with this teacher several times in the past with some success. However, this teacher is usually quick to want students tested for ADD (attention deficit disorder). The teacher has worked in this elementary school for twenty-three years and has gained respect from other teachers and administrators for her teaching efforts. In your experiences working with this teacher, she is generally cooperative but also "lets you know" that she has been working in public education for twenty-three years and can usually "pinpoint" the problems in students.

Application of Consultation to Case Study

Using Kahn's (2000) solution-focused approach to this case study, the following steps could be taken by the school-based consultant (i.e., the school counselor).

Presession and Initial Structuring. The school counselor (consultant) would want to help facilitate the teacher's (consultee) understanding of David's strengths and resources. For example, despite David's problem behaviors, there may be areas that he is strong in (e.g., always completing classroom assignments, effort in work, good writing/reading skills, or appropriate playground behavior). The purpose here is to identify or reframe David's internal strengths and resources.

Establishing Consultation Goals. Here, the school counselor facilitates the teacher in establishing a concrete goal, or goals, for the target behavior(s) in David, as well as prioritizing the goal(s). For example, David is bullying, shoving, and knocking things off other students' desks. Which of these are the most important to focus on? After choosing the target behavior(s) to be changed, the school counselor can ask the teacher, "What is the minimal amount of change that you are willing to accept" (Kahn, 2000, p. 251). Because the primary concern might be David's aggression toward other students, the agreed-upon change might focus on decreasing the number of incidents in which David engages in certain aggressive behavior(s).

Examining Attempted Solutions and Exceptions. Once the targeted behavior(s) for consultation has been identified, the school counselor explores with the teacher various solutions and exceptions that have already been tried by the teacher. For example, the teacher may have changed the location of David's classroom seat several times previously, or is not aware of previous dynamics that may have worked given the often fast pace of classroom instruction. If the teacher cannot think of any previous solutions or exceptions, then the scheduling of classroom observations by the school counselor may help identify strategies that are already working, or simply need more consistency.

Helping Consultees Decide on Solutions. If previous solutions or exceptions have been identified, then the school counselor can help the teacher become more consistent with her implementation. For example, if moving David's seating assignment periodically works in reducing his aggressive behavior, then perhaps continuing to do so will continue to reduce the incidences of the behavior. This step might also include suggestions from the school counselor on reducing the behavior based on the previous step's classroom observations. In this case, the school counselor should facilitate the teacher in exploring the possibilities of implementing any of the suggestions offered.

Summarizing and Complimenting.   An important aspect of the solution-focused approach to consultation, and indeed any approach to consultation, should be summarizing the process and complimenting the teacher (consultee) on her effort and work in the process. For this particular case, the teacher is a twenty-three-year veteran of the classroom, and that should be honored and respected by the school counselor (consultant). Often, teachers are not praised nearly enough for the hard work they do, and in working with a veteran or a new teacher, praise is always welcomed!

This case study in the application of school-based consultation is but one practical approach in the implementation of consultation. Although several approaches have been discussed, it is hoped that individuals learning to be school-based consultants can gain an understanding of this important service delivery approach from reading and learning more about other orientations. My experience in teaching school-based consultation has taught me that people learn much more through practical applications and practicing the necessary skills to become effective school-based consultants. In addition to this sample case study in the application of school-based consulting, two activities that my students have responded to favorably are tag-team consultation and videotaping consultation skills (see Appendix A). Both of these activities require students to practice and develop their consultation skills, receiving helpful feedback in the *here-and-now* (see Appendix B) from other students and myself of their skills development. Despite the approach of school-based consultation preferred, all perspectives require the development of basic helping skills (see Appendix A and Davis [2003] for specific helping skills needed for school-based consultants).

School-Based Consultation in a Diverse Society

The United States has always been a diverse country by virtue of indigenous populations and through immigration (both voluntary and forced). It is only in the last several decades that existing and increased diversity within this country has begun to be embraced and valued more fully, although there is much room for continued growth. The latest U.S. Census (2000) demonstrated that perhaps the country is even more diverse than previously thought, as respondents for the first time had the option of choosing more than one race and/or ethnicity to define themselves, and many did so. For example, I was able to claim both my Cherokee and European heritage! This diversity is equally reflected in public schools, increasing with each year, and calling upon school counselors to provide school-based consultation services that are sensitive to all students and their families.

As with much of the literature on multicultural and/or cross-cultural counseling, consultation across cultures shares as a priority the consultant both acknowledging and having knowledge of cultural differences (Cross, 1988; Dettmer, Dyck, & Thurston, 1999; Huff & Telesford, 1994; Jackson & Hayes, 1993; Lynch & Hansen, 1992; Pinto, 1981) if effective consultation is to take place. In fact, what Pinto (1981) wrote over twenty years ago still holds true today. Effective cross-cultural consultation results when consultants have knowledge of cultural differences, acknowledge these differences, accept these differences, and adapt appropriately to these differences by effectively contrasting their values with those of their consultees. Known as Client-Centered Adaptive, Pinto's method of consulting uses a process in which the consultant's interaction style matches the preferences and comfort level of the consultee. For example, Brown (2001) and Srebalus and Brown (2001) build on Pinto's work by suggesting that such cultural subtleties as level of eye contact, time orientation, and personal space can all have an effect on how the consultee might regard and value the consultant and consultative process. In addition, other mediating cultural factors such as age, social class, gender, sexual orientation, and ability level can necessitate consultants' adjusting their styles to match those of the consultees. In short, current research at all levels of counseling and consulting supports consultants acknowledging these differences in a caring, empathic, and genuine manner, as well as how learning about these differences can be honored and used in the consultation process.

Ethical Issues in School-Based Consultation

The integrity of the school counseling profession is governed by its ethical guidelines and standards of practice. No school counselor should engage in either counseling or consulting relationships until they fully understand their ethical obligations. Specifically germane to professional school counselors are the Ethical Standards for School Counselors (American School Counselor Association [ASCA], 1998), which in many ways reflect the Code of Ethics and Standards of Practice of the American Counseling Association (ACA, 1995). The importance of and purposes for established ethical guidelines were summarized well by Van Hoose and Kottler (1978) as follows: (a) for the self-regulation of the counseling profession as opposed to governmental regulation and interference, (b) establishing behavioral standards for professional groups, (c) protecting the public, and (d) protecting professionals from malpractice by providing guidelines for judgment of their actions.

The ethical standards set forth by both ASCA (1998) and ACA (1995) address a variety of issues regarding the roles of professional counselors, for which being a consultant is one. For all counselors, it is not a question of if, but when they will have to refer to their ethical guidelines in the decision-making process of counseling or consulting. Several decision-making steps and processes, as well as principles guiding ethical behavior, are found in the consultation literature and are briefly described here.

Although the codes and ethics that guide behavior in the counseling profession are comprehensive, they may also not be specific enough for definitive answers to the potential dilemmas that might arise (Baker, 2000). Thus, to help in understanding better the process of ethical decision making, Nassar-McMillan and Post (1998) have established a six-step sequential ethics decision-making scheme as follows:

1. Identify the dilemma.
2. Identify and clarify one's values about the issue.
3. Refer to the appropriate code of ethics.
4. Determine the nature and dimensions of the dilemma.
5. Generate potential courses of action.
6. Consider possible consequences of all options, evaluate potential effects of what appears to be the best option, and implement a course of action.

In addition to steps in the ethical decision-making process of consultation, there are also some basic principles of ethical behavior. Kampwirth (2002) summarized the work of Brown et al. (2000), who relied on the contents of the APA and ACA codes as they applied to consultation:

1. *Competence:* Counselors should only provide services within the scope and boundaries of their competence based on training, education, and supervised experience. Although the specific type of training, education, and experience are not delineated in codes of ethics, CACREP (2001) in its standards for accrediting school counseling programs requires school counseling students to complete at least 48 hours in their program, for which the following competencies regarding consultation must be met:

    a. Strategies to promote, develop, and enhance effective teamwork within the school and larger community;
    b. Theories, models, and processes of consultation and change with

teachers, administrators, other school personnel, parents, community groups, agencies, and students as appropriate;

c. Strategies and methods of working with parents, guardians, families, and communities to empower them to act on behalf of their children; and

d. Knowledge and skills in conducting programs that are designed to enhance students' academic, social, emotional, career, and other developmental needs.

2. *Protecting the welfare of clients*: This is the most important of all principles. It is imperative that the consultant regard the welfare of all the constituents in the consulting process (i.e., consultee, students, administrators, parents).

3. *Maintaining confidentiality*: As with counseling, consultation processes remain confidential unless the consultant learns of abuse of others or threats to self or others. Consultants should explain these limits to confidentiality.

4. *Responsibilities when making public statements*: Related to confidentiality, in the event school-based consultants who work internally have an opportunity to speak to the external publics, they do not disclose information gained during internal consulting unless appropriate consent has been given.

5. *Social and moral responsibility*: Consultants' behaviors and statements are consistent and congruent with, and guided by, the best interest of the people they serve. Equally, the imposition of values, as well as inappropriate physical and sexual behavior, is unethical.

6. *Relationship with other consultants*: School counselors will not be the only professionals conducting consultation within the schools. Several professionals (e.g., school psychologists, special educators, teachers, administrators, external consultants) may all be speaking and advocating for the best interest of the same child. It can be easy for a school counselor to feel they "know" the students better than anyone else. Respecting the opinions of these individuals is placed in the role of collaborator and coordinator of school-based services and teams.

By following the guidelines set forth by ASCA and/or ACA, school counselors conducting school-based consultation services maintain the integrity of the school counseling profession, protect the welfare of their clients and publics, and protect themselves in the process.

▼ Future Trends in School-Based Consultation

Given large discrepancies in counselor-to-student ratios, providing consultation services is one way school counselors can use their time and skills to influence as many people within the school as possible (Gerler, 1992). Although consulting in the schools is a widely accepted function and role of the school counselor, it still is not as clearly understood as the counseling function and role (Baker, 2000). Although there appears to be an increase in emphasis on school-based consultation by school counselors, there are few studies appearing in professional counseling journals that specifically explain how it is to be implemented and what the outcomes are.

The current state of school-based consultation is in an early stage of development. The school counseling profession shares with other related educators (i.e., special educators, school psychologists, and administrators) a strong interest in using consultation as an indirect service delivery approach for working with students. However, like these other school-based professions, this interest has far outdistanced any theoretical or empirical knowledge base (West & Idol, 1987). In determining future trends and directions in school-based consultation, West and Idol's findings and suggestions seem just as valid today as they did fifteen years ago. They are summarized here:

1. Definitions of consultation need to be more operationalized, linking the definition to concrete consultation goals that are congruent to specific theoretical orientations and models.
2. Current research does not appear to rely upon a strong, well-tested theoretical base for the triadic nature of the consultation process.
3. Several existing models of consultation are not clearly linked to a specified knowledge base for problem solving (with the exception of the solution-focused consultation model).
4. More effort needs to be made in aligning consultation programs with particular models, which will help determine the types of interactions and interventions that might result.
5. Not clearly defined, nor linked to a particular theory/model are the roles, responsibilities, and functions of consultants and consultees.
6. The problem-solving process of many theories and models are not clearly characterized by a set of progressive steps/stages, and are not often linked to a particular theory/model.
7. Rather than building a knowledge base for identifying and understanding the variables that influence and interact within the consultation process

(i.e., input, process, outcome), the focus of consultation research has been largely upon the final outcome only.

As West and Idol's (1987) findings suggested, clearly more research is needed specifically linking all aspects of consultation practice to theory and models and vice versa, as well as more theory and model building. One way to begin accomplishing this is to encourage practicing school counselors, and counselors-in-training, to document their school-based consultation practices and outcomes, linking specific models of consultation implemented to outcomes. For example, in my university's school counseling program I have begun requiring school counseling interns to implement at least two different models of consultation (solution-focused, behavioral, etc.) and documenting the processes and outcomes of the interventions. Second, I am currently helping these school counselor interns to write up and publish their results in case-study format. It is hoped that through these case studies in school-based consultation we can begin to clearly understand the relationship between specific models used and their outcomes (e.g., what appears to work or not work in specific situations).

To conclude, although there are many complex factors to consider in the future trends and directions of school-based consultation, four are specifically stated here: (a) more research is needed to specifically link all aspects of consultation practice to theory and models; (b) more theory and model building are needed; (c) briefer models of school-based consultation (i.e., solution-focused and some behavioral approaches) will be more practical in an age of increased accountability; and (d) more interdisciplinary networking and research across professions within schools will increase the empirical base from which all professions can draw.

Summary and Concluding Remarks

It is my hope that through this chapter school counselors in training and other readers have gained a better understanding of how to help create change within the school environment using school-based consultation services. As was mentioned earlier, consultation is recognized by the American School Counselor Association (1998) as one of the 3 Cs (i.e., counseling, consultation, and coordination), with collaboration adding a fourth C (Baker, 2000; Myrick, 2003). Because school counselors are in a position to provide collaborative and consultative services for the benefit of the student body, they have an opportunity to work closely with various school professionals in order to provide a better educational experience for children and adolescents.

In addition, since school-based consultation is still a relatively new service delivery approach, I have proposed here a combination of several "established" theories, as well as emerging approaches to school-based consultation, for school counselors-in-training to consider. Although numerous articles and books have been published regarding the importance of school counselors' conducting school-based consultation, there still exists little research that specifically relates the interactive processes and outcomes of school counselors' conducting school-based consultation, as well as specific models employed.

Through a combination of theories and activities (see Appendix A) discussed in this chapter, one further hope is that nascent school counselors will be encouraged to practice the development of their consultation skills within the discussed theories and approaches before they enter the schools (through internships and employment). Equally important, school counselors should be encouraged to collaborate on documenting and writing up their school-based consultation findings for publication. Encouragement of publication from mentoring school counselor educators and supervisors is strongly recommended in order to further our understanding of school-based consultation. Guidelines for publishing in school counseling can be found in the works by Davis and Sink (2001) and Sink (2000).

APPENDIX A

Suggested Activities for Developing Consultation Skills

School-based consultation involves not only the learning of various approaches and methods for conducting consultation but also the development of specific skills necessary to facilitate the consultation process. Specifically, the development of skills training in consultation requires school counselors to develop and demonstrate basic helping skills germane to the consulting relationship (e.g., collaboration, active listening, reflection statements, clarification, and information gathering).

Suggested by Davis (2003) in the teaching and development of basic consultation skills, the following two activities, (a) tag-team consultation and (b) feedback regarding videotaping of consultation skills, can be helpful tools in accomplishing the development of such skills. These are discussed and illustrated below.

Tag-Team Consultation

My experience has been that most people in the beginning of their training and the on-the-job experience are apprehensive about videotaping their skills. As further development in defining and honing consultation skills within a supportive environment before videotaping, this exercise is offered as a way for you, in collaboration with peers, to practice your skills. First, individuals are divided into groups of four or five. One person in each group acts as the consultee throughout this exercise, while the others in the group rotate acting as the consultant. An experienced leader or facilitator has devised already a likely school-based scenario that includes a diversity issue in recognition of the importance of multicultural concerns within the consulting process (Jackson & Hayes, 1993). The person acting as consultee for this exercise receives his or her part, typed on a piece of paper. The remaining members of the group act as the consultants in the scenario, each also receiving his or her part on a piece of paper, and not completely aware of one another's scenario description. Each scenario is role-played in front of the entire group.

As the consulting scenario progresses, each individual within the group has the opportunity to act as the consultant. The live role-play demonstration commences and is observed by all others, as well as the facilitator. Once the first consultant has reached a likely impasse, or is relieved by the facilitator, the next member-consultant takes over the consulting role. The leader then facilitates a brief large group discussion on both the strengths and the areas for further development of the specific consultant's skills before proceeding to the next member-consultant within the group. The next member-consultant within the group then picks up where the previous member-consultant left off. This process continues until all in the group have completed the scenario and received feedback from observing the entire group and leader regarding basic communication skills.

Videotaping Consultation Skills

Recognizing the value of group process in the audio- and/or videotaping of skills (CACREP, 2001), this exercise involves individuals forming groups of four or five to videotape consultation skills. Each person in this group has the opportunity to serve as a consultant and a consultee, while others in the group observe the videotaping process, waiting their own turn to serve as either. For example, in a group of four, each person acts as a consultant and consultee at least once. This means that each person receives a separate scenario (scenarios they are likely to face in their school experiences as professional school counselors), alternating round-robin consultant and consultee.

Throughout the next two or three group meetings, individuals are given the opportunity to have his or her consulting video role-play viewed and reviewed by the entire group. During the playback, the facilitator pauses the video periodically to elicit comments from the member-consultant concerning his or her reactions to what he or she is doing well thus far, as well as what they might do differently in retrospect. The rest of the group members are also asked for their feedback. In addition, group members are given a consultation video-review feedback form (see Appendix B) to complete anonymously during the video viewing.

Upon completion of the video review, the facilitator collects all the video-review forms from members. Before the next practice session, the facilitator writes a summary of the overall feedback from the entire group regarding each member-consultant's video and includes some comments of his or her own. The facilitator also notes the member-consultant's effort in applying consultation theory and process, as well as some specific skills demonstrated in the video role-play (i.e., reflection statements, clarifications, summarizing, data gathering). Peer feedback can help identify areas of strengths and areas for further development for the member-consultant.

Consultation Rating Form

Consultant's Name _____

For each of the following statements/questions, please circle the number on the scale that most accurately reflects your perceptions/feelings toward the consultant.

1. How did you assess the consultant's role during this meeting?

   (*expert*)   1   2   3   4   5   6   (*collaborator*)

2. How did you sense that the consultee regarded the consultant?

   (*subordinate*)   1   2   3   4   5   6   (*colleague*)

3. To what extent did the consultant impose her or his values on the consultee?

   (*great extent*)   1   2   3   4   5   6   (*not at all*)

4. To what extent did the consultant create an atmosphere of trust and acceptance?

   (*not at all*)   1   2   3   4   5   6   (*great extent*)

5. How effective was the consultant in clarifying the problem?

   (*ineffective*)   1   2   3   4   5   6   (*very effective*)

6. How consistent was the consultant in her or his approach?

   (*inconsistent*)   1   2   3   4   5   6   (*consistent*)

7. How effective do you think the consultant was during this meeting?

   (*ineffective*)   1   2   3   4   5   6   (*very effective*)

What do you believe were the consultant's strengths in this meeting?

What do you believe are some skills for further development in the consultant?

REFERENCES

Alderman, G. L., & Gimpel, G. A. (1996). The interaction between type of behavior problem and type of consultant: Teacher's preferences for professional assistance. *Journal of Educational and Psychological Consultation, 7,* 305–314.

American Counseling Association (ACA). (1995). *American Counseling Association code of ethics and standards of practice.* Alexandria, VA: Author.

American School Counselor Association (ASCA). (1997). *Position statement on counselor-to-student ratio.* Alexandria, VA: Author.

American School Counselor Association (ASCA). (1998). *Ethical standards for school counselors.* Alexandria, VA: Author.

Baker, S. B. (2000). *School counseling for the twenty-first century* (3rd ed.). Upper Saddle River, NJ: Merrill/Prentice Hall.

Bandura, A. (1977). *Social learning theory.* Upper Saddle River, NJ: Merrill/Prentice Hall.

Berg, I. K. (1994). *Family based services: A solution-focused approach.* New York: Norton.

Bergan, J. R., & Tombari, M. L. (1976). Consultant skill and efficiency and the implementation and outcomes of consultation. *Journal of School Psychology, 14,* 3–14.

Brown, D., Pryzwansky, W. B., & Schulte, A. C. (2000). *Psychological consultation: Introduction to theory and practice* (5th ed.). Needham Heights, MA: Allyn & Bacon.

Brown, D., Spano, D. B., & Schulte, A. C. (1988). Consultation training in master's level counselor education programs. *Counselor Education and Supervision, 27,* 323–330.

Brown, D. (2001). An eclectic, culturally sensitive approach to consultation in mental health settings. In C. Salvador (Ed.), *Counseling and psychotherapy: A practical guidebook for trainees and new professionals* (pp. 405–436). Boston: Allyn & Bacon.

Clemente, R., & Collison, B. B. (2000). The relationship among counselors, ESL teachers, and students. *Professional School Counseling, 3,* 339–348.

Cole, C. G. (1991). Counselors and administrators: A comparison of roles. *NASSP Bulletin, 75*(534), 5–13.

Conoley, J. C., & Conoley, C. W. (1992). *School consultation: A guide to practice and training* (2nd ed.). Upper Saddle River, NJ: Merrill/Prentice Hall.

Coyne, J. (1987). Depression, biology, marriage, and marital therapy. *Journal of Marital Therapy, 13,* 393–408.

Coyne, J., Kahn, J., & Gotlib, I. (1987). Depression. In T. Jacob (Ed.), *Family interaction and psychopathology* (pp. 509–529). New York: Plenum Press.

Council for the Accreditation of Counseling and Related Educational Programs. (2001). *2001 Standards.* Retrieved November 14, 2002, from http://www.counseling.org/cacrep/2001standards700.htm

Cross, T. (1988). Services to minority populations: What does it mean to be a culturally competent professional? *Focal Point, 2,* 1–3.

Davis, K. M. (2001). Structural-strategic family counseling: A case study in elementary school counseling. *Professional School Counseling, 4,* 180–186.

Davis, K. M. (2003). Teaching a course in school-based consultation. *Counselor Education & Supervision, 42,* 275–285.

Davis, K. M., & Garrett, M. T. (1998). Bridging the gap between school counselors and teachers: A proactive approach. *Professional School Counseling, 1,* 54–55.

Davis, K. M., & Sink, C. A. (2001). Navigating the publication process II: Further recommendations for prospective contributors. *Professional School Counseling, 5,* 56–61.

de Shazer, S. (1985). *Keys to solution in brief therapy.* New York: Norton.

Dettmer, P., Dyck, N., & Thurston, L. (1999). *Consultation, collaboration, and teamwork* (3rd ed.). Boston: Allyn & Bacon.

Dinkmeyer, D., & Carlson, J. (2001). *Consultation: Creating school-based interventions* (2nd ed.). Philadelphia, PA: Brunner-Routledge.

Dougherty, A. M. (1999). *Psychological consultation and collaboration in school and community settings* (3rd ed.). Pacific Grove, CA: Brooks/Cole.

Fine, M. J. (1992). A systems-ecological perpsective on home-school intervention. In M. J. Fine & C. Carlson (Eds.), *The handbook of family-school interventions: A systemic perspective* (pp. 1–17). Needham Heights, MA: Allyn & Bacon.

Fine, M. J., & Carlson, C. (Eds.). (1992). *The handbook of family-school interventions: A systemic perspective.* Needham Heights, MA: Allyn & Bacon.

Fisch, R., Weakland, J., & Segal, L. (1982). *The tactics of change.* San Francisco: Jossey-Bass.

Gerler, E. R., Jr. (1992). Consultation and school counseling. *Elementary School Guidance & Counseling, 26,* 162.

Gutkin, T. B., & Curtis, M. J. (1990). School-based consultation: Theory and techniques. In C. Reynolds & T. B. Gutkin (Eds.), *The handbook of school psychology* (pp. 577–613). New York: Wiley.

Haley, J. (1980). *Leaving home.* New York: McGraw-Hill.

Haley, J. (1986). *Uncommon therapy: The psychiatric techniques of Milton H. Erickson.* New York: Norton.

Haley, J. (1987). *Problem-solving therapy* (2nd ed.). San Francisco: Jossey-Bass.

Hinkle, J. S. (1993). Training school counselors to do family counseling. *Elementary School Guidance & Counseling, 27,* 252–257.

Hinkle, J. S., & Wells, M. E. (1995). *Family counseling in the schools: Effective strategies and interventions for counselors, psychologists, and therapists.* Greensboro, NC: ERIC/CASS.

Huff, B., & Telesford, M. C. (1994). Outreach efforts to involve families of color. In the Federation of Families for Children's Mental Health. *Focal Point, 10,* 180–184.

Hughes, J. (1994). Back to the basics: Does consultation work? *Journal of Educational and Psychological Consultation, 5,* 77–84.

Idol, L., & Baran, S. (1992). Elementary school counselors and special educators consulting together: Perilous pitfalls or opportunities to collaborate? *Elementary School Guidance & Counseling, 26,* 202–214.

Jackson, D. N., & Hayes, D. H. (1993). Multicultural issues in consultation. *Journal of Counseling & Development, 72,* 144–147.

Juhnke, G. A. (1996). Solution-focused supervision: Promoting supervisee skills and confidence through successful solutions. *Counselor Education and Supervision, 36,* 48–57.

Kahn, B. B. (2000). A model of solution-focused consultation for school counselors. *Professional School Counseling, 3,* 248–254.

Kampwirth, T. J. (2002). *Collaborative consultation in the schools: Effective practices for students with learning and behavior problems* (2nd ed.). Upper Saddle River, NJ: Prentice Hall.

Kaplan, L. S. (1995). Principals versus counselors: Resolving tensions from different practice models. *The School Counselor, 42,* 261–267.

LaFountain, R. M., & Gerner, N. E. (1996). Solution-focused counseling groups: The results are in. *The Journal of Specialists in Group Work, 21,* 128–143.

Lynch, E. W., & Hansen, M. J. (1992). *Developing cross-cultural competence: A guide for working with young children and their families.* Baltimore: Paul H. Brooks.

Madanes, C. (1981). *Strategic family therapy.* San Francisco: Jossey-Bass.

Madanes, C. (1984). *Behind the one-way mirror: Advances in the practice of strategic therapy.* San Francisco, CA: Jossey-Bass.

Madanes, C. (1990). *Sex, love, and violence.* New York: Norton.

McCarthy, M. M., & Sorenson, G. P. (1993). School counselors and consultants: Legal duties and liabilities. *Journal of Counseling & Development, 72,* 159–167.

Meichenbaum, R. (1977). *Cognitive-behavior modification: An integrative approach.* New York: Plenum Press.

Mendoza, D. W. (1993). A review of Gerald Caplan's theory and practice of mental health consultation. *Journal of Counseling & Development, 71,* 629–635.

Metcalf, L. (1995). *Counseling towards solutions.* West Nyack, NY: The Center for Applied Research in Education.

Minuchin, S. (1974). *Families and family therapy.* Cambridge, MA: Harvard University Press.

Moore, A. S., & Davis, K. M. (2002). *Weight management groups with adolescents: How school counselors and school nurses can collaborate.* Manuscript submitted for publication.

Mostert, D. L., Johnson, E., & Mostert, M. P. (1997). The utility of solution-focused, brief counseling in schools: Potential from an initial study. *Professional School Counseling, 1,* 21–24.

Mullis, F., & Edwards, D. (2001). Consulting with parents: Applying family systems concepts and techniques. *Professional School Counseling, 5,* 116–123.

Murphy, J. J. (1994). Working with what works: A solution-focused approach to school behavior problems. *The School Counselor, 42,* 59–65.

Murphy, J. J. (1997). *Solution-focused counseling in middle and high schools.* Alexandria, VA: American Counseling Association.

Myrick, R. D. (2003). *Developmental guidance and counseling: A practical approach* (4th ed.). Minneapolis, MN: Educational Media.

Nassar-McMillan, S., & Post, P. (1998, March). *Ethics reconsidered.* A program presented at the annual meeting of the North Carolina Counseling Association, Chapel Hill, NC.

Newman, J. L. (1993). Ethical issues in consultation. *Journal of Counseling & Development, 72,* 148–156.

Papp, P. (1983). *The process of change.* New York: Guilford.

Paull, R. C., & McGrevin, C. Z. (1996). Seven assumptions of a solution-focused conversational leader. *NASSP Bulletin, 80*(579), 79–85.

Pfeiffer, J. W., & Jones, J. E. (Eds.). (1974). *A handbook of structured experiences for human relations training* (Vol. 3, pp. 14–15). La Jolla, CA: University Associates.

Pinto, R. F. (1981). Consultant orientations and client system perceptions. In R. Lippitt & G. Lippitt (Eds.), *Systems thinking: A resource for organizational diagnosis and intervention* (pp. 57–74). Washington DC: International Consultants Foundation.

Ponec, D. L., & Brock, B. L. (2000). Relationships among elementary school counselors and principals: A unique bond. *Professional School Counseling, 3,* 208–217.

Pugach, M. C., & Johnson, L. J. (1988). Rethinking the relationship between consultation and collaborative problem solving. *Focus on Exceptional Children, 21,* 1–8.

Randolph, D. L., & Graun, K. (1988). Resistance to consultation: A synthesis for counselor-consultants. *Journal of Counseling & Development, 67,* 182–184.

Rowley, W. J. (2000). Expanding collaborative partnerships among school counselors and school psychologists. *Professional School Counseling, 3,* 224–228.

Santa Rita, E. (1996). *The solution-focused supervision model for counselors teaching in the classroom.* (ERIC Document Reproduction Service No. ED 393 524).

Sheridan, S. M., & Colton, D. L. (1994). Conjoint behavioral consultation: A review and case study. *Journal of Educational and Psychological Consultation, 5,* 211–228.

Sheridan, S. M., Eagle, J. W., Cowan, R. J., & Mickelson, W. (2001). The effects of conjoint behavioral consultation: Results of a 4-year investigation. *Journal of School Psychology, 39,* 361–385.

Sheridan, S. M., & Kratochwill, T. R. (1992). Behavioral parent-teacher consultation: Conceptual and research considerations. *Journal of School Psychology, 30,* 117–139.

Sink, C. A. (2000). Navigating the publication process: Recommendations for prospective contributors. *Professional School Counseling, 3*(4), ii–iv.

Sklare, G. B. (1997). A solution-focused approach for school counselors. Newbury Park, CA: Sage.

Srebalus, D. J., & Brown, D. (2001). *Becoming a skilled helper.* Boston: Allyn & Bacon.

Stanton, D. (1981). Strategic approaches to family therapy. In A. S. Gurman & D. P. Kniskern (Eds.), *Handbook of family therapy* (pp. 361–402). New York: Brunner/Mazel.

Stanton, D., Todd, T., & Associates. (1982). *The family therapy of drug abuse and addiction.* New York: Guilford.

U.S. Bureau of the Census. (2000). *2000 U.S. Census.* Washington, DC: U.S. Government Printing Office.

Van, L. (1999, April). *Academic solutions: Solution-focused counseling addresses school performance.* Symposium conducted at the American Counselor Association World Conference, San Diego, CA.

Van Hoose, W. H., & Kottler, J. (1978). *Ethical and legal issues in counseling and psychotherapy.* San Francisco: Jossey-Bass.

von Bertalanffy, L. (1968). *General systems theory: Foundations, development, applications* (Rev. ed.). New York: Braziller.

Webster's Collegiate Dictionary (2nd ed.). (1997). New York: Random House.

West, J. F., & Idol, L. (1987). School consultation (part I): An interdisciplinary perspective on theory, models, and research. *Journal of Learning Disabilities, 20,* 388–408.

West, J. F., & Idol, L. (1993). The counselor as consultant in the collaborative school. *Journal of Counseling & Development, 71,* 678–683.

CHAPTER 10

Community-Focused Consultation: New Directions and Practice

Fred Bemak, Sally Murphy, Carol Kaffenberger

George Mason University

Introduction, Rationale, and Definitions

Schools in the United States continue to face significant challenges in educating contemporary youth. Society has become far more complex with, for example, the advances of technology, changing demographics, changing family structures, unsafe school environments, immigration issues, and so on (Bemak, 2002; Bemak & Chung, 2003; Bemak & Hanna, 1998). These and other factors contribute to a significant gap in academic achievement among different ethnicities, racial groups, and students from both ends of the socioeconomic spectrum (The Education Trust, 1998).

Many of the problems inherent in today's schools that interfere with the academic performance of students are psychological and sociological in nature. Drugs and alcohol, unsafe sexual activity, family problems, gangs, physical and sexual abuse, teenage pregnancy, violence, racism, discrimination, homelessness, poverty, and chronic absenteeism all have their roots in psychosocial issues. Within the school environment it is essential to attend to these complex and interrelated problems in order to ensure that all children receive an education in a safe and healthy environment.

The person best positioned and educated to do this work within the school is the school counselor. Based on their training in individual, group, and family counseling, human growth and development, consultation, and human relations, they are in the unique position of having learned specific skills to address these very difficult issues. Yet they are generally limited in their ability to effectively do this work, given the overwhelming student-to-counselor ratios ranging from 300 to 1,000 students per counselor and assignments by administrators to do "busy work" and testing rather than provide counseling services that will enhance academic achievement. Thus, we believe school counselor partnerships with community representatives are indispensable to address these crucial and pressing issues facing today's youth. Within these partnerships is the essential need for community-focused consultation, whereby the school counselor works closely with outside agencies. Therefore, this chapter provides an overview of community-focused consultation from the vantage point of the school counselor working within a comprehensive program, exploring best practices, the role and function of the school counselor, salient research, ethical issues, cultural diversity, and future trends.

Expanding the Definition of Consultation

Consultation has been defined as a relationship in which two or more persons work together to define a problem, establish goals, develop a plan, assign responsibilities, and implement the agreed-upon strategies (Caplan & Caplan, 1993). Dougherty (2000) further defined consultation as "a process in which a human service professional assists a consultee with a work-related (or care-related) problem with a client system, with the goal of helping both the consultee and the client system in some specific way" (p. 11). We believe that these definitions together provide a good basis for consultative relationships. However, we expand this characterization to include individuals or groups of individuals representing agencies or institutions, so that community-focused consultation is defined as two or more agencies or institutions working together. Thus, the school counselor may represent the school system when working with consulting agencies. Such agencies or systems may include social services, mental health, family services, or juvenile services. Typically, consultation is used to assist a client or system address a particular problem.

The consulting relationship involves three roles: the consultant, the consultee, and the client (e.g., student, teacher, or administrator) or client system (Caplan & Caplan, 1993; Dougherty, 2000). Again, we enlarge this definition to include groups of individuals as well, so that it may be consultants, consultees, and clients or client system*s*. Consultants provide expertise and facilitate the consulting process, whereas the consultees seek information or help for the client or system. Sometimes consultants and consultees are considered peers, but more often the relationship is defined as unequal based on need (Dougherty, 2000). We recommend a modification of this traditional definition and argue that the relationship in community-focused consultation is far more effective if it is based on mutuality and equality rather than on an expert-client model. The consultees need information or help with an identified client problem. The clients or the system(s) are the third member of the consultation relationship and usually the focus and beneficiary of the consultation process. In community-focused consultation, the clients are members of the school and the consultants are representatives of community agencies or systems.

The School Counselor as a Liaison

Although many schools do not have true collaborative partnerships with community agencies, we strongly suggest that community-focused consultation in the school setting is an essential direction. The community agency can provide direct services to the school through the school counselor, who functions within the school as a liaison and conduit for the information and knowledge gained by the community-focused consultation. The counselor can also provide information and knowledge from the consultation to teachers, parents, and administrators about how to address specific problems such as chronic absences, behavioral problems, or school violence. Thus, in the community-focused consultation model, the school counselor receives consultation from community agency personnel and in turn becomes a consultant within his or her own school or district by providing assistance to teachers and administrators within the school environment.

Here's an example of how this process might work: After receiving community-focused consultation from mental health clinic personnel (e.g., a clinical social worker) about aggressive behavior, the school counselor serves as the resource person/consultant within the school setting, helping teachers and administrators better understand the causes and strategies of intervention to deal with this problem. The same would hold true regarding chronic truancy, whereby the school counselor may, for instance, consult with juvenile services and community police programs to gain a better understanding of intervention strategies for students with high rates of absenteeism. The school counselor then may follow up the consultation with juvenile services and the community police with advice and program development for the school system, working closely with teachers and school administrators.

Because consultation is a vital skill for school counselors, it is essential that this be included in graduate-level and in-service training. For example, in the George Mason University program we not only have a consultation course, but also have embedded consultation practice in practicum and internship courses. Since consultation is a primary function of the school counselor and is considered to be a fundamental service in a comprehensive school counseling program as described in the school counselor role definition by the American School Counselor Association (ASCA, 1999), we believe it is critical for school counselors to have extensive training in the theory and practice of consultation.

Ensuring Cultural Relevancy in Community-Focused Consultation

It is essential that educational systems engage in a systematic evaluation of how they are teaching values and tolerance, and combating racism, inequities, and discrimination. As alluded to earlier, it has been clearly documented that there are major educational gaps among cultures, racial groups, and ethnicities (The Education Trust, 1998). As such, we strongly advocate that educational systems must effectively address these differences in order to do a far better job of decreasing the achievement disparities. Our conviction is consistent with the ongoing concerns that educational systems have not adequately responded to culturally diverse ethnic and racial groups, which further demonstrates that issues of diversity have not and are not valued (Locke, 2003). Given the changing demographics and growing regions where formerly labeled "minority" populations are now "majority" populations, there is a tremendous need to carefully attend to cultural diversity in our school environments. In fact, ASCA (1992) supports our contention by asserting that it is an ethical obligation of school counselors to be competent in multicultural counseling. We firmly believe that with regard to community-focused consultation there must be heightened sensitivity to cultural differences, different cultural learning styles, intergroup relations, and multicultural interventions, which all significantly contribute to the relationships between schools and community agencies in the consultation process.

Theoretical Orientation and Background

Community-focused school consultation identifies a particular kind of consultation where community agencies, such as mental health centers or social service agencies, and schools work together in a collaborative relationship to provide programs and services to clients and client systems (Dougherty, 2000). The presumption is that community agencies and schools have a vested interest in addressing mutual problems and can more efficiently and effectively share responsibility for the solution to problems. The school counselor's role in community-focused consultation is to seek consultation services from outside agencies as well as to supply consultation to community agencies. The alliance of community and school is beneficial to both systems. School counselors can contribute to the community agency's understanding of how schools work and discuss issues facing the students within the academic environment, while the agencies can provide knowledge and expertise and participate in the development of joint programs for children and families. The relationship that develops between school counselors and community agencies can provide schools with additional resources and specialized expertise while giving community agencies new and different perspectives about students and their families. Such relationships result in the strengthening of schools and school counselors and community agencies in meeting the comprehensive needs of all children.

To illustrate these mutually beneficial contributions, we share this scenario. A school counselor consulted with a multicultural counseling center about the parenting practices of Sudanese refugee families. The school counselor profited from the culturally sensitive information offered by the agency about family practices and expectations that may be unusual or unfamiliar to the school counselor and was able to establish in-service training for the teachers and school administrators. In turn, the counseling center benefited from establishing a relationship with school personnel and knowledge about school practices, regulations, and resources that are helpful in working with Sudanese families.

The terms *consultation* and *collaboration* are often used interchangeably (Dougherty, 2000). In community-focused consultation there is also an interchangeability of terms, although in our definition of community-focused consultation we are emphasizing consultation by the community agencies in cooperation with the school counselor. One primary difference in the terms is that collaboration is aimed at a shared decision-making responsibility with many participants alternately assuming the role of consultant and consultee (Thousand, Villa, Paolucci-Whitcomb, & Nevin, 1996), with an underlying assumption that the consultee has a greater sense of ownership in the problem-solving process.

Traditional Models of Consultation

Because community-focused school consultation is a particular type of consultation, it is important to clearly understand the differences between conventional consultation models and community-focused consultation as we are defining it. Conventional consultation can be grouped into two theoretical types, one based on case or client-focused consultation and the other based on program consultation. Traditional consultation models are derived from three-way or triadic relationship models where a consultant serves as the expert, providing information and recommendations to the consultee that in turn benefit the client.

Four Triadic Models of Consultation

There are generally four triadic models of consultation discussed in the counseling literature: client-centered consultation model, consultee-centered consultation model, behavioral consultation model, and program-centered administrative model (Dougherty, 2000; Keys, Bemak, Carpenter, & King-Sears, 1998a). The *client-centered consultation* involves the consultee seeking help with a client problem, where the consultant provides recommendations and resources to the consultee, and may also work directly with the client. In *consultee-centered consultation*, the consultant works primarily with the consultee, helping the consultee gain the skills and information to assist the client. In this model, the consultee is the primary beneficiary. The *behavioral consultation* model involves operationalizing recommendations to the consultee, whereas program-centered administrative consultation focuses on program assessment and development utilizing the consultant's expertise to conduct program evaluation and make recommendations based on mental health theory and organizational systems. Generally, community-focused consultation is more focused on broader issues that relate to system-to-system issues, and thus relies on the principles of the *program-centered administrative model*. Less frequently, the community-focused consultation model also includes focusing on a client-centered problem (client-centered consultation model), skill acquisition for the school system through the school counselor (consultee-centered model), and instituting specific recommendations (behavioral consultation model).

Four Stages of Consultation

Like counseling experience, the general consultation process takes place in stages. These four phases are entry, diagnosis, implementation, and disengagement (Dougherty, 2000; Keys, Green, Lockhart, & Luongo, 2002). During the *entry stage* the consulting relationship is explored, there is a preliminary discussion of the problem, and contractual arrangements are formalized. During this phase the preliminary work begins, meaning that the consultant(s) enters the system, works to gain trust of the members of the school, and deals with resistance.

The *diagnosis stage* involves gathering information, defining the problem, setting goals, and brainstorming possible interventions. During the *implementation stage*, or the action stage, the consultant(s) provides resources or trains the school counselor to implement recommendations, the intervention is agreed upon, a plan of action is agreed upon, and an evaluation of the intervention is conducted. During the final phase of consultation, *disengagement*, the consultation process is evaluated, plans for integrating the intervention in the school are made, and termination of the formal relationship is accomplished.

Community-Focused Collaborative Consultation

A form of consultation called *collaborative consultation* has emerged in response to the complex problems facing schools and community agencies. Collaborative consultation is defined by Idol, Nevin, and Paolucci-Whitcomb (1994) as "an interactive process that enables groups of people with diverse expertise to generate creative solutions to mutually defined problems" (p. 1). Collaborative consultation is a relatively new form of school counseling consultation (Keys et al., 1998a) that is responsive to the demands placed on schools seeking to provide educational, health, and mental services to children. It involves three functions: (a) school counselors working collaboratively with other professionals in schools, (b) school counselors providing leadership in facilitating community agency collaboration and consultation services, and (c) school counselors working collaboratively with parents (Bemak, 1998). While the focus of this chapter is community-focused consultation, the reality is that as school counselors seek consultation with community agencies, collaborative relationships are forged.

Stages of Community-Focused Consultation

The stages of community-focused collaborative consultation differ from the traditional stages of consultation mentioned earlier. Community-focused collaborative consultation is best described as a problem-solving process (Melaville, Blank, & Asayesh, 1993). In this approach to consultation there are several stages, including *coming together*, *defining a shared vision*, *developing a strategic plan*, and *taking action*. The major difference between community-focused collaborative consultation and traditional consultation is that the separate organizations (e.g., school, mental health or social service agencies) link to form a new system or partnership (Keys et al., 1998a, p. 129) that is more equal by design. This distinction is felt primarily in the first two stages of community-focused collaborative consultation where the counselor is working to facilitate the partnership.

Responsibility for the definition of the problem, the development of the plan, the implementation, and evaluation of the plan is shared among all members of the team, with valued input and recommendations by all parties.

◤ A New Model of Consultation with a Community Focus

We believe that different models of consultation are appropriate for different developmental issues and problems and that "one shoe does not fit all." Keys et al. (1998a) described how traditional models of consultation are useful for typical developmental problems experienced by students and families but are not responsive to the complex problems of youth at risk for school failure or other serious problems. Furthermore, traditional models seem to limit the involvement of the school counselor and community agency counselor's impact on the respective systems, leaving consultation more to administrators while underutilizing or not utilizing the expertise and skills of the school counselor. Since school resources and budgets can no longer meet all of the needs of students and families (Wang, Haertel, & Walberg, 1995), the use of the school counselor's expertise in new and more innovative models of school counseling has the potential to provide an important additional resource when school counselors and administrators work collaboratively with communities.

As school personnel are asked to provide more and more services to students, and student needs increase, new models of consultation and collaboration with community agencies and community-based resources are required (Adelman & Taylor, 1997, 2002; Bemak, 1998). School counselors must be very involved with community agencies. For example, many schools enforce the zero tolerance of drug and alcohol use. Although this goal is highly commendable, there are no commensurate programs designed to achieve this objective so it results in being a consequence rather than a successful prevention program. Thus, there is a critical need to strengthen relationships with community agencies delivering drug and alcohol interventions in order to come closer to the goal of not using alcohol or drugs.

An example of a creative community-focused consultative relationship between a school and a community agency was in one urban community where the school approached an agency with expertise in drug and alcohol programming and interventions. The agency, through close collaboration with the school counselor, delivered day and inpatient drug treatment to students. In addition, the agency provided consultation to schools about setting up programs on-site, while simultaneously substance abuse counselors went into the schools to conduct small group counseling sessions. The school counselors facilitated consultation by the drug treatment agency with the schools and coordinated public school teachers willing to provide academic support and school-related counseling to students in their day treatment and inpatient centers.

It is clear to us that fresh models of community-focused consultation are required. This need has been affirmed by other experts (Adelman & Taylor, 1993, 2002; Flaherty et al., 1998). During the last ten to fifteen years, a call for more responsive mental health services has given rise to a variety of new approaches to consultation and collaboration (Green & Keys, 2001; Henggeler, 1994; Ho, 2001; Hobbs & Collison, 1995; Keys et al., 2002). The models differ according to who is providing mental health and social services to children and where the services are located. Full-service schools describe models that bring mental health and social services to children and families within the school (Dryfoos, 1994, 1998). Ho's (2001) family-centered integrated service model describes, for instance, a systems perspective of service provision where school counselors direct services to children and families and collaborate with community agencies to integrate services. Bemak and Cornely's (2002) School and Family Integration (SAFI) model provides an innovative method of community-focused consultation among marginalized families and their relevant schools.

School Reform and Community-Focused Consultation

The school reform movement is attempting to address the educational problems facing all of our schools, especially for impoverished urban and inner-city schools. Recognizing that schools cannot address all of the concerns alone, school reformers have sought more involvement with community agencies (Weist, 1997). Recently, school counselors have been examining their role in the school reform movement and how they can be more effective in using community resources (Adelman & Taylor, 2002; Bemak, 2000; House & Hayes, 2002). Visionaries and school reformers are conceptualizing innovative ways to organize schools. As such, it is imperative to develop a new and efficient model for community-focused consultation.

The delivery of community-focused consultation continues to evolve. As school counselors participate in the school reform dialogue, they are also developing new roles and better ways of addressing the needs of all children (House & Hayes, 2002). To help foster these changes, the American School Counselor Association (2003) launched their National Model for school counseling, which expands and reconceptualizes the role and function of school counselors (Hatch

& Bowers, 2002). Consultation in this new model is considered a component of a comprehensive school counseling program's delivery system. It is both a responsive service and a systems support activity. Underlying the development of this model is a belief that school counselors can no longer afford to work in isolation as they respond to the needs of children. Accessing the resources and expertise of the community and working collaboratively with school and community teams through community-focused consultation is therefore important in the work of school counselors.

The Education Trust has also contributed to the discussion about how school counselors can become actively involved in the school reform movement. For example, the National Initiative for Transforming School Counseling, funded by The Education Trust and DeWitt Wallace, is a research effort that focused on defining a new role for school counselors, and how counselor preparation programs need to change to prepare school counselors for their new roles (Perusse & Goodnough, 2001). The contemporary vision for school counselors includes community-focused consultation as a component of three of the five strands describing the role of school counselors, including the work with leadership teams, advocacy for all students in schools, and participation on teams and collaboration with other professionals inside and outside of school. School counselors, by virtue of their relationship with community agencies and knowledge of community resources, are uniquely positioned to address issues of equity and the educational disparities present in U.S. schools (House & Hayes, 2002). Accessing community agencies by acting as both consultant and consultee, and working collaboratively with community agency providers, is an important task school counselors bring to the school reform agenda that no other professional in the school setting is trained to perform.

Redefining the School Counselor's Role

Bemak (2000) described three new roles for counselors working with community agencies that relate closely to community-focused consultation. The first role is to provide *outreach linkage*, by connecting counselors to services in the community, such as juvenile services, mental health, and social services. School counselors can function as conduit to resources in the community by referring teachers, students, and families to community resources and accessing those resources themselves to address particular issues in schools. It is extremely important that school counselors are aware of all the services available in their community. Becoming familiar with community agencies and resources requires school counselors to take advantage of opportunities to visit agencies, compile a resource list, and possibly interview community agency counselors. A good place to start learning about your community is through community-based resource guides and on the Internet. You can locate the names of community agencies and social services using the city, county, or state web page (e.g., http//mentalhealth.about.com/). It is also possible to request a copy of the community handbook listing agencies and services available in your city or county. School counselors can also network with other counselors and social workers in neighboring schools to share information about unique resources, referral sources, and community agencies available in the community.

The second new role is *coordinating services* introduced to the school, such as a mental health clinic run by a community agency. As it becomes more common for community mental health services to be located in schools, school counselors must be able to coordinate and facilitate service provision. School counselors are needed to help community agency counselors enter the school community and gain access to students and teachers. Counselors will play a pivotal role in supporting and facilitating the work of the community agency providers as they conduct their work in schools. In this role, school counselors may be responsible for conducting planning meetings, facilitating the referrals, gaining permissions, and implementing recommendations of the community mental health counselor. Recently, this was illustrated in a local school that received a grant to provide mental health counseling to low-income students in the school. The community mental health counselor worked with the professional school counselor to gain access and acceptance in the school. The school counselor worked closely with school administrators, teachers, and other resource personnel to facilitate meeting space and scheduling. The school counselor consulted with the community mental health counselor, the classroom teacher, and the parents to develop appropriate counseling goals. With the help of the school counselor, the mental health counselor was able to provide group counseling to eighteen children in the school in three different groups.

The third new role is to develop *prevention and intervention programs* in collaboration with community agency personnel with programs that can be located in either the school or the community. The forging of school-community alliances concerning the issues of substance abuse and violence prevention has been a common response to these school and community issues. School counselors can help community agencies understand the concerns of schools and students and develop programs that respond to the identified needs. These agencies provide an excellent example of how schools and communities can pool their resources to analyze shared community concerns and develop responsive programs. The school counselor is trained and prepared to understand the existing issues and contribute to their solutions.

Changing Community-Focused Consultation Models

Altering traditional service delivery models is obviously quite difficult (Bemak, 1998; Keys & Bemak, 1997; Keys, Bemak, & Lockhart, 1998b) given the entrenched structure and norms that are inherent to schools and community agencies. Also, people within these organizations find it hard to change their behavior even though they understand that what they are doing is often ineffectual. Obstacles to providing improved services for children have found a lack of coordination among agencies. This has resulted in duplication and fragmentation of services, deficits in funding to support services and programs that transcend traditional boundaries, and gaps in family support services in communities (Bemak & Cornely, 2002; Collins & Collins, 1994; Gibelman, 1993; Kaffenberger & Seligman, 2002). Adelman and Taylor (1997, 2002) have described the need for restructuring how schools access community health and human services, yet remain cautious, believing that the way schools link these services is affected by the school reform movement.

Because organizations are difficult to change, it is important to address the issues of resistance. Bemak (1998) identified two sources of resistance to change: personal and institutional. He described how *personal resistance* is the result of reluctance to accept new ways of organizing roles and responsibilities, comfort levels with current practices, and lack of confidence in working collaboratively with other professionals. With reference to this chapter, we suggest that personal resistance is already evident in school counselors and community agency staff who are trained in institutional practices that are not conducive to community-focused consultation. *Institutional resistance* comes from discrepancies between what is publicly said and what is actually practiced, and further enhanced by a lack of administrative support, limited budgets, and lack of incentives to work collaboratively with other institutions.

Clearly, overcoming barriers and resistance to move toward creative models of community-focused consultation involves new practices that go beyond the current accepted customs (Bemak, 2000; Flaherty et al., 1998). School administrators and school counselors together need to redefine roles and responsibilities for school counselors, document areas of success in order to secure administrative support for new programs and processes, become better trained in collaborative and interdisciplinary ways of working, restructure school and community resources, and thus rethink how budgets are allocated, and understand traditional and innovative models of consultation.

Literature Review on Community-Based Consultation

Although community-focused consultation is a part of the school counselor's role, it has been a low job priority. In fact, we postulate that the urgency of understanding the importance of this role is only now emerging. Henggeler (1994) summarized the recommendations made by the American Psychological Association's Task Force on Innovative Models of Mental Health Services for Children, Adolescents and their Families, which were based on research findings that mental health services for children were not addressing their psychological needs and that service delivery was inadequate. Suggestions for change included the call for system-level modifications, where service delivery is moved from the community to the home, school, and neighborhood settings. This has a profound effect on community-focused consultation and the school counselor's role.

Providing comprehensive community-based mental health services in schools fosters collaboration and interventions that offer an important step toward prevention. The federal Department of Health and Human Resources reported that providing timely comprehensive community-based mental health services reduced hospital admission days by 39 to 79 percent and reduced average days of detention by 40 percent (SAMHSA, 1998). We urge that these services be offered in schools through a community-focused consultation model.

More efficient service delivery models are required as the need for services that are beyond the scope of the school increases. In order to more adequately respond to the expanding needs of children and families, the number of school-based mental health programs is growing (Adelman & Taylor, 1993, 2002). Approximately 20 percent of youth have emotional problems severe enough to require professional help, and yet only one-fifth of these children and their families will receive the help they need (Hoagwood, 1999). It is estimated that students with severe emotional problems miss more school than any other disability category and that 47 percent of these students drop out of school (Institute of Medicine, 1997). An alarming statistic relating to school dropouts is that 73 percent of the students who drop out are arrested within five years of leaving school. This is the type of problem that could be well addressed by community-focused consultation between the school counselor and community agencies.

It would be helpful to assess the effectiveness of other community-based mental health programs located in schools. One statewide study (Lapan, Gysbers, & Sun, 1997) evaluated school-based mental health services within the context of a comprehensive school counseling program. They concluded that students who attended schools that provided fully implemented mental health services were more academically successful than children attending schools without such resources.

Another study compared the usefulness of school-based comprehensive health centers to managed care health centers located outside of the schools (Kaplan, Dalonge, Guernsey, & Hanrahan, 1998). The researchers found that adolescents who had access to school-based mental health centers were ten times more likely to take advantage of the school-based services. An important finding was that the implementation of school-based health services led to reduced use of emergent and urgent after-hours visits to mental health clinics and improved access and treatment for mental health and substance abuse problems.

Additional research is necessary to evaluate the need for and effectiveness of community-focused consultation practices. School counselors are increasingly making use of data to assess the value of the academic, mental health, and social needs of students. As school counselors develop new ways of working with community agencies, and innovative ways of using resources, ongoing program evaluation becomes necessary. We suggest that action research be conducted. School counselors can use exiting data and develop their own evaluation instruments to assess the effectiveness of existing programs. For example, in the previous case of the school where eighteen children were receiving counseling at school from a community mental health counselor, the school counselor could use attendance records, grades, discipline records, and standardized tests to evaluate the effectiveness of the program. The school counselor could also develop a simple instrument to evaluate how parents, teachers, and administrators perceive the effectiveness of the program. Using these tools of evaluation, the school counselor will be in a position to assess the impact of such a program as it relates to the goals of public education and to make program recommendations.

Ethical and Legal Considerations in Community-Focused Consultation

Today, perhaps more than ever before, school counselors must be aware of the legal and ethical responsibilities that are intrinsic to their role. The issues and concerns that impact students are more complex and serious in nature than they were forty years ago. In an effort to more effectively help students with these issues, school counselors frequently consult with community services or agency counselors. It is imperative that, during any consultation discussion, school counselors remain keenly aware of, and adhere to, the ethical codes of conduct of the profession.

Both the American Counseling Association (ACA, 1995) and ASCA (1998) have developed ethical standards and practices that govern the work of school counselors, and include guidelines that are applicable to community-focused consultation. It is important to be aware of these standards because they provide important guidelines for the work of the school counselor. We present and illustrate here some of the more relevant guidelines.

The ACA ethical document (1995) highlights two specific concerns that relate to consultation and subsequently community-focused consultation. The first two subsections (B.6.a & B.6.b) are under the area that addresses confidentiality. The first standard warns the counselor to respect the client's right to privacy and that any discussion about a client (e.g., students or teachers) must be for professional reasons only.

The following situation exemplifies this ethical concern. One Monday morning, students and staff came to school and learned that, over the weekend, a senior girl, Julie, attempted suicide. Two of Julie's former teachers knew she had been in outside private therapy for three years and knew from the parent that the school counselor had parental permission to communicate with the therapist. The school counselor was also aware of three other suicide attempts in the community during the past six months. The two teachers knew two of the other three students who had attempted suicide. The teachers were very concerned. They approached the counselor and requested information about the one girl and the other students. They demanded from the school counselor to know what had been going on in the students' homes and in therapy. Although the counselor realized the teachers were genuinely concerned for the students, ethically, she could not divulge the content of her conversations with Julie's therapist. In this and other situations involving community linkages, school counselors must safeguard the confidentiality of students, which is also applicable to their work with community-focused consultants. Counselors cannot be held ethically or legally responsible if the consultee (in this case, the therapist) is negligent in applying or discarding their advice (Remley & Herlihy, 2001).

The second subsection of the ACA code encourages the counselor, prior to discussing a client, to find our whether the consultant(s) or agencies have an established policy to protect the confidential nature of the material shared between organizations. Similar to other counselors, school counselors have a form that parents or legal guardians of minors must sign before any type of communication about specific students takes place between agencies. The custodial legal guardian must designate, in writing, the type of information that may be shared between parties. Before any conversation can occur, all parties must have a copy of this signed release form and have exchanged signed releases from the involved parties. Therefore, both parties must send each other their copies of the signed release form prior to any further communication.

The second section of the ethical ACA code (Section D.2.a–d) is devoted entirely to "consultation" and has direct relevance to community-focused consultation. In this section, four key points are addressed that relate to the role of the counselor. The standards discuss the fact that consultation with another professional is a desired choice, that there is a need to ensure one has the skills and competencies as a consultant, the importance that the clients (school personnel, students, and/or parents) understand the consultative process, and that the goals of a consulting relationship are clearly understood with an aim toward self-direction and independence.

In addition to a professional code of ethics, mental health professionals, including school counselors, rely on five fundamental ethical principles that govern their practice (Kitchner, 1984) and relate closely to community-focused consultation. *Autonomy and independence* in decision making is one of the principles. Another is *doing good for others to promote human welfare.* This is closely in line with The Education Trust's (1998) transforming school counseling initiative that promotes advocacy and social justice.

An example of this can be found in the school district where the school counselor chairs a multiagency committee. The committee is made up of representatives from social services, the community services board, a juvenile detention center, the court system, welfare agencies, public and mental health agencies, school district administrators, teachers, and other community agencies. The primary goal of every meeting is to discuss issues pertaining to specific students and to look at systemic issues that affect schools and the community. A sample issue discussed was how the school counselors often found themselves in a position of advocating for students and promoting those issues that would result in fair and equitable treatment.

A third principle is *nonmaleficence*, which basically means, "Do no harm." Thus, all community-focused consultation would adhere to this principle in a concerted effort to not injure students or teachers through decisions made through the consultation process. A fourth principle, *fidelity*, focuses on the counselor's obligation to be faithful and trustworthy; in other words, counselors must keep their promises to clients, whenever possible. When a school counselor promises to consult with an outside resource, that promise must be kept, regardless of the counselor's other responsibilities or deadlines. We suggest that this is also applicable to working with community consultants. Finally, the last principle, *justice*, assures clients that counselors will provide equal treatment to everyone. To be more specific, counselors will be just and fair in providing equal treatment to all people. This idea coincides with maintaining a fair and just inter-action with all consultants, keeping this as a major consideration in community-focused consultation.

◢ Technology Concerns in Community-Focused Consultation

Many school counselors are grappling with emerging ethical issues related to technology. This struggle to determine how technology relates to their work also carries over into questions about the relationship of technology to community-focused consultation work. In short, a key responsibility that school counselors face is the ethical concern surrounding consulting and technology (ACA, 1999). As we have already mentioned, one of the primary ethical principles that govern all mental health counselors is that of doing no harm. This principle is especially important as school counselors move beyond the traditional methods of school counseling within their own buildings and practice community-focused consultation.

As counselors integrate technology into community-focused consultation, there are basic ethical considerations to remember. For example, "How are you able to accurately verify identification and competency of the consultants?" and "How does one ensure confidentiality and security of e-mail transmissions, which are considered to be part of a one's records?" It already appears that issues of confidentiality and storage of client records are problematic (Rosik & Brown, 2001) and may pose a problem for community-focused consultation relation-ships. Without direct contact, and limitations about the identification and issues of the consultants, a full and accurate assessment of significant issues may be compromised. An example of this is when a school counselor was working with an outside agency and received an e-mail from one of the consultants from the agency. Was there anything in the e-mail that would be problematic should the records be required for legal proceedings? Was there any information about par-ticular teachers or students in the e-mail? Who else could access the e-mail, and what would be the ramifications to their reading it?

Legally, e-mail correspondence is subject to subpoena. In addition, parents have the legal right to any and all e-mail documents when it concerns informa-tion about their child (Hodge, Gostin, & Jacobson, 1999). Raising these and sim-ilar questions provides an area for thoughtful consideration for school counselors as they work closely with community agencies using Internet technology that is founded on community-focused consultation.

◤ Community-Focused Consultation and the National Standards for School Counseling Programs

ASCA developed the National Standards for School Counseling Programs (Campbell & Dahir, 1997) in order to provide a cohesive, standards-based, developmental program for use by all school counselors. The primary authors, Campbell and Dahir (1997), recommended that "A school counseling program based upon national standards necessitates the involvement of the entire school community to integrate academic, career, and personal/social development of students into the mission of each school" (p. 1). The National Standards are related to all work that school counselors do, including community-focused consultation, where they provide guidelines and definition while focusing on the consultant and consultee. This is particularly important as the school counselor collaborates with community agency personnel, teachers, administrators, parents, community mental health therapists, and medical professionals in an effort to plan and implement strategies to help students achieve academic success.

The National Standards provide a framework for community-focused consultation and the subsequent relationship between school counselors and community agencies by clarifying the problem definition (e.g., academic performance as an ultimate goal) and ensuring a process that is inclusive of needs assessment, discussion, planning, design, implementation, and evaluation. The next section discusses various case examples and actual situations in which the standards helped guide a community-focused consultation process.

◤ Practical Application in Context of K–12 School Counseling Programs

Types of Community-Focused Consultation

Types of community-focused consultation can be viewed on a continuum from traditional to collaborative service delivery models. Within the more traditional model, school counselors engage community agency experts to provide a range of consulting services regarding issues with children (Bostic & Rauch, 1999) based on the expertise of the community agencies and inability of schools to independently provide that service. This service delivery model assists school counselors with student issues, family problems, and problems specific to school objectives by using the expertise of an outside consultant. This outside consultant is typically a community agency counselor or mental health professional with specialized expertise to address the identified problem. An example of this style of consultation is when a school counselor has a number of children from families of divorce who are disruptive in school. There may be an interest in knowing how to better address these children within the school environment. Thus, the school counselor may consult with an agency providing family therapy for children of divorce in an attempt to better understand the dynamics that contribute to behavioral problems, effective interventions within the school context, and ways to cooperate in working with these children.

Another kind of community-focused consultation involves working with a community agency or agencies to provide expertise in dealing with the particular system, school, or generalized student issue. These agencies may provide consultation to parents and school staff following observations and meetings with students, school counselors, teachers, administrators, and/or parents. In the case of a school or program evaluation, the consultant makes specific recommendations for change based on the evaluation. The school counselor is the recipient of the recommendations and either has the authority to implement the suggestions of the consultant or may bring back the recommendations to committees or school administrators.

These two examples of community-focused consultation are helpful with children having problems and may also be beneficial and more commonly used as a model for community-focused consultation when the goal is for systems change within the school (Bemak, 2000; Keys et al., 1998a). It is important to note that these illustrations may not be as effective with more complex school problems, such as delinquency, school violence, or poor performance on state testing, which would require more complex responses (Keys & Bemak, 1997; Keys et al., 1998b).

Another model of community-focused consultation, as noted earlier, involves bringing entire systems in as the consultant. This was done in a program called the Nashville Youth Network (D'Andrea & Daniels, 2000), where an entire community-run program was introduced into a school. The program provided weekly group counseling to youth while an adult leader, identified as the *program consultant* of this group, functioned as consultant by providing information concerning youth services and resources, facilitating group discussions, and helping develop strategies to address problems. By providing an empathic environment, as well as a problem-solving structure, the counselor was able to help this group address real problems and develop proactive responses. This group was particularly concerned about drug and alcohol use in their community. This excellent example of consultation demonstrates how the program consultant assisted the school in developing a drug and alcohol prevention program.

Community-focused consultation has the ability to address more complex and multifaceted problems. A broader scope of programs in the school can be accomplished by adding community interventions within the school environment and is useful to facilitate the prevention of delinquency, substance abuse, and teen pregnancy (Dryfoos, 1998; Wang et al., 1995). Furthermore, this type of consultation can more effectively address the complex causes of poverty and aggression with a multisystemic approach that includes the school and community.

Another example of community-focused consultation was developed by Atkins et al. (1998). Since so few programs consider the complex interaction of factors that cause childhood aggression, Atkins and his colleagues developed an ecological model of school-based mental health services, called Parents and Peers as Leaders in School (PALS), involving multiple systems and services focusing on service delivery in schools. The PALS program helped the school provide the individualized, flexible, and comprehensive mental health services required to address the complex social and emotional needs of low-income aggressive children. PALS aims toward prevention and a reduction in more intensive services like special education placement, hospitalization, or contact with the juvenile justice system. The PALS mental health consultant conducted systematic assessment and developed prevention strategies for school-based aggression at the classroom, peer, individual, and parental levels. Simultaneously, the PALS mental health consultant worked collaboratively with the teacher and the parent to implement strategies.

Community-focused consultation may also target larger school systems rather than just one school. A good example of this involved the development of school district–wide strategies to improve the services offered to children who are chronically ill. A large urban school district, interested in improving the school reentry services to children, secured an outside consultant who had expertise in this area. Initially, the school system invited the consultant to evaluate the need for training and resources among school counselors and to provide awareness workshops to school counselors, resulting in the finding that school counselors felt unprepared and unclear about their role. An outcome was to offer additional training and clearer guidelines concerning how to interface with the multiple agencies serving the chronically ill student. As a result, a community agency alliance was forged among a university, public heath services, physicians, hospitals, and the schools. University and school members of the team collaboratively developed a school reintegration model that conceptualized overlapping services to chronically ill children provided by school counselors, social workers, and public health nurses. Training and a training handbook were developed based on the model. Many medical personnel, including pediatric oncology social workers, child life specialists, and nurse specialists for particular chronic illnesses, attended the training and provided additional links and support for these children.

Examples of Community-Focused Consultation

Program Development.   The coordinator of guidance and counseling services within a large urban local school district contacted George Mason University's counseling and development department to request a consultation about the district's need for advanced and well-trained future leaders and directors of secondary school counseling. Meetings were held between school district personnel and university faculty to discuss how to address this need. Through consultation with a university faculty member, the school district's coordinator of student services made a decision to pursue the joint development of a program that would provide future leadership training of school counselors and meet the need in the school district. The program, based on the consultation services of university counselor educators with the school district's school counseling administrators, resulted in a collaboratively designed 15-credit-hour post-master's certificate program to provide intensive preparation for experienced secondary school counselors to assume counseling leadership roles. The consultation with the counselor educator was instrumental in helping define how to meet the needs of the larger school system. Simultaneously, the program modeled a collaborative partnership, hiring school counseling administrators from within the district to teach some of the courses and actively participate in the program. This example of community-focused consultation is consistent with the concept that shared ownership and mutual expertise are critical components to successful partnerships (Keys et al., 1998a).

In-service Training for Bully/Victim Issues.   A school was having problems with bullying behavior. These problems had been ongoing for three years and, despite efforts to address this issue by teachers and the principal, the bullying behavior continued. Some students in the school were being threatened and harassed on a regular basis. Administrators were at a loss as to how to intervene, and the victims' parents were becoming angry and frustrated with school officials. In desperation, a parent telephoned a known expert for consultation in the area of bully/victim relationships, to provide information and recommendations for her son. The parent discussed the problem with the consultant and learned that bullying was a learned behavior, usually from a significant role model who models aggressive or violent behavior, that one in seven children were in a bully/victim relationship, and that bullying directly affected at least 15 percent of the total school population (Olweus, 1993, 1997). As the parent began to better understand bullying, she became interested in having the consultant work with the school to provide information and intervention strategies for a broader range of parents and teachers.

The parent later approached the school counselor and asked whether the school would be willing to contract with the consultant to better inform the school community how to handle the situation. The school counselor acknowledged that she did not have expertise in this area and approached the school principal, who agreed to contract with the consultant for six schoolwide sessions. The school counselor, parent, and consultant jointly designed a program to provide in-service training for the school community.

Substance Abuse Program in Schools. A school counselor was concerned about some of his high school students who were recovering from substance abuse. He had seen former students drop out of school even after recovery and revert back to drug and alcohol usage, especially at times when they experienced social and academic stress. Given the demands of his job as a school counselor, and his lack of knowledge in substance abuse treatment, he called the county substance abuse program to consult with a substance abuse specialist and request consultation services for the school. They discussed various approaches and types of prevention programs that would complement the school district's substance abuse program, what existed currently, and the perceived needs. They also explored what kind of in-service consultation would be best suited to the culture and policies of the school community and the practicality of longer-range intervention and prevention strategies following the training and community-focused consultation. After reviewing many options, they decided on a specific approach that would take place in the school and allow students to participate. The substance abuse specialist and the school counselor had engaged in a community-focused consultation that was rooted in a partnership between the school (via the school counselor) and a representative from a community agency.

Gang Intervention. Another example of a community-focused consultation was the situation where a school counselor contacted a mental health agency regarding problems with Hispanic gangs in the school. The community agency had a mental health specialist at the area's multicultural counseling center who originally came from Latin America and specialized in working with Hispanic gangs that were comprised of members from El Salvador. The contact by the school counselor resulted in consultation about gang behavior including risks, prevention, and intervention strategies that were unfamiliar to the school counselor. As a result, meetings and intervention strategies were planned that were collaboratively implemented by the mental health agency and the school, as well as ongoing discussions between school counselors and staff from the mental health outreach program.

Safe Passage Schools. Dryfoos (1994, 1998) described her vision for a new way to organize middle schools by calling them Safe Passage Schools. She envisioned a school organized into separate houses of 200 students each, where students stayed together for three years. In addition to a small teaching staff to student ratio, she would hire counselor-mentors who would act as case managers for students with problems as well as looking out for all the students in the house. Counseling services would be part of a Safe Passage Support System that would include psychological services as well as "a family resource center; health, mental health, and dental care center; after-school learning center; after-school recreation; and evening activities for parents and other community members" (Dryfoos, 1998, p. 194). The Safe Passage School is an extension of her earlier work when she described the concept of a Full Service School in 1994. At that time, she recommended that schools bring community services to support the needs of children and families into the schools. In describing the components of a Safe Passage School, Dryfoos (1998) envisions community resources and expertise as playing a central role in schools, with comprehensive community services located in the schools that would house multicomponent, multiagency one-stop health and social services.

◢ Final Thoughts: Trends in Community-Focused Consultation

In this chapter, we suggest that community-focused consultation must be more systematically addressed and fostered, especially since we know that school and community partnerships enhance student performance (Bemak, 2002; Keys et al., 1998a). School personnel cannot continue to work with the complex issues of students, families, and society independent of the issues and realities of the community. Problems cannot be compartmentalized and addressed as single, narrowly focused concerns. Effective education cannot happen without attending to the diverse needs of today's students. We argue here that community resources are essential for more effective educational systems. In addition, schools must access these resources through collaborative partnerships and community-focused consultation that is culturally sensitive and acknowledges the importance of attending to specific cultural needs and issues. The neglect of ecological context also creates critical deficiencies in the important task of education and counseling (Bemak & Conyne, in press; Bemak & Hanna, 1998). In summary, we believe that community-focused consultation is a critical aspect of the future in schools, and has significance for how school counselors define their future roles and work cooperatively with community agencies.

Community-Focused Collaborative Consultation: A Practical Example to Work Through

Case Study: Consultation Between a Local Mental Health Clinic and High School Counselors

After several meetings between the director of counseling services for the local mental health clinic and the head counselor from a large inner-city high school, a proposed interagency collaboration is coming to pass. The director of the community clinic has agreed to allow two master's level psychotherapists who are working on their doctorates in clinical psychology to help counsel those students most at risk for mental disorders. Everyone thinks it's a "win-win" situation. The school counselors benefit by having additional part-time professionals to help out with their large caseloads, and the two therapists earn on-the-job counseling hours that can later be used toward obtaining their psychologists' licenses. Moreover, rather than sending the students and their families across town for care, the therapists will be on-site to assist with personal and family counseling.

Let's process this scenario and at the same time practically review the chapter's content. Jot down your thoughts and feelings in response to these questions:

1. How might this scenario be considered a "community-focused consultation"? _____

   _____

   _____

2. Who are the major players here? Who is(are) the . . .

   ▪ Consultee: _____

   ▪ Consultant: _____

   ▪ Clients: _____

3. How are the school counselors serving as *liaisons*?

_____

_____

4. What issues of *cultural relevancy* might need to be addressed by the school counselors? _____

_____

_____

5. What are some of the ethical and legal considerations in this "community-focused consultation"? _____

_____

_____

6. Let's now look at the stages of community-focused consultation. How might they play out in the above scenario? Note how each one fits.

Stage	
1: Coming together	_____
	_____
	_____
	_____
2: Defining a shared vision	_____
	_____
	_____
	_____

3: Developing a strategic plan	
4: Taking action	

7. What might be some of the "downsides" of such a community collaborative consultation? _____

_____

_____

_____

Note: This appendix was written by Christopher Sink.

REFERENCES

Adelman, H. S., & Taylor, L. (1993). School-based mental health: Toward a comprehensive approach. *The Journal of Mental Health Administration, 20*(1), 32–45.

Adelman, H. S., & Taylor, L. (1997). Addressing barriers to learning: Beyond school-linked services and full-service schools. *American Journal of Orthopsychiatry, 67*(3), 408–421.

Adelman, H. S., & Taylor, L. (2002). School counselors and school reform: New directions. *Professional School Counseling, 5,* 235–248.

American Counseling Association. (1995). *ACA code of ethics and standards of practice.* Retrieved on May 1, 2002, from http://www.counseling.org/resources/ethics.htm

American Counseling Association. (1999). *Ethical standards for Internet on-line counseling.* Retrieved on May 1, 2002, from http://www.counseling.org/resources/internet.htm

American School Counselor Association. (1992). *American School Counselor Association Ethical Standards for School Counselors.* Alexandria, VA: Author.

American School Counselor Association. (1998). *Ethical standards for school counselors.* Retrieved on May 1, 2002, from http://www.schoolcounselor.org/content.cfm?L1 = 1 &L2 = 15

American School Counselor Association. (1999). *Role of the school counselor.* Alexandria, VA: Author.

American School Counselor Association. (2003). *The ASCA national model: A framework for school counseling programs.* Alexandria, VA: Author.

Atkins, M. S., McKay, M. M., Arvanitis, P., London, L., Madison, S., Costigan, C., et al. (1998). An ecological model for school-based mental health services for urban low-income aggressive children. *The Journal of Behavioral Health Services & Research, 5*(1), 64–75.

Bemak, F. (1998). Interdisciplinary collaboration for social change: Redefining the counseling profession. In C. C. Lee & G. R. Walz (Eds.), *Social action: A mandate for counselors* (pp. 279–292). Alexandria, VA: American Counseling Association.

Bemak, F. (2000). Transforming the role of the counselor to provide leadership in educational reform through collaboration. *Professional School Counseling, 3,* 323–331.

Bemak, F. (2002). Paradigms for future school counseling programs. In C. D. Johnson & S. K. Johnson (Eds.), *Building stronger school counseling programs: Bringing futuristic approaches into the present* (pp. 37–49). Greensboro, NC: ERIC Counseling & Student Services Clearinghouse and American Counseling Association.

Bemak, F., & Chung, R. (2003). Multicultural counseling with immigrant students in schools. In P. B. Pedersen & J. C. Carey (Eds.), *Multicultural counseling in schools* (2nd ed., pp. 84–104). Boston, MA: Allyn & Bacon.

Bemak, F., & Conyne, R. K. (in press). Ecological group counseling: Context and application. In R. K. Conyne & E. P. Cook, (Eds.), *Ecological counseling: An innovative approach to conceptualizing person-environment interaction.* Alexandria, VA: American Counseling Association.

Bemak, F., & Cornely, L. (2002). The SAFI Model as a critical link between marginalized families and schools: A literature review and strategies for school counselors. *Journal of Counseling & Development, 80,* 325–334.

Bemak, F., & Hanna, F. (1998). The twenty-first century counselor: An emerging role for changing times. *International Journal for the Advancement of Counselling, 20,* 209–218.

Bostic, J. Q., & Rauch, P. K. (1999). The three R's of school consultation. *American Academy of Child and Adolescent Psychiatry, 38*(3), 339–341.

Campbell, C. A., & Dahir, C. A. (1997). *The national standards for school counseling programs.* Alexandria, VA: American School Counselor Association.

Caplan, G., & Caplan, R. B. (1993). *Mental health consultation & collaboration.* San Francisco: Jossey-Bass.

Collins, B. G., & Collins, T. M. (1994). Child and adolescent mental health: Building a system of care. *Journal of Counseling & Development, 72,* 239–243.

D'Andrea, M., & Daniels, J. (2000). Youth advocacy. In J. Lewis & L. Bradley (Eds.), *Advocacy in counseling: Counselors, clients, & community* (pp. 71–78). Greensboro, NC: CAPS.

Dougherty, A. M. (2000). *Psychological consultation and collaboration* (3rd ed). Pacific Grove, CA: Brooks/Cole.

Dryfoos, J. G. (1994). *Full-service schools: A revolution in health and social services for children, youth and families.* San Francisco: Jossey-Bass.

Dryfoos, J. G. (1998). *Safe passage: Making it through adolescence in a risky society.* New York: Oxford University Press.

The Education Trust. (1998). *Education watch 1998: The Education Trust state and national data book* (Vol. 2). Washington DC: Author.

Flaherty, L. T., Garrison, E. G., Waxman, R., Uris, P. F., Keys, S. G., Glass-Siegel, M., & Weist, M. D. (1998). Optimizing the roles of school mental health professionals. *Journal of School Health, 68*(10), 420–424.

Gibelman, M. (1993). School social workers, counselors, and psychologists in collaboration: A shared agenda. *National Association of Social Workers, 15*(1), 45–53.

Green, A., & Keys, S. (2001). Expanding the developmental school counseling paradigm: Meeting the needs of the 21st century student. *Professional School Counseling, 5,* 84–95.

Hatch, T., & Bowers, J. (2002). The block to build on. *ASCA School Counselor, 39,* 13–19.

Henggeler, S. W. (1994). A consensus: Conclusions of the APA Task Force Report on innovative models of mental health services for children, adolescents, and their families. *Journal of Clinical Child Psychology, 23*(Suppl.), 3–6.

Ho, B. S. (2001). Family-centered, integrated services: Opportunities for school counselors. *Professional School Counseling, 4,* 357–361.

Hoagwood, K. (1999). *Summary sheet: Major research findings on child and adolescent mental health.* Washington DC: National Institute on Mental Health.

Hobbs, B. B., & Collison, B. B. (1995). School-community agency collaboration: Implications for the school counselor. *The School Counselor, 43,* 58–65.

Hodge, J. G., Gostin, L. O., & Jacobson, P. D. (1999). Legal issues concerning electronic health information. *Journal of the American Medical Association, 282*(14), 1466–1471.

House, R. M., & Hayes, R. (2002). School counselors: Becoming key players in school reform. *Professional School Counseling, 5,* 249–256.

Idol, L., Nevin, A., & Paolucci-Whitcomb, P. (1994). *Collaborative consultation* (2nd ed.). Austin, TX: Pro-Ed.

Institute of Medicine. (1997). *Schools and health.* Washington DC: National Academy Press.

Kaffenberger, C. J., & Seligman, L. (2002). Helping students with mental and emotional disorders. In B. T. Erford (Ed.), *Transforming the school counseling profession* (pp. 249–283). Upper Saddle River, NJ: Merrill/Prentice Hall.

Kaplan, D. W., Dalonge, B., Guernsey B. P., & Hanrahan, M. B. (1998). Managed care and school-based health centers: Use of health services. *Archives of Pediatrics & Adolescent Medicine, 152*(1), 25–33.

Keys, S. G., & Bemak, F. (1997). School family community linked services: A school counseling role for changing times. *The School Counselor, 44,* 255–263.

Keys, S. G., Bemak, F., Carpenter, S. L., & King-Sears, M. E. (1998a). Collaborative consultant: A new role for counselors serving at-risk youths. *Journal of Counseling & Development, 76,* 123–133.

Keys, S. G., Bemak, F., & Lockhart, E. J. (1998b). Transforming school counseling to serve the mental health needs of at-risk youth. *Journal of Counseling & Development, 76,* 381–388.

Keys, S. G., Green, A., Lockhart, E., & Luongo, P. (2002). Consultation and collaboration. In B. T. Erford, (Ed.), *Transforming the school counseling profession* (pp. 171–190). Upper Saddle River, NJ: Merrill/Prentice Hall.

Kitchner, K. S. (1984). Intuition, critical evaluation, and ethical principles: The foundation for ethical decisions in counseling psychology. *The Counseling Psychologist, 12,* 43–55.

Lapan, R. T., Gysbers, N. C., & Sun, Y. (1997). The impact of more fully implemented guidance programs on the school experiences of high school students: A statewide evaluation study. *Journal of Counseling & Development, 75,* 292–302.

Locke, D. C. (2003). Improving the multicultural competence of educators. In P. B. Pedersen & J. C. Carey (Eds.), *Multicultural counseling in schools: A practical handbook* (2nd ed., pp. 171–189). Boston: Allyn & Bacon.

Melaville, A., Blank, M., & Asayesh, G. (1993). *Together we can: A guide for crafting a profamily system of educational and human services* (No. PIP 93-1103). Washington, DC: U.S. Department of Health and Human Services, Office of the Assistant Secretary for Planning and Evaluation.

Olweus, D. (1993). *Bullying at school.* Oxford, UK: Blackwell.

Olweus, D. (1997). Bully/Victim problems in school: Facts and intervention. *European Journal of Psychology of Education, 12*(4), 495–510.

Perusse, R., & Goodnough, G. E. (2001). A comparison of existing school counselor program content with the Education Trust initiatives. *Counselor Education and Supervision, 41,* 100–110.

Remley, T. P., Jr., & Herlihy, B. (2001). *Ethical, legal, and professional issues in counseling.* Upper Saddle River, NJ: Prentice Hall.

Rosik, C. H., & Brown, R. K. (2001). Professional use of the Internet: Legal and ethical issues in a member care environment. *Journal of Psychology and Theology, 29*(2), 106–120.

Substance Abuse and Mental Health Services Administration (SAMHSA). (1998). *National expenditures for mental health, alcohol, and other drug abuse treatment.* Washington, DC: SAMHSA, Department of Health and Human Services.

Thousand, J. S., Villa, R. A., Paolucci-Whitcomb, P., & Nevin, A. (1996). A rationale and vision for collaborative consultation. In W. Stainback and S. Stainback (Eds.), *Controversial issues confronting special education* (2nd ed., pp. 205–218). Boston: Allyn & Bacon.

Wang, M. C., Haertel, G. D., & Walberg, H. J. (1995). The effectiveness of collaborative school-linked services. In L. C. Rigsby, M. C. Reynolds, & M. C. Wang (Eds.), *School-community connections: Exploring issues for research and practice* (pp. 283–309). San Francisco: Jossey-Bass.

Weist, M. D. (1997). Expanded school mental health services: A national movement in progress. In T. Ollendick & R. Prinz (Eds.), *Advances in clinical child psychology* (Vol. 19, pp. 319–352). New York: Plenum Press.

PART FOUR

Collaboration and the Future of the Profession

CHAPTER 11

Enhancing Developmental School Counseling Programs Through Collaboration

Susan Keys and Alan Green
Johns Hopkins University

Introduction: Case Examples

Mrs. Elliott, a kindergarten teacher at Woodland Elementary School, asked Karen Johnson, the school counselor, to assist one of her students, Krista, to develop more appropriate social skills. Although Krista settled into the school routine with ease, she is having a difficult time interacting with her peers. Krista likes others to do things her way and can be very disruptive and vocal when this does not happen.

Lincoln Middle School is located in a large urban school district and has approximately 1,400 students. The school has experienced increasing levels of violent and aggressive behavior over the past two years culminating in a student being knifed by another student at the end of the last school year. The principal of Lincoln Middle School has decided to use the summer break to develop a strategic plan for creating a safer school environment and has organized a school-family-community school-safety work group to develop this plan. David McCoy, the school counselor, has been asked to chair this work group.

Jose Rivera is an honor student at Lakeland High School. Jose's family immigrated to the United States from El Salvador four years ago. None of Jose's family has ever attended college, and his mother and father are hopeful that Jose will be the first. They have an appointment set up with Renee Hughes, the school counselor, to discuss the college application process.

These scenarios represent typical situations that school counselors encounter as part of a normal day. As one of the few professionals in the school building charged with overseeing the academic, career, and personal/social development of students (American School Counselor Association [ASCA], 2000), the school counselor's roles and responsibilities are diverse and encompass a broad range of tasks.

Counseling, consultation, and coordination are well-recognized school counselor functions (Keys & Green, 2000) and an integral part of the developmental school counseling model that originated during the late 1960s and early 1970s. In all likelihood, the school counselor will implement aspects of these roles when responding to the above-mentioned scenarios. This chapter introduces a fourth dimension—collaboration—to the school counselor's role and function and examines the implications collaboration has for how school counselors define and execute their role. Questions to be answered include the following: What is collaboration? How is collaboration the same as, or different from, counseling, consultation, and coordination? How do school counselors form collaborative partnerships? and What skills, knowledge, and attitudes do school counselors need in order to function collaboratively? This chapter explores these and other questions as a way of discovering more about the school counselor as a collaborator.

What Is Collaboration?

Collaboration is a specific process that occurs among individuals who have come together to solve problems. Collaboration requires more than one person. School teams are a common vehicle for problem solving and fertile ground for collaboration. School counselors frequently function as members of various school work groups or teams, such as a school improvement team, a special education review team, a school counseling program advisory group, or a student services team. Such teams come together for a specific purpose—to address either a whole school problem (e.g., increase in violence and aggression) or the needs of a specific student. One way a school counselor can provide expertise to such groups is by promoting collaboration as an effective method for accomplishing common goals.

Friend and Cook (1996) defined collaboration as a *style* of interaction between at least two coequal parties who are working together toward a common goal. Collaboration conveys *how* an interaction takes place. The emphasis is on a process that occurs between and among people who engage in teaming or problem solving, not on the problem to be solved or the actual problem-solving activity.

Idol, Nevin, and Paolucci-Whitcomb (1994) also defined collaboration as an interactive process. They stressed that collaboration emphasizes teamwork and recognition by all participants that each person contributes a unique expertise to the problem-solving process. It is integration of this expertise that enables groups of individuals to generate creative solutions to problems that might not have occurred with individuals working alone. In this chapter, we suggest that school counselors need to adopt a posture of collaboration in order to effectively meet the challenges of implementing a comprehensive developmental program in today's school climate.

Defining Characteristics

Friend and Cook (1996) identified the following six characteristics that classify an interaction as collaborative.

Collaboration is Voluntary. People cannot be forced to collaborate. In our example of Lincoln Middle School, the school's principal has invited people to join a work group to address a specific school problem. Just because group participants are in a room together, or sit at a common table, it does not necessarily guarantee that the group will function collaboratively. It is how people engage with one another that determines whether or not the interaction could be described as collaborative. A style of interaction cannot be mandated.

Collaboration Requires Parity Among Participants. If an interaction is collaborative, then all persons involved recognize and respect all participants as equal members of the problem-solving team who have equal decision-making power. If one member on the team is perceived to have greater decision-making power within the group than another person, then collaboration cannot occur.

Let's return again to our Lincoln Middle School example. Suppose the group posits that one of the causes for disruptive and aggressive behavior is the lack of a whole school discipline plan. All members agree that this is a contributing factor in why the school has had difficulty managing student behavior, and the group makes a decision to identify and implement a specific discipline plan by the start of the new school year. This is not the outcome the school principal had in mind when convening this group. The principal had expected an endorsement for the installation of metal detectors and the hiring of a school police officer. If parity exists, group members feel comfortable expressing their views even when these opinions set them apart from another member who holds a position of power outside of the group. Because parity exists as a norm for the Lincoln Middle School work group, David McCoy, the school counselor who chairs the group, felt secure in disagreeing with the principal's expectations.

It is important to note the emphasis on parity "within the group." Outside of the group, individuals may assume different roles and different positions of power and will make decisions based on their authority to do so rather than an ethic of parity. For example, the principal at Lincoln Middle School interacts collaboratively (i.e., values equity in decision making) as a member of the school-safety work group, but outside of the group establishes directives about limits and expectations for teachers and staff related to procedures for office discipline referrals.

Collaboration is Based on Mutual Goals.   People who assemble to solve a problem need to have a common understanding and definition of the problem and a shared vision of what they want to accomplish. Having a common purpose encourages commitment to the problem-solving process. All participants in the Lincoln Middle School work group were in agreement that creating a plan to achieve a safe school environment was their goal.

Collaboration Depends upon Shared Responsibility for Participation and Decision Making.   Collaboration creates an interdependence among team members. Problem-solving tasks are shared, although not all members necessarily assume the same level of responsibility. The expertise of some team members may be more relevant for the problem being addressed, and those members of the team may assume more responsibility for problem-solving tasks.

For example, let's take the case of Jose at Lakeland High School. Jose, his parents, and Ms. Hughes all agree that attending college is an important goal for Jose. As an outcome of their initial meeting to discuss the college application process, each person agrees to take responsibility for certain tasks before the next meeting. Jose agrees to complete the Scholastic Achievement Test (SAT) application, Mr. and Mrs. Rivera agree to attend an information session at the local community college, and Ms. Hughes agrees to research scholarship opportunities for which Jose might be eligible, to identify area colleges to which Jose might consider applying, and to assist Jose with the SAT application. Ms. Hughes agreed to meet with Jose individually before meeting again as a group.

Clearly in this example, Ms. Hughes has taken on the most tasks. Although the division of labor may not be equal, Jose, his parents, and Ms. Hughes all share responsibility for deciding which tasks need to occur and whether these tasks are reasonable.

Individuals Who Collaborate Share Their Resources.   Resources can include skills and knowledge, space, money, time, tangible items, and personnel. Resources need to be freely given, allowing the group to decide how best to use the resources that group members contribute. Offering resources linked with expectations for how those resources will be used limits parity, and without parity, collaboration cannot exist.

Returning to the case example of Lincoln Middle School, assume that a representative (Mr. Harris) of the local health department has joined the school-safety work group. This person oversees a community-based mental health clinic, and clinicians at this clinic work with youth and families from the Lincoln Middle School catchment area. Mr. Harris offers to place a clinician at the school to provide individual and group counseling services. All members of the team are eager to have this extra resource, but most feel the clinician's time would be better spent providing consultation services to teachers related to classroom management. Mr. Harris indicates that if he places a clinician at the school, the clinician's time can only be spent on delivering services that can be billed to Medicaid and other insurance plans.

This situation presents an interesting dilemma for the school-safety team. On the one hand, extra services are valued and useful. On the other hand, the school-safety team has set a goal of establishing a schoolwide discipline plan. Although direct counseling services can support that plan, changing teachers' behavior is deemed a higher priority by the team. Not having flexibility in how the clinician's time would be spent limits the level of collaboration.

Individuals Who Collaborate Share Accountability for Outcomes.   By the nature of their shared decision making and shared responsibility for tasks, the group itself is accountable for outcomes and for revising problem-solving plans that are not moving toward agreed-upon goals.

In the case of Krista, the disruptive kindergarten student, the school counselor, Karen Johnson, consults with Mrs. Elliott, about Krista's behavior. Krista lives with her grandmother, and Mrs. Johnson and Mrs. Elliott invite Krista's grandmother, Mrs. Landers, to attend a meeting to discuss how they might create a more effective learning environment for Krista. At this meeting, the three of them identify a common goal and develop a strategy for encouraging more appropriate behavior. They develop a behavior management plan that Mrs. Elliott agrees to implement with the school counselor's help. Krista's grandmother agrees to stay in weekly phone contact with Krista's teacher to be updated about Krista's behavior. All share ideas for possible tangible reinforcers. The plan is implemented with all participants executing their agreed-upon tasks.

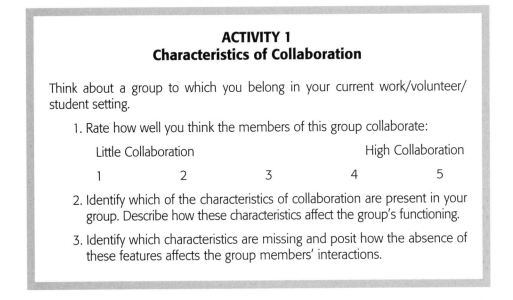

ACTIVITY 1
Characteristics of Collaboration

Think about a group to which you belong in your current work/volunteer/ student setting.

1. Rate how well you think the members of this group collaborate:

Little Collaboration   High Collaboration

1   2   3   4   5

2. Identify which of the characteristics of collaboration are present in your group. Describe how these characteristics affect the group's functioning.

3. Identify which characteristics are missing and posit how the absence of these features affects the group members' interactions.

Context for Collaboration

The concept of collaboration has not been a traditional part of the public school culture. Typically, professional educators have held an expertise in a particular area or areas (i.e., curriculum development, instruction, administration, counseling) and focused on doing their part to achieve educational objectives. Nowadays, school counselors have begun to work across disciplines in order to develop a true comprehensive program.

School counselors are also beginning to understand that the complex needs of students in schools today cannot be adequately addressed by professionals working in isolation from each other. Nor can comprehensive solutions occur if the counselor only focuses on students as isolated individuals. Bronfenbrenner's (1979) systemic-ecological model suggests that the individual student exists within a larger complexity of systems, all of which exert influence, either directly or indirectly, on an individual's behavior, thoughts, and feelings. Bronfenbrenner identified four interrelated systems: (a) the microsystem—which focuses on the relationships among persons within the daily environment, such as family, peers, school, and classroom; (b) the mesosystem—which centers on the interrelationship of the various microsystems, such as the school and family, the classroom and school; (c) the exosystem—or the larger institutions of society, such as government, educational system, service systems; and (d) the macrosystem, or overall cultural system of norms, social policies, and social expectations. According to Bronfrenbrenner's model, one cannot understand an individual without understanding the environmental context that surrounds the individual. Change for the individual is closely connected with change in the systems and structures that surround the individual.

The school counselor works primarily, but not exclusively, within the mesosystem. Collaboration is a vital tool for the school counselor to reach out to the broader systems—family, peer, classroom, school—that need to work together to create risk-free environments that promote positive behavior and well-being.

Regardless of the recognition of the value of collaboration, a lack of understanding persists about how to create collaborative environments. Collaboration has only recently been recognized as a critical component if school counseling is to address the multiple barriers to academic and personal success that can arise in any school setting (Campbell & Dahir, 1997; Green & Keys, 2001; House & Hayes, 2002). Collaboration has been looked upon also in juvenile justice, community mental health settings, and school mental health settings as an essential best practice when dealing with issues that are systemic in nature and origin (Atkins, Frazier, Adil, & Talbott, 2003; Luongo, 2000).

In addition to the theoretical and practice models that support collaboration, there are two key pieces of public policy legislation that value a collaborative-based school counseling model. The first of these, the Individuals with Disabilities Education Act (IDEA; U.S. Department of Education, 1997) called for educating students with disabilities in the least restrictive environment in which their needs can be met. Increasingly, students with disabilities are being integrated into regular education classrooms, requiring that educators, student services personnel (including school counselors), and family members work together to determine optimal service delivery systems (Carpenter, King-Sears, & Keys, 1998). According to this law, every student who has been determined to have at least one type of physical or learning disability must have what is called an Individualized Education Program (IEP). The IEP identifies specific goals and objectives to be pursued in order to meet the needs of the special education student. IDEA stipulates that each IEP is to be created by a collaborative team consisting of at least one regular education teacher, at least one special education teacher, an administrator, representatives of any relevant public agencies that will impact the IEP, the parent(s), and the child if appropriate (U.S. Department of Education, 1997). Collaboration facilitates the ability of school professionals to meet the requirements of this law by creating a team process that integrates professionals from within the school, parents, and others as necessary into the decision-making process used to plan services for students.

The No Child Left Behind Act of 2001 (NCLB; U.S. Department of Education, 2001), signed into law by President George W. Bush in 2002, called for major changes in the way schools meet the academic and associated needs of elementary and secondary students. It is the key piece of legislation that supports the use of collaboration in schools. Primarily, the law called for achieving adequate yearly progress (AYP) toward higher academic outcomes through school accountability, which in turn will affect future school funding. Removing barriers to learning and success is one of the ways this goal will be achieved. School counselors and other student support services providers can act to help schools remove social-emotional barriers through the provision of counseling services and advocating for collaborative teams to better integrate the diversity of support services some students need in order to succeed academically. School counselors can apply their human services and education training to these tasks.

In addition, the Elementary School Counseling Demonstration Program (U.S. Department of Education, 2000), which has also been adopted as part of the NCLB act, calls for the provision of comprehensive developmental school counseling programs to enhance the academic performance of students. By working collaboratively with other school and community professionals, school counselors can provide services and programs that support academic performance. Aligning school counseling program goals with the academic goals of the school is an important first step. The AYP requirements of the NCLB law call for schools to pursue and demonstrate progress toward rigorous academic standards to be measured primarily by national standardized tests. School counseling programs that provide universal (for all students) and targeted (for students at higher risk of school failure) services are directly connected to this broader educational mission by helping to remove social-emotional barriers to learning.

The following example illustrates how such an alignment can occur and how school counselors can be instrumental in helping schools remove barriers to learning.

Grove Elementary School is part of a school district where the school superintendent requires all schools to demonstrate annually adequate progress on the

California Test of Basic Skills (CTBS). The superintendent uses this assessment as a direct means of determining student progress and an indirect means of judging overall school performance. Specifically, each elementary grade level must achieve 75 percent satisfactory performance on the CTBS in order for a school to be given a "passing grade."

Joshua Smith, the Grove Elementary School counselor, chairs the school's School Improvement Team (SIT). The team has just reviewed last year's data for the CTBS. Although the school has met the 75 percent satisfactory mark, there are a large number of third-grade students who barely achieved the satisfactory level on the math portion of the standardized test. Further analysis reveals that a number of the students with marginal math grades have been referred to the office for discipline problems during math time. Mr. Smith has also reviewed teacher-parent contacts related to behavior, and these data suggest a disruptive behavior pattern that originated the previous year when these youngsters were in second grade and now continues to be a problem in the third grade. In addition, math teachers have noted that some of these students fail to complete homework assignments on time and seem to have difficulty understanding class assignments. Mr. Smith suspects that the discipline referrals are connected to the lack of academic success. It is a disappointment to the SIT that the school has not adequately captured these students' potential to achieve. Thinking and planning collaboratively, the team asks Mr. Smith to meet with the third-grade teachers to develop a strategy for addressing academic needs of this group of students.

Mr. Smith meets with the third-grade teachers, who working together develop a multifaceted strategy for those third graders who are below standard in math. The plan includes individualized academic support and interpersonal skill development. The overall goal of the plan is academic success in math. The team also acknowledges that this action plan could potentially help these students in other areas beyond math performance.

The third-grade teachers decide to adjust their instructional schedule to provide fifteen-minute tutorial sessions in math three times per week. They also agree to assign math buddies to students that seem to have the most difficulty completing in-class assignments and allow buddy-pairs to work together during class time.

Mr. Smith agrees to work with the students who have disruptive behavior and low math scores in a small group counseling context. The focus of these group sessions will be to help students learn alternative ways of behaving in the classroom when frustrated by schoolwork. Mr. Smith will also spend some time in the classroom helping students generalize skills learned in group to the classroom setting. Together Mr. Smith and the teachers will also develop a classroom discipline strategy based on reinforcement of positive behaviors. This strategy will be used across all third-grade classrooms. The third-grade teachers agree to spend time with the whole class teaching the expected classroom behavior. Each teacher also agrees to contact parents or other family members (as relevant) to advise them of the new initiative and seek their input. The group decides to reconvene in three weeks' time to exchange information about implementation progress.

This example clearly illustrates the connection between school achievement goals and school counseling program goals. It is important for school counselors to link with other school professionals—to collaborate—in terms of both overall program development and the planning of specific services. Accountability for student achievement is no longer the sole responsibility of teachers and administrators, but rather a shared responsibility of all school personnel, family members, and members of the larger community (House & Hayes, 2002).

School Counselors as Collaborators

School counselors have the responsibility of developing programs that respond to the academic, personal/social, and career needs of students in K–12 schools. Recently, the American School Counselor Association (2003) developed a national model for comprehensive school counseling programs and identified National Standards (Campbell & Dahir, 1997) for the programs that reinforce these three areas of development as the foundation of school counseling programs. You have learned in previous chapters that school counselors perform three primary functions in the delivery of comprehensive developmental programs: counseling, coordination, and consultation. We suggest that these three functions are best executed when the school counselor uses a collaborative style of interaction. In fact, collaboration can be thought of as the common ground that supports the other three functions (see Figure 11.1).

Regardless of the context in which the school counselor works (e.g., directly with individual students in individual or group counseling, with other professionals and family members when coordinating program planning and implementation, or in consultation sessions related to a specific student's needs), collaboration facilitates people's ability to work together. Collaboration is the oil that helps the school counselor's interactions function more harmoniously regardless of the context. Collaboration, like counseling and consultation, is based on trust, mutual respect, and a commitment to positive outcomes.

Some have suggested that only if school counselors function collaboratively will they be able to create programs that are truly comprehensive and integral to

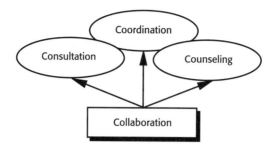

Figure 11.1 Collaboration as Support to Counseling, Coordination, and Consultation.

the well-being of children and youth (Taylor & Adelman, 2000). Schools today face educating a population of students with complex needs who are at risk for school failure, school dropout, substance abuse, and violent and aggressive behavior. Dealing with the multiple and interrelated factors that place students at risk requires multiple, interrelated solutions, and interrelated solutions require collaboration (Taylor & Adelman, 2000). School counselors are an integral link between promoting positive development for students and the interrelated solutions required to do so. To be successful, school counselors cannot function alone. Too many students have too many needs for the school counselor to act from a traditional, primarily direct services–focused model (Keys, Green, Lockhart, & Luongo, 2002). School counselors need to adapt to changing needs by integrating their program into the larger educational program and with prevention programs occurring within the larger community. Such integration requires collaboration within the school building and with partners in the community.

ACTIVITY 2
Responding Collaboratively

Assume you are a school counselor at Ridgeview High School. The school community is greatly concerned about the number of freshman students that become pregnant during the school year. Data from the past three years support this growing trend. Data also indicate that students tend to come from two neighborhood clusters. Your principal has asked the school counseling department to come up with a way to address this problem. Given this concern and your interest in creating a collaborative school climate, identify what might be your next steps.

Next Steps:

_____

_____

_____

Working Collaboratively Within the School

Collaboration actively involves educators, family members, youth, and school counselors as equal partners and experts in a problem-solving process related to a specific issue (Nevin, Thousand, Paolucci-Whitcomb, & Villa, 1990). Collaboration moves the school counselor away from the more traditional role of "a solitary expert" from whom others seek advice (see Figure 11.2) toward the expanded role of "collaborative problem solver," who both imparts knowledge to others and receives knowledge from others (see Figure 11.3). It is this sharing and transferring of knowledge across all members of the team that enables the group to create a more comprehensive solution to the problem. The roles of "experts" in a collaborative style of interaction depend upon the nature of the problem and who has relevant information about the problem. It is the nature of the problem that determines who should be involved at different points in the problem-solving process and to what degree.

For example, let's return to the case of Grove Elementary School and the counselor–math teacher problem-solving group. The counselor-faculty group shared a common goal—improved math success. Together they decided how to go about accomplishing their goal. Each group member shared information and responsibility for tasks related to their areas of expertise. Each group member functioned as an expert. Mr. Smith both received and exchanged information, which allowed for a more comprehensive plan of action. The counselor in this case provided expertise related to classroom behavior management practices and coping skills to use when frustrated. Classroom teachers contributed expertise related to math instruction, math remediation, and classroom management.

The nature of the interactions for team members who collaborate can be

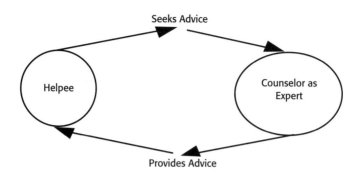

Figure 11.2 Counselor as Solitary Expert.

quite different from the interactions of group members who simply communicate with each other or coordinate separate functions. Team members, who work within a collaborative frame of reference, value and promote the critical elements described earlier. In this particular example, strategies are to be planned and implemented jointly. Mr. Smith will use group counseling activities to reinforce the expected behaviors identified and taught by the team of teachers, and Mr. Smith will deliver some counseling services directly in the classroom. Progress

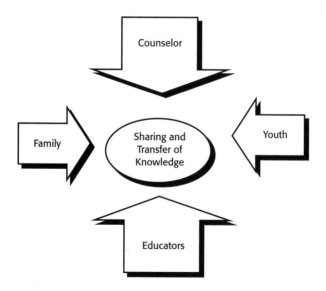

Figure 11.3 Collaboration as Sharing and Transfer of Knowledge.

toward the goal of math success depends upon the each person's contribution to the overall plan of action.

ACTIVITY 3
Developing Collaborative Relationships
Within the School Building

Read the following case scenario. Describe how you, as the school counselor, might change this scenario to engage people more collaboratively.

As the school counselor you have been asked to work with a third-grade student who is new to the school, not attending school regularly, and in danger of failing. The child's classroom teacher tells you the child's mother reports the child is sick on days the child misses school. The classroom teacher, however, suspects the child misses the bus and is not really sick. The child is not doing well academically and is in danger of not passing to the next grade.

The family is from Nicaragua. The mother speaks limited English and sometimes asks an older sibling to translate or speak for her to the teachers and counselor. The father remains in Nicaragua. The family has lived one year in this country. The mother also is in contact with a school-based family liaison who is Latino. The mother frequently asks this person to communicate with the school on her behalf. This liaison works at the school full-time as part of a community-school-family resource project.

The teacher and school social worker feel the school-based family liaison enables the mother to remain less involved at school. Sometimes when the mother calls to say the child is sick, the liaison visits the home and ends up bringing the child to school. The school social worker feels this interferes with a behavior contract she is trying to implement with the child and mother.

Forming Collaborative Partnerships with the Larger School Community

Developing a comprehensive program requires that the school counselor reach out to other service providers and integrate the school's counseling program with other prevention work occurring in the broader community. Program integration underscores the fact that no one agency or institution can provide the full range of services needed for effective prevention work (Lerner, 1995). School counselors provide an important link to other community services and can serve as a school liaison to community-based groups. This means that school counselors who strive to form collaborative relationships with community groups and agencies will spend a certain proportion of their time outside of the building developing these relationships and partnerships. The emphasis shifts from activities that occur solely within the confines of the school building to those that occur in the larger community. The primary work site for the collaborative counselor is the school building. Yet, what is being suggested here is that school counselors need to spend time outside of the building learning about the broader community, connecting with other professionals and community leaders, and learning about community resources and how to create linkages between programs offered within the school and those provided at community settings. For example, assume the school counselor learns that a local church provides a social skills training program for youth. These youth also participate in a grade-level social skills program that the school counselor provides all ninth-grade students. It would be important for the school counselor to learn about the content of the program being offered at the neighborhood church and work collaboratively with the youth minister from the church to establish how the content of each program might be integrated in order to reduce confusion and mixed messages to the youth that attend each program.

Some of the service groups with whom the school counselor needs to be familiar include core social institutions such as child welfare services (designed to protect children and youth) and juvenile justice (designed to protect the public from the wrongdoing of children and youth) (Luongo, 2000). Behavioral health services (e.g., mental health and substance abuse prevention services), although not considered a core social institution, also offer the potential for partnerships (Luongo, 2000). Traditionally, a school counselor's primary contact with such groups was to connect a student with community services (Adelman & Taylor, 1997).

The context for helping changes when the counselor approaches service delivery from a collaborative perspective. Communication among school and community groups, connections among programs, joint planning of program initiatives, and cross-training for professionals from different disciplines become possibilities. Professionals who collaborate begin to organize resources around common goals rather than services or disciplines.

ACTIVITY 4
Discovering Community Resources

This activity requires some time outside of the classroom. To complete this exercise you will need to identify a particular community, which may be the community in which you live or work.

Assume you have been hired as a new school counselor at the local school in the community you have identified. Your school principal has asked that you provide a summary report of community prevention programs that are available to the students and families—including those provided by core service institutions (social welfare, juvenile justice) and behavioral health (health, mental health, substance abuse prevention), and organizations that are not a part of the governmental structure (private and nonprofit providers). Your report should include the names, addresses, and phone numbers of the agencies, a summary of services provided to students and families, how students and families can access these services, typical fees, and whether the service providers have any type of linkage with schools. Identify at least three different agencies, and describe at least three different services in each of the three agencies.

It is particularly important that school counselors reach out to communities that are underrepresented at school functions and teacher conferences. Collaboration draws its strength from diversity. If problem-solving groups are too homogeneous or fail to include those who are not typically engaged by the school, the group misses an opportunity to draw upon untapped expertise.

ACTIVITY 5
Discovering Untapped Resources

Finding informal resources in communities can be difficult (e.g., identifying informal neighborhood leaders can be more difficult than identifying established agencies and services). Using the community you have identified in Activity 4, identify what groups might be underrepresented. Describe what steps you would take to connect with those groups and how you might go about identifying informal leaders within these groups.

◤ Mechanisms to Support Collaboration

The school counselor can also provide leadership within the building for developing mechanisms and support structures to support collaboration among school personnel and family members, and between school personnel, family members, and members of the larger community. Keys and Bemak (1997) proposed that school counselors establish school-family-community mental health teams to guide and direct school counseling programs. This team supplants the more traditional program advisory steering committee that may or may not have community representation. Such a team meets regularly to identify school-family-community needs and strengths, specify mutual goals, develop coordinated and integrated plans for services, oversee communication across participating groups, and make recommendations for change in school, agency, and governmental policies (Bemak & Keys, 2000). This group works closely with the school improvement team to assure an alignment with school goals.

Another school structure that supports collaboration is a case management team. This team might be called different names in different school systems. Some refer to this entity as a child study team, student assistance team, or case review team. Such a team organizes itself around the needs of specific students and actions taken to remediate and respond to problems. Team members share responsibility for overseeing the implementation of plans and the coordination of services across represented groups. Students who are reviewed by this team do not have to be identified as in need of special education services. School counselors also foster collaboration as members of school crisis teams and school safety teams.

In each instance, the school counselor as collaborator works to establish systems and structures within the school to support efforts to organize, coordinate, and integrate services in a way that capitalizes on shared expertise.

◤ Skills and Attitudes for Collaboration

School counselors have three essential areas of expertise to contribute to establishing a collaborative process: (1) an underlying knowledge base from which they can contribute expertise, (2) communication, group process, and problem-solving skills that enhance a collaborative style of interaction, and (3) intrapersonal attitudes supportive of a collaborative group process (Idol et al., 1994).

Knowledge Base

In addition to the communication, group process, and problem-solving skills described below, school counselors can contribute expertise from several additional areas. These include knowledge of (a) normal and abnormal child development, (b) behavioral principles and strategies for facilitating behavior change, (c) strategies for developing social skills, (d) school system policies, procedures, and resources, (e) community resources, and (f) multicultural values and attitudes and what are culturally appropriate expectations and behaviors.

Communication Skills

Creating a group or team atmosphere where people (educators, family members, community agency representatives, and youth) feel their opinions and ideas are valued and respected presents a challenge for a school counselor. When we think of a collaborative group, we think of leadership as a shared function. Collaborative group leadership facilitates parity. This style of leadership is very different from a hierarchical model where expertise rests at the top and group members are responsible for executing a leader's directives but may have less responsibility for decision making.

School counselors, by the very nature of their training in communication skills and group process, have expertise to contribute to the shared leadership of a collaborative group. School counselors facilitate a group's work by using effective communication skills to encourage participation and teamwork. Specifically, school counselors use basic listening skills (e.g., paraphrasing, reflection, clarification, open- and closed-ended questions, summarization) to communicate recognition and understanding of other group members' ideas. A school counselor who facilitates a collaborative group process recognizes and relies on the diverse expertise of group members rather than assuming a more authoritative posture.

Group Process Skills

Facilitating a team or group's interaction is an important function for a school counselor. Bemak and Keys (2000) identified several skills school counselors can use to create a collaborative climate during team or group meetings. These are summarized here.

Establishing a Climate That Conveys Warmth and Welcome to All Members.
Such an atmosphere is particularly important when people attend meetings at the school who are a part of the broader community. Agency representatives and

family members may be unaware of school procedures for visitors or unclear about their role or school expectations for their participation. Previous memories of school may also not be pleasant. Family members who have been contacted repeatedly by the school with negative reports about a child's behavior or academic performance may be hesitant to participate in a "school-initiated" meeting. A school counselor can serve an important function by serving as a liaison from the school to the home and various community groups and agencies. In this role, the school counselor can assure that participants feel welcomed at initial team meetings. Simple things like providing refreshments, making sure all members are introduced, seeing that everyone has a chance to speak and that the group respects each member's contributions, all convey that participants are an important part of the group. School counselors can also make those who are "new to the school" feel welcome by introducing them to the office staff, greeting people when they arrive, seeing that they know the school's sign-in procedures for visitors, showing them where to put their coats, and alerting them to the availability of a phone should they need to make a call.

Establishing Group Norms that Support Collaboration.   As the group moves forward in its work, it is important that the group establish norms that support a collaborative style of interaction. Different groups will establish norms relative to the particular group. The school counselor, however, can assist a group in forming collaborative group norms and is able to bring to the group's attention patterns of behavior that suggest a group norm needs to be created. For example, it is quite typical that people from diverse disciplines have discipline-specific terminology that may be unfamiliar to others. Family members could also be confused by both school and agency jargon. After observing this disconnect with language, the school counselor might point out to the group that the use of jargon creates a barrier to communication. The school counselor might suggest that the group agree that it is fine for anyone to interrupt and ask for clarity if a group member uses terminology or refers to something that is confusing for anyone. Knowing the critical elements of collaboration, the school counselor can help groups establish norms that facilitate a collaborative group process.

Working with school administrators who function within a hierarchical model of leadership may present challenges to the collaborative school counselor. It is difficult to bring about any innovation in a school if the administrator does not support the change. It is important to provide the school administrator with information about collaboration and the advantages of creating a collaborative group process. Many administrators may think they are acting collaboratively—they have asked people to meet—yet how the administrator functions in a meeting may be more authoritative than collaborative. Figuring out ahead of time how open your principal is to a collaborative team process could save time and energy later.

Empowering Group Members.   A group functions collaboratively when all members contribute expertise. Some members may not feel like experts and be hesitant to contribute, particularly if they are new to the group or uncomfortable being in the school building. A school counselor can encourage participation by reaching out to group members, asking for comments, recognizing and reinforcing contributions, visually recording all participants' ideas, asking people to elaborate, bringing ideas that get lost back into the discussion, and encouraging and supporting members who take responsibility for tasks.

Managing Domineering Group Members.   A domineering group member can easily overpower a team that is trying to work collaboratively. On the one hand, the school counselor works to encourage participation by all members, yet needs to limit contributions by any member who disregards others or fails to recognize how he or she limits the contributions of others. Restating, paraphrasing, asking for comments from the group, and reflecting on personal discomfort with the group process are some strategies the school counselor can use to limit a domineering group member. Other strategies include providing a structure for meetings through the use of a written agenda, articulating ahead of time a specified time frame for the meeting, and assigning rotating roles to group members such as facilitator, timekeeper, and note taker.

Facilitating Decision Making.   Most groups with which the school counselor will work are organized to solve a problem—either a whole school problem, such as school violence, or a problem more specific to a student, such as inadequate learning, poor social skills, test anxiety, or the college application process. Groups come together around a common need, identify a common goal, and seek to develop a plan of action to accomplish this goal. Decision making is an integral part of action planning. The school counselor can facilitate this process by ensuring that group members (a) hear each other's ideas, (b) recognize and value differences, (c) evaluate whether or not the alternatives they generate move the group toward or away from their shared goal, and (d) identify potential consequences, including costs and benefits.

Problem-Solving Skills

School counselors are educated to help individuals solve problems. The same problem-solving process that guides a school counselor's actions within an individual counseling session is applicable to helping groups that are charged with solving a schoolwide, classroom, or student-focused problem. Collaborative problem solving involves six steps (Bemak & Keys, 2000), discussed below.

Identify the Problem.   This is a critical first step toward productive teamwork. Frequently, team members have different perceptions of what the problem is. One of the first tasks to which the school counselor needs to attend is making sure the group has a consensus about what problem they are about to solve. Many times, group members like to move ahead to "fixing the problem" or "generating solutions," only to become confused later in the process because their solutions are not tied to a clear definition of the problem. School counselors who are developing collaborative group processes need to assist group members in clarifying perceptions of the problem before moving to solutions, remembering that it is the communication and transfer of knowledge that is essential to collaborative interactions and to problem identification.

Establish Agreed-upon Goals and Objectives.   This is often the most time-consuming and trying part of group problem solving. Goals generally are stated in more general terms, with objectives being more specific and measurable. Group members often lose interest because the process of "solving the problem" slows as goals and objectives are identified and defined. The school counselor's job at this point in the process is to reassure group members, assist the group to use language that is concrete and clear, and build consensus on what the actual goals and objectives should be. Facilitating the process of discussion is an important role.

Generate Strategies.   Group members enjoy this part of problem solving. It is important to allow people time to be creative and to not evaluate potential solutions initially. Acceptance rather than evaluation is particularly important for members who may feel intimidated by the group or by being in the school building. The group process should stimulate ideas, get all ideas out for discussion, and only then begin to evaluate and assess feasibility.

Develop an Action Plan.   An action plan identifies next steps, roles and responsibilities for those involved in executing the plan, and a timeline. If the team is collaborating around the needs of an individual student, the plan may be less complex than the plan that is devised for a whole school problem. A plan that addresses a whole school problem may have phases and subgoals.

Implement the Plan.   The extent to which people integrate their roles and tasks while implementing activities from the action plan reflects the level of collaboration. The exchange and transfer of information characteristic of collaboration continues through this step. Those who implement their roles in isolation from other team members function less collaboratively.

Evaluate Outcomes.   Conducting the evaluation comes after the plan has been executed. It is important to plan the evaluation strategy earlier in the problem-solving process when goals and objectives are being identified. Asking the group to think about how to evaluate an objective helps the team specify objectives that are concrete and helps members think about evaluation criteria long before the evaluation is to occur. Monitoring progress is also a part of evaluating outcomes. Noting whether the plan was implemented and the level of implementation will be useful when trying to interpret results and understand why change may not have occurred as expected. Group members share accountability for outcomes. Group members may also share the monitoring or progress function.

Intrapersonal Attitudes

It is important that school counselors who want to function collaboratively believe in collaboration as an effective problem-solving tool. The collaborative school counselor needs to understand their role as one of direct and indirect service provider. Facilitating a collaborative group process and coordinating action plans for prevention programs are important services that should not be thought of as less important than direct counseling services. Changing how people organize themselves around a problem and changing the mechanisms and structures that support problem solutions can have a more far-reaching effect than changing the thoughts, behaviors, and attitudes of an individual.

Student achievement is an overriding concern of schools. Schools exist for students to learn. It is important that school counselors understand the goals of the school and work to align their school counseling program with these broader system goals. Counselors who fail to see their role in support of the overarching goal of academic success run the risk of alienating teachers.

School counselors also need to perceive the school as a complex system with many subsystems (e.g., classrooms, faculty, students, family, community) and to recognize that these systems have various rules, which may be written or unwritten. School counselors should be aware and open to these rules and willing to adapt their behavior to the requirements of these larger systems. For example, the rules for entering a teacher's classroom can vary from teacher to teacher. Some teachers are quite willing to have the counselor enter to observe a student without prior notice. The counselor can enter, sit down, observe, or be free to move about the room, becoming a part of whatever activity is occurring. Other teachers might resent the counselor's visit without advance notice and may see the counselor as intrusive. Detecting the unwritten rules in a system is as important as learning the more formal, explicit rules.

School counselors who bump up against system rules with which they disagree or who have difficulty getting faculty to be receptive to the innovations that are a part of collaborative efforts can become frustrated and discouraged. Not all schools are open to change. Resistance occurs frequently and should be expected, and not taken personally. A school's effort to maintain the status quo can be quite powerful. The counselor may do everything right, and still some members of the system may resist what the counselor recommends. The counselor may begin to resent the challenges presented by the school and may lose a sense of objectivity. Reframing challenges as opportunities and seeing resistance as a systemic reaction to change rather than a personal affront are important actions and attitudes to help the counselor maintain objectivity.

School counselors need to be comfortable adopting a "one down" posture (Keys et al., 2002). To be effective as a collaborator, the school counselor needs to interact in ways that are nonthreatening to others' territory. By the nature of their expertise, school counselors could be perceived by others as intimidating. School counselors who seek acceptance by the faculty or family subsystems should minimize status differences between themselves and teachers and family members (Cherniss, 1997). Acknowledging the expertise of the other person, seeking advice, asking for assistance, asking for the other person's perspective and suggestions, and being open to trying new approaches are all ways the school counselor can overtly recognize another person's skills and knowledge, and covertly maintain a "one-down" position (Keys et al., 2002).

Identifying and Overcoming Barriers to Collaboration

One of the biggest barriers to collaboration is time. People in schools are very busy and face increased pressure to have positive academic outcome for all students. Bringing people together for problem solving initially might not seem an efficient use of resources. Collaboration takes more time than working as a single individual. Collaboration adds a great deal when the diversity of expertise unleashed through collaboration results in an effective solution that would not have been available had people worked individually.

Attitudes toward change are another potential barrier. People often feel most comfortable with the status quo and resist having to do things differently. Working in small steps and reinforcing incremental changes can be important in gaining acceptance of a new practice.

Scheduling and coordinating meeting times can be problematic if the school does not have a mechanism that allows people to come together. Creating team structures can help schools overcome this barrier. Administrative support for collaboration will be essential. For example, when the staff at Walnutwood Elementary school wanted to implement new procedures for conducting parenting conferences, the changes were introduced by the school improvement team, which consisted of well-respected teachers and the two school administrators. The new procedures were implemented one grade level at a time, beginning with the kindergarten and first-grade levels. This was done because the upper-grade-level teacher teams had been at the school the longest and typically resisted change. As the changes were initially implemented, the benefits were shared among all of the staff, which ultimately reduced resistance to the new process.

Ethical Issues

Collaboration in schools brings together parents and family members with different professionals who work within and outside of the school. This means that educators and noneducators work together to achieve the ultimate common goal of meeting the needs of students. Often these collaborators come from different personal and professional backgrounds that affect one's perspective, values, and ethics. Although collaboration could set the stage for a conflict of values and perspectives, the common goal of what is in the best interest of the student or students should be the guiding light throughout the collaborative process. Collaboration should begin and end with a strong emphasis on ethics. Consideration of diverse perspectives is the hallmark of collaboration and should not be stifled.

Collaborators should have a clear sense of why collaboration is necessary and what might be the benefits of such an approach. It is important to clarify purpose and to identify motivation to collaborate—genuine assistance versus passing the responsibility for working with "problem kids" on to others.

Clarification of confidentiality as a group norm is also important. What are the parameters of confidentiality? When might information be shared? What parental/guardian permissions are required? How might different group members perceive this norm? These are important questions to be answered within problem-solving groups, particularly when working with different cultural groups that may not be clear about what this term means. Griesel (1992) reminded us that along with bringing the expertise of various professionals to bear on the education of children comes the dilemma of having various professional guidelines for ethics and various consequences for compliance and noncompliance. School counselors, for example, are bound by the ethical code of the American School Counselor Association (ASCA, 1998). This code of ethics, which was developed by professional school counselors, sets forth very explicit regulations for dealing with confidentiality. These regulations may be different from those of administrators, teachers, or other community-based professionals. Ethical codes and prior experiences influence each person's understanding of confidentiality. Others who collaborate may be restricted in what they can share by policies that dictate what can be discussed without informed consent (i.e., agency policies limit what social workers employed by social service agencies can share with other agencies and groups about children under their case management).

Professional integrity should be the driving force of all actions when working on behalf of students. Having clearly defined ethical guidelines will ensure that integrity will not be deserted. In a school where professionals have created a climate of collaboration, ethical guidelines will over time become well established. It is important, however, to indoctrinate new group members about ethical guidelines when they become a part of the process.

ACTIVITY 6
Developing Ethical Guidelines

Imagine you are a member of the School Improvement Team that is going to work on a plan to decrease the number of conduct violations taking place in and around the school. After an initial assessment of the problem, the group asks neighborhood community leaders, family members, local police, and mental health professionals to help solve this problem. Before the group assembles, you must decide what matters pertaining to ethics are important regarding the task at hand.

   1. What are some of the ethical issues of concern?

2. How might confidentiality be addressed among all group members? How will this be discussed at the initial meeting?

3. What kinds of confidential information could potentially be shared in a meeting?

4. Should nonprofessional members of the group only be exposed to nonconfidential information?

5. What parameters should be established for the sharing of confidential information given the group's composition?

6. Should the group decide to seek informed consent, what steps might be needed to establish this procedure?

Salient Research

Collaboration in schools has become more commonplace within the past decade. As mentioned previously, there have been a number of key legislative developments within special education that have made collaboration a necessity and a requirement for meeting the needs of students with special needs (Cramer, 1998). Data to support the use of collaboration and the effects on outcomes for students are limited. One recent investigation of several partnerships implemented in a large northeastern urban school district produced formative and summative data to support positive outcomes through collaboration (Kopacsi & Walker, 2000). In particular, researchers were interested to determine if the multiple school reform efforts implemented throughout the school district were effective. In this study, collaboration was a central part of school reform and the evaluation of reform efforts. In all, nine projects were evaluated, each one involving multiple partners in schools and across agencies that serve schools. Among the findings reported in the final report, collaborations were found to be effective in meeting the comprehensive nature of school reform and student needs. Collaboration, for example, was found to promote shared understanding of different concerns and expectations of program objectives.

Qualitative evaluation of the district's kindergarten reform program revealed that child-centered classrooms were more effective than teacher-directed ones in meeting the needs of children. The idea of using this strategy came from the collaborative efforts of university scholars, school teachers, and administrators. A quantitative investigation of the program revealed that achievement outcomes for students placed in classrooms designed by the university partnership were more positive on the district test than for students placed in traditional classrooms.

Others working in a nonschool context failed to find a connection between service integration and positive child outcomes (Glisson & Hemmelgarn, 1998), but did find positive effects for organizational climate. Preliminary research on collaboration efforts in schools beyond special education indicate favorable results. One thing is clear, however: More research is needed. These initial findings do suggest that by having varied perspectives on the planning, implementation, and evaluation of educational strategies, students and families have a better opportunity to experience school success.

Implications for School Counseling in the Twenty-First Century

School counselors and their programs have always responded to the needs of students and to the changing trends within education. At the beginning of the twenty-first century, student needs and educational trends require that school counselors continue to adjust their programs to remain responsive. In order to be successful, students in the twenty-first century must negotiate multiple challenges. Changing societal and family dynamics and peer pressure, in addition to increased academic demands, call for sophisticated approaches to providing support for the development of academic, social, and emotional skills. As school systems engage in reform efforts to meet these needs in ways that rely on multiple partnerships within and outside of the school building, school counselors must also be prepared to participate and even manage these partnerships.

The typical school counselor of the past, working diligently from an independent perspective to meet the social, academic, and emotional developmental needs of the student, is in for an uphill battle. Collaboration is a strategy that has been employed in other human service fields as well as in special education to meet today's needs. Partnering equally with other professionals on behalf of students affords school counselors the opportunity to integrate their skills knowledge and services in the most efficient manner. Collaboration is also a tool that can propel family members into the helping process. ASCA (2000) specifies that school counseling programs be comprehensive and developmental in nature. Collaboration as it is defined and elaborated on in this chapter propels school counselors who run comprehensive developmental counseling programs toward partnerships for student success.

REFERENCES

Adelman, H., & Taylor, L. (1997). Addressing barriers to learning: Beyond school-linked services and full service schools. *American Journal of Orthopsychiatry, 67,* 408–421.

American School Counselor Association. (1998). *Ethical standards for school counselors: Revised.* Retrieved on July 18, 2002, from http:www.schoolcounselor.org

American School Counselor Association. (2000). *National standards for school counseling programs.* Retrieved on July 18, 2002, from http:www.schoolcounselor.org

American School Counselor Association. (2003). *The ASCA national model: A framework for school counseling programs.* Alexandria, VA: Author.

Atkins, M. S., Frazier, S., Adil, J. A., & Talbott, E. (2003). School-based mental health services in urban communities. In M. Weist, S. Evans, & N. Lever (Eds.), *Handbook of school mental health: Advancing practice and research* (ch. 12). New York: Kluwer.

Bemak, F., & Keys, S. (2000). *Violent and aggressive youth: Intervention and prevention strategies for changing time.* Thousand Oaks, CA: Corwin Press.

Bronfenbrenner, U. (1979). *The ecology of human development: Experiments by nature and design.* Cambridge, MA: Harvard University Press.

Campbell, C. A., & Dahir, C. A. (1997). *The national standards for school counseling programs.* Alexandria, VA: American School Counselor Association.

Carpenter, S., King-Sears, M., & Keys, S. (1998). Counselors + educators + families as a transdisciplinary team = more effective inclusion for students with disabilities. *Professional School Counseling, 2,* 1–9.

Cherniss, C. (1997). Teacher empowerment, consultation, and the creation of new programs in schools. *Journal of Educational and Psychological Consultation, 8,* 135–152.

Cramer, S. G. (1998). *Collaboration: A success strategy for special educators.* Boston: Allyn & Bacon.

Friend, M., & Cook, L. (1996). *Interactions: Collaboration skills for school professionals.* White Plains, NY: Longman.

Glisson, C., & Hemmelgarn, A. (1998). The effects of organization climate and interorganizational coordination on the quality and outcomes of children's service systems. *Child Abuse & Neglect, 22,* 401–421.

Green, A., & Keys, S. (2001). Expanding the developmental school counseling paradigm for urban schools in the 21st century. *Professional School Counseling, 5,* 84–95.

Griesel, P. (1992). *Ethics of collaboration: A quest for guidelines.* (ERIC Document Reproduction Service No. 360235).

House, R. M., & Hayes, R. L. (2002). School counselors: Becoming key players in school reform. *Professional School Counseling, 5,* 249–256.

Idol, L., Nevin, A., & Paolucci-Whitcomb, P. (1994). *Collaborative consultation.* Austin, TX: Pro-Ed.

Keys, S., & Bemak, F. (1997). School-family-community linked services: A school counseling role for changing times. *The School Counselor, 44,* 255–263.

Keys, S., & Green, A. (2000). School Counseling. In D. Capuzzi & D. Gross (Eds.), *Introduction to the counseling profession* (3rd ed., pp. 299–315). Needham Heights, MA: Allyn & Bacon.

Keys, S., Green, A., Lockhart, E., & Luongo, P. (2002). School consultation. In B. Erford (Ed.), *Transforming the school counseling profession* (pp. 171–190). Upper Saddle River, NJ: Merrill/Prentice Hall.

Kopacsi, R., & Walker, E. M. (2000, April). *Multiple voices and mixed methodologies to support comprehensive school reform.* Paper presented at the annual meeting of the American Educational Research Association, New Orleans, LA.

Lerner, R. M. (1995). *America's youth in crisis: Challenges and opportunities for programs and policies.* Thousand Oaks, CA: Sage.

Luongo, P. (2000). Partnering child welfare, juvenile justice, and behavioral health with schools. *Professional School Counseling, 3,* 308–314.

Nevin, A., Thousand, J., Paolucci-Whitcomb, P., & Villa, R. (1990). Collaborative consultation: Empowering public school personnel to provide heterogeneous schooling for all—or, Who rang that bell? *Journal of Educational and Psychological Consultation, 1,* 41–67.

Taylor, L., & Adelman, H. (2000). Connecting schools, families, and communities. *Professional School Counseling, 3,* 298–307.

U.S. Department of Education. (1997). *Individuals with Disabilities Education Act Amendments of 1997.* Retrieved on September 5, 2002, from http://www.ed.gov/offices/OSERS/Policy/IDEA/

U.S. Department of Education. (2000). *Elementary School Counseling Demonstration Program of 2000.* Retrieved on September 3, 2002, from http://www.ed.gov/legislation/FedRegister/announcements/2000-2/041800d.html

U.S. Department of Education. (2001). *No Child Left Behind Act of 2001.* Retrieved on September 5, 2002, from http://www.ed.gov/offices/OESE/esea/

CHAPTER 12

Looking Ahead: The Future School Counselor

Christopher A. Sink
Seattle Pacific University

Responding to current social and political pressures and public demands for change, educational leaders feel pressured to tinker with and, in some cases, reinvent the schooling process. As was pointed out in Chapter 1 and subsequent chapters, school counseling is not immune to the influence of these educational trends. Early on, the profession had the unofficial goal of providing vocational and career information to students. Later, educational guidance was added to the counselor's job description. Detouring a bit from this initial path, school counselors around the 1960s also began to address students' social-emotional needs. Unfortunately, counselors shouldered the major responsibilities of the position with limited support from other educators. However, by the 1970s and 1980s and the advent of guidance and counseling programs, the load began to be shared by relevant school personnel. Comprehensive school counseling programs allow school counselors to work with students and their caregivers in ways that are more closely aligned with the American School Counselor Association's (ASCA, 1999c) role statement and its National Model (ASCA, 2003), as well as with the information presented in this text.

The aims of this concluding chapter are twofold. First, several of the key themes discussed in the previous chapters are reviewed. Second, the major developments in professional school counseling that will influence practice for at least the near future are considered.

Review of Principal Themes

Not only did the first chapter review the profession's one-hundred-year history, it also emphasized the need for emergent school counselors to learn the common language of the field, as well as addressed the most important school counseling roles and competencies. Salient concepts for new counselors to understand include the fundamental differences between counseling, coordination, consultation, guidance, and collaboration. Moreover, terms like *systems thinking*, *developmental theory*, *best practices*, and *comprehensive school counseling programs* were clarified.

In the following chapter, Littrell and Zinck argued that a significant change was needed in the way school counselors conduct individual counseling. No longer should traditional therapeutic approaches (e.g., Gestalt, Psychodynamic, Rational Emotive Therapy) serve as the backbone of school counseling programs' responsive services. These authors provided evidence that short-term, solution-focused approaches were not only effective but also workable in school settings, where counselors' time is at a premium given their large caseloads. Complementing well the goals of comprehensive programs, brief individual counseling tends to be goal directed and readily adaptable to a variety of student and family concerns.

From the menu of responsive services, Jacobs and Schimmel reiterated in Chapter 3 the value of group counseling for school counseling programs. They explained in a practical way how group work is an effective and helpful means to deliver information, support, and remediation to students. Similarly, Whiston and Bouwkamp's chapter on peer mediation and peer and family counseling reinforced the use of these interventions to advance the goals of comprehensive school counseling programs and, in the process, better serve the needs of their constituents. In particular, Whiston and Bouwkamp maintained that school counselors are in a good position to support and counsel families using family counseling interventions, for they (a) have an extensive knowledge of the inner "workings" of their school systems, (b) are well-informed about child and adolescent development, and (c) are schooled in family dynamics and effective counseling interventions.

The book's next section included four chapters on the school counselor's role as program coordinator. Gysbers and Henderson's contribution (Chapter 5) discussed how to form, implement, and administer comprehensive guidance and counseling programs as a method to foster a variety of student developmental skills. These main elements, among other relevant topics, were covered in their chapter: guidance curriculum, individual planning, responsive services, system support activities (e.g., program management and development, public relations), and assorted resources needed to operate and sustain the program.

As a follow-up to Chapter 5, three central dimensions of comprehensive programs were explicated. First, Sears's practical overview of large group guidance curriculum development and instruction provided a clear blueprint for beginning school counselors to use in support of children and youth. By adopting a developmental perspective, classroom guidance was shown to be an effective component of comprehensive programs. Dovetailing nicely with this chapter, Hughey's discussion in Chapter 7 of career and educational planning emphasized the significance of students developing a coherent school-to-work or school-to-education pathway. Moreover, because career planning is a lifelong process, Hughey encouraged school counselors to include in their work systematic, intentional, and relevant learning experiences that will realistically prepare students for their future life roles. Capping this section, Chapter 8 addressed the valuable part results-based program evaluation plays in the overall coordination of systemic approaches to school counseling. Lapan provided a helpful literature review as well as a useful scaffold for conducting school-based evaluation research.

In the third section, the authors examined a couple of key aspects of the "dual" consultation role. Davis (Chapter 9) elaborated on the significance of school-based consultation as a conduit to support change within the school environment. Further, he summarized a flexible and generic approach to the school-based consultation process that could be readily adapted to most K–12 settings. Subsequently, Bemak, Kaffenberger, and Murphy advocated for the development of community-based consultation skills. They recommended that school counselors, in a culturally sensitive manner, should avail themselves of external resources through collaborative partnerships and community-focused consultation. Finally, Keys and Green focused on how school counselors must use their collaborative skills and associated interpersonal strategies in their relations with students, families, school staff, and community representatives. Underscoring Bemak et al.'s theoretical position (see Chapter 10), Keys and Green framed the collaboration role from a social-ecological perspective. In a sense, collaboration was portrayed, and rightly so, as the essential "glue" that keeps elements of school counseling programs together and well functioning. Collaboration is a consistent theme running through the effective use of the 3 Cs Plus (counseling, coordination, consultation, and guidance). Before discussing some of the profession's future challenges, take a few minutes to assess your learning.

Self-Evaluation

- Which chapter themes and ideas are you still unsure about and need to further review?

- As you read the above summary, what topics were the most interesting to you? Why?
- As a way to translate the chapters' major themes to the "real world," go back now through each one looking for those areas that resonate—and those that do not—with your school experiences.
- As you continue to shadow experienced school counselors, ask them how they use any of these ideas in their daily practice.

What Issues Should Stay on School Counselors' Radar Screens?

To anticipate and prepare for the coming years, it is important to carefully consider the major practical challenges and research concerns facing school counselors during this decade. In closing, therefore, this section attempts to look ahead and envision the profession's near future. The first big concern for school counselors is the rate and nature of societal change.

Societal Issues

Even the casual observer notices that certain elements of American society undergo fairly rapid change. Typical examples other than technological innovations include major shifts in community values and mores, educational processes, family structures, community health, social conditions, and sociopolitical perspectives (see, e.g., Erford, 2003, and Schmidt, 2003, for additional details). Drawing primarily from data published in the U.S. Census Bureau's (2000) Statistical Abstract of the United States, several of these areas are considered here.

The Changing Family.   Obviously, societal evolution reflects the ongoing reconfigurations of the family unit. Recently, Meyers, Varkey, and Aguirre (2002) showed that a family's health can be significantly predicted by important socio-economic variables (i.e., education and income), the mother's levels of personal maturity and depression, as well as the amount of stress families are under, their social support network, and parenting style. As such, an increasing number of families with low incomes and headed by parents with little education appear to be at risk for relationship problems, leaving children in a precarious position. Adding to this sobering reality, about 50 percent of marriages currently end in divorce or separation, again leaving children and youth to cope with major personal and social disruptions. Students are living in families that are quite different from those of their grandparents. Other than the shrinking nuclear family, some of the family structures one might see in schools are single-parent homes, blended families (e.g., biological and stepchildren living under one roof), families headed by a grandparent(s), children in foster care homes, and families where the major caregivers are not the biological parents (e.g., families of adopted children).

Even though parental/family engagement in the schooling process is essential for the educational development of youngsters (Feuerstein, 2000; Giles, 1998), school counselors no longer can count on strong public support. The overall level of family involvement in students' academic lives, especially for disadvantaged families (e.g., families with low socioeconomic status), appears to be a serious concern among researchers and educators (e.g., Desimore, 1999; Feuerstein, 2000). Mental health issues of students and families are complex and multilayered, requiring creative and innovative interventions. School counselors need to find better ways to be multisystemic in their approaches to working with students and their caregivers (Keys & Lockhart, 1999). Moreover, parental education as suggested by ASCA (1999a) may become one of the mainstays of school counseling, where parents/caregivers are provided with ongoing support, involving, for example, short-term family counseling, referrals to outside agencies, parenting classes, and other relevant workshops (Cicero & Barton, 2003).

Cultural and Ethnic Diversity.   As alluded to in Chapter 1 and elsewhere, large cities have become a rich tapestry of people groups and a large percentage of schools in these areas now reflect this reality. Programs and interventions have been devised, with some success, to sensitize nonminority students and educators to the cultural, ethnic, and religious differences within the student body (Sogunro, 2001). Unfortunately, John F. Kennedy's (1963) goal for Americans some forty years ago remains largely unrealized.

> It ought to be possible, in short, for every American to enjoy the privileges of being American without regard to his race or his color. In short, every American ought to have the right to be treated as he would wish to be treated, as one would wish his children to be treated.

As a result, counselors must assume a more active role in fulfilling Kennedy's dream and ASCA's (1999b) position statement on multicultural counseling: "School counselors take action to ensure students of culturally diverse backgrounds have access to appropriate services and opportunities promoting the individual's maximum development."

Injustice and inequity of opportunities can be redressed to some degree through comprehensive school counseling programs. For instance, Sink (2002a) recently suggested that multicultural education could be infused within comprehensive programs through these activities: (a) altering student developmental competencies to include relevant multicultural outcomes; (b) using large group guidance lessons as a way to engage students on diversity issues; (c) beginning the multicultural citizenship formation process in the early elementary years; and (d) encouraging parental and community involvement in diversity education. Specifics on how this might be accomplished are also included in this article as well as in Pedersen and Carey's (2003) text on multicultural counseling in schools.

To augment the above recommendations, school counselors can implement Sogunro's (2001) "10-point recipe" addressing how to teach multicultural education in schools.

The 10-Point Recipe (Sogunro, 2000)

- Study different cultural groups through literature and oral presentations by people from various cultures living in the community.
- Encourage parents to tell their children about their cultures.
- Ask students to talk about their culture themselves.
- Examine and develop appreciation for differences and similarities in cultures.
- Encourage students to reflect on their experiences based on the cultures studied.
- Encourage reinforcement of ethical values in student homes.
- Demonstrate the knowledge, skills, and attitudes necessary to contribute to the success of others.
- Form students into groups to work on projects related to cultures different from theirs.
- Involve students in role-playing the different cultures they have learned about.
- Complement class activities and progress with related field trips, tours, and so forth. (p. 22)

In sum, school counselors of the twenty-first century must demonstrate their multicultural competence to meet the needs of all students (Holcomb-McCoy, 2003). They need to also establish, implement, and reinforce interventions that help children and youth learn about and appreciate each other.

Sexual Orientation of Youth.   Although highly controversial within various sectors of American society, the gradual trend in public education to openly address the sexual orientation of youth will be with us for at least the foreseeable future. ASCA (2000) recently reframed the topic as a developmental concern that school counselors must consider:

> Professional school counselors are committed to facilitating and promoting the fullest possible development of each individual by reducing the barriers of misinformation, myth, ignorance, hatred and discrimination based on sexual orientation. Professional school counselors are in a field committed to human development and must be sensitive to the use of inclusive language and positive modeling. ASCA is committed to equal opportunity and respect for all individuals regardless of sexual orientation.

It is therefore imperative that nascent school counselors educate themselves on this issue. To reiterate, effective school counseling programs address the concerns of all students.

Other Areas of Social Change.   Recent overviews by Thompson (2002) and Cobia and Henderson (2003) have cataloged many of the other most pressing social concerns confronting school counselors. For example, these writers suggested that issues such as poverty, lack of opportunities for minority children, inadequate adult supervision during the nonschool hours, sexually transmitted diseases, substance abuse, teenage pregnancy, and community and school violence could be major concerns for years to come. To help students with these issues, school counselors, as suggested above, may soon be involved at some level with designing and implementing various (a) before- and after-school interventions for students at risk, (b) ways to bring community services into the school environment, and (c) collaborative projects with external agencies (e.g., community health, law enforcement, social services, faith-based institutions) to create out-of-school support networks. Weaving these useful ideas into the fabric of comprehensive school programs will no doubt be challenging.

School Reform, Academic Achievement, and "High Stakes" Testing

Chapter 1 explored the counselor's role in supporting school reform, so the issue is only briefly explored here. Schools, as we know, are under intense pressure by local, state, and federal mandates to produce better-educated students. On the surface, this seems like a noble goal, but in reality, high-placed educational policymakers and politicians have operationalized this goal in terms of higher student achievement test scores. Raising standardized test scores can be particularly troublesome for many low-income, inner-city, and rural schools, where resources are scarce and staff morale is low.

According to Cobia and Henderson (2003), school leaders and various related associations (e.g., National Association for College Admission Counseling, 2000) recommend that school counselors become more involved in educational reform and testing. Put more plainly, school counselors must assist in the process of reshaping schools where academic excellence is not the exception, but the rule. Regrettably, some writers think counselors have already missed the boat on this issue (Erford, House, & Martin, 2003). In short, professional school counselors can no longer afford to be nonchalant about their part in school reform; they must take a larger role in helping schools enhance their academics as well as in student assessment. Future school counselors, as an aspect of the reform process, will have to do a better job at (a) managing school testing programs, (b) providing strong advocacy for assessment fairness, and (c) helping students, parents, teachers, and administrators coherently interpret the assessment results (Guidon, 2003).

Within the context of reform, school counselors will also need to be more accountable for the outcomes of their comprehensive programs (Gysbers & Henderson, 2000). They will have to document more clearly how school counseling programs can help students with their educational needs and contribute positively to the school climate (Lapan, 2001). To do so, they must learn not only advanced assessment skills, but also how to conduct program evaluation research (e.g., Myrick, 2003; Schmidt, 2003; Whiston, 2003). In other words, new school counselors will need to become *educational leaders* in their particular districts (Clark & Stone, 2000).

Technological Innovation

While greatly affecting our daily lives, the rate and sophistication of technological innovation can be intimidating. Even newer and more improved hardware and software as well as better methods of electronic (e) communication are always around the corner. The "less" complex e-functions like e-mail, PowerPoint presentations, Internet web surfing (Sabella, 2003), computer-based assessment, and e-databases challenge our skill level. In recent years, school counselors have been encouraged to use various forms of advanced technology in guidance and counseling programs and in their work with students (e.g., Hohenshil, 2000; Sabella, 2000; Sabella & Booker, 2001). Apparently, their advice has been heeded. These e-practices affect student-counselor relationships; for instance, students and family members can send e-mail to the school counselor, go online to conduct research on a particular problem, and seek out resources and support services using the Internet. Finally, distance learning, career and educational planning, counseling, and testing via the Internet may soon become a reality for many students. It is therefore essential that counselors stay on top of these innovations, regularly updating their skills (Sabella & Booker, 2001).

Implementation of a National Model for School Counseling Programs

As indicated in Chapter 1, the national model for school counseling programs (Bowers & Hatch, 2002; ASCA, 2003) is available and ready for implementation. The model complements well the National Standards for School Counseling Programs (Campbell & Dahir, 1997) established in the late 1990s. Briefly, the implied goals of the ASCA document are to help school counselors implement a comprehensive program that is, for example, preventive in design, developmental in nature, an integral part of the total educational program, systematic in the delivery of its components, collaborative, and data-driven. Students are closely monitored to see if they are demonstrating the desired outcomes as outlined in the program goals and related developmental competencies. Moreover, academic achievement is a central theme. The publication clearly states, "Counselors are expected to consistently monitor *academic progress and achievement* [italics added]" (Bowers & Hatch, 2002, p. 14). Finally, similar to Gysbers and Henderson's (2000) comprehensive guidance and counseling program, elements of the national model include the following: foundational components (beliefs and philosophy), delivery system (guidance curriculum, individual student planning, responsive services and systems support), management systems (management agreements, advisory council, use of data, action plans), and accountability (results report, school counselor performance evaluation, and program audit).

Areas for Future Research

In a recent article, Sink (2002b) discussed several areas deserving of further school counseling research. The major research agenda for the early twenty-first century should include an examination of the (a) effectiveness of comprehensive school counseling programs, (b) utility of adding other developmental domains to our programs, (c) communitarian approach to schooling, and (d) value of service integration models. These are summarized below.

Comprehensive Guidance and Counseling Programs

Over the past decade or so, the effectiveness of comprehensive programs in meeting their stated goals has received some attention in the school counseling literature (see, e.g., Gysbers & Henderson, 2000; Lapan, 2001, for a review, and Lapan's chapter in this book). Initial outcomes research is fairly promising. For example, it appears that these programs help students master various developmental competencies and improve the learning environment. However, much work still needs to be done (Whiston, 2003). New school counselors can assist in the process of collecting relevant outcome data. Here are a few sample questions for further research:

- Are students demonstrating outside of the school building mastery of various life skills?
- Are school counselors effective in their delivery of the comprehensive programs?
- How do parents and community members perceive the effectiveness of the programs?
- What areas of student functioning are not being addressed by the majority of comprehensive programs?
- How is the collaboration process working among all relevant parties inside and outside the school building?
- In what ways are comprehensive programs contributing to the academic achievement of students?

"New" Developmental Domains

Because students are multidimensional beings, school counselors also need to support children and youth in important developmental domains beyond those specified in most comprehensive guidance and counseling programs (i.e., educational, personal/social, and career; Gysbers & Henderson, 2000). For example, in an ethical manner, students' emotional (Denham, 1998; Greenspan, 1997; LeDoux, 1996; Saarni, 1999; Salovey & Sluyter, 1997), "spiritual" (Burke & Miranti, 1992, 1995; Kelly, 1995; Richards & Bergin, 1997; Sink, 1997), and citizenship development (MacDonald & Sink, 1999; Mustaine & LaFountain, 1993; Sink, 2002a) should be nurtured. Counselors could benefit from research in these "supplementary" areas, focusing on how they could be successfully encouraged within the context of school counseling programs.

Schools as Communities of Learners

Given that comprehensive guidance and counseling programs are supposed to aid in creating a positive school climate (Lapan, 2001), the "schools as learning communities" research could be an important literature base to consult (e.g., Baker, Terry, Bridger, & Winsor, 1997; Battistich, Solomon, Watson, & Schaps, 1997; Battistich, Solomon, Kim, Watson, & Schaps, 1995; Kohn, 1996; Osterman, 2000). The communitarian approach seems to contribute to a safe and nurturing school environment (Tolan, Guerra, & Kendall, 1995), reducing, for example, school bullying and other forms of violence and increasing prosocial behavior (e.g., better conflict resolution skills) in students (see, e.g., Sink & Rubel, 2001, for a review). In summary, creating a sense of community in our schools is an objective school counselors can work toward in their buildings. How comprehensive school counseling programs can integrate these findings deserves further study.

Service Integration Models

More recently, school counselor educators and others have suggested that schools need to become "full service" institutions, where community agencies and support services are brought together under one roof (e.g., Adelman, 1993; Arellano & Arman, 2002; Keys & Bemak, 1997; Taylor & Adelman, 2000). For example, mental health agencies would work together on school campuses to help students and families with their concerns. One good example is the Children First program in Denver, Colorado, which currently serves seventeen schools (Arellano & Arman, 2002). As a school-based multiagency program, Children First serves collaboratively the mental health needs of underrepresented populations. Conceptually, the practice makes good sense; however, rigorous efficacy research is limited. Several issues remain: Is the "one-stop Wal-Mart-type" services approach the way schools should go in the future? What role should school counselors play in this model? Is there adequate funding to do the collaboration well?

Final Thoughts

The chapters in this book have underscored how important school counselors are to the overall educational process. They are the principal support personnel for students and their caregivers, as well as for teachers and administrators. Without school counselors, critically needed student services would be uncoordinated and less effective. Only about twenty years ago, leading counselor educators characterized the future of school counseling in fairly negative terms (e.g., Carroll,

1985; Drury, 1984). Fortunately, these prognostications were inaccurate—in fact, quite the opposite was true. Gysbers and Henderson (2001) indicated that twenty-first-century school counselors are now the beneficiaries of their predecessors' strong vision and hard work. The profession is transforming itself for the better, and the outlook is quite promising (Erford, 2003).

Naturally, as you gain additional experience, you will want to enhance and update your skills and knowledge base. Professionals do this on a regular basis. Here are some of the key areas to focus on as you move through your school counseling career:

- Develop and update the skills necessary to serve *all* students;
- explore innovations in educational and counseling theory and practice;
- implement well-designed comprehensive school counseling programs;
- advocate for yourself and your school's or district's programs;
- collaborate with other school counselors, other school personnel, and with community agencies and programs;
- measure carefully student and program accomplishments and needs;
- create a sense of community in their schools; and
- demonstrate a high degree of professionalism. (Sink, 2002b)

A Final Challenge

Students and their families deserve only the best you can offer. It is hoped that you will join the scores of counselors who already bring to school each day their extraordinary caring, commitment, and competence. Your unique gifts and contributions are badly needed to make the profession's transformation complete.

An Eye to the Future: Closing Self-Reflections

1. What future concerns might you envision for the profession?
2. Imagine yourself as a professional with ten years of experience; now, what do you want to "look" like? What do you want your educational colleagues to say about your practice?
3. How do you hope to grow professionally and personally over the next ten years?

REFERENCES

Adelman, H. S. (1993). School-linked mental health interventions: Toward mechanisms for service coordination and integration. *Journal of Community Psychology, 21,* 309–319.

American School Counselor Association. (1999a). *Position statement: Family education.* Retrieved October 20, 2003, from http://www.schoolcounselor.org/content.cfm?L1 = 1000&L2 = 19

American School Counselor Association. (1999b). *Position statement: Multicultural counseling.* Retrieved October 20, 2003, from http://www.schoolcounselor.org/content. cfm?L1 = 1000&L2 = 26

American School Counselor Association. (1999c). *The role of the professional school counselor.* Retrieved November 25, 2002, from http://www.schoolcounselor.org/content. cfm?L1 = 1000&L2 = 69

American School Counselor Association. (2000). *Position statement: Sexual orientation.* Retrieved November 24, 2002, from http://www.schoolcounselor.org/content.cfm? L1 = 1000&L2 = 31

American School Counselor Association. (2003). *National* model *and* RAMP. Retrieved October 20, 2003, from http://www.schoolcounselor.org/content.cfm?L1 = 10

Arellano, K. M., & Arman, J. F. (2002). The Children First program: A school-based mental health collaborative. *Journal of Humanistic Counseling, Education & Development, 41,* 3–13.

Baker, J. A., Terry, T., Bridger, R., & Winsor, A. (1997). School as caring communities: A relational approach to school reform. *School Psychology Review, 26,* 586–602.

Battistich, V., Solomon, D., Kim, D., Watson, M., & Schaps, E. (1995). Schools as communities, poverty levels of student populations, and students' attitudes, motives, and performance: A multi-level analysis. *American Educational Research Journal, 32,* 627–658.

Battistich, V., Solomon, D., Watson, M., & Schaps, E. (1997). Caring school communities. *Educational Psychologist, 32,* 137–151.

Bowers, J. L., & Hatch, P. A. (2002). *ASCA national model for school counseling programs* [draft]. Alexandria, VA: American School Counselor Association.

Burke, M. T., & Miranti, J. G. (Eds.). (1992). *Ethical and spiritual values in counseling.* Alexandria, VA: Association for Religious and Value Issues in Education.

Burke, M. T., & Miranti, J. G. (Eds.). (1995). *Counseling: The spiritual dimension.* Alexandria, VA: American Counseling Association.

Campbell, C. A., & Dahir, C. A. (1997). *Sharing the vision: The national standards for school counseling programs.* Alexandria, VA: American School Counselor Association.

Carroll, M. R. (1985). School counseling—What does the future hold? *NASSP Bulletin, 69*(485), 2–5.

Cicero, G., & Barton, P. (2003). Parental involvement, outreach, and the emerging role of the professional school counselor. In B. T. Erford (Eds.), *Transforming the school counseling profession* (pp. 191–207). Upper Saddle River, NJ: Merrill/Prentice Hall.

Clark, M., & Stone, C. (2000). The developmental school counselor as educational leader. In J. Wittmer (Ed.), *Managing your school counseling programs: K-12 developmental strategies* (2nd ed., pp. 85–81). Minneapolis, MN: Educational Media.

Cobia, D. C., & Henderson, D. A. (2003). *Handbook of school counseling.* Upper Saddle River, NJ: Merrill/Prentice Hall.

Denham, S. A. (1998). *Emotional development in young children.* New York: Guilford.

Desimore, L. (1999). Linking parent involvement with student achievement: Do race and income matter? *Journal of Educational Research, 93,* 11–30.

Drury, S. S. (1984). Counselor survival in the 1980s. *The School Counselor, 31,* 234–240.

Erford, B. T. (Ed.). (2003). *Transforming the school counseling profession.* Upper Saddle River, NJ: Merrill/Prentice Hall.

Erford, B. T., House, R., & Martin, P. (2003). Transforming the school counseling profession. In B. T. Erford (Ed.), *Transforming the school counseling profession* (pp. 1–20). Upper Saddle River, NJ: Merrill/Prentice Hall.

Feuerstein, A. (2000). School characteristics and parent involvement: Influences on participation in children's schools. *Journal of Educational Research, 94,* 29–40.

Giles, H. C. (1998, May). *Parent engagement as a school reform strategy* (Digest—ERIC Clearinghouse on Urban Education). Retrieved November 25, 2002, from http://eric-web.tc.columbia.edu/

Greenspan, S. I. (1997). *The growth of the mind and the endangered origins of intelligence.* Cambridge, MA: Perseus.

Guidon, M. H. (2003). Assessment. In B. T. Erford (Ed.), *Transforming the school counseling profession* (pp. 331–355). Upper Saddle River, NJ: Merrill/Prentice Hall.

Gysbers, N. C., & Henderson, P. (2000). *Developing and managing your school guidance program* (3rd ed.). Alexandria, VA: American Counseling Association.

Gysbers, N. C., & Henderson, P. (2001). Comprehensive guidance and counseling programs: A rich history and a bright future. *Professional School Counseling, 4,* 246–256.

Hohenshil, T. H. (2000). High tech counseling. *Journal of Counseling & Development, 79,* 365–368.

Holcomb-McCoy, C. C. (2003). Multicultural competence. In B. T. Erford (Ed.), *Transforming the school counseling profession* (pp. 317–330). Upper Saddle River, NJ: Merrill/Prentice Hall.

Kelly, E. W. (1995). *Spirituality and religion in counseling and psychotherapy.* Alexandria, VA: American Counseling Association.

Kennedy, J. F. (1963, June). *Radio and television report to the American people on civil rights.* Retrieved November 23, 2002, from http://www.cs.umb.edu/jfklibrary/j061163.htm

Keys, S. G., & Bemak, F. (1997). School-family-community linked services: A school counseling role for changing times. *The School Counselor, 44,* 255–263.

Keys, S. G., & Lockhart, E. J. (1999). The school counselor's role in facilitating multisystemic change. *Professional School Counseling, 3,* 101–107.

Kohn, A. (1996). *Beyond Discipline. From compliance to community.* Alexandria, VA: Association for Supervision and Curriculum Development.

Lapan, R. T. (2001). Results-based comprehensive guidance and counseling programs: A framework for planning and evaluation. *Professional School Counseling, 4,* 289–299.

LeDoux, J. (1996). *The emotional brain: The mysterious underpinnings of emotional life.* New York: Touchstone.

MacDonald, G., & Sink, C. A. (1999). A qualitative developmental analysis of comprehensive guidance programmes in schools in the United States. *British Journal of Guidance and Counselling, 27,* 415–430.

Meyers, S. A., Varkey, S., & Aguirre, A. M. (2002). Ecological correlates of family functioning. *The American Journal of Family Therapy, 30,* 257–273.

Mustaine, B. L., & LaFountain, R. M. (1993). Some thoughts on the future of school counseling. *Guidance and Counselling, 8,* 30–39.

Myrick, R. D. (2003). *Developmental guidance and counseling: A practical approach* (4th ed.). Minneapolis, MN: Educational Media.

National Association for College Admission Counseling. (2000). *National association for college admission counseling statement on counselor competencies.* Retrieved August 30, 2002, from www.nacac.com/downloads/policy_couns_competencies.pdf

Osterman, K. F. (2000). Students' need for belonging in the school community. *Review of Educational Research, 70,* 323–367.

Pedersen, P. B., & Carey, J. C. (2003). *Multicultural counseling in the schools: A practical handbook* (2nd ed.). Boston: Allyn & Bacon.

Richards, P. S., & Bergin, A. E. (1997). *A spiritual strategy for counseling and psychotherapy.* Washington, DC: American Psychological Association.

Saarni, C. (1999). *The development of emotional competence.* New York: Guilford.

Sabella, R. A. (2000). School counseling and technology. In J. Wittmer (Ed.), *Managing your school counseling programs: K-12 developmental strategies* (pp. 337–357). Minneapolis, MN: Educational Media.

Sabella, R. A. (2003). *SchoolCounselor.com* (2nd ed.). Minneapolis, MN: Educational Media.

Sabella, R. A., & Booker, B. (2001). *Using technology to promote your guidance and counseling program among stake holders.* Retrieved December 2, 2002, from http://coe.fgcu.edu/faculty/sabella/bootcamp/promoting.pdf

Salovey, P., & Sluyter, D. J. (Eds.). (1997). *Emotional development and emotional intelligence: Educational implications.* New York: Basic Books.

Schmidt, J. J. (2003). *Counseling in schools: Essential services and comprehensive programs* (4th ed.). Boston: Allyn & Bacon.

Sink, C. A. (1997). Spirituality and faith development of schoolchildren: Implications for school counseling. *Religion and Education, 24,* 59–66

Sink, C. A. (2002a). Comprehensive guidance and counseling programs and the development of multicultural student-citizens. *Professional School Counseling, 6,* 130–137.

Sink, C. A. (2002b). In search of the profession's finest hour: A critique of four views of 21st century school counseling. *Professional School Counseling, 5,* 156–163.

Sink, C. A., & Rubel, L. (2001). The school as community approach to violence prevention. In D. S. Sandhu (Ed.), *Faces of violence: Psychological correlates, concepts, and intervention strategies* (pp. 417–437). Huntington, NY: Nova Science.

Sogunro, O. A. (2001). Toward multiculturalism: Implications of multicultural education for schools. *Multicultural Perspectives, 3*(3), 19–33.

Taylor, L., & Adelman, H. (2000). Connecting schools, families, and communities. *Professional School Counseling, 3,* 298–307.

Thompson, R. A. (2002). *School counseling: Best practices for working in the school* (2nd ed.). New York: Brunner-Routledge.

Tolan, P., Guerra, N., & Kendall, P. C. (1995). A developmental-ecological perspective on antisocial behavior in children and adolescents: Toward a unified risk and intervention framework. *Journal of Consulting and Clinical Psychology, 63,* 579–584.

U.S. Census Bureau. (2000). *Vital Statistics.* Retrieved November 16, 2002, from http://www.census.gov/prod/2001pubs/statab/sec02.pdf

Whiston, S. C. (2003). Outcomes research on school counseling services. In B. T. Erford (Ed.), *Transforming the school counseling profession* (pp. 435–447). Upper Saddle River, NJ: Merrill/Prentice Hall.

APPENDIX

American School Counselor Association Ethical Standards for School Counselors

Revised June 25, 1998

Preamble

The American School Counselor Association (ASCA) is a professional organization whose members have a unique and distinctive preparation, grounded in the behavioral sciences, with training in clinical skills adapted to the school setting. The school counselor assists in the growth and development of each individual and uses his or her highly specialized skills to protect the interests of the counselee within the structure of the school system. School counselors subscribe to the following basic tenets of the counseling process from which professional responsibilities are derived:

- Each person has the right to respect and dignity as a human being and to counseling services without prejudice as to person, character, belief, or practice regardless of age, color, disability, ethnic group, gender, race, religion, sexual orientation, marital status, or socioeconomic status.
- Each person has the right to self-direction and self-development.
- Each person has the right of choice and the responsibility for goals reached.
- Each person has the right to privacy and thereby the right to expect the counselor-counselee relationship to comply with all laws, policies, and ethical standards pertaining to confidentiality. In this document, ASCA specifies the principles of ethical behavior necessary to regulate and maintain the high standards of integrity, leadership, and professionalism among its members. The Ethical Standards for School Counselors were developed to clarify the nature of ethical responsibilities held in common by school counseling professionals.

The purposes of this document are to:

- Serve as a guide for the ethical practices of all professional school counselors regardless of level, area, population served, or membership in this professional Association;
- Provide benchmarks for both self-appraisal and peer evaluations regarding counselor responsibilities to counselees, parents, colleagues and professional associates, schools, and communities, as well as to one's self and the counseling profession; and
- Inform those served by the school counselor of acceptable counselor practices and expected professional behavior.

A.1.   Responsibilities to Students

The professional school counselor:

a. Has a primary obligation to the counselee who is to be treated with respect as a unique individual.
b. Is concerned with the educational, career, emotional, and behavioral needs and encourages the maximum development of each counselee.
c. Refrains from consciously encouraging the counselee's acceptance of values, lifestyles, plans, decisions, and beliefs that represent the counselor's personal orientation.
d. Is responsible for keeping informed of laws, regulations, and policies relating to counselees and strives to ensure that the rights of counselees are adequately provided for and protected.

A.2.   Confidentiality

The professional school counselor:

a. Informs the counselee of the purposes, goals, techniques, and rules of procedure under which she/he may receive counseling at or before the time when the counseling relationship is entered. Disclosure notice includes confidentiality issues such as the possible necessity for consulting with other professionals, privileged communication, and legal or authoritative restraints. The meaning and limits of confidentiality are clearly defined to counselees through a written and shared disclosure statement.
b. Keeps information confidential unless disclosure is required to prevent

clear and imminent danger to the counselee or others or when legal requirements demand that confidential information be revealed. Counselors will consult with other professionals when in doubt as to the validity of an exception.

c. Discloses information to an identified third party who, by her or his relationship with the counselee, is at a high risk of contracting a disease that is commonly known to be communicable and fatal. Prior to disclosure, the counselor will ascertain that the counselee has not already informed the third party about his or her disease and he/she is not intending to inform the third party in the immediate future.

d. Requests of the court that disclosure not be required when the release of confidential information without a counselee's permission may lead to potential harm to the counselee.

e. Protects the confidentiality of counselee's records and releases personal data only according to prescribed laws and school policies. Student information maintained in computers is treated with the same care as traditional student records.

f. Protects the confidentiality of information received in the counseling relationship as specified by federal and state laws, written policies, and applicable ethical standards. Such information is only to be revealed to others with the informed consent of the counselee, consistent with the counselor's ethical obligation. In a group setting, the counselor sets a high norm of confidentiality and stresses its importance, yet clearly states that confidentiality in group counseling cannot be guaranteed.

A.3. Counseling Plans

The professional school counselor:

works jointly with the counselee in developing integrated and effective counseling plans, consistent with both the abilities and circumstances of the counselee and counselor. Such plans will be regularly reviewed to ensure continued viability and effectiveness, respecting the counselee's freedom of choice.

A.4. Dual Relationships

The professional school counselor:

avoids dual relationships which might impair her or his objectivity and increase the risk of harm to the client (e.g., counseling one's family members, close friends, or associates). If a dual relationship is unavoidable, the counselor is responsible for taking action to eliminate or reduce the potential for harm. Such safeguards might include informed consent, consultation, supervision, and documentation.

A.5. Appropriate Referrals

The professional school counselor:

makes referrals when necessary or appropriate to outside resources. Appropriate referral necessitates knowledge of available resources and making proper plans for transitions with minimal interruption of services. Counselees retain the right to discontinue the counseling relationship at any time.

A.6. Group Work

The professional school counselor:

screens prospective group members and maintains an awareness of participants' needs and goals in relation to the goals of the group. The counselor takes reasonable precautions to protect members from physical and psychological harm resulting from interaction within the group.

A.7. Danger to Self or Others

The professional school counselor:

informs appropriate authorities when the counselee's condition indicates a clear and imminent danger to the counselee or others. This is to be done after careful deliberation and, where possible, after consultation with other counseling professionals. The counselor informs the counselee of actions to be taken so as to minimize his or her confusion and to clarify counselee and counselor expectations.

A.8. Student Records

The professional school counselor:

maintains and secures records necessary for rendering professional services to the counselee as required by laws, regulations, institutional procedures, and confidentiality guidelines.

A.9.   Evaluation, Assessment, and Interpretation

The professional school counselor:

a. Adheres to all professional standards regarding selecting, administering, and interpreting assessment measures. The counselor recognizes that computer-based testing programs require specific training in administration, scoring, and interpretation which may differ from that required in more traditional assessments.
b. Provides explanations of the nature, purposes, and results of assessment/ evaluation measures in language the counselee(s) can understand.
c. Does not misuse assessment results and interpretations and takes reasonable steps to prevent others from misusing the information.
d. Uses caution when utilizing assessment techniques, making evaluations, and interpreting the performance of populations not represented in the norm group on which an instrument is standardized.

A.10. Computer Technology

The professional school counselor:

a. Promotes the benefits of appropriate computer applications and clarifies the limitations of computer technology. The counselor ensures that: (1) computer applications are appropriate for the individual needs of the counselee; (2) the counselee understands how to use the application; and (3) follow-up counseling assistance is provided. Members of under represented groups are assured equal access to computer technologies and are assured the absence of discriminatory information and values in computer applications. b. Counselors who communicate with counselees via internet should follow the NBCC Standards for WebCounseling.

A.11. Peer Helper Programs

The professional school counselor:

a. has unique responsibilities when working with peer helper programs. The school counselor is responsible for the welfare of counselees participating in peer programs under her or his direction. School counselors who function in training and supervisory capacities are referred to the preparation and supervision standards of professional counselor associations.

B. Responsibilities to Parents

B.1. Parent Rights and Responsibilities

The professional school counselor:

a. Respects the inherent rights and responsibilities of parents for their children and endeavors to establish, as appropriate, a collaborative relationship with parents to facilitate the counselee's maximum development.
b. Adheres to laws and local guidelines when assisting parents experiencing family difficulties that interfere with the counselee's effectiveness and welfare.
c. Is sensitive to cultural and social diversity among families and recognizes that all parents, custodial and noncustodial, are vested with certain rights and responsibilities for the welfare of their children by virtue of their role and according to law.

B.2. Parents and Confidentiality

The professional school counselor:

a. Informs parents of the counselor's role with emphasis on the confidential nature of the counseling relationship between the counselor and counselee.
b. Provides parents with accurate, comprehensive, and relevant information in an objective and caring manner, as is appropriate and consistent with ethical responsibilities to the counselee.
c. Makes reasonable efforts to honor the wishes of parents and guardians concerning information that he/she may share regarding the counselee.

C. Responsibilities to Colleagues and Professional Associates

C.1. Professional Relationships

The professional school counselor:

a. Establishes and maintains professional relationships with faculty, staff, and administration to facilitate the provision of optimal counseling services. The relationship is based on the counselor's definition and description of the parameter and levels of his or her professional roles.

b. Treats colleagues with professional respect, courtesy, and fairness. The qualifications, views, and findings of colleagues are represented to accurately reflect the image of competent professionals.

c. Is aware of and optimally utilizes related professions and organizations to whom the counselee may be referred.

C.2. Sharing Information with Other Professionals

The professional school counselor:

a. Promotes awareness and adherence to appropriate guidelines regarding confidentiality; the distinction between public and private information; and staff consultation.

b. Provides professional personnel with accurate, objective, concise, and meaningful data necessary to adequately evaluate, counsel, and assist the counselee.

c. If a counselee is receiving services from another counselor or other mental health professional, the counselor, with client consent, will inform the other professional and develop clear agreements to avoid confusion and conflict for the counselee.

D.   *Responsibilities to the School and Community*

D.1.   Responsibilities to the School

The professional school counselor:

a. Supports and protects the educational program against any infringement not in the best interest of counselees.

b. Informs appropriate officials of conditions that may be potentially disruptive or damaging to the school's mission, personnel, and property while honoring the confidentiality between the counselee and counselor.

c. Delineates and promotes the counselor's role and function in meeting the needs of those served. The counselor will notify appropriate officials of conditions which may limit or curtail her or his effectiveness in providing programs and services.

d. Accepts employment only for positions for which he/she is qualified by education, training, supervised experience, state and national professional credentials, and appropriate professional experience. Counselors recommend that administrators hire only qualified and competent individuals for professional counseling positions.

e. Assists in developing: (1) curricular and environmental conditions appropriate for the school and community; (2) educational procedures and programs to meet the counselee's developmental needs; and (3) a systematic evaluation process for comprehensive school counseling programs, services, and personnel. The counselor is guided by the findings of the evaluation data in planning programs and services.

D.2. Responsibility to the Community

The professional school counselor:

collaborates with agencies, organizations, and individuals in the school and community in the best interest of counselees and without regard to personal reward or remuneration.

E.   *Responsibilities to Self*

E.1. Professional Competence

The professional school counselor:

a. Functions within the boundaries of individual professional competence and accepts responsibility for the consequences of his or her actions.
b. Monitors personal functioning and effectiveness and does not participate in any activity which may lead to inadequate professional services or harm to a client.
c. Strives through personal initiative to maintain professional competence and to keep abreast of professional information. Professional and personal growth are ongoing throughout the counselor's career.

E.2. Multicultural Skills

The professional school counselor:

understands the diverse cultural backgrounds of the counselees with whom he/she works. This includes, but is not limited to, learning how the school counselor's own cultural/ethnic/racial identity impacts her or his values and beliefs about the counseling process.

F. *Responsibilities to the Profession*

F.1. Professionalism

The professional school counselor:

 a. Accepts the policies and processes for handling ethical violations as a result of maintaining membership in the American School Counselor Association.

 b. Conducts herself/himself in such a manner as to advance individual ethical practice and the profession.

 c. Conducts appropriate research and reports findings in a manner consistent with acceptable educational and psychological research practices. When using client data for research or for statistical or program planning purposes, the counselor ensures protection of the individual counselee's identity.

 d. Adheres to ethical standards of the profession, other official policy statements pertaining to counseling, and relevant statutes established by federal, state, and local governments.

 e. Clearly distinguishes between statements and actions made as a private individual and those made as a representative of the school counseling profession.

 f. Does not use his or her professional position to recruit or gain clients, consultees for her or his private practice, seek and receive unjustified personal gains, unfair advantage, sexual favors, or unearned goods or services.

F.2. Contribution to the Profession

The professional school counselor:

 a. Actively participates in local, state, and national associations which foster the development and improvement of school counseling.

 b. Contributes to the development of the profession through sharing skills, ideas, and expertise with colleagues.

G. *Maintenance of Standards*

Ethical behavior among professional school counselors, Association members and nonmembers, is expected at all times. When there exists serious doubt as to the ethical behavior of colleagues, or if counselors are forced to work in situations or abide by policies which do not reflect the standards as outlined in these Ethical Standards for School Counselors, the counselor is obligated to take appropriate action to rectify the condition. The following procedure may serve as a guide:

1. The counselor should consult confidentially with a professional colleague to discuss the nature of a complaint to see if she/he views the situation as an ethical violation.

2. When feasible, the counselor should directly approach the colleague whose behavior is in question to discuss the complaint and seek resolution.

3. If resolution is not forthcoming at the personal level, the counselor shall utilize the channels established within the school, school district, the state SCA, and ASCA Ethics Committee.

4. If the matter still remains unresolved, referral for review and appropriate action should be made to the Ethics Committees in the following sequence:
   - state school counselor association
   - American School Counselor Association

5. The ASCA Ethics Committee is responsible for educating—and consulting with – the membership regarding ethical standards. The Committee periodically reviews and recommends changes in code. The Committee will also receive and process questions to clarify the application of such standards. Questions must be submitted in writing to the ASCA Ethics Chair. Finally, the Committee will handle complaints of alleged violations of our ethical standards. Therefore, at the national level, complaints should be submitted in writing to the ASCA Ethics Committee, c/o the Executive Director, American School Counselor Association, 801 North Fairfax, Suite 310, Alexandria, VA 22314.

H.   *Resources*

School counselors are responsible for being aware of, and acting in accord with, standards and positions of the counseling profession as represented in official documents such as those listed below:

American Counseling Association. (1995). *Code of ethics and standards of practice.* Alexandria, VA. (5999 Stevenson Ave., Alexandria, VA 22034) 1 800 347 6647 www.counseling.org.

American School Counselor Association. (1997). *The national standards for school counseling programs.* Alexandria, VA. (801 North Fairfax Street, Suite 310, Alexandria, VA 22314) 1 800 306 4722 www.schoolcounselor.org.

American School Counselor Association. (1998). *Position Statements.* Alexandria, VA.

American School Counselor Association. (1998). *Professional liability insurance program.* (Brochure). Alexandria, VA.

Arrendondo, Toperek, Brown, Jones, Locke, Sanchez, and Stadler. (1996). Multicultural counseling competencies and standards. *Journal of Multicultural Counseling and Development.* Vol. 24, No. 1. See American Counseling Association.

Arthur, G.L. and Swanson, C.D. (1993). Confidentiality and privileged communication. (1993). See American Counseling Association.

Association for Specialists in Group Work. (1989). *Ethical Guidelines for group counselors.* (1989). Alexandria, VA. See American Counseling Association.

Corey, G., Corey, M.S. and Callanan. (1998). *Issues and ethics in the helping professions.* Pacific Grove, CA: Brooks/Cole. (Brooks/Cole, 511 Forest Lodge Rd., Pacific Grove, CA 93950) www.thomson.com.

Crawford, R. (1994). Avoiding counselor malpractice. Alexandria, VA. See American Counseling Association.

Forrester-Miller, H. and Davis, T.E. (1996). A practitioner's guide to ethical decision making. Alexandria, VA. See American Counseling Association.

Herlihy, B. and Corey, G. (1996). ACA ethical standards casebook. Fifth ed. Alexandria, VA. See American Counseling Association.

Herlihy, B. and Corey, G. (1992). Dual relationships in counseling.

Alexandria, VA. See American Counseling Association.

Huey, W.C. and Remley, T.P. (1988). Ethical and legal issues in school counseling. Alexandria, VA. See American School Counselor Association.

Joint Committee on Testing Practices. (1988). Code of fair testing practices in education. Washington, DC: American Psychological Association. (1200 17th Street, NW, Washington, DC 20036) 202 336 5500

Mitchell, R.W. (1991). Documentation in counseling records. Alexandria, VA. See American Counseling Association.

National Board for Certified Counselors. (1998). National board for certified counselors: code of ethics. Greensboro, NC. (3 Terrace Way, Suite D, Greensboro, NC 27403-3660) 336 547 0607 www.nbcc.org.

National Board for Certified Counselors. (1997). Standards for the ethical practice of webcounseling. Greensboro, NC.

National Peer Helpers Association. (1989). Code of ethics for peer helping professionals. Greenville, NC. PO Box 2684, Greenville, NC 27836. 919 522 3959. nphaorg

Salo, M. and Schumate, S. (1993). Counseling minor clients. Alexandria, VA. See American School Counselor Association.

Stevens-Smith, P. and Hughes, M. (1993). Legal issues in marriage and family counseling. Alexandria, VA. See American School Counselor Association.

Wheeler, N. and Bertram, B. (1994). Legal aspects of counseling: avoiding lawsuits and legal problems. (Videotape). Alexandria, VA. See American School Counselor Association.

Ethical Standards for School Counselors was adopted by the ASCA Delegate Assembly, March 19, 1984. The first revision was approved by the ASCA Delegate Assembly, March 27, 1992. The second revision was approved by the ASCA Governing Board on March 30, 1998 and adopted on June 25, 1998.

Contributors

Foreword, Chapters 1 and 12

Christopher A. Sink, Ph.D., NCC, LMHC, is a professor of school counseling and psychology at Seattle Pacific University. He is the former editor of *Professional School Counseling* (the scholarly journal of the American School Counselor Association) and continues to serve on the journal's editorial board. For many years, Dr. Sink was also an associate editor for the refereed publication *National Association for Laboratory Schools Journal.* Prior to joining the professorial ranks, Dr. Sink served for many years as a secondary and community college counselor. He recently received two distinguished service awards by state counseling organizations for his work on fostering comprehensive school counseling programs in the state of Washington. He has published extensively (over thirty-five publications) in the areas of educational psychology and school counseling. His current research and teaching interests focus on the role of school counselors in preventing school violence, promoting citizenship education, and developing systemic approaches to educational restructuring, including comprehensive guidance and counseling programs and the school-based communitarian movement. Dr. Sink works and consults with school districts around the country as a comprehensive school counseling program developer and evaluator. He is married to a middle school teacher and is the father of two teenagers. Chris can be reached via e-mail at csink@spu.edu or by telephone at (206) 281-2453.

Chapter 2

John M. Littrell, Ph.D., is a professor in the Department of Educational Leadership and Policy Studies at Iowa State University. He serves as the program coordinator for the counselor education program, which specializes in an integrated-curriculum approach to school counseling. Littrell is the author of thirty-plus articles and five chapters in professional journals and books. During a Faculty Improvement Leave during the 1985–86 academic year, Dr. Littrell was a Fulbright Professor in Malaysia. His current area of interest is brief counseling, a way of speeding up the process of change. Dr. Littrell has presented twenty-five national and international brief counseling workshops for the American Counseling Association. Recently, he authored *Brief Counseling in Action* and produced five brief counseling videotapes. Currently, he is coauthoring a research-based book, *Counselor as Educational Leader: Transforming a School Culture,* based on an analysis of an outstanding elementary school counselor. In his spare time, he writes short-story mysteries based on famous counselors and therapists who solve murders that occur in their practice. Freud's story is titled *Death on the Analyst's Couch.*

Kirk Zinck, *Ph.D., LMFT,* is a clinician for a community mental health center in coastal Alaska. Commuting by air taxi, he provides clinical services to three "off road" villages with indigenous populations. He also maintains a limited private practice of counseling, consulting, and training. Dr. Zinck's professional experience includes school and clinical counseling, clinical supervision, graduate instruction, and research. He has conducted professional trainings in the United States and abroad. He has authored and coauthored publications and instructional media focused on brief counseling, counseling adolescents, and transformational processes of adult couples. Dr. Zinck is a clinical member of the American Association for Marriage and Family Therapy, a National Certified Counselor, and a National Certified School Counselor.

Chapter 3

Ed Jacobs, *Ph.D.,* is coordinator of the counseling program at West Virginia University, where he has been teaching group counseling for over thirty years. Professional publications include twenty-five articles in books and journals as well as three books on counseling techniques: *Impact Therapy, Creative Counseling Techniques: An Illustrated Guide,* and *Group Counseling: Strategies and Skills,* which is now in its fourth edition. Dr. Jacobs has been recognized for his outstanding contribution to the field of group counseling by being selected as a Fellow in the Association for Specialists in Group Work. He is on the advisory board for the National Association for Cognitive-Behavioral Therapists. Each year, Ed presents throughout the United States, Canada, and Europe over forty workshops on Impact Therapy and group counseling for school districts, agencies, and organizations.

Chris Schimmel, *M.A.,* is an instructor in the counseling program at Marshall University Graduate College in South Charleston, West Virginia, where she primarily teaches preservice school counselors and oversees off-campus programs for the college. She is a former school counselor, having worked at all levels in public schools. Ms. Schimmel has traveled the country providing workshops to school counselors on the topic of group counseling as well as use of theory and Impact Therapy.

Chapter 4

Susan C. Whiston, Ph.D., is a professor at Indiana University in the Department of Counseling and Educational Psychology. She has been teaching school counseling students since 1986 and has published many articles related to the empirical support for school counseling. Prior to receiving her doctorate from the University of Wyoming, she worked at the secondary-school level as a counselor for low-income students.

Jennifer Bouwkamp, M.S., is currently a Ph.D. student in counseling psychology at Indiana University and received her master's degree from the University of Kansas in 2001. She is interested in public health issues, positive psychology, and attachment theory.

Chapter 5

Norman C. Gysbers, Ph.D., is a professor in the Department of Educational and Counseling Psychology at the University of Missouri-Columbia. He received his B.A. degree (1954) from Hope College and his M.A. (1959) and Ph.D. (1963) degrees from the University of Michigan. Dr. Gysbers's research and teaching interests are in career development, career counseling, and school guidance and counseling program development, management, and evaluation. He is the author of sixty-five articles in seventeen different professional journals, twenty-seven chapters in published books, fourteen monographs, and fifteen books including *Career Counseling: Process, Issues, and Techniques,* second edition, 2003 (with Mary Heppner and Joseph Johnston); *Leading & Managing Your School Guidance Program Staff,* 1998 (with Patricia Henderson); and *Developing and Managing Your School Guidance Program,* third edition, 2000 (with Patricia Henderson). In 1981 he was awarded the National Vocational Guidance Association's National Merit Award and in 1983 the American Counseling Association's Distinguished Professional Service Award. In 1989 he received the National Career Development Association's Eminent Career Award, and in 2000 he received the National Career Development Association's President's Recognition Award. Dr. Gysbers was editor of the *Career Development Quarterly,* 1962–1970; president of the National Career Development Association, 1972–73; president of the American Counseling Association, 1977–78; and vice president of the American Vocational Association, 1979–1982. Currently, he is editor of the *Journal of Career Development.*

Patricia Henderson, *Ph.D.,* is currently a consultant and counselor educator. Having spent nineteen years as a counselor educator, she is currently teaching at the University of Texas at San Antonio and Our Lady of the Lake University. Prior to this, she spent thirty years as a school counselor supervisor and administrator. Of those years, the last nineteen were as director of guidance at Northside Independent School District in San Antonio. By the end of her tenure at Northside, she was leading the work of approximately two hundred professional school counselors. She is author or coauthor of nineteen articles and chapters, and nine books and monographs. She is coauthor with Norman Gysbers of *Developing and Managing Your School Guidance Program,* which is now in its third edition and continues to be the American Counseling Association's best-selling publication over time. Its companion, *Leading and Managing Your School Guidance Program Staff,* is recognized as an important text in the newly emerging doctoral programs in school counseling. She has been an active leader in professional counseling associations at the local, state, and national levels and has received awards for being an exemplary practitioner, writer, and researcher.

Chapter 6

Susan Jones Sears, *Ph.D.,* is currently an associate professor and coordinator of the school counseling program in the College of Education at the Ohio State University. Dr. Sears is director and principal investigator of OSU's Transforming School Counseling Initiative (TSCI). OSU is one of six sites in the United States, chosen by the DeWitt Wallace Fund/Education Trust, to implement TSCI, a national initiative to improve the preparation of school counselors. In addition to the TSCI grant, she has written and directed several grants focusing on the counselor's role in School-to-Work and Tech Prep and the career development of adolescents. Dr. Sears has consulted throughout the United States on counselor licensure, career development of adolescents, and the development of school counseling programs. She has published extensively in those areas including four books and eight book chapters. Dr. Sears is the recipient of twelve national and state awards for outstanding leadership and service to the counseling profession.

Chapter 7

Ken Hughey, *Ph.D.,* is a professor in the Department of Counseling and Educational Psychology at Kansas State University. From 1992 to 1998, he served as associate director of counseling for High Skills, a project funded by the DeWitt Wallace-Reader's Digest Fund to Kansas State University. His previous work experience includes high school math teacher, high school counselor, administrator, and facilitator of workshops for displaced workers. In addition, Dr. Hughey served as the editor of Professional School Counseling from 2000 to 2002. He served on the editorial board of *The School Counselor* and *Professional School Counseling,* and is currently on the editorial board of the *Journal of Career Development.*

Chapter 8

Rich Lapan, *Ph.D.,* is a professor in the Department of Educational, School, and Counseling Psychology at the University of Missouri-Columbia. For the past fourteen years, he has been involved in training professional school counselors. He earned a B.A. in philosophy from St. Anselm's College, an M.A. in existential/ phenomenological counseling from Duquesne University, and a Ph.D. in counseling psychology from the University of Utah. Prior to earning his doctorate, Rich worked for several years as a master's level counselor in several school settings and residential treatment programs for adolescents. He is the proud father of three daughters and lives with his wife, Sharon, in Columbia, Missouri. He can be reached at LapanR@missouri.edu.

Chapter 9

Keith M. Davis, *Ph.D., NCC, NCLSC,* is currently an assistant professor in the Department of Human Development and Psychological Counseling at Appalachian State University, Boone, North Carolina, and teaches a course in school-based consultation within the program. He has also worked in the North Carolina public schools for ten years as a high school teacher, high school and elementary school counselor, family therapist, and consultant to school systems for teaching and counseling with Native American students and families.

Chapter 10

Fred Bemak, *Ph.D.,* is currently a professor and program coordinator for the Counseling and Development Program in the Graduate School of Education at George Mason University. As a member of the National Advisory Board of the

American Association of Higher Education, he helped design the National Initiative to Transform School Counseling and was later a recipient of a Dewitt Wallace-Readers Digest Fund grant through The Education Trust to transform school counseling. Dr. Bemak has presented, consulted, and given seminars throughout the United States and internationally in over thirty countries. His work has focused on youth and family populations identified as being at risk and cross-cultural counseling. He has directed several federal and state programs, including Upward Bound and the Massachusetts Department of Mental Health Region I Adolescent Treatment Program, and held numerous grants focusing on addressing problems faced by today's youth. In addition, Dr. Bemak has published extensively in these areas. He is a former Fulbright Scholar, a Kellogg Foundation International Fellow, and a recipient of the International Exchange of Experts and Research Fellowship through the World Rehabilitation Fund. He continues to consult in schools and communities with marginalized and disenfranchised youth and families.

Carol Kaffenberger, Ph.D., is currently an assistant professor at George Mason University in the Counseling and Development Program in the Graduate School of Education. She teaches counseling skill and theory classes, and supervises field experience for master's students seeking school counseling licensure. Dr. Kaffenberger is a trainer for the Education Trust, Transformation of School Counseling initiative. Previously, she was a school counselor and a special education teacher. Her research interests include school reentry for children with chronic illness, and the transformation of school counselors. She has written professional articles on school reentry issues and the role of school counselors in school reform. Carol has written book chapters on school reentry, the use of empathy in counselor education, and the clinical role of school counselors. She has developed and conducted training workshops for school reintegration teams and counseling skills for higher education counseling centers. Professional presentations include school reentry for the chronically ill, the transformation of school counselors, school counselor leadership, and using technology in counseling.

Sally Murphy, Ph.D., is an assistant professor and clinical coordinator in the Counseling and Development Program, Graduate School of Education at George Mason University, Fairfax, Virginia. Dr. Murphy has worked in a variety of educational roles over the past thirty-plus years including her current role as a university professor, a professional school counselor, and an elementary school teacher. She has given numerous presentations at state and national professional conferences and has conducted workshops for school districts and local school communities on topical issues related to bully/victim relationships, school counseling leadership, and the transformation of school counseling. In her role as clinical coordinator, Sally focuses on improving the quality of the clinical field experience and site supervision. She and her husband live in northern Virginia.

Chapter 11

Susan Keys, Ph.D., is an associate professor in the Department of Counseling and Human Services, in the School of Professional Studies in Business and Education at Johns Hopkins University. Dr. Keys is also the associate director for education of the Johns Hopkins University Center for the Prevention of Youth Violence. She has been active in the field of school counseling as counselor, consultant, and counselor educator for over twenty-five years. Dr. Keys has published extensively on innovative models for school counseling and collaborative consultation. Her other interests include interprofessional development and education, school violence prevention, leadership in urban schools, and school mental health. Recently, she completed a postdoctoral fellowship in children's mental health services research at the Johns Hopkins University's Bloomberg School of Public Health. At present, Dr. Keys is co-principal investigator of an intervention study investigating the effects of school discipline practices on aggressive behavior of elementary school children.

Alan Green, Ph.D., is an assistant professor and coordinator for the school counseling and field placement program at Johns Hopkins University. In addition, he is the principal investigator of Project Inspiration, a federally funded grant for the development and refinement of an urban elementary school counseling model being implemented in the Baltimore City Public System in Maryland. Previously, Dr. Green was a research assistant and adjunct professor at the Metropolitan Center for Urban Education at New York University. Here he worked as project director of a federally funded Safe and Drug Free Schools data collection project with New York City Public Schools. Dr. Green's research interests are in urban education, academic underachievement among African Americans, and the use of data to improve schools.

Name Index

Subject Index